An IDEA a DAY...
365 GREAT BUSINESS IDEAS
FOR EACH DAY OF THE YEAR

An IDEA a DAY...
365 GREAT BUSINESS IDEAS
FOR EACH DAY OF THE YEAR

The ideas in the book are compiled from titles in the 100 Great Ideas series published by Marshall Cavendish Business

Cover design: Opalworks Co Ltd

Published by Marshall Cavendish Business
An imprint of Marshall Cavendish International

PO Box 65829
London Ec1p 1ny
United Kingdom
info@marshallcavendish.co.uk

and

1 New Industrial Road
Singapore 536196
genrefsales@sg.marshallcavendish.com
www.marshallcavendish.com/genref

Marshall Cavendish is a trademark of Times Publishing Limited

Other Marshall Cavendish offices:
Marshall Cavendish Corporation. 99 White Plains Road, Tarrytown NY 10591–9001, USA • Marshall Cavendish International (Thailand) Co Ltd. 253 Asoke, 12th Floor, Sukhumvit 21 Road, Klongtoey Nua, Wattana, Bangkok 10110, Thailand • Marshall Cavendish (Malaysia) Sdn Bhd, Times Subang, Lot 46, Subang Hi-Tech Industrial Park, Batu Tiga, 40000 Shah Alam, Selangor Darul Ehsan, Malaysia

A CIP record for this book is available from the British Library

ISBN 978-981-4328-64-7

Printed and bound in the United Kingdom by CPI Mackays, Chatham ME5 8TD

CONTENTS

INTRODUCTION

What are the greatest business ideas ever? People have their own favourites, for example: Henry Ford deciding consumers, and his motor company, would benefit from standardised, mass-produced vehicles; or Bill Gates deciding software, not hardware, was where the fortune lay in computing. Ideas are great not simply because of immediate benefits; they are great because they provide inspiration and a way of working that others can follow.

This is a book about some of the best ideas used in business. Some are simple—sometimes almost embarrassingly so—while others are based on detailed research and brilliant intellect. Most are perennial, as their logic, simplicity or value will help them endure; while others are, to be honest, rather faddy. What unites these business ideas is their proven power and potency. They are not only insightful and useful but they have worked: often in a brilliant way or despite great adversity.

Each idea is presented in a standard format and approach: a short description of the idea, followed by an example or two of how the idea was implemented previously, and then finally practical guidelines on making the idea work for you or your organisation. Each idea has been carefully researched and drawn from businesses and business people, past and present, from around the world. The criteria for selecting an idea are its impact, appeal and applicability.

As a result, the book provides a fascinating, stimulating, thought-provoking and practical guide to the world of great business ideas. We hope it will inspire and stimulate you to think about the way you do business; enable you to understand what makes a great business idea; and encourage you to adapt and implement some of the best concepts in business. Before embarking on the latter, it might be valuable to examine the guiding principles.

IMPLEMENTING GREAT IDEAS

Having a great idea is one thing, making it succeed is quite another. Many brilliant ideas remain hidden because of poor execution, while others that should never get out of the focus group too often do. So, what are the rules when implementing great business ideas, where are the pitfalls and how can they be overcome?

It's useful to understand three guiding principles. First, implementing great ideas requires a balance between a big picture view and detailed planning, both are vital. Second, personal responsibility and flexibility are vital. Too often, people complain that circumstances have changed so it is not possible to implement the idea. This overlooks an eternal truth: the fact that things will always change. What matters is adopting a flexible, resourceful attitude. It's not what you know that matters, but how you react to what you do *not* know. Finally, there is no quick solution, no silver bullet or magic formula. Instead, success can be achieved with a few simple techniques and strong leadership.

One leadership skill that assumes special significance when implementing ideas is *visioning*. This means inspiring a sense of purpose and belief by communicating a simple, clear, compelling vision to those involved. This then provides a touchstone to guide decisions, focusing the way people think and work. Also, if people have a shared sense of purpose it is easier to initiate actions to achieve that purpose. Visioning is valuable because it promotes teamworking and consistency with everyone working towards the same goal.

A vision of how the idea will succeed needs to come from the leader and it should have several essential characteristics. It needs to be powerful, painting a clear picture of the future as well as exciting and inspiring people. It needs to be easily communicated, desirable and realistic. The vision needs to be specific and 'real-world' enough to guide decision-making and, finally, it should also be adaptive: able to accommodate individual initiatives and flexible enough to allow for changing conditions.

You can get people to understand and support the vision by: communicating in an exciting and practical way, speaking positively so that people are intrigued, challenged and motivated. It also helps to be honest and open about your plans. Encourage people to see what the vision means for them and bring the vision to life, ideally with examples.

A great vision needs to be balanced with detailed planning and monitoring, proving the point that great leaders balance a big picture view with a detailed approach. So, don't leave things to chance, especially technology. Prepare a plan and set realistic and challenging goals that are specific, measurable and time-constrained. Also, look to achieve progress steadily and 'grow' your idea; keep it simple, test and practice, rather than rushing things. Next, monitor and measure progress; remember that what gets measured gets managed. Finally, stay flexible and ready to make adjustments. The implementation plan needs to be capable of coping with changing circumstances. If it is too rigid or inflexible then it is likely to fail.

Another valuable technique is to *manage risk and adopt a questioning approach.* There are no downsides: questioning will help you be prepared for any eventuality, stay on track and build confidence. For example, consider: what could go wrong? Where are the risks and how are these being managed? Are we delivering the most valuable aspects of this idea? What adjustments do we need to make? Scenario planning is a great technique to help you understand the issues.

Questioning is also useful because it supports another useful technique: the need to develop empathy. Too many ideas fail because they don't view the innovation through the eyes of people outside the immediate implementation team. Empathy can be achieved by understanding different motivations and priorities; for example, consider how you and others might react or behave in certain situations.

Several specific leadership skills are also significant when implementing ideas. It's vital to build a strong team and then give that team energy, belief and focus. Leaders also need to be decisive, as well as managing and securing resources, encouraging creative thinking, communicating and providing feedback, managing performance and developing a 'no blame' culture. All of these are prerequisites for a strong implementation team.

There are several practical steps that leaders can take to help new ideas succeed. For example, it is important to confront problems early and remove any constraints, such as bureaucracy, that block implementation. This shows determination, provides inspiration and helps set the pace. Also, support people: help them develop their skills and achieve their potential. This will help improve the quality of implementation as well as sustaining success.

Avoiding the Pitfalls

The way people think affects the way that ideas are applied. For example, the *status quo trap* biases us towards maintaining the current situation—even when better alternatives exist—due to inertia or the potential loss of face if the current position was to change. The *sunk-cost trap* inclines us to perpetuate the mistakes of the past, because the investment involved makes abandonment of previous decisions unthinkable. The *over-confidence trap* occurs when a decision maker has an exaggerated belief in their ability to understand situations and predict the future. The *prudence trap* leads us to be over-cautious when estimating risk. There is a tendency to be very risk averse and is likely to occur when there is a decision dilemma—when the decision maker feels both the current approach and alternative courses carry risks.

In addition to these thinking flaws, there are two potential pitfalls resulting from the culture or environment of the organization: *fragmentation and groupthink*. Fragmentation occurs when people are in disagreement, either with their peers or their superiors. Usually, the expression of emerging dissent is disguised or suppressed. Groupthink is the opposite of fragmentation, occurring when the group suppresses ideas that are critical or not in support of the direction in which the group is moving. The group appears to be in agreement or certain but is neither. The longer it lasts, the more entrenched and 'normal' it becomes. It can be very difficult to reverse.

So, what are the solutions? The first step is to *be bold* and don't fear the consequences of decisions—we tend to over-estimate the consequences, good and bad, of our choices. We also tend to discount our ability to make the right choice because of 'loss aversion': the view that a loss will hurt more than a gain will please. Next, *trust your instincts and emotions*. We have evolved to make good decisions and manage their implementation. Sometimes, quick decisions work best precisely because you have picked up on key pieces of information quickly. More time can simply lead to information-overload and other distractions. Also, be prepared to *play devil's advocate*—searching for flaws and failings will strengthen your decisions. Other important points are to avoid irrelevancies, reframe decisions and view issues from a new perspective. Finally, don't let the past hold you back: dare to be different. Possibly the greatest aspect of implementing new ideas is the fact that they lead to greater progress and success.

There are 365 ideas in this book, providing you with one business stimulant a day for the whole year. But there are no hard and fast rules for reading and using this book. We simply hope that these ideas will provide you with the inspiration to find out more or stimulate your thinking along new, creative lines, resulting in business and personal success.

STRATEGY
HAVE A VISION
Jonathan Gifford

A VISION SETS out a view of what the organization should look like in the future and of the way in which it will have changed the world. A really successful vision will inspire an organization, and affect every decision that is taken.

The idea

The Wal-Mart Stores retail group is one of the world's largest public corporations in terms of revenue. The founder, Sam Walton, said, "If we work together, we'll lower the cost of living for everyone ... we'll give the world an opportunity to see what it's like to save and have a better life."

"Saving people money to help people live better" is still the company's vision. The vision of Microsoft Corporation is "To help people and businesses throughout the world to realize their full potential". Google's vision is "To organize the world's information and make it universally accessible and useful". Nike aims "To bring inspiration and innovation to every athlete in the world".

A vision should be specific enough to guide people's future behavior, but sufficiently general to allow for changing circumstances, and to allow the organization to use its initiative in deciding how best to achieve the vision.

Some visions are apparently stark and simple and need to be "unpacked" to reveal all of the organization's values but, in the best examples, all of these values are implied in a simple, bold statement.

Wu Xiaobing, president and MD of pharmaceutical company Wyeth China, says, "To me, the most important thing for a leader is to create a vision and get everyone on the management team to believe, be convinced and excited and work for that. In most cases, if there is a vision, people will work hard together to create a miracle. If you are only dealing with daily business, and even if you are busy every day, you won't go very far and you won't have breakthrough. The leader must have a good vision, and then people will become inspired." The corporate vision of Wyeth is "To be the world's best pharmaceutical company". It unpacks this vision to reveal the goal of "developing innovative new medicines that really make a difference to people's lives and address significant areas of unmet medical need."

In practice

- A vision sets out a future that the organization seeks to bring about. It is a statement of where the organization hopes to get to, what it aspires to be and what change it intends to bring into people's lives.
- A vision should be simple and bold; it is not a definition of the organization's role—this is set out in the mission statement.
- The vision should inspire the organization, give it purpose and act as a reference point for every decision. It should persist through changing circumstances and different strategies.

MOTIVATION
MAKING YOUR EMPLOYEES PROUD
Jeremy Kourdi

A COMPANY WITH a positive self-image and sense of pride will be more unified and efficient, with a stronger "employer brand." When employees respect and appreciate the organization they work for, then their productivity, quality of work, and job satisfaction increase.

The idea

Are your employees proud of working for your business? This sense of pride may result from the organization's purpose, success, ethics, the quality of its leadership, or the quality and impact of its products. An example of this is Taylor Nelson Sofres (TNS), a leading market information company, with over 14,000 full-time employees across the world. It collects, analyzes, and interprets information for clients, provides research on business and market issues, and conducts social and political polling.

The firm's network spans 70 countries, and has been largely assembled through acquisition. Consequently, employees were often more loyal to their local "in-country" TNS business than to the group, which seemed remote or foreign. However, when one of its executives was caught in the tsunami in South Asia in December 2004, TNS donated $250,000 to UNICEF to aid relief operations. This altruism brought the company together, as employees were pleased to be working for an organization with values that they respected.

As TNS illustrates, simple and positive gestures can achieve impressive results in terms of employee satisfaction, pride, and motivation.

In practice

- Carry out acts of corporate social responsibility—such as donation, fundraising, or simply enacting more compassionate business practices. These all serve to make current and potential employees feel proud to work with your organization.
- Ask employees what they value—what would they like their employer to do?
- Provide opportunities for employees to engage in fundraising and volunteering activities.
- Avoid negative business practices. Employees will be less motivated to work within an organization that is viewed negatively in society.
- Remind employees of the ways their services benefit society; how the everyday tasks they perform make a positive difference within society.

MARKETING
ADD SOME VALUE
Jim Blythe

WHATEVER BUSINESS YOU are in, there is a strong likelihood that you have competitors who offer something similar—and it is a racing certainty that there are alternative solutions out there for customers' problems, as seen from the customer's viewpoint. For instance, someone in the restaurant business might feel complacent because there are no other restaurants in town, but not recognize that a local cinema is competition in the "where shall we go for a night out?" category.

Adding value means finding something that will mark you out from your competitors *in the eyes of the customers you are hoping to attract.* What is good value for one person is poor value for another.

The idea

When Peter Boizot founded PizzaExpress in 1965, pizza was virtually unheard of outside Italy: there were no pizzerias at all in London. Early on, Boizot latched on to the idea of providing something extra—he started by having live jazz bands performing in the restaurants (many well-known jazz musicians got their start by playing at PizzaExpress in Soho). Nowadays, the restaurants often have live music, but many host art exhibitions or have other types of live performance. The point is the company is aiming for an "artsy" audience who will enjoy this type of added value.

PizzaExpress has a Members' Club: for a subscription (currently £45 a year) members become entitled to four vouchers a year for free menu items plus a free glass of wine, to free desserts when dining early, free entry to the PizzaExpress Jazz Club, and a £10 gift voucher for every ten meals purchased.

Offering extra value has enabled PizzaExpress to withstand competition, and to keep its brand intact in the face of the "pile 'em high and get 'em out there" approach of American pizza chains. PizzaExpress is able to charge more for its pizzas than these big chains, because the added value makes them worthwhile—the higher prices also deter the kind of downmarket customers PizzaExpress wants to discourage.

In practice

- Only offer added value that your target customers will appreciate.
- Price accordingly—people do not mind paying more if they are getting more.
- Ensure that what it costs to add the value is less than the premium your customers will pay.
- Promote the added value—they already know about your product.

PUBLIC RELATIONS
DEVELOP A COMPANY HISTORY
Jim Blythe

STORYTELLING IS PROBABLY the oldest form of entertainment human beings have. We all love a good story—which is why we have so many conversations, why we delight in telling each other what happened to us last week, and why we like to listen to such stories. We like history, too, which is why costume dramas are so popular on TV.

Company histories combine these elements to create something that is truly of interest.

The idea

Many large companies publish their corporate histories on their websites. H. J. Heinz, for example, has a detailed history of the company on its site, going back to the days when a young Henry Heinz grew horseradish to sell to local grocery stores. The history emphasizes Henry's personal values of thrift, honesty, and fair dealing (with the clearly stated implication that this is how the company is run to this very day).

The Heinz history is illustrated, is interactive, and is comprehensive. Not all companies would have the resources to create such a web page, but even the smallest company can make a human-interest story from their history: Lucie's Farm, a supplier of Highland beef, tell the story that their founders (Craig and Marjorie Walsh) first became interested in rearing Highland cattle after seeing the film *Rob Roy*. They are now the leading breeders of these cattle outside Scotland: the farm even has its own crest. This kind of story is a great deal more interesting than features about the quality of the beef, or the problems of rearing hairy cattle in a warmer climate than they have been used to.

In practice

- Emphasize the human aspects of your history. No one's interested in your balance sheet.
- Put your history on your website and in your printed promotional material.
- If your history is interesting enough, see if someone will make a documentary about you.

STRATEGY
ESTABLISH YOUR MISSION
Jonathan Gifford

THE ORGANIZATION'S MISSION statement is different from the leader's vision, which is a view of how the ideal future would look. The mission statement is about the present; about what the organization does, for whom and why. When it is well defined and clearly presented, the mission can be as inspiring as the vision: it gives people clear and immediate goals and targets.

The idea

Jack Welch, chairman and CEO of General Electric from 1981 to 2001, defines the ideal mission statement with characteristic force.

"In my experience, an effective mission statement basically answers one question: How do we intend to win in this business? ... It requires companies to make choices about people, investment, and other resources, and it prevents them from falling into the common mission trap of asserting they will be all things to all people at all times ... Effective mission statements balance the possible and the impossible. They give people a clear sense of the direction to profitability and the inspiration to feel they are part of something big and important. Take our mission at GE as an example. From 1981 through 1995, we said we were going to be 'the most competitive enterprise in the world' by being No. 1 or No. 2 in every market— fixing, selling, or closing every underperforming business that couldn't get there."

There could be no doubt about what this mission statement meant or entailed. It was specific, descriptive, with nothing abstract going on. And it was inspirational too, in its global ambition. General Electric's vision was "To be the most competitive enterprise in the world". Its mission was "To be No. 1 or No. 2 in every market".

John Mackey, co-founder and CEO of the USA's natural and organic foods retailer, Whole Foods Market, says this about his company's mission:

"The business has a mission or deeper purpose beyond maximizing profits to the shareholders ... Our mission is ... to sell the highest quality natural, organic foods in the world. And that's our deepest mission. And then we organize our stakeholders around that mission, satisfying the customers, team-member happiness and excellence, increasing shareholder value through profits and through growth and taking care of the communities and the environment ... we're mission-driven in that we try to fulfil those core values which include, but go beyond, simply maximizing profits."

Whole Food's *vision* is encapsulated in its motto: "Whole foods, whole people, whole planet".

In practice

- Vision is about the relatively distant future; mission is about the present.
- A mission statement spells out what the organization offers, to whom and why, and how it intends to achieve that mission.
- A clear mission statement is inspiring in itself, since it sets out clearly what the organization will do and how. It sets clear goals for the team.

COMPETITION
INSTANT RECOGNIZABILITY
Jeremy Kourdi

CREATING A DISTINCTIVELY packaged product will secure it a lasting place in the memory of customers, convey an image, and ensure it stands out among other choices, making it easy for people to recognize instantly.

The idea

How to successfully differentiate your product is a much-debated issue in marketing and product development departments. While superior levels of customer service and quality are important, it should be recognized that people can be visually reliant when forming a first impression of a product. Consequently, packaging your product in an appealing and instantly recognizable way provides a valuable head start in the battle for differentiation.

The flat-sided, sapphire-colored bottle used to market Bombay Sapphire dry gin is instantly recognizable thanks to its striking, translucent design. It can be recognized without having to see the product name on the bottle. With this bold, style-savvy approach, potential customers are instantly drawn to the product and their curiosity piqued. Should customers wish to buy the product again, they can find it quickly and easily in an array of cleverly packaged choices. The dry gin manufacturer emphasized its design credentials by awarding the Bombay Sapphire Prize—the world's biggest international glass design award. By taking design seriously, it pushed itself further toward pole position in its market.

It is a tactic used by Coca-Cola, whose distinctively curvy, long-necked glass bottle wrapped in the distinctive red and white logo is a symbol of American consumer culture—instantly recognizable on the crowded soft drinks shelves in supermarkets.

Possessing a distinctive design allows people to form emotional attachments to your product and to use it as a status symbol. Your packaging becomes an extension of your logo—don't neglect it, and don't be content to merely conform to the industry standard: seek to surpass it.

In practice

- Pay attention to small details in product design: well-crafted lines and curves have a subtle impact.
- Sexuality can be important. Products with a design that loosely mirrors the shape and form of the female body (such as a Coke bottle) are supposedly more appealing (they may make a talking point, providing an added dimension to marketing).
- Intangible products, such as financial advice, are not excluded from the challenges of good product design. Managing the customer experience and designing offices and marketing campaigns are activities that benefit from good product design to make these products and services more eye-catching, enjoyable, and memorable.
- Consider hiring a professional product expert for advice on what design will best work for your customer offering.

A GOOD FIRST IMPRESSION
Patrick Forsyth

YOU ONLY GET one chance to make a good first impression. That statement may be a cliché, but it is true. In sales terms another maxim is almost more important: first impressions last. However you look at it, selling is easier if first impressions lead people to positive conclusions, and prompt thoughts like: that's a good start—so far so good—I like that, now what comes next?

Sometimes this can be achieved simply and it is specific to the individual; it is something they do. Sometimes, more rarely perhaps, the impression stems from the whole company, and more rarely still, it is something that achieves a real wow factor.

The idea
At international construction machinery company JCB ...

Here is a company that certainly wows first-time visitors to its factory in the English Midlands, especially those who come from overseas. Its product needs demonstrating so it no doubt has visitors aplenty. Imagine: you fly from wherever—Peru or Paris—and even if you are not familiar with the country, you know that the place you will visit is a significant journey from London. (You imagine the usual hazards of any journey—traffic, hold-ups and so on.) But your hosts say they will meet you at Heathrow Airport, London, so that sounds a little easier.

Then the meeting turns out to be a brief connection to the company helicopter and a very straightforward direct flight, of only an hour or so, which lands you in the landscaped grounds surrounding the factory.

Not everyone can run to a company helicopter, but attention to any detail at first contact that will give the right impression is worthwhile and helps set the scene for the subsequent meeting. The helicopter may be a dramatic way of doing things, but it is really only one way of providing extra service and convenience to customers. This is true of the individual, several individuals, or the organization itself.

In practice

- Seek to make genuine service, rather than gimmicks, enhance customer acceptance.
- Ensure that there are management processes to consider/ approve expenditure on such things (though not necessarily of this magnitude!).

MARKETING
GIVE THE PRODUCT AWAY
Jim Blythe

GIVING THE PRODUCT away might seem crazy—but in some cases it is the only way to establish it in a new market. When a product is revolutionary, few people want to be the first to try it, so asking them for money up front often simply creates a barrier. In some cases, this is just something we have to live with, but if owning the product means that the customer will have to buy repeatedly, giving away something that creates a dependency is good business.

There are many examples in practice of products that are sold cheap, with the company making its money on the peripherals. Spare parts for cars are an example—the cars are sold relatively cheaply, but genuine spares are expensive, because that is how the manufacturer makes money. There is no reason at all to be wedded to the idea that every product that leaves the factory gates has to have a price tag on it, and many companies have succeeded admirably by giving products away.

The idea

When King C. Gillette invented the safety razor he was working as a salesperson for a bottle-cap manufacturer. He conceived the idea for a disposable razor when his cut-throat razor got too old to be resharpened: he fairly easily developed a way of making the blades and the razors to hold them (the first blades were made from clock springs) but economies of scale meant that the blades could only be profitable if he could manufacture them in their millions. He needed a quick way of getting men to switch over from cut-throat to disposable razors, so he decided to give the product away.

Gillette gave away thousands of razors, complete with blades, knowing that few men would go back to using a cut-throat razor once they had experienced the safety razor. Within a few days they would need to buy new blades, so Gillette had created an instant market, limited only by his capacity to give away more razors.

In time, once the product was established in the market and the first users (the innovators) had started telling their friends about the product, Gillette was able to start charging for the razors themselves. However, the razors were always sold at close to, or even below, the manufacturing cost—the company makes its money on selling the blades, which cost almost nothing to produce and which can be sold for a premium price.

In time, other shaving systems came along (plastic disposables, for example) that superseded Gillette's idea, but the basic marketing idea remains and is still used to this day.

In practice

- Identify products that carry a long-term commitment to buying peripherals, spares, or other consumables.
- Decide your target market—there is no point giving out freebies to all and sundry if they aren't going to follow through and buy your product later.
- Make sure you have good intellectual property rights (patents, etc.) so that nobody can enter the market with knock-off consumables that work with your giveaway product.

STRATEGY
BUMPER-STICKER STRATEGY
Jeremy Kourdi

A FIRM SHOULD be able to summarize its business and approach in a single concise statement.

The idea

Quick and effective communication is viewed by many as a cornerstone of modern business. In light of this, it seems natural that many organizations have developed a way of summing up the most important aspects of their business in a memorable and impressive "bumper-sticker" tagline. Notable examples of organizations that use this tactic include:

- *Virgin*: "Debunk the establishment, business as fun." This statement reinforces the company's image as rebellious, confident, and daring within the corporate world.
- *BMW*: "The ultimate driving machine." Underlining its status as the most superior luxury-car brand, BMW strives to appear as the most impressive option in a competitive market where status is vital.
- *Federal Express*: "Guaranteed overnight delivery." Showing off its core competency and proposition in three words, this statement reminds customers of its reliability and speed, while reminding employees of the importance of timely delivery.

The benefits of a good bumper-sticker slogan are not just in winning over customers—it can be useful for communicating with employees too. While the examples mentioned were for entire companies, they can be used at all levels within an organization, and adjusted for different teams, departments, and strategic initiatives. This helps teams work together toward a common goal, as well as clarifying complex sales campaigns so they can be fully understood. Bumper stickers also help salespeople understand which points to emphasize.

Customer-focused taglines cement your brand's image among your consumer base, capture their attention, and remind them of the quality of your services. Make sure you have one for your business or job.

In practice

- Decide which specific aspects of your product offering or corporate strategy should be emphasized in the tagline.
- Work it into your company's advertising, wherever possible. It should come to be symbolic of your firm's values and services.
- Show a clear differentiation from your competitors.
- Promise value. See it from your customers' point of view—have you clearly outlined the advantages for them?
- Consider what is unique about your business organization that will allow you to carry out the strategy in a superior way to your competitors.
- Ensure employees are committed to the goal and take it to heart.

VALUES

ESTABLISH YOUR VALUES

Jonathan Gifford

AN ORGANIZATION NEEDS a vision and a strategy, but it also needs a value system. These values will affect every aspect of corporate culture, and can ensure that every employee understands how he or she is expected to behave in any circumstance.

The idea

The Texas-based American low-cost airline, Southwest, established itself on a platform of exceptional customer service. Its former president, Colleen Barrett, explains how the company's values are nailed to its mast: "Our mission statement is posted every three feet, all over every location that we have, so if you're a customer, you've seen it. It's to follow the Golden Rule—to treat people the way that you want to be treated, and pretty much everything will fall into place." Every employee needs to be able to take this fundamental approach to heart, says Barrett: "We hire for attitude and we train for skill, and we are far more likely to terminate someone for attitude and behavior and lack of respect than just about anything else."

Dieter Zetsche, chairman of Daimler AG and head of Mercedes Benz Cars, highlights four values that form the heart of the company's culture: passion, respect, integrity and discipline. Every Daimler employee must have a passion for cars; respect must encompass customers, colleagues, business partners and shareholders; integrity dictates that every employee anywhere in the world adheres to the highest ethical standards. The fourth value is discipline.

"When we talk about discipline," says Zetsche, "what we mean is the ability to choose the truth over convenience."

Subroto Bagchi is a co-founder of MindTree, a global IT solutions consultancy with headquarters in Bangalore, India, and New Jersey, USA. The young company asked its employees to choose the values that would define the organization. Now, says Bagchi, the company places alignment with its core values first in its recruitment and appraisal policies.

"The responses were synthesized into five key values. These are Caring, Learning, Achieving, Sharing, and Social Sensitivity. We now find that these have been internalized. These have been embedded into our performance management system and our recruitment system. We certainly believe that value alignment precedes competence. The world is full of competent people ... If values are in place, competence can always be developed."

In practice
- An organization's values usually emerge naturally from its original vision, but the team needs to explore these values so that they are clear to all.
- The values must be widely publicized; managers must work hard to ensure that they have been understood by everyone in the organization.
- A lapse in behavior by any member of the team can be

surprisingly damaging; a team that has internalized the values can be trusted to behave in the best interests of the organization in every situation.

- Alignment with the organization's values is of primary importance in recruitment and promotion: skills can be taught; not everyone has the right attitude.

PUBLIC RELATIONS
CONSUMER SCIENCE SELLS STORIES
Jim Blythe

TWENTY-FIRST-CENTURY people often seem to be obsessed with themselves (which is a feature they probably have in common with nineteenth-century, eighteenth-century, or even twelfth-century people).

This being the case, periodicals often like to publish research that tells us something interesting about ourselves or about others we might know—and such research can be turned to your advantage.

The idea

A very large amount of research about consumer behavior is published every year in academic journals. Most of it passes unnoticed, and indeed a lot of it is hardly worth a mention anyway, but sometimes research will come up with a really interesting snippet. If it's relevant to your business, it can lead to a story in the mainstream press.

For example, a piece of research revealed that people who wear contact lenses are four times more likely to attract a partner in a nightclub than are people who wear glasses. This was of great use to a contact lens company.

Trawling through academic journals need not take up a great deal of time—usually university libraries are happy for you to browse the journals section provided you don't borrow anything or make a nuisance of yourself to the librarians, and you usually only need to read the abstracts anyway to know if the article is any use. An hour or two is likely to produce two or three articles you could draw on.

Such research, of course, carries a great deal of credibility. You should have little trouble in establishing your bona fides with the periodicals you send the story to.

In practice

- Contact the authors of the articles and tell them what you are planning. This is a courtesy, and it may lead to further information and/or research findings being forthcoming.
- Make a note of the source of your information. The newspaper will want to know where you found the research.
- If necessary, work with the researchers to produce more useful results in the future.

MARKETING
FEEL-GOOD ADVERTISING
Jeremy Kourdi

RATHER THAN SIMPLY presenting customers with a manifesto of reasons to purchase your product, try to entertain, intrigue, or reassure them.

The idea

It can be tempting when creating an advertising campaign just to focus on why your product is superior and how you can persuade customers to purchase it. But the reality is that most of the people you reach with your advertising will be cynical and overloaded with other campaigns. Consequently, they have little interest in an unsolicited, short statement about why your product is better. This means you should find a new way of talking to them. Creating a marketing campaign that potential customers find amusing, fascinating, or heart-warming will help you reach even the most jaded consumer.

Cellphone company Orange devised its "Orange Wednesdays" offer of free cinema tickets for customers, through a series of adverts that aired before movies in Britain, which humorously lampooned the movie and advertising industries. The short clips showed movie stars unsuccessfully attempting to pitch ideas to an "Orange Film Commission," only to be shot down because the movies did not do enough to promote Orange cellphones. Over-the-top and deliberately laughable suggestions were made to the aspiring movie-makers, including "making the fourth in the trilogy" for *Lord of the Rings*, and renaming it "Lord of the Ring Tone." These non-traditional adverts satirized advertising, while subtly attempting to win customers and form positive brand associations.

Dove, a leading provider of skin and hair care products, implemented a feel-good advertising promotion with its "Campaign for Real Beauty." Straying from the typical approach of cosmetic companies using attractive models, Dove encouraged customers to feel happy about the way they look naturally. Using models with a "realistic" appearance, Dove encouraged women to have a positive body image regardless of conventional beauty standards. British newspaper *The Times* commented on the campaign: "Dove presents a refreshing antidote to the jaundiced narcissism of the professional supermodel hired to sell beauty products."

By rebelling against some of the negative or traditional practices in advertising, Dove and Orange created goodwill and positive brand awareness, while entertaining and amusing potential customers.

So don't just make your customers feel better about your product: make them feel better about themselves.

In practice
- Understand the sense of humor, social concerns, and typical "personality" of your target market.
- Consider involving entertainers in your ad campaigns to provide a memorable comic edge.
- Integrate any corporate social initiatives your company is undertaking into your advertising campaign.
- Do not feel pressured to fit your product into conventional

advertising. Be critical and adapt your marketing into a more lively and customer-focused offering.

CUSTOMERS
KNOW YOUR CUSTOMER'S MOTIVATIONS
Jim Blythe

IF WE KNOW what makes our customers tick, we can offer them solutions that will appeal to their innermost motivations. Sometimes we need to look beyond the obvious—for example, few men buy aftershave, and few women buy sexy underwear. In the case of aftershave, most of it is bought by women to give as a gift to their husbands or boyfriends, and sexy underwear is bought by men to give to wives and girlfriends. This is part of the fantasy of what we would like our partners to be—less smelly, and more sexy.

Likewise, most men (left to their own devices) probably would not buy deodorant. Deodorant is not a gift purchase, though, so manufacturers need to consider why a man WOULD buy deodorant. What is the motivation?

The idea
Lynx deodorant is the world's biggest-selling deodorant spray for men. In most of the world it is sold as Axe, but in Britain that brand name was already registered so it had to have a new name. The brand owners, Unilever, decided that the only reason men buy deodorant is because they think it will make them more attractive (or at least less repellent) to women.

The company therefore developed the concept of the "Lynx effect." In the advertisements, a geeky-looking guy sprays himself liberally with Lynx and is immediately mobbed by women. The ads are tongue-in-cheek, of course: no one really expects that women are that easily persuaded, but subconsciously the message gets through that smelling better will improve your chances with women.

The idea actually grew from an earlier Unilever product, Impulse. This was a body spray for women, and the advertising showed men doing something romantic after catching a whiff of the Impulse-sprayed woman—for example, chasing after her down the street with a bunch of flowers. The motivation is similar: while the Lynx-sprayed men enjoy the idea of a lot of sexy women chasing them, the Impulse-sprayed woman enjoys romantic encounters with attractive, non-threatening men.

In each case, the key lies in finding out what the real motivation is for buying the product.

In practice

- Find the hidden motivator. Is it sex? Security? Respect of others? Often these are totally separate from the apparent "surface" motivation.
- It is OK to make the advertising a bit of a fantasy. Nobody really believes advertising anyway—it all operates on the subconscious level.
- Make the characters in your advertising believable. People relate best to people who they perceive as being like them.

SALES

ADOPT THE RIGHT ATTITUDE

Patrick Forsyth

SALESPEOPLE OFTEN ASK me what the key to sales success is. Would that it was so simple! Success comes not from one thing, but is largely in the details: the approach, the techniques used—and the attitude that people take to it. This is more than just the ubiquitous "positive mental attitude" beloved of many a book on how to be successful (in selling or anything else). It comprises a number of attitudes, including:

- A conscious and considered awareness of the psychology of

selling and how it works. The best salespeople always seem to have a clear understanding of what they are doing and of deploying the right approaches at the right moment.

- A customer focus: because the psychology of decision making and buying demands this and it is a foundation for success.
- A will to win and an ability to not allow any rejection along the way to cramp their style. As few (if any) salespeople have a 100 percent strike rate this is simply necessary.
- Persistence: because not every order comes easily or instantly.
- Creativity: even a superficial reading of this book shows the need for that.
- An awareness that selling is a dynamic process. It cannot be done by rote in the same way forever. What works for one person today may need to be done differently for someone else next week, certainly next year. Good salespeople keep their approaches updated.

There are no doubt more, though some will stem from those listed. Attitudes underpin action, so how we think about things is as important as what is done. Thus it is helpful if you have habits that act to remind you of the attitudes you should adopt and maintain.

The idea
In computer giant IBM ...

All I want to stress here is one aspect of the power of attitude, which is given weight by being favored by such a large, well-known organization. According to marketing guru Philip Kotler, a maxim used in every IBM internal training course is that whoever a salesperson is talking to, they should conduct the meeting as if they are about to lose the order. Holding such a thought will help strengthen everything that is done, making it thorough and maximizing persuasiveness.

In practice
- Identify those attitudes you can usefully display.
- Work at displaying them (this may go beyond your natural persona).

EXECUTION
MAKE IT HAPPEN
Jonathan Gifford

ALL OF A leader's great plans come to nothing if they are not successfully executed. Leaders make things happen.

The idea
Michael Eisner, former CEO of the Walt Disney Company, now runs the privately held investment company Tornante.

As Eisner says about execution, "The problem is not the ideas, the problem is getting them executed. And I don't or cannot remember a successful movie or television show that we've ever made that I didn't get many letters saying, 'That was my idea,' or 'Oh you did a movie. It was just like something I was thinking about doing.' And what I want to say is, 'Well, why didn't you do it?' And the problem is that it is a big step from having an idea flow from out of your head, and getting it on a piece of paper, getting people around you to think it's a good idea, finding a writer, putting on a show—look how hard it is to put on a show in High School!"

Louis Gerstner, previous CEO of IBM, says that making it happen is possibly more important than developing a brilliant new strategy—which may, in any case, be highly risky. "Execution—getting the task done, making it happen—is the most unappreciated skill of an effective business leader. In my years as a consultant, I participated in the development of many strategies for many companies ... It is extremely difficult to develop a unique strategy for a company; and if the strategy is truly different, it is probably highly risky. The reason for this is that industries are defined and bound by economic models, explicit customer expectations, and competitive structures that are known to all and impossible to change in a short period of time ... So, execution really is the critical part of a successful strategy. Getting it done, getting it done right, getting it done better than the next person is far more important than dreaming up new visions of the future."

In practice

- Many people have good ideas; few actually carry them out; fewer still carry them out with excellence.
- Businesses are constrained by well-known economic and market factors that limit the scope for truly original new strategies. Your competitors almost certainly have the same ideas that you do. The leader who executes those ideas most successfully—who makes things happen most effectively—wins.

MARKETING
IMAGINE ...
Andy Maslen

ONE OF THE simplest techniques for getting your reader to engage with your copy is to ask them to use their imagination. And the simplest way to do this is to use the verb "imagine." Telling people to imagine something engages far more of their brain than simply writing about your product.

Instead, you give them license to daydream—a far more pleasurable activity than reading. Then all you have to do is create a place for them where that daydream leads, inexorably, to interest in whatever you're selling.

The idea
From dreamcarhire.com, a sports car hire firm
As a self-confessed petrolhead, I love everything to do with fast cars. And I guess like a lot of people, I'd love to tool around in a Ferrari for a day—or longer. But until that lottery win or inheritance from a mystery millionaire relative, it's going to have to stay as just a dream. Or is it? Because, of course, for every dream we in the West can conjure up, there's at least one outfit catering to its fulfillment. In the case of sports car hire, there are dozens, from membership clubs to straightforward hire companies.

Flicking through the back pages of *Top Gear* magazine, I came upon a really great ad for dreamcarhire.com. As an aside, it follows the ideal ad layout, as used by great copywriters from David Ogilvy and John Caples on down: picture, headline, body copy, call to action, logo.

We have a full-width photo of a glossy black Ferrari F430, landscape blurred behind it. But it's the headline that really brings you up short and lets the ad do its work:

Imagine yourself behind the wheel of a supercar

It's a powerful little eight-word phrase, supercharged by the word "imagine." Why? Because that's precisely what the reader is doing anyway. So the copywriter has tapped directly into the motivation of the reader. They could have just written ...

You could be driving this supercar

But then we're left feeling, "Yeah right, but only for a day." It's a downer.

Or

Driving a supercar needn't cost the earth

But now we're focused on cost, even as the copywriter strives to sell the benefits of hiring. But the "imagine" headline takes us beyond the sell, beyond the close, into the territory the copywriter wants us to inhabit: *life with the product.*

In practice

- Start by thinking about how the world would look to your reader if they did the thing you wanted them to. Create a quick pencil portrait of this scene.
- Write some copy starting with the phrase "Imagine a world in which you ..." Now complete it with the details of your pen portrait. New paragraph: "It's all possible when you ..."

BRANDING
BUILD A CORPORATE BRAND
Jim Blythe

THE CORPORATE BRAND is the overall impression the company gives to its publics, as opposed to the individual brands given to the firm's products. Building a corporate brand gives the firm a higher profile with its customers as well as with other publics, and gives credibility in all sorts of places.

Building a corporate brand is often something that companies regard as "a nice thing to have if we could only afford it" but in fact is the signal to your customers that you are passionate about what you do, and serious about being the best in your field, not just planning to earn a crust from the business. It also signals to your employees that they are working on something special: rather than working in a quarry, they are helping to build a cathedral, for example. Finally, it signals to government and local authority people that you are a firm to be taken seriously, a big player (even if you aren't).

The idea
When Edward Stobart was a child growing up in 1960s Cumberland, he (like many other little boys) liked playing with toy lorries. When he became a man, he was able to play with big lorries—he took over the family's haulage concern (part of their agricultural supplies business) and grew it into the Eddie Stobart Ltd. freight logistics empire.

Stobart knew from the outset that he needed a strong corporate brand. There were hundreds of other companies out there, many of them much longer established, so unless he was going to compete on price (which in business is the last refuge of the incompetent) he would have to compete on credibility and integrity.

Stobart gave all his trucks women's names (his first were named after prominent female performers of the seventies such as Suzi Quatro and Dolly Parton) and insisted that his drivers be smartly dressed in collars and ties at all times. Driver training is still a major part of Stobart's success—apart from hiring nice people to start with, the company trains drivers to be courteous to other road users and (of course) to customers, and to take a pride in their vehicles.

From a customer viewpoint, taking a delivery from a Stobart driver makes a welcome change from some of the greasy oafs who turn up at the warehouse demanding a signature. All Stobart staff are expected to adopt a "can-do" attitude, finding ways to accommodate customer expectations.

Eddie Stobart is now the best-known haulage company in Britain— it even has its own fan club, and people collect models of the Stobart vehicles. No small achievement for a trucking company!

In practice

- Be prepared to spend money on building your corporate brand.
- Be different from everybody else—latch onto something the others aren't offering.
- Be passionate and committed to your brand—if you aren't, no one else will be.

SALES

GETTING PEOPLE TO GIVE YOU TIME
Patrick Forsyth

MANY SALESPEOPLE NEED to take steps to get people to give them their undivided attention, to spend sufficient time with them and to do so willingly because they believe it is useful. But ...

People are busy, these days pressure on time seems to be greater than ever before, and anything other than a realistic attitude to this is unlikely to help you sell successfully. Clearly a more professional approach is more likely to be seen as relevant, but the more imaginative salespeople can take specific action to maximize time spent.

The idea
In a major international airline ...

There is a particular salesperson known internally as "the donut man." Given that part of his job is to call regularly on travel agents and brief their staff on new developments (such as new routes, fares, and special offers), he has a problem. If he does this one person at a time, then even in a medium-sized city agency it could take a long time to brief everyone. The agency will not let him do it with everyone at one time—telephones must be answered and business must continue. So he has evolved a cunning plan: he arranges to see half the staff at a time, and promises to arrive "bearing gifts." At the appointed time he appears with a tray of coffees, teas, and donuts from a nearby café. Half the staff takes a break together, they gather round, and he can brief them in a convivial atmosphere. When he has finished the staff swap: the now briefed group go back on duty, and the other half take a break. They all like it. They pay attention. And they look forward to his next visit.

Most important, they are up to date, and well able to steer their customers toward this particular airline in their day-to-day work.

In practice
- Think about how your customers' businesses work and aim to fit in with their special nature.
- Sometimes something unconventional can fit this criterion and work well; stay open-minded.

CHANGE
SEEK OUT CHANGE
Jonathan Gifford

BRINGING ABOUT CHANGE is the primary function of leadership. Change is frightening because it is, by definition, a leap into the dark. However, change is unavoidable: market conditions can shift quite suddenly and with little or no warning.

Leaders must instil a sense of open-mindedness in the organization and encourage the team to explore new ideas.

The idea

Harvard Business professor and author John Kotter writes: "Leadership produces change. That is its primary function." Leaders must set the direction for change, and Kotter points out that this is not the same as planning: "Planning is a management process ... primarily designed to help produce orderly results, not change." Making a change or coping with change is, by definition, risky. It takes us into unfamiliar territory where no established management processes can help us.

Richard Branson, chairman of Virgin Group, is frank about the fact that change is not welcome: "It's no good saying 'Prepare for change' or 'Embrace change' ... The bald fact is, change, most of the time, is a threat. It's the thing that wants to kill you. And let's face it: one day, it will." But Branson is proud of his own group's record: "What delights me is the way the company has continued to innovate its way out of trouble. A defensive, conservative, cautious mindset—a natural enough reaction when things get tough—can kill you stone dead in a competitive marketplace. When your existence is threatened, you have to change. This is one of the hardest lessons to learn in business, because it is so counter-intuitive."

In practice

- Leadership is primarily about change and involves risk. The leader's function is to choose the right direction for change.
- The environment in which organizations operate can change quite suddenly. Leaders need to create an attitude throughout the organization that expects change and is willing to adapt.
- Leaders should encourage an environment of constant innovation. Organizations that actively seek out change are more likely to stay ahead of the game.
- When a change in the outside world takes the organization by surprise, internal change is essential. Keeping on doing the same thing will not work.

FORGET IMPACT, GO FOR UNDERSTANDING

Andy Maslen

THERE'S A REAL temptation when designing press ads (or briefing them) to go for high impact designs. Brightly colored headlines, eye-catching illustrations or photography, unusual typefaces or layouts. Yet only one of these will do anything to increase the proportion of people stopping at your ad who can actually understand it. Want to have a guess which one?

If you plumped for the illustrations, well done. Everything else, while full of impact, decreases comprehension of the body copy. Next time you're reading a newspaper or magazine, compare the look of the editorial matter to the advertising. Notice the difference. Unless it's a very trendy new magazine aimed at sk8er boyz and girlz (or something similar), the editorial is mostly set in black type (usually a serif typeface) on a white ground. Not so the ads. Hmmm. I wonder why.

The idea
From Colin Wheildon, the only man ever to have researched and made public the scientific relationship between design and comprehension

That's some build-up, huh? But it happens to be true. Wheildon, a journalist and son of a typesetter, set out to research the effects of different typefaces and layouts on reader comprehension. Wheildon's book is called, in its latest edition, *Type & Layout: Are you Communicating or Just Making Pretty Shapes?*. Buy it. You won't be disappointed. (Your designer might be.)

In it, Wheildon systematically reveals the effects of such art directors' favorite devices as sans-serif body copy, body copy set into unusual shapes, images and captions, ragged versus justified setting, bright color headlines, column width, and so on.

In what is, for me, probably the most telling example, he researched the effects of setting ad headlines in black, versus low and high croma colors (dark blue and bright red for example). Poor comprehension of body copy jumped from 14 percent of research subjects for ads with black headlines to 65 percent for ads with red headlines. Good comprehension dropped from 67 percent to 17 percent when the same color switch was made.

Giving a worked example, he says that if an ad in a national newspaper gains a million readers with a black headline, it will gain 1.6 million readers if you set the headline in bright red. Great, so job done? Er, no. Because, although it has more impact, the red-head ad only delivers 240,000 people who understand it thoroughly, compared to 670,000 for the original. And if they don't read the body copy, they miss the selling message.

In practice

- Color does attract additional readers for your ad, but try using it in non-type elements such as backgrounds or photographs.
- Your designer will probably never have heard of Colin Wheildon and will, in any case, dispute his findings. Run a test.

SALES
FIND THE DECISION MAKER
Patrick Forsyth

ANY SELLING TECHNIQUE must be directed to the decision maker, whoever that is (it may be more than one person). Identifying who you are talking to and what role they play is vital. Sometimes your contact will have a specific brief: perhaps they are a "recommender," asked by a decision maker to check things out. If you feel other people are involved in the buying decision, you need to engineer a link to them, or better still a meeting with them.

The idea

From a major Volvo car dealer ...

It is said that the most important thing in selling a car is to get the prospect to sit in the driver's seat, with taking a test drive coming a close and linked second. So far so good, but what happens when you have identified that a family is involved and yet only one of the key players comes to the dealership? This might be either a male or female partner, and who is to say which of the pair is the more important? Once you have persuaded this person to take a test drive, one ploy that can be used here is to organize the route so that in its latter stages it goes close to the prospect's home. (This assumes they live within reach, but most likely they do, or why would they go into that dealership?) Then as the drive is nearing completion the salesperson suggests a stop at the house, using an appropriate phrase such as "Let your wife have a look."

This creates a meeting within a meeting. Suddenly the salesperson has both halves of the decision-making duo together, and can tackle the remaining stage of the sale with both of them. All being well, the drive will already have made a good impression, and seeing the car parked on their own driveway helps stimulate the prospects' imagination.

This is a novel response to the problem of involving all decision makers. It is well tailored to the way such sales work, and uses a suggestion that is likely to be seen only as a helpful addition to what is being done.

In practice
- Always explore and identify who the true decision maker is for your prospect, and remember the decision may involve several people.
- Make your sales approach suit, and if possible be special to, all the people involved.

LEADERSHIP
BE HUMAN
Jonathan Gifford

WHILE THE ORGANIZATION does not want to see a leader's every passing humor, it does need to see his or her core, relevant emotions: passion, concern, dedication, hope, conviction.

At times the organization will want to see compassion and friendliness. Leaders also need to encourage the organization to explore its own humanity and to benefit from uniquely human talents such as creativity and ingenuity.

The idea

Roger Ailes is a media advisor who worked on President George Bush's 1988 presidential campaign. He subsequently advised New York Mayor Rudolph Giuliani on his media presentation techniques and went on to become president of Fox News Channel and chairman of Fox Television Stations Group. Ailes advised Giuliani to stop reading his scripts to camera.

"Forget it. Just take your glasses off and start talking, and we'll get it right. If you feel angry, communicate it. Sad, communicate it. Mopey, communicate it. Let people know that you're a human being and the rest will take care of itself."

Jun Tang, Microsoft China President, reminds us that the workplace is not an emotionally neutral place where people assemble simply to make a living.

"In China, the company is as important as the family. When you have a problem, you can talk to your company management. If you are unhappy, you can discuss it with your colleagues."

Harvard Business School Research Fellow, Gary Hamel, makes a significant point: "There seems to be something in modern organizations that depletes the natural resilience and creativity of human beings, something that literally leaches these qualities out of employees during daylight hours. The culprit? Management principles and processes that foster discipline, punctuality, economy, rationality, and order, yet place little value on artistry, nonconformity, originality, audacity, and élan. To put it simply, most companies are only fractionally human because they make room for only a fraction of the qualities and capabilities that make us human. Billions of people turn up for work each day, but way too many of them are sleepwalking. The result: organizations that systematically under-perform their potential."

In practice

- Do not try to turn yourself into a robot in the belief that your emotions are irrelevant or a distraction to your team. Let the team see your human qualities.
- The organization does not want to see your less noble emotions (spite, anger, frustration), but it welcomes the emotions that you bring to your role as leader: passion, hope, conviction, enthusiasm.
- Your team cannot be inspired by you if they cannot relate to you as a person. If you are undergoing an emotional experience— the birth of a child, pride in your family, a bereavement—share some of this with your colleagues.
- Emotions are not the only significant human qualities: try to harness the other human qualities of the organization: ingenuity, creativity, resilience.

PUBLIC RELATIONS
TAKE THE FIGHT TO THE ENEMY
Jim Blythe

OFTEN, PR EXERCISES are aimed at publics without being specifically directed at an "enemy." In other words, if a firm is under attack, the tendency is to counter the attack in the minds of the public without directly confronting the other organization.

Obviously there is always a risk of retaliation in kind, and much depends on the nature of the exercise—but many organizations can and do use guerrilla tactics to take the fight to the enemy. Even if you don't use this idea yourself, you need to be aware that someone might use it against you!

The idea

Friends of the Earth is a pressure group dedicated to environmental issues. It is an organization that is almost entirely driven by PR: it lobbies government and industry to reduce waste, reduce the carbon footprint, and generally behave responsibly toward the environment.

During one of its campaigns to combat the use of non-returnable plastic bottles, FOE deposited 1,500 bottles outside a Schweppes bottling plant. This blocked the company's gates, but more importantly it created a photo opportunity for the local press and TV companies. Although Schweppes are clearly not the only company who use these bottles, FOE's action certainly left them with a public relations problem—and not one that could easily be explained away with a press release or two.

Generating a high-impact event like this takes planning and coordination, but the effects are likely to be large and far-reaching.

In practice

- Always try to do something that has a visual impact.
- Ensure that the press will be there on the day.
- If you are likely to be on the receiving end of something like this, enter a dialog with your enemies first!

PROFITABILITY
WHO SETS THE SELLING PRICE?
Anne Hawkins

FOR THE VAST majority of businesses, the market sets the selling price for the product or service you have chosen to offer. You try to position yourself so that you can maximise the price you can charge (and still win the business) by being the one the customer prefers to buy from—because of your great quality, service, relationships, etc.

The idea
Everyone knows that Selling price – Costs = Profit.

So if the price is set by the market, does that mean you shrug your shoulders and abdicate responsibility for how much profit your business makes?

Of course you don't. You manage your costs.

It is important to start by understanding precisely what your customer is buying from you. Having established this, your task is now to align your business to meet those market needs in the most cost-effective way. Just as the market will not reward you for providing features of a product or service that it doesn't value, neither will it pay you a premium just because you have chosen to make it or deliver it inefficiently. In some instances, this requires a massive shift in culture.

For many years, defence contracts were negotiated on a cost-plus basis, with the selling price being determined by what the product cost to make plus an agreed percentage for profit.

Questionably not the most effective use of taxpayers' money, as of course the higher the supplier's costs, the greater the profit they made.

Nor a great incentive for supplier cost-control!

Businesses unused to having to foot the bill for the cost of their inefficiencies have been rudely awakened by the advent of competitive tendering and, even more of a challenge, cost-down contracts where they are committed to make year-on-year reductions in price.

There's only one way to reduce prices and still maintain profit margins—and that's to improve costs.

Now there's an incentive!

In practice

* Look at your offerings through your customers' eyes and make sure you understand what gives your products or services value.
* Having eliminated the cost of providing features that your customer doesn't need, look to how you provide those valued characteristics in the most cost-effective way by eliminating waste.

TOP TEAM

BUILD THE PERFECT TOP TEAM
Jonathan Gifford

THE TOP TEAM transforms the leader's ideas into action. It is easy for leaders to imagine that they should recruit a top team of people who are similar to themselves. The ideal top team is a healthy mix of attitudes and abilities.

The idea

Leaders should actively "recruit to their weaknesses" and seek out people who are good at what they themselves are less good at. We all resist this, partly because we are afraid that the other person may succeed where we fail. We are also instinctively drawn to people who are like ourselves.

Daisy Poon built a food export business in China before looking for other business opportunities. During a trade visit to Japan, she was impressed by the Japanese Ajisen Noodle restaurant chain, whose meals also reminded her of the broth-based noodle dishes that her mother made when she was a child. She won the licence to develop the brand in China and opened her first restaurants in Hong Kong and then Shenzhen. The Ajisen Noodle chain is now one of China's leading fast-food chains.

"My view is that teamwork is fundamental. The people in your executive management team are very important. We have around four or five people on the team. One works on operations, one on finance, one on human resources management ... We have some disagreements in our work, but we try to complement each other ... Within the team, there has to be someone who can take the fight to the market place, someone who is tolerant and calm, someone who can keep things under control, and someone who thinks in greater detail. You have to have these different traits within one team, and the skill to organize all these people is crucial."

In practice

- A leader is primarily a strategist and a decision maker. Most if not all implementation should be carried out by your team.
- Select your top team with great care; look for people with different skills and abilities who will complement you and each other.
- Self-confident leaders do not need to feel that they know all of the answers or that they are superior to the rest of the team. They are the team leader.
- The leader's job is to keep this team functioning smoothly and heading in the chosen direction; great diplomatic skills will be required.
- The top team will need to be constantly "upgraded" to meet new challenges—but if the team was chosen well, this will require advice, training and motivation rather than replacement.

COMMUNICATION
MAY THE BEST MAN WIN
Patrick Forsyth

IT IS OFTEN said that the sheer power of a presentation can act to influence the outcome regardless of content. Thus a better presented plan may gain acceptance for a plan that is actually no better than, or even inferior to, another that is less well presented.

The idea

When your skills are such that it is viable, engineer presentations in situations where judgement might normally be made without such a formal input, so that in competitive situations your presentational power helps carry the day and get you what you want.

In practice

- This is clearly a factor in sales where competing suppliers vie to impress a potential customer, but it can be just as useful internally and may win you acceptance of plans, budgets and more that might otherwise be lost to you.
- Make the suggestion, "Perhaps it would help if I made a short presentation about this," in a low key way without it being obvious why you are doing so. Sometimes this will get someone else who initially hoped not to present having to do so alongside you, sometimes it means your case will include a presentation while a competitive pitch will not—in either case, you can create an advantage.
- It is clearly sensible to have an accurate idea of how well a competitor might perform before using this idea.

PUBLIC RELATIONS
PIGGYBACK ON CELEBRITY NEWS
Jim Blythe

CELEBS ARE ALWAYS in the news—that's what they do. Often, they are shown doing something silly, or something exciting, or wearing something inappropriate. Any celeb picture offers an opportunity for somebody to generate a story—especially if the celeb is doing something that relates to your business.

The key to success is keeping your antennae out, and always thinking "How can I turn this to my advantage?"

The idea

When Britney Spears was photographed driving with her eight-month-old son in the front of her car, in a forward-facing baby seat, slumped to one side, one enterprising child safety consultant generated a story about wanting to give Britney Spears lessons in child safety. This story gave people the subconscious impression that the consultant was ACTUALLY giving Britney Spears advice, which of course was not the case and was, in fact, never stated.

There are plenty of other possibilities—a celebrity who is caught drink-driving might provoke a response from a soft-drinks company or a driving school (or even a law firm). A star who appears in an ill-fitting suit might prompt a story from a tailor or a style consultant, a celeb caught "in flagrante" with a co-star might get some gratuitous advice from a hotelier or a florist.

Piggybacking on a celebrity's news value might seem a little cruel, but of course the celebrity is only too happy if the story runs and runs—after all, they are the arch-publicists, or they are nothing!

In practice

- Keep watching the news—especially the tabloids.
- Ideally, only pick up on things that have made the front page. You

are producing a secondhand story, after all, which will weaken its impact.

- Be very quick—the same day if possible. If you wait a day, the original story is old news.

PROBLEM-SOLVING
DEEP-DIVE PROTOTYPING
Jeremy Kourdi

A DEEP-DIVE PROCESS is a focused, team approach to developing solutions to specific problems or challenges. It is intended to harness the ideas of everyone in a team in a creative, stimulating, focused, energetic, fun, and useful way.

The idea
A deep dive is a combination of brainstorming and prototyping (where an initial potential solution is explored and developed). This is an approach that anyone leading a change initiative can use to identify actions that can move a business forward. A deep dive can be completed in an hour, a day, or a week.

The main stages in the deep-dive process are:

- Building a varied team.
- Defining the design challenge.
- Visiting experts.
- Sharing ideas.
- Brainstorming and voting.
- Developing a fast prototype.
- Testing and refining the prototype.
- Focusing on the prototype and producing a final solution.

In practice
IDEO, a prominent American design company, believes that there

are several stages in deep-dive prototyping (for further information see *The Art of Innovation: Lessons in creativity from IDEO, America's leading design firm* by Tom Kelley and Jonathan Littman).

- Understand your market, customers, technology, and perceived constraints.
- Observe people in real-life situations.
- Synthesize and organize the key themes from the first two phases.
- Visualize: this often involves intensive brainstorming and discussion. Imagine new concepts and ideas around the main themes of the design.
- Prototyping is next, and this involves building ideas and physical brainstorming.
- Refine and streamline your ideas. Again, brainstorm ways to improve the prototype and overcome obstacles, and narrow and focus your concepts. Evaluate and prioritize your ideas, and decide how they will be implemented.

Other valuable aspects of creative problem solving that may be applied when time is tight include:

- Trying first (and asking for forgiveness later).
- Test marketing.
- Ensuring that teams are as varied and diverse as possible.
- Seeking external input.
- Reducing, and virtually eliminating, hierarchy.
- Involving people, generating a sense of play, and working without boundaries.
- Being flexible about working arrangements.
- Accepting that it is all right to try and fail.
- Imposing a deadline, while allowing people the time to be creative.

SALES
BE AVAILABLE
Patrick Forsyth

It is, of course, a fact that often it is tedious dealing with customers who will not make up their mind. You want confirmation now. They want to think about it (which reminds me of the saying that when a customer says "I'll think about it and let you know"—*you know*). But what matters most is the customer's timetable, rather than the seller's. However long they mull things over for, whatever sort of gap appears between one contact and another (and there is a need here to keep in touch and take an initiative in following up), when they are ready to act, they are ready to act.

It can be galling to spend time creating interest, keeping in touch, perhaps over some time, and then finding that you lose business because you were not available when they actually wanted to say "Let's talk."

The idea
In the world-renowned Raffles Hotel in Singapore ...

The general manager here, who certainly sees a key part of his role as selling, gives his personal cellphone number to many of his guests. Given the international nature of the business, with guests coming from time zones all over the world, this seems like a formula for a sleepless life. Not so. The number is only usually passed on personally, so the manager can judge something about the value and hazards of doing so. If it is done right, with a little description about its use, then its use is evidently not abused (well, not often!). The manager gets a few time-wasting calls at odd hours of the day, but reports that, generally speaking, it is a valuable tactic and one that "definitely produces business."

It allows contact in a way that customers see as very convenient—allowing them to make contact at the top of the hotel's organization when they want—and their being given such a number is seen as an unusual gesture, one they appreciate.

There is a direct link here for most people, one that applies to contact with an organization or an individual by phone, email and in other ways.

In practice
- Use modern technology such as the cellphone—but do not regard its use as routine, make it special.
- Be seen to "go the extra mile."

PROFITABILITY
WHERE THERE'S A PROBLEM THERE'S A COST
Anne Hawkins

IF YOU WANT to run a cost-efficient business, you need to be able to complete the Working Capital cycle (from cash back into cash again) as fast as you can and with minimum effort.

Working capital cycle

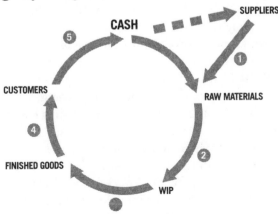

The idea

Every time you deviate from the shortest, most efficient, route to your destination on the working Working Capital cycle (your customer paying you for what you've done), you've wasted time and money.

Wherever there's a problem on the journey there is a cost. And that journey is extremely hazardous with loads of opportunity for getting it wrong.

In fact when you think about it, it's amazing you ever complete the journey 'right first time'!

Do you ever buy the wrong things from your suppliers? If you do, and you have to scrap the stuff off, you may as well have just sat in the corner of the office dropping £50 notes into the shredding machine.

Do you ever bring in temporary labour who may not have been adequately trained and then end up rejecting goods? More work for the shredding machine.

Do you ever get your materials and your labour right, but having failed to maintain your equipment properly end up producing scrap? The shredding machine awaits.

Do you get your materials, your labour and your equipment right but find out that you didn't quite understand the customer's specification ...

The possibilities are endless. As are the opportunities to improve.

In practice

- Learn to recognise when people are dropping £50 notes into the shredder—obvious examples include scrap and where work has to be re-done.
- If you look carefully you will find people beavering away spending their entire working lives at the shredder—because they are employed to 'cover up' an imperfect process or carry out unnecessary tasks.
- Get rid of the shredder by getting to the root cause of problems and then fixing them—permanently.

MANAGING
BE MERITOCRATIC
Jonathan Gifford

IT IS ESSENTIAL to recognize and reward people on the basis of their merit.

Nothing demotivates colleagues more effectively than the belief that other people are being rewarded for reasons that have nothing to do with talent, effort and results.

A true meritocracy also demands that people who produce exceptional results are rewarded more highly than other people and that the brightest and the best are identified as future managers and leaders.

The idea

The first and fundamental aspect of a meritocracy is even-handedness. Walter Wriston, former CEO of Citicorp, describes the motivating force of being seen to operate in a meritocratic way.

"People like to be on a winning team. If they think that [management] know what they are doing and treat their people with respect, and that they are running a meritocracy, people will be motivated. We always made it clear that we didn't care about family status, or the color of your passport, or your race or gender; all we cared about was if you could do the job. I think that has a tremendous motivating force."

Anne Mulcahy, chairman and former chief executive officer of Xerox Corporation, was formerly the company's vice president of human resources. This taught her the importance of candid assessment and persuaded her that people normally get very little honest feedback from their companies.

"It became very much a mantra for me, to [create] a culture that assessed people accurately and really dealt with people fairly. The other piece is the importance of talent development. Not everybody is created equal, and it's important for companies to identify those high potentials and treat them differently, accelerate their development and pay them more. That process is so incredibly important to developing first-class leadership in a company. I think sometimes companies get confused with egalitarian processes that they think are the fairest, and that is not what companies need. Companies need to be very selective about identifying talent and investing in those leaders of the future."

When Carly Fiorina took over as CEO of Hewlett Packard in 1999, she also felt the need to put in place a rigorous system of differentiation.

"We would move away from the peanut butter approach of spreading ratings and merit pay evenly across the organization. Managers were expected to evaluate employee performance honestly and stand behind their decisions. Step by step we would learn to become, once again, a meritocracy."

In practice
- Colleagues must be treated even-handedly. People must be selected and rewarded on the basis of their talents and abilities only.
- In a meritocracy, harder work and exceptional efforts are rewarded above the average. Spreading reward evenly is not meritocratic.
- The most talented must be identified as potential managers and leaders of the futures.
- It must be open to anybody in the organization to be able to join this team of potential leaders.

PUBLIC RELATIONS
PUT IN SOME STYLE
Jim Blythe

MANY COMPANIES AND brands come to be seen as staid: being boring is not always a bad thing, but for a brand that has been exciting in the past, it is not a good place to be. Moving a brand or a company to a different place in people's minds is often essential, but requires some effort to overcome the inertia of most people's thinking.

Reviving an established product is a problem that faces most firms at one time or another. Doing so is a balancing act between creating a new concept for the product on the one hand, and the risk of alienating loyal customers on the other.

The idea
The Vespa scooter, manufactured by Italian company Piaggio, has been around since 1946. Vespa is actually Italian for wasp, a reference to the buzzing noise the scooter makes: it has an iconic status deriving from the 1950s and 1960s, when it was a stylish alternative to the motorcycle.

In more recent years, though, its popularity suffered a decline, so Piaggio decided to revive the brand. Piaggio's British PR agency invited British celebrities to design their "dream Vespa," the designs to be created in reality by a vehicle customizing company. Bridget Jones author Helen Fielding designed one with accessories for the modern woman, for example, while photographer David Bailey designed a fur-covered version.

At the same time, a parallel competition was run for the general public: the winner would have their design displayed at Sotheby's, and would be given their own customized version of a Vespa ET2 scooter.

The winning design was used for publicity purposes by Vespa

before being handed over to the lucky winner, but the celebrity designs were auctioned in aid of the charity Action on Addiction. The company even found a scooter customized by Salvador Dalí in 1962, and borrowed it from the Guggenheim Museum for the campaign.

The campaign as a whole generated a very large number of media permutations—it involved celebrities, a public competition, a charitable element, and even a High Street store element (Vespas were exhibited in the windows of Top Shop as part of the competition publicity). Overall, the campaign generated over 60 million opportunities to see, based on print media readership alone.

In practice

- Make sure you get a lot of entries for your competition: publicize it widely, or better still involve the media directly by offering prizes to their readers.
- Involve a charity. Celebrities are more likely to take part if there is a charitable element, but their main reason for doing this kind of thing is to increase their own exposure.
- Look after your celebrities. They get asked to do a lot of charity gigs, so they deserve to be put in a nice hotel, taken out for a good dinner, etc.
- Provide plenty of photo opportunities.

SELF-HELP
TACKLING THE TYRANNY OF THE URGENT VERSUS THE IMPORTANT
Patrick Forsyth

It can sometimes be curiously difficult to decide certain priorities (even with Pareto's law in mind. Asking why brings us to the vexed question of the urgent versus the important. The urgent and the important are different in nature, yet both generate pressure to deal with them "before anything else."

The idea

It may help to think here of four categories—things that are:

- Urgent and important.
- Important but not urgent.
- Urgent but not important.
- Neither important nor urgent.

Overall, the key is to think first and make considered decisions before letting particular circumstances push you into doing anything first, or just trying to do everything. Things that need action taking fast you must then either do, or delegate, at once. Things that will wait should not just be put on one side, but scheduled so that they get the time they deserve and are also completed.

In practice

- The principle described above may seem difficult; indeed, it *is* difficult. But the difficulty is, at least in part, psychological. We usually know what is most in need of action, yet somehow the pressures of circumstances combine to give some things an "unfair"—and inappropriate—advantage and we allow that to dictate the decision and give something priority. This is a prime area where resolve is more important than technique, where there is no magic formula, and making the right judgments in a considered way must become a habit if we are to remain organized in the face of such pressures.

SALES
AGREE THE IMPOSSIBLE
Patrick Forsyth

PRICE IS ALWAYS a sensitive issue in selling. Buyers want value for money, they want a bargain, and they may want to negotiate. They might unashamedly challenge the price you quote in order to try to obtain a better one. Indeed they may well genuinely reckon the original price is too high, and be unprepared to buy at that level. So faced with a challenge on price, what do you do?

The idea
From direct computer provider Dell ...

When customers say the price is too high, they may well intend it to close the conversation: it is too high for them, and they will not buy, and that's it. If you agree with them—"You are right, Mr Customer, the price is way too high"—that will probably be the last thing they expect. Although they had closed their minds to further debate, they now open them again and want to know what's going on.

Of course, there's more to this idea than just agreeing. Although you might say this, it will not be what you mean, and you must continue the conversation in a way that makes this clear. This is a technique that works well with any product going through technological change, something that is permanently the case with computers. This may not be a technique you meet in every branch of a retail chain, but I have heard it used well by Dell. How does it work? The salesperson might explain, yes, it is a high price for a computer, but not for a laptop that can be used on the move, or (going into more detail) for a laptop with such an exceptionally long battery life as this one.

In other words the price is described as high if the product were much less valuable than it is, but as necessary, understandable, good even, for what the product actually is. Then your description locks it in to key benefits.

In practice
- Any important feature may be highlighted to make this approach fit, and it can work well for a range of products and services.
- Not only does it work, it also surprises, and customers concentrate at once when you agree with something that they had expected would start an argument. It's an idea that can move a sales conversation from stalemate to discussion and agreement.

MANAGING
COLLABORATE
Jonathan Gifford

LEADERS MUST COLLABORATE with their colleagues and work together with them to achieve the organization's goals. People are no longer motivated by the old hierarchical style of leadership; they need to be consulted and inspired.

The idea
In the early days of industrialization, corporations looked to the military as the ideal model for an efficient corporate structure. Harvard Business School professor and business author, Bill George, looks back on his early days at Harvard.

"In my 1960s class at Harvard Business School, our professor cited the Department of Defense ... as the most iconic organization. Business followed their lead, as General Electric, General Motors, AT&T, and Sears became their role models. By century's end, the latter three were in long-term decline, while GE was revolutionized by Jack Welch. Hundreds of other organizations like Kodak, Motorola, and Westinghouse followed similar patterns of self-destruction. The hierarchical model simply wasn't working. In retrospect, it seems obvious people weren't responding to 'top-down' leadership."

Amongst other reasons for this shift, George cites the fact that today's knowledge-workers are less prepared to simply trade their time for money and to follow a set of instructions. They look to find satisfaction and meaning in their work, and expect a collaborative relationship with the organization.

Marten Hansen, management professor at the University of California, writes about the cultural change that has come about in what is expected in leadership style.

"Over the past 20 years we have lived in an era that has worshipped the managers as heroes that ride into town and make things great. They make the decisions, they call the shots, they are the geniuses. Now that one-star model is becoming outdated. We need collaborative leaders that harness the collective intelligence around them."

Leaders themselves must adopt a more collaborative style, but Hansen warns that collaboration throughout the organization must be focused.

"The goal of collaboration is not collaboration but better results. This means that you should only collaborate when it is the best way to improve performance; many times it is better to work independently." Hansen recommends that leaders carefully select which projects colleagues should collaborate on (and which not), that they understand the barriers that currently prevent employees from collaborating, and find management solutions that tear down those barriers.

In practice

- A leader is the leader of a team. Working with a team involves real collaboration.
- Colleagues want to find satisfaction and meaning in their work. They need to be inspired and involved.
- The point of collaboration is to get better results. Not every project will benefit from collaboration—but most will.
- Look for structural issues that prevent colleagues from collaborating with each other.

MARKET RESEARCH
FIND THE USP
Jim Blythe

THE USP OR unique selling proposition is what makes your product stand out from everyone else's. However, what you think the USP is may not be the same as what your customers think it is—a restaurateur might, for example, think that the quality of the food is the USP whereas it may be that the waiters and waitresses are exceptionally attractive people.

Finding the USP may involve carrying out some basic market research, but it will certainly pay off when you come to design your promotional campaign.

The idea

K Shoes is a small shoe manufacturer based in Kendal, in the English Lake District. The company is known for producing good-quality, sensible footwear rather than high-fashion shoes: K shoes last longer and wear better than other shoes, and one might be forgiven for assuming that this is about as good a USP as one could hope for.

However, some basic research among K shoe wearers revealed something else—K shoes don't squeak. Even when new. For the wearers, this was the true USP, and was (for them) a sign of the quality of the shoes.

K Shoes used this information to develop an advertising campaign in which the advantages of non-squeak shoes were promoted in a humorous way. For example, one K Shoes advert showed a wife sneaking up on her husband while he was dining with another woman and dumping a bowl of noodles on his head. No other shoes would allow her to do this.

Knowing why people buy from us enables us to play to our strengths.

In practice
- Determine your USP from the customer's viewpoint—not yours.
- Build the USP into all your promotion.
- If you don't have a USP, get one—or you won't survive long.

ELIMINATING WASTE (*MUDA*)
Jeremy Kourdi

IN THE RUSH to focus on revenue, many businesses forget to consider the importance of business process and the effects of waste. Put another way, businesses that strive to remain streamlined and well organized have a significant advantage over those that lack efficiency.

The idea

For decades, leading Japanese companies directed their cost management efforts toward *muda* (waste elimination). Western companies mirrored the success of this "Japanese Miracle" of the 1970s and 1980s. Concepts of just in time (JIT) and waste elimination meant that new terms, such as process analysis, process mapping, and re-engineering, became part of the business lexicon. The idea of process analysis is to think of business activities as a chain of events, perhaps from the beginning of the manufacturing process through to the end, and to break down the chain of activities into very discrete, yet identifiable, tasks.

Following difficulties in the 1970s, senior managers at Harley-Davidson visited Honda's motorcycle facility at Marysville, Ohio. The difference between Honda's facility and Harley-Davidson's was dramatic in terms of layout, production flow, efficiency, and inventory management. The managers decided that Harley-Davidson needed to introduce a business-wide JIT manufacturing initiative called MAN (Materials As Needed). Production operations were brought together, reducing the amount of resources required for material handling. Harley-Davidson reduced both the amount of supplies received too early and the inventory produced too early. This also reduced the space required for manufacturing, which liberated additional space to increase production.

Caterpillar, a leading manufacturer of agricultural and construction machinery, had a similar experience. During the 1980s, Caterpillar's cost structure was significantly higher than that of its principal competitor—the Japanese firm Komatsu. Caterpillar concluded that Komatsu's "flow" process was more efficient than Caterpillar's method of moving parts and partially finished products through the production process. It undertook a significant plant rearrangement initiative called PWAF (Plant With a Future). The new flow process reduced the distances between operations, which improved material handling expenses, inventory levels, and cycle time to make each product. In some cases, cycle time was reduced by as much as 80 percent.

In practice

- Analyze your production process for inefficiency and wastage. Ask the people who run the processes how they could be improved. This applies to service businesses as well as manufacturing and process industries.
- Create a clear, workable plan for reducing areas of inefficiency and replacing them with streamlined operations.
- Decide what success will look like, how it will be measured, and when it will be assessed.
- Be cautious when introducing the new plan. Changes to any process can have unforeseen consequences—be aware of these possible problems and be ready to make adjustments to compensate for them.

LEADERSHIP
BE PASSIONATE
Jonathan Gifford

PEOPLE ARE UNLIKELY to follow any leader who does not manage to convey the passion that they have for their cause. Leaders are also very unlikely to find the necessary energy and commitment needed to lead successfully unless they feel passionately about the field in which they work, and about the success of the organization that they lead.

The idea

Richard Branson, chairman of Virgin Group, has always been driven in business by passion and excitement—by doing the things that interest him. This, in turn, is what makes him able to excite other people.

"At its heart, business is not about formality, or winning, or 'the bottom line', or profit, or commerce, or any of the things the business books tell you it's about. Business is what concerns us. If you care about something enough to do something about it, you're in business ... What really matters is what you create. Does it work or not? Does it make you proud?"

Harvard Business School professor, Allen Grossman, ex-CEO of Outward Bound, says that only genuine passion for what you do allows you to put in the hard work needed to ensure success.

"I haven't found a satisfactory substitute for just working your butt off. Virtually everyone I know, whether they be governor, president, the head of a public company, or whether they're at Harvard, Yale, or wherever, the common denominator is real commitment and focus. If you're not passionate, maybe self-discipline or whatever set of emotions you have, including guilt, might help you work hard. But most people who are really successful are also passionate. It is the wonderful ingredient that brings happiness with success."

Robert Mondavi, the California winemaker who helped to transform the reputation of North American wines, says that being passionate about what you do turns work into enjoyment.

"Interest is not enough. You must be passionate about what you do if your want to succeed and live a happy life. Find a job you love, and you will never have to work a day in your life."

In practice

- If you are not passionate about what you do, you will not be able to bring other people with you; if your work does not fill you with excitement, you will not be able to find the energy for the hard work that your role as leader requires.

- Passion is not only about drive and ambition; it is about fun, excitement and self-fulfilment.
- Don't keep this passion to yourself: spread it around. Nothing is more infectious than a person's genuine passion for any subject.

SALES
STRAWBERRIES AND CREAM
Patrick Forsyth

ONE SURE WAY to sell more is to link selling one thing to selling another. This is true from a marketing perspective—for example cellphones and call revenue, or computer printers and toner cartridges—but it is also true of selling. Historically, for obvious reasons, it has been known as the strawberries and cream technique.

The idea
Check out the Amazon website ...

The way to make this idea work is to envisage links between one thing and another, or better still one thing and a whole raft of others. The past masters of this are Amazon. Visit the Amazon website and notice how it is set up. Whatever you do on it—just view something, add it to a wish list, or buy it—the system makes use of what you appear interested in to make other suggestions to you.

For example, if you're looking at books, it will provide links based on the author, the kind of book, the subject of non-fiction titles, and more. That the system works well in terms of human psychology is demonstrated by how addictive it is. As a habitual book buyer I can spend a long time following a track through the system to see if it puts something interesting, unknown, and perhaps surprising in front of me.

It is worth examining your own product range to see how different things can be made to link together. Bear in mind that some links will be obvious, but others will not. All that matters is that there is a logic that is recognized by the customer. Linking purchases can save time and hassle: so someone selling paper to an office might also offer spare cartridges for the printer (among other things). Paper is, after all, not much use without ink.

This technique can link effectively to others. For example, some companies vary prices on the basis of combinations of product, so paper might be offered at a lower price to those customers buying a toner cartridge, or depending on the quantity ordered. Now just to practice what I preach, let me suggest that if you bought this book, maybe you would also find another one helpful. If you want something on how to excel in your career, look no further: *Detox Your Career* by Patrick Forsyth (Cyan/Marshall Cavendish Books) is readily available.

In practice
- Again regular analysis is necessary here.
- This makes a useful topic for sales meetings, when different combinations can be explored or exchanged.

MARKETING
RESPECT YOUR CONSUMER
Jim Blythe

MARKETERS HAVE A bad habit of talking about "the consumer" as if they are one person. Consumers are in fact all different—they are a lot like people in that respect—and they are in fact us. We all resent being patronized, but many marketers do this with astonishing regularity. People discount advertising statements (in fact in most cases they don't even read them) and most of us can spot bullshit pretty well. We are all consumers—if we can see through marketers and their cunning ploys, so can everybody else.

The difficulty is always to encapsulate the concept of customer respect in a way that staff can relate to when they are working with people. It's easy for our staff to get into the habit of seeing our customers as simply cannon fodder, or walking wallets, rather than as human beings with their own needs, wants, and skills. If you need an example, try dealing with the care workers of a friend who is a wheelchair user—or better still, use a chair yourself for a day and see how people treat you.

The idea

David Ogilvy was one of the giants of the advertising industry. He was responsible for telling us that the only sound in a Rolls-Royce at 60 mph is the sound of the clock ticking, for example. What he told his staff was equally important—among many Ogilvy-isms, two stand out. The first is: "The consumer is not a moron—she's your wife!" We have to keep reminding ourselves that our consumers are not stupid, they are people just like us.

The second one is "People do not buy from bad-mannered liars." Yet so many marketing communications (especially telephone marketing approaches) are both bad-mannered and untrue. Somebody calling from India, claiming to be called Sharon, and immediately asking about how much one has left on one's mortgage, is clearly bad-mannered and lying.

These two statements should be up in letters of fire in every marketing department in the country.

In practice

- Remember that your staff may not have the same commitment to the business that you have.
- People often forget that consumers are people too—there is nothing wrong with reminding them.
- Putting up signs to remind people has a long history—IBM's "Think!" signs, Bill Clinton's "It's the economy, stupid!" sign, and many others have worked well.
- Don't forget the lesson yourself, especially when dealing with somebody difficult!

TEAMWORK
THE RULE OF 150
Jeremy Kourdi

COWORKERS FIND SOCIALIZING, teamworking, and associated activities (such as innovating, collaborating, and sharing knowledge) much easier to achieve when they are placed in groups of less than 150. In this way, larger corporations gain the benefit of smaller groups that are often closer, more energetic, entrepreneurial, supportive, and better.

The idea
A fascinating example of an organization that clearly understands the benefits of collaboration is Gore Associates, a privately held, multi-million-dollar high-tech firm based in Delaware. As well as manufacturing the water-resistant Gore-Tex fabric, the firm also produces products for the semiconductor, pharmaceutical, and medical industries.

Gore is unique because of its adherence to the rule of 150. This approach is based on anthropological research highlighting the fact that humans can socialize in large groups because, uniquely, we are able to handle the complexities of social arrangements. However, there is a limit to the bonds people can make, and this is reached at around 150. In groups larger than 150, complicated hierarchies, regulations, and formal measures are needed, but below 150 these same goals can be achieved informally.

Consequently, Gore limits the size of each office so it is below 150. Gore has 15 plants within a 12-mile radius in Delaware and Maryland, each with a close-knit group of employees who understand each other and work well together. This approach emphasizes the benefits of collective management such as communication, initiative, and flexibility, and it has enabled a big business with thousands of employees to retain the attitude of a small, entrepreneurial start-up. The result is a rate of employee turnover that is a third of the industry average, and sustained profitability and growth for over 35 years.

In practice

- Divide your workforce into groups or branches of under 150 people.
- Institute a strong managerial system to oversee smaller "branches" and ensure they are coordinated and efficient.
- Encourage a sense of community and teamwork within groups. The "rule of 150" simply means that it will be possible for workers to form positive bonds with all of their coworkers—extra measures should be taken to ensure that this actually happens.
- Develop a sense of team across groups of 150. This means finding ways for people to communicate and collaborate across the whole business, rather than developing a series of competitive, separate groupings.

SALES
GET THEM NODDING
Andy Maslen

ONE OF THE oldest tricks in the sales book is to get your prospect to agree with you. Not on any earth-shattering subject like "do you want to buy this fridge?" but on an altogether less controversial plane. Classically, you suggest, on meeting your prospect, that it's a "nice day, huh?" Provided it isn't raining, you should get a noncommittal "Sure is."

But that "Sure is" is anything but noncommittal, because your prospect just agreed with you. Once they agree with you on a small point they're much more likely to agree with you on a big one. The trick is timing. You work through a few more easy questions and before they know it, your new best friend finds everything you say pretty uncontroversial. *Then* you ask for the order.

The idea
From a business-to-business mailshot
For the opening to a direct mail letter aimed at corporate managers, I adopted just such an old-school approach:

> Would you agree with me that running a business in Eastern Europe calls for a unique mix of skills? Skills observed in successful executives like you?

Kinda hard to disagree with that, wouldn't you say? Combined with some fairly obvious flattery, it almost forces the reader to say "yes." Which is all I wanted at this stage.

If you've figured out or researched what makes your reader tick, you have all the ammunition you need for this type of opening. It works for any kind of reader, and in ads, emails, landing pages, Adwords, or mailshots. Let's take a few examples ...

- Parents: do you ever worry about your kids' education?
- Middle managers: people like us are the driving force in the business, aren't we?
- Home cooks: would you be interested in a foolproof recipe for wow-factor chocolate cake?
- Retirees: is it time seniors were given more respect?
- Competitive swimmers: want to know how to reduce turbulence?

Once you have their first nod, try to build on it with another one. Then you need a little body-swerve to bring them around to your point. "Well," you say, "in that case, you may be very interested in what I have to say next." Or, "Of course you do, we all do. And that's why I have developed this foolproof way of ..."

In practice
- Allay your reader's fears that you're about to sell to them by asking them to agree with you on some inconsequential point.
- Or tap into their deeper motivation by suggesting something they hold to be true and asking them to agree with that.

43

DO SOMETHING VERY, VERY PECULIAR
Jim Blythe

IN ORDER TO stand out, you have to be different. Sometimes this means doing something that seems absolutely crazy—and might actually BE crazy. On the other hand, it doesn't pay to look foolish. It's a fine line between being startling and being stupid.

In recent years the fast-food industry has undergone marked changes. Competition has increased dramatically, with American fast-food restaurants covering the world and British home-grown versions losing ground. People have become a great deal more sophisticated in their eating habits, too—the chips-with-everything tradition of British cooking has taken a downturn as people have become more attuned to healthy eating and more exposed to good-quality world cuisine. Rising standards of living and better home cooking have also led to the downfall of many British catering institutions such as roadside transport cafés and fish-and-chip shops.

The idea
Little Chef is an icon of roadside eating for British motorists. Established for 50 years, the chain has served up literally millions of meals, mainly traditional British fast-food mainstays such as all-day breakfasts and pie and chips.

In 2007, though, the company went into receivership, victim of falling customer demand and increased competition from chains such as McDonald's and Burger King. The restaurants were seen as old-fashioned, unhealthy greasy-spoon cafés. Chief executive Ian Pegler decided to pull off a PR coup by recruiting world-renowned chef Heston Blumenthal to revamp the menus.

Blumenthal runs what is often called the world's best restaurant, and quite clearly is neither acquainted with, nor has much sympathy for, the greasy fry-up approach to cooking. He has no real qualifications for turning around a restaurant like Little Chef (although he did eventually come up with some excellent ideas, after one or two false starts). His value lay in the PR effect of employing him in the first place—in fact, Channel 4 made a documentary about the whole process, generating considerable publicity in the national press.

Pegler could have chosen from several other celebrity chefs with better track records in turning restaurants around (Jamie Oliver and Gordon Ramsay are two obvious examples), but choosing Blumenthal was a better PR coup precisely BECAUSE he was a square peg in a round hole.

In practice

- Doing something peculiar always has more news value than doing the obvious.
- Whatever you do must work out in the end, or you will look ridiculous. Blumenthal did, eventually, manage to create some excellent new dishes for Little Chef.
- What you do must be backed up by news coverage: make sure the appropriate media are involved from the start.

INNOVATION
MIX THINGS UP
Jonathan Gifford

ORGANIZATIONS NEED A constant flow of new ideas. Bringing together people from different cultures, experiences or fields of expertise creates an environment that is more likely to generate innovation.

The idea

Frans Johansson, author of *The Medici Effect*, argues that innovation is encouraged when different cultures and ways of thinking come together to spark off new ideas. He recommends bringing together teams from diverse backgrounds and cultures and introducing new people to the team: many breakthrough discoveries are made by people who are either young, or who have recently moved into a new field of expertise; these people see things with fresh eyes.

Johansson cites a multi-disciplinary team of researchers at Brown University, Rhode Island, who pioneered research in using brain signals alone to control a cursor on a computer screen: the signals were interpreted using advanced statistical techniques, allowing the computer to turn the brain signals into workable instructions; the neuroscientists could not have done this without the statisticians or the other experts in the team.

In another example, a telecommunications engineer became intrigued by the way in which colonies of insects find the most efficient route to a source of food. His new understanding of biological mechanisms enabled him to find radical new solutions for the routing of electronic signals.

Jane Jacobs, a Canadian writer whose most influential book on urban planning, *The Death and Life of Great American Cities*, was published in 1961, was a passionate believer in the importance of diversity in urban areas. Jacobs argued that the existence of a variety of different kinds of buildings with different purposes within the same area—high- and low-rent residential properties, industrial and commercial premises, warehouses and artists' studios—creates a vibrant environment which brings many different kinds of people together and sets up the possibility of chance encounters and the exchange of ideas. Streets should be kept short; there should be many chances to turn corners, see new things and meet new people.

Jacobs used New York's Greenwich Village as a good example of a mixed urban community that has helped to create and support a successful and vibrant community.

In practice
* Leaders need to create an environment in which the organization is constantly searching for better ways of doing things and new opportunities.

- Employing and bringing together people from different backgrounds, cultures and fields of expertise helps to create an atmosphere that encourages innovative ways of thinking.
- Move people around: find reasons to bring people together with new colleagues and different departments. Set up teams for special projects that come together and then disband, or teams that have a rapidly changing membership.
- Create spaces where colleagues can meet in unplanned ways.
- Broaden your own experience. Consider some apparently radical career options that would expose you to new ways of thinking. Take up new interests that take you away from your usual path.

MARKETING
COMMUNICATE IN A RELEVANT WAY
Jim Blythe

SOMETIMES THE PRODUCT'S unique selling proposition can be tedious. Whatever the real benefits, it is sometimes just not exciting enough for consumers to get worked up about. Injecting some excitement is often a matter of being creative about the advertising message—and turning a drawback into an advantage.

The idea
Grolsch is a Dutch beer aimed at mature males who consume premium brands. The beer itself tastes pretty much like any other Dutch lager beer, and during the 1990s it became marginalized by the more aggressively marketed Stella Artois, Budweiser, and Kronenbourg 1664 brands. The company's advertising agency, The Leith Agency, was tasked with repositioning the brand in order to double sales by 2002, and replace Kronenbourg 1664 as the number two premium brand by 2010.

The distinctive feature of Grolsch is that it is brewed more slowly than other beers. This gives it a fuller flavor, but telling consumers that it is brewed longer for a fuller flavor is a message that came across as dull and not very relevant. The agency identified the consumers' prevailing view of the Netherlands: that it is a laid-back, easygoing place. This perception of the Netherlands and the Dutch is what the agency hung the campaign on.

The new campaign featured a Dutch hero showing that things are better when they are not rushed. The first advert showed bank robbers attacking a bank that was only partly built. The Dutch hero shouts "Schtop!" and the endline "We only let you drink it when it's ready" was flashed up on the screen.

The end result was that Grolsch exceeded the planned sales target of doubling sales by a margin of 75,000 barrels (a 58.4 percent increase overall). By combining country-of-origin effects with the product's USP, The Leith Agency created an award-winning, and business-winning, campaign.

In practice
- Take a look at your advertising slogans and check if they are boring. If you've been using the same one for more than three or four years, it's probably boring.
- Find a humorous or startling way to convey the USP.
- Look for a further feature of your product to link the USP to—for example, place of origin, the way it is made, the age of the firm, and so forth.

BRANDING
BRAND SPACES
Jeremy Kourdi

DEVELOPING STYLISH AREAS that are decorated and designed to appeal to your target market, even if they do not sell your core products, will reinforce your image and help customers appreciate the distinctiveness of your products and brand.

The idea

One of the trendiest new ideas in marketing, brand spaces advocates creating stylish spaces—perhaps a bar, art gallery, lounge, or exhibition hall—that may not be directly related to your main product but where individuals are immersed in your brand image. Practiced by leading companies such as Apple, ING Direct, Kodak, Google, and Nokia, there has been a dramatic increase in the number and quality of brand spaces.

French car manufacturer Renault uses brand spaces with a high level of commitment and panache, running four brand spaces in Buenos Aires, Bogota, Mexico City, and Paris. Its latest project, the Terrasse Renault in Mexico City, is impressively designed, and centers on "a bar with wooden latticing, through which visitors can glimpse the Renault zone, where car prototypes are exhibited." Occupying prime real estate in global cities and offering gourmet cuisine, art galleries, and seamlessly blended marketing, the Renault brand spaces are characteristic of the concept. Renault describes its brand spaces as "hosting artistic, cultural and sporting events in keeping with the brand's universe to reinforce Renault's energy and identity as a visionary, warm and innovative brand."

The innovative design of brand spaces includes Nokia's "silence booths" for people seeking temporary quiet and calm at music festivals; Coca-Cola's "Red Lounges" designed to provide multimedia experiences to teenagers in malls in Illinois and Los Angeles; and Microsoft's Xbox 360 Lounge in Tokyo incorporating VIP rooms, multimedia opportunities, and even Xbox-themed mixed drinks.

With an increase in lifestyle brands, brand spaces can reinforce your organization as part of an idealized culture and aesthetic that is sculpted to the tastes of your target demographic. Brand spaces help sell directly and indirectly. They also build the value of your business by generating understanding of—and affinity for—your brand.

In practice

- Consider where your target demographic market would choose to go to enjoy their free time and use your brand space to create an idealized version of it.

- Recognize the variety of options you have when creating a brand space; focus on individuality.
- Remember that the aesthetic and physical design of the brand space is usually vital.
- Choose which specific aspects of your company's service and image will be portrayed in the space.
- Provide a range of activities for visitors to enjoy.
- Decide what the emphasis of your brand space will be—for example, convenience, culture, excitement, or relaxation.
- Choose your location carefully—whether you choose an airport, shopping center, music festival, or simply a city street to be home to your brand space, is the first step to ensuring the project is a success.

MANAGING TIME
BEWARE FAVORITES
Patrick Forsyth

THIS MAY SEEM an odd one, but it is potentially even more time-wasting than putting off things that you do not like or that you find difficult. Many people spend a disproportionate amount of time on the things they like doing best and, perhaps, also do best. This is perfectly natural and there are various reasons for it. An important one is that any concentration on what you like is what seems to produce the most job satisfaction. This is fine if that satisfaction comes simply from doing whatever it is and the thing itself is necessary, though the danger is that you may be prone to some over-engineering, doing more than is necessary, putting in more time and sometimes producing a standard of quality or excellence that is just not necessary.

But there can be more sinister reasons for this practice. For example, it may be because:

- You are using one task to provide an excuse to delay or avoid others (difficult or unfamiliar things, perhaps), telling yourself, with seeming reason, that you are too busy to get to them.

- You are concerned about delegating (a subject covered separately) and worry that a task is not a candidate for this, so you go on doing it yourself and go on over-engineering.
- You find the work conditions of one task too tempting, such as a low-priority job that involves visiting an attractive location new to you, for instance; this is something that is compounded by the opposite being true of the priority task.
- You find some aspect of the task fun; as an example, this happens to some people who have a fascination with computers, and they spend hours devising, say, a graphic representation of some figures when something simpler would meet the case just as well.

All these and other reasons can cause problems. The practice is frankly all too easy to engage in, we are all prone to it, probably all do it to some extent, and thus we all have to be constantly on our guard against it. Usually it continues because it is easy not to be consciously aware that it is happening.

The idea
Avoid what is sometimes called "cherry picking." The answer here is to really look, and look honestly, as you review your tasks and your regular work plan for examples of this happening. Better still, look for examples of where it might happen and make sure that it does not. Of all the points in this book, I would rate this as in the top few best potential time savers for most people. Do not be blind to it—it is so easy to deny it happens. Check it out and see how much time you save. And, who knows, maybe some of the extra things you can then fit in will become tomorrow's favorite tasks.

In practice
- Self-generated interruptions can be surprisingly time-consuming and their frequency can be one of the surprises that often emerge from keeping a personal time log. It is easy to be blind to them and, at the risk of being repetitive, it is logical to watch for these before the ones involving other people or outside circumstances as their cause.

I THINK, THEREFORE I FAIL ...

Patrick Forsyth

MOST, IF NOT all, of the problems you may anticipate in speaking formally can be removed or reduced by preparation.

Preparation can quite literally make the difference between success and failure, and can turn something routine into something memorable.

The idea

As part of your preparation, "talk your way to success"—think positively.

In practice

- Psychologists say that more than seventy per cent of what is called "self-talk" about speaking formally is negative. This refers to all those thoughts that start with: "I'm not sure I can..." or "It won't be..." Understandable perhaps, but doubts can all too easily become a self-fulfilling prophecy and many that arise in this way are intangible and not factually based. You need to combat this by thinking positively. Imagine it going well. Visualize the detail of particular elements working as you planned. Do so repeatedly and beat negative thoughts into submission (having addressed and solved any specific and tangible problems). Why not imagine the applause too?

- The time for this thinking is as you prepare. And bear in mind that the single most common reason why things sometimes do not go well is because the person concerned gave insufficient time to preparation. Bear in mind too that, quite simply, what you do in preparing creates the certainty that it will go well.

- So the rule should be: Prepare – Practice – Present, and think positive. If the practical issues are addressed, you can then put irrational fears on one side, recognizing them for what they are.

SALES
NOT JUST LOGICAL
Patrick Forsyth

PEOPLE NEED A reason to buy. Especially with technical or complex products, and certainly in areas of industrial and business-to-business purchasing, buyers make logical decisions. They weigh up the evidence and see how something stacks up. They compare one supplier with another. But it is not just logical factors that influence their final decision. What else is involved?

The idea
From world-famous Harvard Business School ...

Some years ago Harvard Business School carried out research with top American buyers to ascertain how much logic and how much emotion was involved in buying decisions. To many people's surprise the results showed that 84 percent of all buying decisions are based on emotion. Certainly if someone is purchasing something like a wedding gift, or a wedding dress for that matter, one would expect there to be some emotion involved—perhaps a lot. But what about say a heat exchanger, or a forklift truck, or a machine lathe: surely not?

But it is a fact: emotion does matter, and it matters particularly when the package of more technical matters in evidence is evenly balanced between competitors. If there is apparently not much to choose between two (or more) technical cases, people will search for something else that they can use to swing the balance; and the deciding factor can then become emotional. They choose the product because the salesperson selling it remembers their birthday, gets on best with them, makes a point of recognizing that they are pressed for time, or any of a hundred and one little things that make an impression and appeal.

In practice
- Never underrate what may seem to be peripheral factors; indeed

you can do worse than to seek some out, especially when you judge that a decision is a finely balanced one.

- For example, if there are a dozen books on the shelf under the heading "Sales," the cover of the one you choose may suddenly become disproportionately important to your choice. That's why I worry about the blurb for something like this volume. It's a common principle.

MARKETING
WISH YOU WERE HERE
Andy Maslen

HAVE YOU EVER got a postcard in your morning's post and *not* read it? Me neither. There's something compelling about that small, stiff piece of card that says "Read me." So why not consider putting that factor to work for you in your marketing campaigns?

Postcards have a number of advantages over traditional mailpacks. They're cheaper, there's no need for an envelope, they have instant visual appeal, they only need one hand to read, they have a "fun factor," and they look less daunting. As a series, you can also use them to communicate a complex idea in stages, drip-feeding information to your target without overtaxing them.

The idea
From a computer services company
I once wrote an eight-card series for this client, promoting a new IT maintenance contract. The idea was to stimulate awareness among corporate IT managers and build their database.

We announced on the first card that there would be a quiz on the final one with a prize of a day's tank driving. The hook was that the questions would relate to the information provided on the first seven cards—a big incentive to look out for them and keep reading.

They achieved maximum exposure for minimum outlay and gained lots of new names for their database, too.

Because you don't need an envelope, you can also throw away the rule book about acceptable sizes. Yes, you can have an A5 or an A6 postcard. But why not try a half-page A4 vertical format? Or a 100mm square? Or a circle? There are cost considerations, as always, but talking to your printer (or designer) will help you balance creativity against paper wastage.

Whatever you do with it, your postcard—mono, two-color, or full color—adds another component to your marketing campaigns, increases your flexibility, and gives your customers/prospects a break from the run of mailshots they're used to.

In practice
- Once you've printed your postcard, you can use it different ways. As a self-mailer, an insert, a flyer, an exhibition giveaway, or a component of your press kit.
- Why not investigate digital printing for your postcard? You can incorporate your target's name (and any other variable data you like) into the design. In color.

PERFORMANCE
CREATE AN ENTREPRENEURIAL CULTURE
Jonathan Gifford

STUDIES SHOW THAT successful entrepreneurs do not have better ideas than other people: they have more ideas, and work harder to try to turn them into reality. They have many failures, but occasional big successes.

The idea
William Weldon, CEO of pharmaceutical giant Johnson & Johnson,

talks about the way in which his organization encourages groups of people to form mini business units to explore new product areas.

"We have what we call internal ventures ... who may put forward a recommendation for something that can be done ... So they put together a business plan, present it, put together a budget with it and then we allow that group to go off and work on that. We create other environments ... where we may bring people from the consumer, pharmaceutical and medical device and diagnostics groups together to share what they are doing. And, out of that, they will generate ideas where they can work together to bring products forward. It's usually better when they generate them rather than when we try and impose upon them."

Carol Bartz, CEO of Yahoo! and previously head of Autodesk, Inc, says, "I think the best way is for a CEO to create a culture that allows people to experiment and fail and not be ostracized for that. Innovation comes from experimentation; it comes from ideas, it comes from trying things and it comes from taking risks. You need a culture and environment that says taking risks is not only acceptable, but is rewarding. A few years back, when I was CEO of Autodesk, I had a saying: 'Fail, fast forward'. What it meant was, try something and if you fail, figure it out as fast as you can and move forward. Rather than be afraid to try anything because you might be wrong."

The inventor, James Dyson, works hard at encouraging new ideas. "Getting rid of that cynicism about new ideas is terribly important if a company is to succeed. When someone has a good idea I say, 'That's great'. I don't reject it; I look at it. It is about praising people who have good ideas and protecting them because ideas are fragile things."

In practice
- An organization that is not constantly producing innovative ideas will quickly be overtaken by the competition.
- The organization itself is the best source of ideas about productive and profitable innovation. Try to create an entrepreneurial atmosphere throughout the organization.

- Teams can be brought together temporarily to work up and present new ideas. Bring together people from different disciplines with a wide variety of skills. Keep initial costs low.
- The majority of ideas will not be taken forward. Reassure colleagues that this is normal and inevitable. People must gain recognition for trying. Never criticize a team for "failing"—they have explored a good idea; it didn't work out.
- Give the few successes a lot of recognition, to encourage the teams working on other projects.
- Encourage teams to generate their own new ideas to explore. Never criticize or run down a new idea.

PUBLIC RELATIONS
END IN -EST
Jim Blythe

INTEREST IN THE biggest, the smallest, the fastest, the slowest, and the silliest will always attract people's attention ("most" is another good word). Such stories are automatically interesting, and are almost always sure-fire winners with the media because they lend themselves to eye-catching headlines.

This preoccupation with extremes is what makes people buy *Guinness World Records*, and is also a driver for people buying newspapers. Such stories often make the TV news as well, and there have even been several TV shows dedicated to extremes of weight, height, and even silliness.

They also tend to generate lively photographs, which alone is a good reason for using them, but it isn't always obvious how to link the biggest, smallest, silliest thing to your company.

The idea
Arlo Guthrie of Consult the Guru tells the story of a competition

he once ran to find Britain's Most Destructive Dog. This was to promote a treatment for dogs that destroy things, and it provoked tremendous interest among the dog-owning public, who rushed to enter their pooches in the competition.

The hands-down winner, though, was a dog that destroyed its owner's car. The resulting headline, "My Dog Ate My Ford Fiesta," had reporters on the doorstep of the "lucky" winner straightaway.

Using the word "most" or any word ending with "-est" automatically raises the stakes—but it may need to be engineered into the campaign.

In practice

- Run a survey or a competition to find your "most" or "-est."
- Ensure that you get permission from the person you want to feature, and preferably get a contract for future rights.
- Make full use of any photo opportunities.

MARKETING
THE TIPPING POINT
Jeremy Kourdi

THE SPREAD OF products or ideas and the decline of others are rarely understood. Writer Malcolm Gladwell has developed the idea of the "tipping point": a compelling theory about how an idea becomes an epidemic. The "tipping point" is the dramatic moment when everything changes simultaneously because a threshold has been crossed—although the situation might have been building for some time.

The idea

Malcolm Gladwell likens rapid growth, decline, and coincidence to epidemics. Ideas are "infectious," fashions represent "outbreaks," and new ideas and products are "viruses." Gladwell explains how a factor "tips"—when a critical mass "catches" the infection, and passes it on. This is when a shoe becomes a "fashion craze," social smoking becomes "addiction," and crime becomes a "wave." Advertising is a way of infecting others.

Several factors are significant in making sure that an idea "tips":

1. *The law of the few.* Epidemics only need a small number of people to infect many others. This is apparent with the spread of disease: it is the few people who socialize and travel the most that make the difference between a local outbreak and a global pandemic. Similarly, word of mouth is a critical form of communication: those who speak the most (and the best) create epidemics of ideas. There are three types of people: connectors, mavens, and salespeople.
   - *Connectors* bring people together, using their social skills to make connections. They are key agents in the spread of epidemics, as they communicate throughout different "networks" of people. Masters of the "weak tie" (a friendly, superficial connection) can spread ideas far.
   - *Mavens*—information specialists—also connect with people, but focus on the needs of others rather than on their own needs, and have the most to say. Examples of mavens include teachers.
   - *Salespeople* concentrate on the relationship, not the message. Their "sales" skills, with mastery of non-verbal communication and "motor mimicry" (imitating the person's emotions and behavior to gain trust), afford them a pivotal role in persuading others.

2. *The stickiness factor.* With products or ideas, how attractive they are matters as much as how they are communicated in determining whether they spread. To reach a tipping point, ideas have to be compelling and "sticky." (If something is unattractive, it will be rejected irrespective of how it is transmitted.) The information age has created a stickiness problem—the "clutter" of messages we face leads to products and ideas being ignored. To create epidemics, it is essential to

make sure the message is not lost in this clutter, and to ensure the message is "sticky."

3. *The power of context.* Changes in the context of a message can tip an epidemic. Given that people's circumstances, or context, matter as much as their character, a tipping point can be controlled by altering the environment they live in. This has many implications for businesses, from employee performance to generating sales.

An example of the tipping point is "broken windows theory." One person, seeing a single broken window, may believe there is an absence of control and authority, making them more likely to commit crimes. In this way, small crimes invite more serious crimes, spawning a crime wave. This theory was used in New York City in the 1990s by the chief of police, William Braxton. The "zero tolerance" approach that targeted minor crime (eg fare-dodging and vandalism) led to a dramatic fall in crime overall. Although other factors may have contributed to the crime reduction, this example highlights the power of context.

In practice

- Choose a compelling, attractive proposition or idea to spread. Understand what will make it appealing and emphasize these factors to key contacts.
- Identify and develop links with key contacts—people with connections ("connectors" or networkers); people with knowledge and influence ("mavens" such as teachers or journalists), and people with influence ("salespeople" such as celebrities).
- Choose the right time to spread the idea, making sure that the environment is receptive and that the idea is relevant and timely.
- Read *The Tipping Point* by Malcolm Gladwell.

MARKETING
BRING A FRIEND
Jim Blythe

FRIEND-GET-FRIEND promotions are very common, but persuading people to sell to their friends can be problematic. People often feel embarrassed to do this, and some research conducted in the 1950s by two American academics (Leon Festinger and James M. Carlsmith) brought out an interesting phenomenon: people who are offered a big reward for persuading a friend to do something are LESS likely to succeed at it than are people who are offered a small reward. This is because people offered a small reward will persuade because they are themselves persuaded—people offered a large reward do so because of the reward.

In many cases, offering a reward to someone for recommending a product makes them feel as if they are betraying a friendship—not the result the company would like, and yet many bring-a-friend schemes do exactly that, offering ever-larger rewards as a way of persuading people to pass on a friend's name.

The idea
Laphroaig is a Scottish single-malt whisky distilled on the island of Islay. It is the strongest-flavored whisky available, so for some people it is too powerful, for others it is a rare treat. Obviously the quality comes at a price—but for its devotees the price is well worth paying.

The distillery has a "Friends of Laphroaig" organization that devotees can join. Periodically, the distillery asks "Friends" for the names of three or four friends, to whom the distillery will send a small bottle of the whisky as a gift. There is nothing in this for the "Friend"—the other person gets the whisky. What it does do is enable the distillery to expand the number of people who know the product, with the added advantage that the "Friends" are likely to choose people who they think will enjoy the product. Obviously there may be some abuse of the system—choosing three teetotaller friends in order to obtain three free miniatures of the whisky is one obvious possibility—but in general people are very fair about it, because it is after all a very generous offer.

The idea can be extended in other ways—banks might offer £25 to be deposited in the friend's account, a gym might have a "bring-a-friend" day with a free gift or discount to the friend if he or she joins the gym, a hotel might offer a free room to a friend.

In practice
- The offer needs to be something that the friend will appreciate and benefit from.
- The reward to the recommender is the thanks of a friend—there is usually no need to offer anything to the recommender.
- The reward needs to connect directly to the product—a sample or a trial period, for example.
- If you do give a reward to the recommender, try to make it something they can share with the friend.

SALES
CLOSE CONTACT
Patrick Forsyth

MANY CUSTOMERS CHECK out potential purchases on the internet these days. This means that by the time someone makes contact with an individual business they have done their research and may see the process of selection and buying as well on the way. But this can create long-distance contacts from customers who are not physically near the salesperson. There's a good side to this: it exposes salespeople to prospects with whom they would never otherwise have had any contact. But how do you get closer?

The idea
From a Volvo dealership ...

One industry in which this internet checking now goes on is car sales, including secondhand ones. People can check out possibilities and prices, and when they have an idea of the kind of car they want, they can see a list of every car for sale in the country that meets their exact criteria and where it is to be found. Then they can contact the appropriate dealer, who may be on the other side of the country. At that point they want to hear about the car, gleaning details beyond the basic description of year, color, and so on. If they are still interested, they will doubtless resolve to go and have a look at it.

One salesperson I spoke to in my local Volvo dealership has cracked this one. He offers to drive the car to the prospect (or maybe to meet them halfway). This surprises people, and that surprise helps him gauge the seriousness of their intent. This is important because a journey costs time and money, but if he is confident he's found a good prospect, then it can pay dividends. Indeed my informant claims a good strike rate. After all, he does not suggest this to anyone he suspects of time wasting.

In practice
- Review how e-marketing is affecting the way your customers behave. (It will likely be changing and need regular review.)
- Adapt your approach to fit with their new practice.

CRISIS MANAGEMENT
CREATE A CRISIS TEAM
Jim Blythe

BAD THINGS HAPPEN in most industries from time to time. Some industries are especially prone to newsworthy incidents—airlines are an obvious example—while others may go for years without anything happening that would hit the headlines. However, if a crisis does occur, it is amazing how fast it can turn from a simple, solvable problem into a PR disaster.

For many firms, such a crisis can be enough to destroy the company. When a Pan American Airlines flight was destroyed by terrorists over Lockerbie, the company suffered a PR disaster when it emerged that warnings had been given about a bomb on the aircraft. The fact that PanAm received an average of four bomb warnings a day made no difference to the public perception: shortly afterward, PanAm went out of business.

The problem was that PanAm did not have an effective crisis management protocol.

The idea

Many companies have a well-established crisis team who anticipate scenarios that may create PR problems, and work out solutions in advance. When Eurolines, the European long-distance bus company, suffered a crisis, they had a plan in place. A Eurolines bus from Warsaw to London was hit by a lorry in Germany, injuring a number of passengers (some seriously). The company's crisis team were ready: some passengers were hospitalized in Germany, some were given the option of returning to Warsaw, others were given the option of continuing to London.

At the London end, a large hotel was booked to receive passengers. Medical staff were on hand to provide help (although of course all injured passengers had already received medical care in Germany) and interpreters were available. The passenger list was checked to determine the nationalities of passengers—not all were Poles, since some had traveled to Warsaw from Lithuania, Latvia, Estonia, and even Russia to meet the connection in Poland. Rooms were booked for all passengers and also for friends or family who had expected to meet the coach. Eurolines' operations director was also present, as well as the PR officer, to field questions from the press and specifically to prevent reporters from harassing passengers for comments. A buffet was provided for all those present, and the following day Eurolines issued free tickets for onward connections in Britain, recognizing that many passengers would have missed their connections or whoever was meeting them in London.

The organization was exemplary: efficient, effective, and geared to creating goodwill all around. Such a slick approach does not happen by accident—it only happens through careful planning and rehearsal.

In practice

- Choose the right people to be on the team. They need to be senior enough to carry credibility with the firm's publics, and to understand the possible problems and solutions.
- Arrange for the crisis team to meet regularly to consider possible scenarios.
- Practice—do dummy runs.
- Ensure that team members know how to deal with the press—having someone say "No comment" to every question is a PR disaster in itself.

CUSTOMERS
BEING SPACES
Jeremy Kourdi

CREATING PLACES WHERE people want to be—whether to socialize, relax, or simply carry out everyday activities such as reading or working—can become a profitable product.

The idea

At first glance, this concept appears similar to "brand spaces." However, there is a crucial difference: "being spaces" make the idea of a desirable social setting the chief selling point and core product—a fundamental aspect of the business.

Being spaces are particularly popular in cities where cramped apartments, claustrophobic offices, and sometimes unsafe public areas prompt people to seek a more relaxing change of scene. Trend Watching, an organization documenting consumer trends, described the concept of being spaces as "... urban dwellers trading their lonely, cramped living rooms for the real-life buzz of commercial living-room-like settings, where catering and entertainment aren't just the main attraction, but are there to facilitate small office/living room activities like watching a movie, reading a book, meeting friends and colleagues, or doing your admin."

While many successful businesses, such as coffee house franchise Starbucks and book retailers Borders, blend the idea of a being space with other products, there is an increasing number of businesses devoted to providing customers with nothing other than simply a place to be. Paragraph NY is one such company. With monthly memberships from $100, it provides a 2,500 square foot loft space near Union Square divided into a writing room and a lounge area. Members can work in library-style cubicles or relax and socialize with other members—a modern home from home.

In practice

- Design the space carefully and functionally—emphasize style and comfort, and use soft furnishings and room dividers to absorb sound, ensuring your being space remains convivial and relaxed.
- Provide opportunities for both socializing and relative privacy within the space.
- Consider raising revenue by selling advertising in the being space. While you should not allow advertising to compromise the aesthetic feeling, sophisticated, cutting-edge, and carefully placed adverts can enhance customers' perceptions and be useful.
- Even if you do not wish to have a being space as your primary business venture, you can incorporate some of the principles into your business to entice potential customers.

MARKETING
GIVE PEOPLE A GLIMPSE BEHIND THE SCENES
Andy Maslen

PEOPLE *LOVE GETTING* insider information. For certain readers the idea that there's an elite group, somewhere, all having a wonderful time at their expense is sufficient motivation to stump up the cash for whatever you're selling. It's why headlines promising to reveal "the 7 secrets of professional manicurists" do so well.

Even people who *are* members of an elite worry that there may be a super-elite to which they are denied access. Perhaps because they are latecomers, or not of the right class, or from the wrong side of town. At every level of society, you have these anxieties about station and you can play on them to achieve your goals.

The idea
From an IT company
In the middle of a series of press ads for this IT services supplier, we decided to try something different. Rather than addressing the reader directly, in the second person singular—"you"—and talking about the usual benefits, we'd create a "fake" memo from the managing director to the marketing manager. The idea—conceit wouldn't be too harsh—was that, somehow, the memo had been printed in place of an ad, thus "revealing" the company's plans to its customers.

The memo read something like this:

> Dear James,
> Just wanted to remind you that our prices are going up next month. We should probably let customers know beforehand so they get the chance to book next year's support contract at this year's prices.
> Maybe a new ad? Or a mailing?
> I'll leave the details to you.
> Karen

The ad was designed to look like an internal memo, and set off-center against what appeared to be a normal page of editorial.

Opposite the ad we ran a bound-in insert with a straight presentation of the deal on offer and a booking form.

The results were good, better than the control. I guess people just liked the idea that someone had goofed and they could take advantage of this little piece of insider information. Even though it was a deal we could have presented in a straight ad, it just looked more interesting this way.

In practice

- If you decide to try this approach, make sure you nail the internal tone of voice. Imagine you're recording a meeting then just type up what you overheard.
- You could even create a little giveaway based on giving the recipient the inside track. Use words such as "revealed," "exposed," or "discovered."

LEADERSHIP
ENGAGE PEOPLE'S EMOTIONS
Jonathan Gifford

A LEADER'S VISION must connect with people at an emotional level if it is to change their behavior.

The idea

Robert McKee is a successful screenwriter, lecturer and author who believes that leaders need to use the art of storytelling to engage the team at an emotional level.

"A big part of a CEO's job is to motivate people to reach certain goals. To do that, he or she must engage their emotions, and the key to their hearts is story. There are two ways to persuade people. The first is by using conventional rhetoric, which is what most executives are trained in. It's an intellectual process, and in the business world it usually consists of a PowerPoint slide presentation in which you say, 'Here is our company's biggest challenge, and here is what we need to do to prosper'. And you build your case by giving statistics and facts and quotes from authorities. But there are two problems with rhetoric. First, the people you're talking to have their own set of authorities, statistics, and experiences. While you're trying to persuade them, they are arguing with you in their heads. Second, if you do succeed in persuading them, you've done so only on an intellectual basis. That's not good enough, because people are not inspired to act by reason alone. The other way to persuade people—and ultimately a much more powerful way—is by uniting an idea with an emotion. The best way to do that is by telling a compelling story. In a story, you not only weave a lot of information into the telling but you also arouse your listener's emotions and energy."

Storytelling, says McKee, expresses how and why life changes. Stories "display the struggle between expectation and reality in all its nastiness".

When Greg Dyke, previous Director General of the BBC, set about instigating a programme of culture change called *Making it Happen*, his vision was to make the BBC "the most creative organization in the world".

He commissioned a series of short films that celebrated the achievements of the BBC's unsung heroes. "These films, and dozens of others like them, opened the eyes of BBC people to the scale and range of the organization and made them proud of what was being achieved and of those involved. The real point about *Making it Happen* was that it engaged people's emotions, not just their brains. Cultural change is above all an emotional experience, not an intellectual one."

In practice

- People can be convinced by a compelling argument, but this may not change their behavior. To motivate and inspire people, a leader needs to engage their emotions.

- We all tend to remember and understand events as a series of stories; this is how we try to make sense of what we experience.
- In compelling stories, something that is desired is thwarted by antagonistic forces that must be overcome.
- A leader's vision—the struggle that the organization faces to achieve its goal—can be framed as a compelling story.

COMMUNICATION
AGAIN AND AGAIN AND ...
Patrick Forsyth

ONE OF THE things most presenters want to achieve in most circumstances is making a message stick. They do not just want to inform or entertain; they want to have a more lasting effect— changing views or behavior or prompting action to be taken later.

The idea
The idea is to repeat things. Repetition is a fundamental help to grasping a point. Repetition is a fundamental help to... sorry. But it is true. It does not imply just saying the same thing, in the same words, repeatedly. Repetition takes a number of forms. You do not want to overdo this principle but to use it judiciously.

In practice
- Repetition can be used in a variety of ways, for instance:
  - Things being repeated in different ways (or at different stages of the same presentation)
  - Points made in more than one manner: for example, being spoken and written down (in a handout or on a slide)
  - Using summaries or checklists to recap key points
  - Reminders over a period of time (maybe varying the method— phone, email or meetings that follow up a presentation)
- Slides are essentially a form of repetition. You hear something and you see something. More than that: at a presentation, you may have considerable repetition:

- An agenda sent in advance makes a general point
- The introduction starts from the general (prior to moving to the particular)
- A point is made (maybe more than once)
- A slide is shown about it
- An example or anecdote is used to illustrate it (maybe with a summary point at the end, or even another slide)
- A summary mentions the point again (with another slide, perhaps)
- A handout mentions it in writing (and includes copies of slides used)

- This is a fair bit of repetition. It can be overdone of course (perhaps as in the introduction to this point here), but it is also a genuinely valuable aid to getting the message across, especially when used with the other factors now mentioned.
- Never forget: people really are more likely to retain what they take in when they see or hear it more than once, and in different ways. (Okay, enough repetition!)

POSITIONING

REPOSITION INTO A BETTER MARKET

Jim Blythe

SOMETIMES A BRAND has been promoted to a target audience that is disappearing, or at least turns out to be less attractive than another audience. The brand might be doing perfectly well, but could do better: this is where repositioning comes in.

Repositioning means establishing the brand in a different location in the customer's consciousness. Usually, it means changing the way everybody thinks of the brand—not just the existing customers, but anyone else who might now consider the product. The position of a brand in people's minds is always relative to other brands and products, some of which may not be direct competitors—people often say that a product is "the Rolls-Royce of ...", for example.

Repositioning takes time and effort, but the payoffs can be very large indeed.

The idea

Lucozade is a carbonated glucose drink available throughout Britain and in many other countries. It was originally developed as a drink for people convalescing after serious illnesses—the glucose provided quick energy, and the bubbles gave people's digestive systems a boost. As a way of nourishing someone whose appetite might be poor it succeeded very well, and was in fact an iconic brand.

However, during the 1980s it became clear that there were a great many more healthy people than sick people. General improvements in healthcare and aftercare meant that Lucozade had a shrinking market—while at the same time interest in taking up sport was on the increase as more people had leisure time to fill.

A series of TV advertisements showing decathlete Daley Thompson drinking Lucozade helped to reposition the product. Handy-sized bottles were used instead of the larger one-pint bottles Lucozade originally came in, and the drink was sold through vending machines and at sports clubs.

Nowadays, Lucozade uses Lara Croft as its role model, and the repositioning is complete. Sales have multiplied, but more importantly the product's future is secure in a growing market, rather than the shrinking market it occupied previously.

In practice

- Before deciding to reposition, be very sure that you want to lose the market you are already in.
- You cannot occupy two positions at once—if you reposition, you lose the position you already have.
- Be very clear about the position you want to occupy—consider the competitive issues particularly.
- Anticipate retaliation from competitors in the new market.
- Keep your promotion consistent with the new position.

62 STAND UP TO CUSTOMERS

Patrick Forsyth

THERE IS AN old saying that if you appear to be like a doormat, you should expect people to walk all over you. Sometimes a customer relationship can feel like this. Some customers are not just demanding (aren't they all?) but take extreme liberties that demand something that goes beyond any definition of even excellent service. Such a relationship is costly, at worst reducing or removing the profitability of the business.

The idea

Seen in a market research company in Hong Kong ...

Situated in Hong Kong, this company has offices and clients around the Asian region. At one time the staff of one of its largest clients were causing the manager they dealt with considerable problems. The clients' disorganization was at the root of the problem. They were forever canceling or changing meetings and demanding attendance at others at short notice. They commonly telephoned demanding that the manager rush to one of their many regional offices at a moment's notice, with the need to travel from, say, Hong Kong to Singapore compounding the problem. This sort of situation costs time and money, and ultimately threatened the viability of a carefully costed project. Being sales and service oriented, the manager's instinct was to respond helpfully, to manage somehow to accommodate them. In this case this just compounded the problem.

The client was of the "give us an inch and we'll take a mile and a half" school (aren't they all? you may say again). Every helpful act simply made them feel that anything demanded would be responded to positively. Ultimately, if demands go up and up, something must be done. But it is a question of degree. Where do you draw the line? Perhaps the best answer is sooner rather than later, despite the instinct to help on each individual occasion, and the real fear that saying "No" will jeopardize the client relationship.

In this case a line was drawn. The manager said "No" to a particularly inconvenient request, and reminded the clients of the terms of the assignment. Surprise, surprise—the clients, who clearly understood what they had been doing, respected his refusal and began to act differently. Profitability returned. The client relationship was improved. More assignments were booked.

In practice
- Sometimes the right thing to do is to stand up to customers.
- The trick is to decide when and how powerfully you need to react.

DIRECT MARKETING
WHAT NOT TO PUT ON YOUR ORDER FORM
Andy Maslen

WHENEVER I GET a mailshot in the post, or look at a direct response ad in the paper, I always read the order form first. It's become a little game ... seeing whether they've gone for the easy option or been creative. And specifically, I look at the headline.

I get a point every time I see the words "Order form." So far I have roughly 85 million points. Why, after getting all the way through the sales process to the close, do these copywriters shrug their shoulders and start *labelling* things? There has to be something more compelling to write than "Order form" doesn't there?

The idea
From order forms labeled "Order form"
When you're writing a direct response ad or mailshot, I'm willing to bet you write the order form last. We all tend to think linearly

about copywriting, starting from the outside in. So, outer, letter, brochure, response device. Which means by the time we get around to the order form itself, we're feeling just a couple of steps away from the finish line.

The result is often recourse to the boilerplate bin. Need a headline? "Order form" should do it. After all, it *is* an order form. But that's precisely my point. There are plenty of clues to tip off even the doziest reader that this is, indeed, the order form. Credit card symbols, lines for entering their personal details, return address, direct debit mandate, and so on.

And it's not as if we resort to labeling any other parts of the pack. The outer envelope, for example, rarely carries the line "Outer envelope." And I'm fairly sure I've never seen a sales letter with "Top flap" written above the body copy.

If you were selling face to face, and the customer had just agreed to buy from you, would you say, "Great! Can I just get you to fill in this form?" No! You'd say, "Great! Let's just get this paperwork done and I can give you your free steak knives." In other words, turn the close into another pleasurable part of the process, not form-filling.

There are lots of things you could write that would keep the smile on the customer's face long enough for you to close the sale. Recap the main benefit, for example. Or remind them of what they'll lose if they don't buy.

In practice
- Write your order form first. That way you come to it fresh.
- Treat the order form as an ad in its own right. Spend some time thinking of a headline that encourages the reader to make the purchase. "Order now" is far, far better than "Order form."

CREATE SOME "HOW-TO" TIPS
Jim Blythe

PEOPLE ARE CONSTANTLY looking for expert advice, and there is no doubt that running a business makes you more knowledgeable than you were before. Sharing that knowledge (without giving away all your trade secrets) is a good way of attracting attention to yourself, but more importantly it demonstrates that you know what you are doing, and can be trusted.

Demonstrating trust is a good way of generating trust. Trusting people with some of your knowledge won't make them go elsewhere—it will tend to make them want to trust you with their business.

The idea
Write a series of "how-to" tips for the layperson. For example, if you are in the building trade, some tips on how to check your house over to make sure it will withstand winter may well generate some business—and it is exactly the kind of advice people will want to cut out and keep. Someone finding a problem has your number to hand, and can tell you exactly what they need you to do.

Likewise a hairdressing salon can give tips on looking after hair between visits, a restaurant could publish recipes, or a driving school could issue advice on safe driving. The possibilities are endless, and almost any business could benefit from this approach.

In practice
- Write tips that people can easily understand, and that are useful to the layperson.
- Don't worry that it will harm your business—people are more likely to come to you, since they will trust your knowledge.
- Make yourself available for interviews for the newspapers or even broadcast media (radio shows often bring in experts).

COMPETITION
HARDBALL
Jeremy Kourdi

COMPETING MEANS STRIVING to get ahead of the competition, but hardball goes further: it is about relentlessly developing and then sustaining a clear gap between you and your nearest rivals. It is highlighted in the article "Hardball Strategies" (*Harvard Business Review*, September 2006, by Lachenauer, R.; MacMillan, Ian C.; van Putten, Alexander B.; Gunther McGrath, Rita; Stalk, George Jr.).

The idea

It is fashionable to think that playing tough is doomed to failure: that playing hardball is inherently cynical, bereft of virtue, values, or decency, and lies behind the high-profile failures of Enron and others. This is untrue. Hardball does not mean being criminal or even unethical, but it does mean being determined and single-minded.

Wal-Mart became hugely profitable and the biggest retailer in the world by explaining to suppliers exactly how goods should be delivered. Suppliers were given computer information enabling them to track consumer purchases and to help manage inventory, they were told when to resupply Wal-Mart warehouses, and told to deliver only full truckloads at a given time. This system, which is constantly refined, enables Wal-Mart to remove wastage and cost from its supply chain, improving efficiency and margins.

In practice

Hardball has several guiding principles. First, strive for "extreme" competitive advantage. Regulators may worry about market dominance, hardball players do not. Dominance only occurs in extreme situations, and is rightly prevented, but, by trying to dominate, a firm becomes better and actually benefits customers. This links closely with two other points: know the limits to what you can do, and go no further. It is vital that your business is accepted in the markets where you operate, so go as far as possible without alienating customers and communities.

Several key questions will help you decide the limit. Is the action good for the customer? Does it break any laws? Will it directly hurt a competitor? Will it antagonize increasingly influential special interest groups? The right and only answers are, in order: yes, no, no, and no. Serving a customer better than anyone else is vital; targeting a competitor without producing any real benefit for the customer is unnecessary and counter-productive (customers may resent you).

Also important is the need to maintain a relentless focus on competitiveness. This means taking action in two ways. Instill a competitive, customer-focused, entrepreneurial culture, understand what your competitive advantage is—and then exploit it ruthlessly and continually.

Two other points are significant. Use your competitors' weaknesses to your advantage, but avoid going head to head or competing directly. The danger of direct confrontation is that you will focus too much on competitors at the expense of customers. Finally, develop the right attitudes in yourself and your colleagues. Most people have a natural will to win, so use this. This requires restless impatience, an action-oriented approach, and a desire to change the status quo and constantly improve.

ONLINE MARKETING
BE PROMINENT ON GOOGLE
Jim Blythe

THE INTERNET HAS, of course, wrought many changes in the way businesses operate. One of the major ones is in corporate communications, simply because people no longer sit around waiting for companies to communicate with them. Typically, people seek out information online, and in fact control the flow of information.

This has major implications for public relations. People seek out information from sources that they find agreeable, either from the viewpoint of being familiar and easy to use or from the viewpoint of having content that matches with the individual's own views. People are not passive recipients of information, and the internet allows them to take this further by choosing which company's websites they go to.

The idea

Ensuring that your website comes up in the first ten search results is the aim. This is because few people go beyond the first page of their Google search, and most only look at the first one or two pages. Choosing the right keywords when setting up your site is crucial, as is ensuring that the site content contains words that people are likely to use when searching the internet.

In larger firms, media relations tends to be relegated to the "nice to have if only we could afford it" list. Having an effective web presence is an important way to maintain a high PR profile at little or no cost.

In practice

- Choose your keywords carefully, based on what your publics are likely to enter into their search engines.
- Ensure that your content will not disappoint.
- Visit the website regularly yourself and encourage others to do so—this tends to move it up the list in terms of search results.

SALES

CLIMB THE STAIRS

Patrick Forsyth

MANY BUSINESSES NEED a constant supply of new prospects. Prospecting—and cold calling—is not most salespeople's favorite activity. The trick to ensuring that you have a constant supply of new people to talk to is to have a number of methods, where each lends itself to regularly producing some new names. These might include everything from combing directories or association membership lists to simple observation—who's moving into that new building under construction.

The idea

I first observed this being done by the representative of a printing firm ...

Any salesperson has to create personal effectiveness in terms of time. Prospecting must not take too long, and you do not want to undertake labyrinthine research when something simpler will do the job. The salesperson I am thinking of here worked in central London. He wanted to find customers within a tight radius of the printing works to minimize travel time, and had hit on what he called the climbing stairs method of prospecting. This he did specifically to try to find new customers close to existing ones.

Every time he visited a customer in an office block, he took the stairs (on the way down is easiest!) and checked out what other organizations were operating in the building. If he found a likely prospect, it only took a moment to nip in and ask a few questions at reception. Occasionally he met a decision maker as a result. More often he got information and names, and could make a more considered approach later. It was a very time-effective method. The same sort of thing can be made to work in a variety of different circumstances, for example on an industrial estate. Sometimes the notice listing occupants in the lobby is helpful, but actually seeing the front door or going in allows a better judgment to be made about potential.

In practice

- Anything like this can be made a habit. Something that takes little time but can be done regularly day after day is especially useful.
- Prospecting is as much a question of attitude as of technique. Those who think about it positively are rarely short of someone new to talk to.

BUSINESS SKILLS
FOCUS ON THE WILDLY IMPORTANT
Jonathan Gifford

IT IS EASY to become distracted and even overwhelmed by the sheer number of things that apparently have to be done. Highly effective leaders focus on a small number of core goals that will have a significant effect on a wide range of other targets.

Concentrating on these "wildly important" issues clears the mind and is a key factor in achieving improved productivity and a better work-life balance.

The idea

Stephen Covey, management and leadership author and co-founder of the FranklinCovey Company, says, "You need to narrow your focus down to the one, two or three most important goals you must achieve. These goals are so important that if you don't achieve them, nothing else you achieve really matters much."

This kind of prioritization, says Covey, is essential for effective leadership, and should also cascade through the whole organization.

"The bottom line is, when people are crystal clear about the most important priorities of the organization and team they work with and [have] prioritized their work around those top priorities, not only are they many times more productive, they discover they have the time they need to have a whole life."

Progress towards achieving the key goals must be measurable; key activities that demonstrate progress towards achieving the core goals should be selected and monitored weekly.

Martha Lane Fox, co-founder of lastminute.com, talks about the need for leaders to "get out of the detail" to focus on the really important issues.

"Good leaders know when to get into the detail and know when to get out of it again. I often see people who immerse themselves in detail for comfort. They busy themselves with meetings and all the things you need to do daily in a business while being too scared to think, 'What could really transform this business?' or, 'What direction is this business going in five, 10 or 15 years time?' Mind you, in lastminute.com's time frame, it was five, 10 or 15 months' time."

In practice

- Focus on the core achievements that are most essential to achieving your overall goals. Choose not more than three "wildly important" goals.
- Ensure that the team understands these goals and prioritize their own activities to focus on achieving the core overriding goals.
- Choose key measures that will indicate progress towards achieving these goals; monitor progress and make the results visible to everyone as frequently as possible—ideally weekly.
- Step back from the detail of the job whenever possible; changing circumstances will affect what needs to be done to achieve the goals.
- Successful prioritization will improve the efficiency of the organization as a whole and free up everyone's time, improving productivity and work-life balance.

SALES COPY
CREATE CURIOSITY
Andy Maslen

IT's BEEN SAID that curiosity is one of the big psychological triggers or motivators. And it stands to reason. We *are* curious. It's in our genes. All higher primates start exploring their world as soon as they can. We puzzle over things. We love figuring things out. Almost as soon as they learn to talk, human children start asking, "Why?"

Which is excellent news for us copywriters. We can use our readers' natural curiosity to draw them into our copy. Because, wouldn't you know it, the answer to all their questions can be had for the price of the product we're promoting.

The idea
From *Personal Computer World*, an IT magazine

The readers of—and subscribers to—*Personal Computer World* (*PCW*) are well educated, mostly male, and mainly IT professionals. I was commissioned to write a direct mail letter that would be run as a test against the existing letter (the control). Like a lot of copywriters, I find the opening the hardest to settle on. Not because I can't get started, but because I can't decide which among several appeals will pay off with the best results. (Well, if I could, I'd be psychic and probably not writing copy for a living.)

I decided, finally, that male pride in being a technical expert, coupled with good old-fashioned fear of falling behind the pace, would form the bedrock of the letter. But how to start? Here's what I eventually wrote:

> Dear Mr Sample,
> I think you are like me. You're passionate about technology and you want the best you can afford. More than that, though:

That first six-word sentence does several things. It invites the reader to read it because it's so short. It implies that the rest of the letter will be easy to read. And, crucially, it piques the reader's curiosity. This was a two-page letter, so I assumed the reader would glance over the page to see who the letter was from. The Editor in this case. So the question my opening sentence plants in the reader's mind is, "*How* am I like the Editor of *PCW*?" It is also a subtle piece of flattery. By opening like this, I engaged directly with the reader's own sense of self worth *and* encouraged him to read my next sentence. In other words, I began training him to read past sentence breaks.

In practice

- Use curiosity as a motivator if you can, but be sure to link it to an appeal to the reader's self-interest. In this example, he was curious to find out how he resembled an authority figure in IT.
- A simple technique to get or keep people reading is to tell them that, "In a moment I am going to reveal to you the XYZ industry's dirty little secret."

STRATEGY
PICK THE SEGMENTS NOBODY ELSE WANTS

Jim Blythe

THERE IS A tendency for firms to aim for the most attractive groups of customers all the time—the wealthiest, or the youngest (on the assumption that they will have a longer life as customers), or those with the highest usage rates for the product. This is fine, except that everybody else is targeting the same groups, so you can expect some fierce competition.

This was particularly the case for the older consumers. Companies assumed that elderly people on pensions would have little money to spend and would probably already have most of what they wanted. What these companies had not noticed is that many older people have generous occupational pensions, low fixed outgoings (having paid off their mortgages, and having relatively few loans) and also more leisure time to enjoy activities.

The idea

This is the market Saga tapped into. Originally, Saga targeted the over-60s, offering vacations that catered for people who were prepared to pay a small premium for extra care. Saga understood their customers' needs—while they ensured that less mobile people got the help they required (for example, older Saga customers rarely need to carry their own baggage), they also recognized that most people in their sixties are fit, active, and interested in adventures. Saga moved vacations for the elderly away from coach trips to Blackpool or the Lake District toward adventure breaks in the Amazon Rain Forest and activity weekends. The company also retains a greater degree of flexibility than other package companies—recognizing that many Saga customers have children or siblings living abroad. The company allows people to combine a tour of (say) Australia with the possibility of staying on for a few weeks afterward in order to visit relatives.

Focusing on a segment nobody else wants means having the opportunity to capture the entire segment with little or no competition—Saga are now able to offer many services other than vacations to this age group, having established their credibility in the market.

In practice
- Know your segment. Get to understand their needs in detail.
- Find a segment nobody else wants—even people with very little money still buy something.
- Look for opportunities to sell a wider range of products to your segment—in other words, base your approach on the segment, not on the products you want to sell.

LEADERSHIP
STICK TO THE VISION
Jonathan Gifford

THE VISION OF an organization can be quite simple, but the right vision has a profound effect on the organization's behavior, and can guide it through periods of great change and difficulty.

The idea
Ruben Vardanian is chairman and CEO of Troika Dialog, Russia's leading private investment bank. When the company was founded

in 1991, its guiding vision included principles that would guide the company through the turbulent times following the dissolution of the Soviet Union and the founding of the Russian Federation, as the old government planning system was replaced by free financial markets.

The company established core principles from the outset: to position itself for the long-term and as a client service organization and to benchmark the company against international standards. It was the only investment bank in Russia to employ external auditors to report on their first year's losses. The company turned down business from clients who were being offered very high guaranteed rates of return by other investment companies.

"Looking back today, that seems easy to say, but at the time it was quite tough. We didn't know if we would have money to pay salaries at that time. But I knew it would be wrong, and I knew sooner or later we would be paid back for it. This is why you need to have a dream. You need to have a vision ... You need to understand what kind of things you will do and what kind of things you will not do."

Andrea Jung, chairman and CEO of Avon Products Inc, talks of the company's vision, dating back to its founding in 1886, which was to empower women to run their own independent businesses under the Avon banner.

"The whole legacy that comes with being 122 years old has good and bad aspects. Now that we're a $10-billion-plus company there is a completely different set of requirements. Running the company today is completely different; the global marketplace is different; the competition is different; the consumer is different; the selling requirements for our Representatives are different. Everything has changed around the company—except, luckily, the original mission. So I as the CEO have always to ask myself how I can make sure the company stays fit for the future without neglecting its heritage and its history. ... It is a unique thing to have a founder who believed in 1886 that women, who could not even vote at that time, should be empowered to run their own independent businesses ... luckily through all the decades of the company and all the transitions, that has remained the constant vision."

In practice

- The right vision will help to guide an organization through difficult times and help it to make the right decision.
- Part of a leader's role is to interpret the vision for current conditions and to present it to colleagues in contemporary terms.
- The vision will guide leaders and the organization though periods of great change; everything else may be altered and developed, but the vision remains the same.

MANAGING TIME
USE A "DOCUMENT PARKING" SYSTEM
Patrick Forsyth

PROBLEM: YOU MAY have many things on the go at any one time, and in physical terms they may be represented by a single sheet of paper or a batch of correspondence. Many of them do not need action, or rather nothing can be done immediately. Such items are what so often constitute the ever-present pending tray that makes many a desk groan under its weight. The net result is that you spend a great deal of time either shuffling through the heap to locate things, or checking things in there to see what you might in time do about them.

The nature of some of the material makes the problem worse. Say one item can only be dealt with when certain monthly performance figures are published; in that case, to keep checking may well be both time-consuming and useless, as no action can be taken until a later stage anyway. Further, constant reviewing can achieve little in advance of knowing what the figures say, as there are many different possibilities in terms of what they might predicate.

The idea

If you suffer this sort of situation, you need a parking place for such things, somewhere safe yet guaranteed to trigger prompt action at the appropriate moment. You need what is called a Prompt (or Bring Forward) File. This means you take an item and decide when you will be able to progress it. This may be at a specific time (when the monthly figures arrive), or it may not (just six weeks on, or longer, at the start of the next financial year). Then you simply mark it with the date on which you next want to see it and file it, with other similar items, in date order. Then forget it. Waste no more time even thinking about it. You do not have to, because every day you, or your secretary, can check the file and take out anything marked with that day's date. At which point you can either act or, occasionally, give something another date and move it forward.

In practice

- A couple of provisos must be borne in mind. First, you may want to limit the total quantity of items (or A–Z list them) as something will happen occasionally that means you need to take action earlier than you thought, and you will need to retrieve an item from the file and action it ahead of the date you originally set. Second, you may want to link it to a diary note, especially if you have no secretary. This is a simple, easy to set up, common-sense idea that works for many people.

COST CUTTING
YOU TELL ME WHAT WE NEED TO DO!
Anne Hawkins

THERE IS A wealth of experience and talent in the workforce that all too often gets overlooked. If improvement activities are left to managers then the business is missing a huge opportunity.

The idea

Don't leave most of your players sitting on the bench.

Even when you're looking at the 'big picture' rather than telling people what needs to be done in terms of reducing costs and improving efficiency, it may be helpful to give them an opportunity to work it out for themselves.

An uncanny resemblance

This large manufacturing company in the metals sector had just run a series of financial awareness courses for managers from across the business. The trainer was then asked to repeat the sessions for the trade union representatives. It was thought it would be helpful to improve their basic financial understanding in preparation for a meeting with management to discuss steps to resolve poor profit performance and perpetual shortages of cash.

Rather than repeating the earlier sessions, the trainer adopted a different approach. Delegates were given the opportunity to 'buy' a business that they could 'run' using 'money' to purchase materials, turn them into products and then ship them out to customers. After taking a look at how the business worked, the delegates accepted the offer to buy and, as the new owners, set about their work. As they re-enacted one financial year after another, our new capitalists became increasingly frustrated by the lack of any return on their investment and muttered threats about closing the business down and moving on could be heard. Then the penny dropped—the business they were 'running' was a mirror image of the company they worked for. Understanding why there was a need to act, the delegates started to come up with their own ideas for improving performance ... that bore a remarkable resemblance to the agenda for their forthcoming meeting.

In practice
- Recognise that relying on a small proportion of the workforce for ideas is wasting a great opportunity.
- If you want your co-workers to embrace change and join the fight against waste you have to lead from the front and be convincing about the benefits on offer ... and the risks of lagging behind your competition.
- Remember that many will ask "What's in it for me?"—so make sure you have your answers ready!

MARKETING
PRECISION MARKETING
Jeremy Kourdi

DECIDE WHO YOUR ideal customers are—then decide where they go, what they do, and what they want. Use this information to target them precisely at key points in their everyday lives.

The idea
Precision marketing involves asking four questions—who, what, when, and how—to create a sharply effective marketing strategy.

ABN, a bank wishing to court wealthy Dutch customers, created a lounge at Amsterdam's Schiphol Airport for the exclusive use of its Preferred Banking clients (account holders with savings or investments exceeding €50,000, or a monthly income exceeding €5,000). The elite lounge was open daily from 6 am to 10 pm, providing meeting space, internet access, refreshments, foreign currency exchange, and a place to relax amid the rush of traveling. With this project, ABN showed a clear understanding of precision marketing:

- *Who its customers were*: comfortably wealthy individuals traveling from the Netherlands.
- *What they wanted*: a place to enjoy relaxation and luxury when traveling.
- *When they wanted it*: between 6 in the morning and 10 in the evening, when the majority of flights depart and arrive.
- *How to deliver it*: creating an exclusive lounge that provided the amenities valued by affluent travelers.

What makes precision marketing special is its ability to reach its target audience and to meet their preferences in a memorable way, promoting a robust product that can withstand competitors.

In practice

- Make sure you target the right market by gaining access to reliable market research—for example, via web marketing. Precision is the vital element of precision marketing!
- Hold brainstorming sessions where each of the "four questions" of precision marketing are considered in depth.
- Consider what precision marketing strategy you would realistically be able to carry out that surpasses your competitors' current efforts.
- Find ways to enhance your marketing and your offer. Keep it fresh, appealing, targeted, and distinctive.

LEADERSHIP
SET A GOOD EXAMPLE
Jonathan Gifford

ONE OF THE most difficult aspects of being a leader is that you are constantly on show. Everything that you do is seen by the organization and by a wider public. Leaders have no option but to set a good example in everything that they do.

The idea

Sir John Harvey-Jones, previous chairman of UK chemical giant ICI, points out that the organization may read significance into what is, in fact, a moment of irritation or a bad mood, and that it is dangerous to appear in public when one is not at one's mental and physical best.

"One of the penalties of leadership is indeed that people watch your mood in a way which you do not allow for ... I remember another occasion on which, in my anxiety to ensure that I spoke to a management course, I came straight off the overnight plane from America to address them. I barely had time for a shave before I appeared ... I felt very virtuous and proud until I got the feedback, which was that they were concerned that perhaps I was losing my grip! Entirely my own fault, but it certainly taught me not to assume that one can perform tasks beyond one's physical capability."

Reuben Mark, previous chairman and CEO of Colgate-Palmolive reminds us that a corporate leader's integrity must be unquestionable and that leaders must demonstrate integrity in all things, not just in major issues of corporate governance. Leaders cannot be seen to be "bending the rules".

He highlights the case of Tyco chief executive Dennis Kozlowski, who paid restitution for tax evasion after admitting that works of art that he had declared to be for the company's use were in fact on display in his New York apartment. Empty cartons supposedly containing the artworks were sent to a warehouse. Mark talks about the impact on a worker handling those empty cartons: "He knows that the boss is cheating on taxes. How can you really expect that warehouseman to be honest in his job when the example he's getting is just the opposite? With everything you do as a leader, you've got to think not only, 'Is it the right thing for me to do?' but, 'Is it right for the organization?'"

In practice

- Setting a good example applies as much to relatively unimportant issues, such as the impression that you gave at the last presentation, as it does to serious issues about your personal behaviour.
- Leaders must try to avoid seeming bad-tempered, irritable or moody since people are likely to interpret this as being significant.
- Avoid taking on more than you are physically capable of.
- Integrity on major issues of governance is taken for granted. Integrity on lesser issues is just as important. If a leader bends the rules, the team will assume that they can do the same.

DESIGN
USE THE PACKAGING
Jim Blythe

PACKAGING IS, AT its most basic, there to protect its contents from the environment and vice versa. However, packaging can do so much more—it can inform customers about the product, advise people about different possible ways of using the product, promote other brands in the firm's portfolio, and so forth.

Most brand managers are familiar with these aspects of packaging, and so this is all standard stuff—but some firms go further, and provide customers with some fun or extra utility from the packaging. For example, in France mustard is commonly packed in wine glasses, so that the customers can use the pots afterward. In many developing countries packaging is recycled to make oil lamps or to decorate houses. In some cases, the packaging can be designed just for fun.

The idea
French mineral water bottler Evian wanted to package its water in a plastic bottle that could be easily recycled. Most plastic bottles take up considerable space in recycling bins, even though the bottles are mostly empty space—so Evian designed a bottle that crushes down to a much reduced size.

What the company had not bargained for, though, was that people actually enjoyed the sensation of crushing the bottles. Finishing a bottle of mineral water just to enjoy crushing the bottle may seem a bit bizarre—but in fact the crushable bottle created a small, but discernible, USP in a crowded market. After all, water is water—the product relies heavily on other factors to differentiate it from its competitors.

In practice
* Watch what people do with the packaging. There may well be a good idea in there for you.

- Think of ways the packaging can add value—but remember it still has to sit on retailers' shelves.
- Packaging might be the only USP you have—exploit it!

SALES
THE POWER OF DESCRIPTION
Patrick Forsyth

EVERYONE IN SELLING must know the concept of features and benefits, and that, to use an old phrase, you sell the sizzle and not the sausages. People buy something because of what it does for them, or means to them; that is, they buy because of its benefits. As a result, sales messages should predominantly be benefit-led: you talk about the benefits, and use the features as factors that demonstrate how a benefit can be delivered. So far so good, yet prevailing practice is by no means perfect, and the world is full of salespeople busily talking about features. Certainly I find that significant numbers of people attending courses on sales techniques do not really understand the difference between features and benefits.

Even when you clearly understand the difference, the way benefits are described is a key factor in making a successful sales pitch and obtaining agreement.

The idea
From a manufacturer of catering equipment ...

Selling a range of cookers, grills, water heaters, and other items for hotels, restaurants, and various such establishments certainly involves a degree of technical detail, but let's just concentrate on a couple of simple facts. Imagine too that a busy café is the intended customer.

One feature of a flat grill is its size. Say the model being sold has a cooking area of 800 square centimeters. Perhaps not many people can instantly imagine what that looks like. But if you say it can cook a dozen eggs simultaneously (*because* it has an 800 sq cm surface area), and tie this in to the "rush at breakfast time," everyone in the catering business will be able to call a picture instantly to mind, and see the advantage.

Similarly, to sell a twin 8 pint water heater, you would do best not to emphasize the 8 pint capacity, but to refer to its ability to dispense both tea and coffee at the same time.

Descriptions like this, which are not only benefit-oriented, but also focused on the customer's specific situation, are worth a great deal. They link to the customers' experience, and prompt their imagination. I could probably give 99 more examples of this kind of thing, and fill up the rest of the book with them, but that might not make for the most helpful of manuals.

In practice

- Bland or inappropriate description—lazy description, if you like—can dilute a good case to the point where it will persuade no one.
- Good, powerful descriptions, as described above, are, however, a prerequisite of successful selling. This is something every salesperson needs to work at to get right.

ONLINE MARKETING
GET ON YOUTUBE
Jim Blythe

YouTube has been the online phenomenon of the century so far. It allows people to post pretty much anything they want to on video, provided it isn't pornographic or libellous or otherwise illegal.

People like to see themselves on telly, and a huge number of people have taken advantage: everything from professionally produced clips down to cellphone videos appear on YouTube, and clips come in from all over the world.

Of course, outright commercial plugs aren't permitted, but that's not what PR is about anyway.

The idea

An artist named Valentina from California decided to expand interest in her work beyond galleries. She wanted the opportunity to explain her thinking, and show people the process of making the artworks, so she had herself filmed actually painting a new work, and giving a running commentary.

The idea took off, and she now posts a new "episode" every Sunday. Eager YouTube viewers "tune in" each week to watch her paint, and she now has a worldwide following.

Not all of these people will buy a painting, of course, but galleries have certainly picked up on what she is doing: her profile has been raised considerably. And that, as they say, is PR in action.

In practice

- YouTube will edit you out if you are overtly commercial rather than just interesting.
- Have the actual filming done as professionally as possible, but without the "Hollywood" touch. YouTube is about people, not about slick production.
- Keep it personal. Talk about yourself, not the company (although you can, of course, mention the company too).

BUSINESS SKILLS
STOP BEING JUDGEMENTAL
Jonathan Gifford

IT IS VERY easy for leaders to pass judgement on colleagues. To some extent this might be seen to be part of a leader's brief. In fact, being judgemental switches colleagues off more effectively than any other leadership error, and achieves almost nothing positive by way of compensation.

The idea
Leadership development consultant and author, Marshall Goldsmith, lists "passing judgement" as one of the unconscious bad habits that prevent us from being better leaders.

He recommends a test: "For one week, treat every idea that comes your way from another person with complete neutrality ... Don't take sides. Don't express an opinion. Don't judge the comment." Goldsmith recommends that we simply say "Thank you". This will greatly reduce the amount of time spent having pointless arguments with colleagues, he says. More importantly, "people will begin to see you as a much more agreeable person, even when you are not in fact agreeing with them. Do this consistently and people will eventually brand you as someone whose door they can knock on when they have an idea." Similar "judgemental" bad habits listed by Goldsmith include routinely starting our sentences with "no", "but", or "however" or, in effect, "let me explain why that won't work".

Morgan McCall, business author and professor at the Marshall School of Business has written about "why leaders derail". He interviewed the peers and colleagues of apparently successful leaders whose careers had come to a sudden end.

"Insensitivity was the most commonly reported flaw among derailed executives in our research and one of the sharpest differentiators between derailed and successful executives. Humiliating managers in front of peers or subordinates, cutting people off, demeaning others' ideas—everyone who has ever worked for an insensitive boss ... knows the story and the incredible visceral response such treatment generates. Power and intimidation can produce compliance, but insensitivity can lead to lack of support at crucial junctures, failures of subordinates to pass on important information, active sabotage, loss of ideas from below, and a host of counterproductive activities. Organizations seem quite willing to overlook the flaw of insensitivity as long as someone gets results, but at the higher levels of management, alienating people in most cases assures that good results will not be sustained over time. It can't be very useful to have large numbers of people eager to see one fail."

In practice

- Passing judgement is something we all do without thinking; we feel obliged to make our views known. This is not helpful and can have negative effects.
- Practice being neutral. When people bring ideas and comments to you, just say "Thank you".
- Look out for other habitual negative responses that are, in effect, judgemental.
- Leaders who are judgmental to the point of being insensitive, and even abusive, lose all support. This limits their effectiveness.
- Insensitive and judgemental behavior can reach a critical point, at which leaders can suddenly be asked to step down.

COMPETITION
DEFINE YOUR OPPONENT
Jim Blythe

KNOWING YOUR OPPONENT is one thing—defining them in the minds of your publics is another. Most PR exercises are about defining the organization in the minds of its publics, but this is only half the story, especially when one is confronted with a persistent opponent who cannot be placated.

The problem is made worse by the fact that people often identify with the underdog, which means that direct attacks on opponents are very likely to backfire. Subtlety is needed! The way forward for many organizations is to use wording that conveys a solidly positive image, forcing opponents to take up the negative stance.

The idea

By categorizing yourself in a positive way it is easy to imply that your opponents are categorized in a negative way. The topic of abortion is an extremely emotive one, for example: those in favor of it categorize themselves as "pro-choice," which means that any opponents immediately categorize themselves as "anti-choice." Those same opponents categorize themselves as "pro-life," which tends to make opponents categorize themselves as "anti-life" in the public consciousness.

For firms in less emotive industries, there is the possibility of categorizing the firm as "pro-jobs" or "on the side of economic growth in the region." This immediately wrong-foots opponents, who then need to justify their own positions.

Forcing opponents into a negative position provides you with an immediate advantage in establishing your own credibility in the minds of your publics. Unless your opponents are very slick, you will have gained the high ground.

In practice

- Find the positives.
- Choose the positive that forces your opponents into a negative position.
- Do not muddy the waters—keep plugging the positive term you have decided on.
- Be prepared for retaliation. Your opponents will probably respond in kind.

ONLINE MARKETING
FLOG IT ON EBAY
Jim Blythe

MARKETING IS ABOUT creating profitable exchanges. Even the word derives from the kind of street market that represents the ultimate in buyer–seller interaction. Street markets are dying out in most industrialized countries due to the economies of scale that exist for large firms (whether retailers or manufacturers).

Taking a product direct to market has many advantages, though. It means that the supplier and the buyer can get together without any intermediaries, which means that it is easier to get a clear idea of what customers want and need. It means that middleman profit margins are taken out of the equation (although wholesalers and retailers usually earn their profit margins by increasing efficiency). It means that the seller has more control over the whole process, in conjunction with the buyer.

Doing the whole thing online has obvious advantages.

The idea
eBay has been around since 1995, and was originally founded as an auction site for consumer-to-consumer deals. At the time, it was more like an online jumble sale or auction than a true street market—but since then things have moved on.

Many companies now sell goods on eBay. The site allows companies to set up "booths" from which they can sell goods, at a fixed price rather than through an auction. Having a booth can be extremely cost-effective, especially considering the number of potential customers you might reach.

In practice
- eBay customers are likely to be price-sensitive bargain hunters. You may need to keep your prices down.

- eBay has strict rules—you need to be sure you understand them and agree with them.
- This idea works best for well-known brands. Remember that potential customers cannot easily inspect the products.
- Be prepared for people to return products they are not happy with, as they would in any other mail-order situation.

DIFFERENTIATION
AVOIDING COMMODITIZATION
Jeremy Kourdi

WHEN A PRODUCT becomes easily interchangeable with other products of the same type, it is said to become a "commodity." The process of a previously differentiated and specialized product becoming interchangeable is known as commoditization. While it is believed to increase overall economic efficiency, it can be difficult for individual companies to handle. Economic value and profits come from scarcity, whereas commoditization can curtail the potential for profit.

The idea
A famous example of commoditization is the microchip industry. While microchips started out as a specialized innovation that commanded a high price, they gradually became mass produced and interchangeable. This commoditization altered the nature of the microchip industry, increasing competition and decreasing profit margins.

Harrah's Entertainment, a gaming corporation that operates hotels and casinos in America, recognized that traditional attempts made by casinos at avoiding commoditization—such as creating increasingly garish and noticeable designs—were becoming stale and ineffectual. It decided that the most effective way to avoid becoming an interchangeable commodity would be to establish an increased level of customer communication and gratification.

A loyalty program was introduced where valuable customers were rewarded with significant gold-, platinum-, and diamond-level privileges. Harrah's CEO Gary Loveman commented, "When I started, this business was commoditized—you have a big box and gaming tables. Your challenge is to differentiate yourself from the other big boxes."

While commoditization is viewed as the largely inevitable fate of many products, companies can increase their chances of avoiding it by differentiating themselves, recognizing when commoditization is about to occur, and taking steps to ensure their product remains on the cutting edge.

In practice

- Find new ways to make your product or service distinctive, and avoid letting your product become an undifferentiated commodity.
- Ensure that some aspect of your product remains specialized, unique, and valuable for your customers.
- Consider the potential for commoditization when deciding to invest in growth industries.
- Utilize intellectual property protection laws, and create products or services that cannot be easily mimicked by competitors.

COLLABORATION
HELP YOUR ALLIES TO HELP YOU
Jim Blythe

IN MANY BUSINESS situations, you will have allies. These are companies that sell to the same target audience, but do not compete directly with you. For example, people who read the local paper obviously live locally and are therefore within your catchment area; having the local paper on your side would be a good thing.

Sometimes it is possible to operate on a larger scale—especially if you have a large number of possible allies.

The idea

When Tate Modern (the London art gallery) opened its doors it needed to attract the kind of audience that would enjoy modern art, and especially the kind of avant-garde exhibits that Tate Modern was planning to show.

Tate Modern's marketing team developed a profile of the type of person they thought would be in their target group (always an excellent starting point for any marketing activity). This included the type of restaurant they were likely to patronize, the type of coffee shop they would prefer, and the type of bar they would drink in—not businesses that would compete directly with an art gallery, but ones that would attract a similar audience.

Tate Modern arranged to supply Tate-branded chopsticks to Japanese restaurant chain Wagamama, and 6 million Tate-branded disposable coffee cups to the Coffee Republic coffee shop chain. Finally, the gallery supplied Tate Modern-branded beer to the fashionable Mash restaurant.

From the viewpoint of the restaurants and bars, being associated with Tate Modern was in itself prestigious: having the gallery supply them with free disposables also helped their bottom line. At the same time, getting the brand across in a novel and interesting way to 6 million coffee drinkers was achieved at a relatively low cost—this sophisticated audience would be difficult to reach in any conventional way.

In practice

- It is absolutely essential to begin by identifying your "typical" target customer—which other goods and services they buy, where they like to go on vacation, which magazines they read, and so forth. Be as detailed as possible.
- Find a giveaway that helps your allies either to sell more themselves or to save money.
- This idea works best if your allies can see an advantage in being allied to you.
- Be careful in your choice of allies—be sure that they will use your branded products effectively and in a way that enhances your status.

- Be very clear with your allies about how the partnership will work—what are the boundaries?

PLANNING
PLAN FOR EVERY CONTINGENCY
Jonathan Gifford

WHEN MAKING ANY important decision, it is a great advantage to have thought through, in detail, several possible options that best serve different likely contingencies.

The idea

During his time at the Ford Motor Company, Lee Iacocca worked with Robert McNamara, who was to become Secretary of Defense under Presidents John F. Kennedy and Lyndon B. Johnson.

Iacocca describes McNamara as "one of the smartest men I've ever met, with a phenomenal IQ and a steel-trap mind. He was a mental giant. With his amazing capacity to absorb facts, he also retained everything he learned. But McNamara knew more than the actual facts—he also knew the hypothetical ones. When you talked with him, you realized that he had already played out in his head the relevant details for every conceivable option and scenario. He taught me never to make a decision without having a choice of at least vanilla or chocolate. And if more than a hundred million dollars were at stake, it was a good idea to have strawberry, too."

Richard Branson, chairman of Virgin Group, stresses the need to plan for the worst kind of contingency—a disaster: "You can take measures to mitigate and manage business risks. Then, if disaster strikes, at least your attention won't be split every which way by other worries. Always, always have a disaster protocol in place. Because if something truly horrific occurs, a lot of frightened people are going to come to you looking for answers."

Business author and Harvard Business School professor, John Kotter, warns against doing too much planning for the long-term, since something unforeseen will inevitably happen and the plans will have to be redone. Similarly, too much unguided short-term contingency planning can absorb a wasteful amount of management time.

"Short-term planning can become a management black hole, capable of absorbing an infinite amount of time and energy. With no vision and strategy to provide constraints around the planning process or to guide it, every eventuality deserves a plan. Under these circumstances, contingency planning can literally go on forever, draining time and attention from far more essential activities."

In practice

- Plan for several contingencies. Hold as much information about these contingencies as you can in your head.
- Plan for disaster; even organizations that do not run the risk of a disaster that can affect its consumers still run the risk of a major incident, such as a fire. Have a business recovery plan in place.
- Don't waste much time on long-term contingency planning: something will change and the plans will be useless.
- Short-term contingency planning must be guided by the organization's overall direction: there is no point in planning for contingencies that are not relevant.

PUBLIC RELATIONS
CREATE A TOP TEN LIST
Jim Blythe

TOP TEN LISTS appear everywhere—Ten Worst Dressed Men, Ten Best Dressed Women, Ten Worst Cars, and so forth. Such lists are often compiled by people who have no particular claim to be able to do so, except for being in an industry with a vested interest.

However, the news media love them. They create a human-interest story, they create debate among the readers, and they often provoke letters to the editor (another way of generating space-filling material).

The idea

Almost any business can create a top ten (or bottom ten) list. The problem is to do it without upsetting the customers, and with a degree of humor attached to it.

Compiling the list itself could simply be a matter of making a judgment yourself, or it could involve a survey or voting system: in some cases, it may be worth while to offer the opportunity for a newspaper to get involved, running the survey and collecting the votes. Understandably, they will want to share in the glory if the story gets picked up elsewhere, but it will undoubtedly guarantee publication of your list in at least one place.

Alternatively, you could have a guest list of judges drawn from your industry, or from the long list of celebrities who are prepared to judge this kind of thing—for a fee, of course.

In practice

- Choose something humorous, but relevant to your business.
- Be careful not to be libellous.
- It doesn't have to be ten—it could equally be five, or even three.
- Consider the possibility of two contrasting lists—best and worst, for example.
- This idea works best if you do it near the end of the year—the worst of 2009, for example, produced in December 2009.

SALES
THE USEFULNESS OF "GATEKEEPERS"
Patrick Forsyth

"THE BUYER" MAY be a person, but it may be more than one person: several working together in some way, the board of directors, or a committee. In any case this or these are probably not the only people that a salesperson meets in the course of dealing with a customer. Others include receptionists, secretaries, assistants, and whoever brings you a cup of tea, if you are welcomed hospitably. More senior people can be involved too. First consider the nature of the gatekeeper description. Gatekeepers are people who can allow or deny access to others, ultimately the decision maker. So a sensible rule here is to never, ever get on the wrong side of someone in that position. Beyond that, though, can you actively canvass their help?

Sometimes the relationships are such that you can draw people in. Saying to one person, "What does Mary think about it?" might bring a response to the effect that they are not involved, but it might prompt a new thought, especially if you have offered a reason that their opinion might help. "Mary has a lot of customer contact, doesn't she? What's her view?" Even bring the other person into the discussion on an ongoing basis. Even where there is no apparent link, people other than the buyer can be useful.

The idea
Allied Carpets: the chatty salesperson ...

George works selling carpets. Many customers come to the store, and other inquiries start with a meeting elsewhere: in a company office, say. George has a rule. When he sits in someone's reception he chats to the receptionist. "What's it like working here?" is a favorite lead-in, and receptionists as a breed are sufficiently put upon to often want to talk. Regularly such conversations lead to additional sales. Perhaps George says he is there to, say, do a quote for the boardroom, but he's told, "But it's the showroom that could really do with a new carpet. You should see the state of it in there." He can sometimes even persuade the receptionist to give him a sight of such a place. Then it is an easy matter to introduce it into a conversation with a buyer, and (economies of scale work well here, he says) often he obtains an additional sale. Maybe he gets a date or two with the receptionist as well.

In practice

- Many people you come across in a customer's organization may be able to assist you to sell.
- Even one small piece of information can be helpful.
- Explore all such contacts (carefully).

MARKETING
MAKE PEOPLE BEHAVE
Jim Blythe

PEOPLE REMEMBER MUCH better if they have to do something: putting people into a position where they feel as if they are already using the product can be a powerful way of getting them to remember the brand. This isn't always easy—car dealers do it by offering people test drives, but for many products this is simply not possible.

One way of doing it is to find a situation where people are already acting in a way that would remind them about the product, and then nudge them a little further.

The idea

Right Guard is a well-known deodorant, widely available but with many competitors. Perhaps surprisingly, there are still many people who rarely, or never, use deodorant: the problem for Right Guard was to promote daily use of deodorant in a market where the Right Guard brand is one of the market leaders.

Accordingly, Right Guard arranged to refit a whole London Underground train, replacing the straps that commuters hold with Right Guard cans. Commuters are already aware of body odors—especially when others raise their arms to hold the overhead straps. Holding the Right Guard can with arms raised in the position people adopt to use the deodorant generated a very powerful message.

Naturally, the train's interior advertising cards and exterior livery were also converted totally to Right Guard—and it certainly did no harm that "Right, Guard!" was at one time a common way of signaling the train's guard that all passengers were aboard.

In practice

- Think about how people use your product.
- Find some other activity that generates similar behavior.
- Be prepared to be creative and make an effort to create the same circumstances for people.
- Back up your promotional ploy with publicity—let the press and news media know what you're doing. Try to make it newsworthy!

ONLINE MARKETING
SUBJECT LINES
Andy Maslen

Do YOU USE emails as part of your promotional mix? If you do, I bet you spend a long time working on the message: lots of nice short sentences (balanced with longer ones, of course); plenty of benefits; calls to action top and bottom; hot buttons. But let me ask you a question ...

How much time do you spend on the subject line? This is the critical part of the package; yet it's often overlooked. It can galvanize your reader into opening the email or it can have them stabbing the Trash button.

The idea
From a company promoting car care products via email
A while back, I had a classic car: a beautiful, two-tone silver/burgundy 1973 Rover V8 Coupé. I probably spent more time polishing it than driving it. (Maybe because it always seemed to be breaking down.) Classic car nuts love lavishing TLC on their vehicles so they're a

natural market for any kind of product that promises a superior shine. Here's the subject line from an American company that makes a range of car (and boat) care products:

Andy, Give Your Cherished Classic a Showroom Shine in Minutes!

We've got my first name (which they'd captured online). People tend to scan their inbox downwards, not left to right like normal reading. So your hot words need to be upfront where they'll get picked up. But right after the name—whammo!—the benefit. In fact it's two benefits. First you can get that wet-look shine that makes you want to park your car where you—and others—can see it. Second you can do it quickly. That sounds like big results for basically no work. (Because everybody's lazy, right?)

If you've come from a direct mail background, you should be a natural. The subject line is your outer envelope. But just look at the height of the bar you have to clear. You've got no color, no paper, no windows showing glimpses of the pack inside, no logo—just a few characters.

And I mean a few. Some years ago now, Anne Holland of MarketingSherpa was recommending 40. In fact with growing numbers of readers opening emails on their BlackBerry, I'd say even 40 characters was pushing it. As inboxes get more and more crowded, people are actively looking for reasons not to open emails of any kind, let alone promotional ones. So the secret is to give them a reason to click. And that means giving them the benefit.

In practice
- Put the good stuff upfront, where people can see it. You can't guarantee your reader will go right to the end of your subject line before deciding whether to open or not.
- Write your message first, then you've got a platform to create a winning subject line.

KEEPING YOUR PRODUCT OFFERING CURRENT

Jeremy Kourdi

MAINTAINING AWARENESS OF the latest market news, consumer concerns, and cutting-edge technologies will stimulate sales and build a loyal client base.

The idea

One of the most effective ways to keep your company current and cutting-edge is to cultivate an awareness of changing consumer concerns. Understanding your customer is vital to good business, but clients are not fixed in their desires. Their needs and wants change regularly, and for a variety of reasons—to claim you are truly at the forefront of your industry you must maintain knowledge of, and cater to, these changing demands.

Subaru's 2006 marketing strategy is an impressive example of this—every buyer of selected new Impreza, Forester, and Legacy models received £3,000 worth of free fuel vouchers. Customers who purchased any other model in the Subaru range received £1,000 worth of vouchers. This deal, not offered by any of its competitors, connects with the widespread global concern of rising fuel prices.

Instead of offering a traditional reduction in price to stimulate sales, Subaru understood the changing needs and concerns of its clients, and used this to create a truly enticing price incentive. By blending innovation with a willingness to react to the latest market developments, it is possible for businesses to prosper in volatile environments.

In practice

- Talk to your current and potential customers. What do they value? What are their concerns? What do they want?
- Find out what businesses in other industries are doing to attract customers.

- Ask people at all levels of your business, including the "extended family" such as retailers or distributors, how they would keep the product appealing.
- Plan a series of product enhancements and sales initiatives. A constant series of incentives to buy is better than a desperate splurge (or a complacent lack of activity).
- Be prepared to test a range of ideas and initiatives. Find out what works best, where and why, and see whether it can be replicated elsewhere.

MARKETING

LINK YOUR PR AND YOUR ADVERTISING
Jim Blythe

OF COURSE! ALL firms link their PR and their advertising, surely? Not to mention their other communications—sales promotions, personal selling, websites, etc., etc., etc.

However, most firms only make these links in a superficial way, perhaps using the advertising to refer to a particularly successful PR campaign, or creating a PR campaign based around a particular advertisement. Really slick companies will create an integrated campaign based on a combination of communication techniques, each one boosting the other.

The idea
When Sega introduced its Mega-CD games console, the company knew that it had a promotional mountain to climb. The target audience for the product was the marketing-savvy, worldly-wise, cynical, seen-it-all-before teenage market. To reach these people, Sega would have to do something seriously spectacular—so it ran a combined ad and PR campaign designed to intrigue the audience.

First, the company ran ads for fictitious products (a cat food billed as

"Good enough to eat!" showing the cat's owner eating the cat food, and a washing powder called Ecco). The spoof ads ran for some weeks, but would then be "hijacked" by "pirate" TV transmitters promoting the Sega product. Billboard ads were subjected to the same treatment—the corners would apparently be torn off to reveal the Sega ad beneath.

The piracy theme of the ads appealed to the anarchic tendencies of teenagers, but more importantly the spoof caught the imagination of the media and sparked a flurry of editorial coverage commenting on the cleverness of the campaign.

In practice

- Think through your connection between the advertising and the PR elements.
- Beware that the media may not like being spoofed—ensure that they are in on the joke.
- Make sure that your audience gets the joke: sometimes people take things seriously, and then feel silly afterward.

MARKETING
PLAY A GAME
Jim Blythe

GETTING PEOPLE TO be involved with the brand means getting them to build it into their lives. One way is to encourage them to see the brand as fun, and to play around with the product—which is why car dealers allow customers to take test drives. Salespeople call this the puppy dog close: once you've cuddled the puppy, it's hard to give it back!

Obviously this is not always possible with expensive or delicate products, so if that's what you're selling you need to think of some other way of allowing people to be playful with the brand. Sometimes the internet can help.

The idea

When Panasonic launched their Lumix camera range, they needed to promote the key features of the camera—its 10x optical zoom, and its 28mm wide-angle lens. The TV advertising campaign featured the Golden Gate Bridge crumpling up to accommodate someone using an ordinary camera, and the Sphinx coming toward a photographer to show how the optical zoom makes things look better. These campaigns were wonderful and eye-catching—but any marketer knows that advertising alone is never enough.

Panasonic commissioned Inbox Digital to create an online game called Lumix World Golf. The game is based around an 18-hole game of crazy golf played around nine world heritage sites. Players can zoom in and out to judge their shots (as they would with the camera) and can win prizes, offset against signing up for the Lumix e-CRM (customer relationship management) program.

There is, of course, a "tell a friend" button so that people who enjoy playing the game can involve a friend. The game itself is quite addictive and engaging—plugs for the camera are shown between each hole, and players are congratulated or commiserated with according to how well they play each hole.

The site attracted over a million visitors, most of whom found out about the site through friends.

In practice

- The game needs to be professionally executed and slick.
- It needs to connect to the product in a straightforward but fun way.
- It should connect with other promotions to reinforce the message.
- It should ALWAYS have a tell-a-friend button.

MANAGING
WORK WITH THE TEAM YOU HAVE
Jonathan Gifford

AT SOME POINT in their career, most leaders will take over an existing operation and its team. If the operation has been under-performing, there is a temptation to start afresh; to bring in a new team to solve the problem.

The idea

Louis Gerstner, who brought about a remarkable turnaround of the failing computer giant, IBM, in the 1990s, confirms that he decided that it would be wrong to attempt to bring in a new team from outside.

"I think it would have been absolutely naïve—as well as dangerous—if I had come into a company as complex as IBM with a plan to impose a band of outsiders to somehow magically run the place better than the people who were there in the first place. I've entered many companies from the outside, and based on my experience, you might be able to pull that off in a relatively simple industry and under optimal conditions. It certainly wasn't going to work at IBM. It was too big and too complex a structure. More importantly, the company was brimming with talented people, who had unique experience. If I didn't give players on the home team a chance, they'd simply take their talent and knowledge and go somewhere else. I just had to find the teammates who were ready to try to do things in a different way."

Robert Mondavi, founder of California's Robert Mondavi Winery, argues that it is best to work with people as they are. "Understand that you cannot change people. You might improve them, but you can't change anyone but yourself. Accept people the way they are. Accept their differences and work with them the way they are. I learned this after about 70 years of life, and it is amazing what peace of mind I found when I finally understood it."

In practice

- If a leader takes over a failing operation, it is deeply unlikely that the existing team are collectively responsible for the failure. That failure is the responsibility of the previous leadership.
- A new team will not be able to grasp the detail of a large and complex organization quickly enough.
- The talent of the existing team will be lost to the competition if the new leadership fails to engage that talent and to make it part of the recovery plan.
- Anybody who understands the need for a new approach can be part of the recovery.
- Work with people as you find them.

STRATEGY
FIND THE LOST TRIBE
Jim Blythe

ALTHOUGH WE LIKE to think we have moved on a lot from the days of living in the jungle, human beings still retain most of their instincts from our cave-age past. For example, we like to be part of a tribe. Anthropologists recognize that urban people still develop tribal groupings, complete with rituals (secret handshakes, special language or jargon, even special clothing), in order to have a sense of fitting in.

In our hunter-gatherer days, being part of a tribe was essential to survival: fighting off predators and finding food would have required a good-sized group. In modern times, being part of a tribe (whether it's a local street gang or a Rotarian group) is essential to our social well-being, and certainly helps us to survive better.

Tapping into tribal associations offers marketers a chance to create fierce loyalty as well as selling to a larger group than might otherwise be the case, at no greater expense or effort.

The idea

Tatoo is a French telecommunications company, specializing in pagers and cellphones. Pagers were, at one time, the communications tool of choice for teenagers throughout France. Tatoo decided to target the product at primary social groups (groups of friends and family) and so they used images of in-line roller skaters to promote the product. "Tribes" of in-line skaters were recruited to appear in the adverts (rather than use professional actors) so that the adverts conveyed an authentic image to the teenagers.

Tatoo rapidly became the biggest pager supplier in France, and followed on to become one of the largest cellphone companies.

In practice

- Identify the primary groups—these are groups of friends and family.
- This idea works best if your product helps the group to function better together.
- Consider all the other products the tribe uses so that you can identify the tribe members, and sell them other things.

SALES

WORK AROUND INHERENT PROBLEMS

Patrick Forsyth

SOMETIMES THERE ARE problems that you know make selling more difficult, yet by their nature they are seemingly impossible to change. This example, where the hindrance is a physical fact, is taken from one particular industry. Because of the specific circumstances the solution is not one that would be necessary or possible for everyone, but like so many of the ideas here it demonstrates a kind of creative thinking that I applaud, and that you can imitate.

The idea

At a local distributor for Rank Xerox ...

A certain office equipment distributor had an office and showroom in a medium-sized town (say the size of Cambridge in Britain). It was on a prime site but there was one drawback: there was no easy customer parking nearby, and none that was free. The few staff parking spaces were shared with the other businesses in the block in which it occupied the first floor. The company knew that many customers would not buy without a demonstration, and also surmised that the lack of parking put some people off from making a visit. Of course there were a number of things that might have helped, including moving the showroom, and banning the staff from parking on the premises so the spaces could be used for customers instead. One idea worked well, however.

The showroom was open on Saturdays, a day when staff in the offices above did not work. Following an idea generated by one of the team, the company did a deal with its neighbors to use their parking spaces on Saturdays. It then suggested in promotions and telephone prospecting calls that customers might come to a demonstration on a Saturday. This worked well. It soon discovered that for some male customers the attraction was free parking and an excuse to avoid shopping with their partner or family! This change extended the number of demonstrations given and thus saw sales rise.

In practice

- Are there things to do with your sales situation that might be exploited or changed to help your sales? Check.

PUBLIC RELATIONS
DO A RANDOM ACT OF KINDNESS
Jim Blythe

MANY BUSINESSES HAVE strong associations with other businesses that are important to them. For example, estate agents and lawyers have a symbiotic relationship: lawyers rely on estate agents for conveyancing business, and estate agents rely on lawyers for referring people who are (for example) dealing with a deceased relative's house sale, or looking to value a property.

Likewise, lawyers and accountants often feed work to each other, and doctors and chemists work closely together. All businesses rely on someone else—that's the nature of business—so why not recognize the importance of these other firms by committing an act of kindness?

The idea

A law firm in Baltimore, America, knew that they relied on accountants (CPAs) for a large amount of their business. Accountants would often need to refer a client to a good commercial law firm, and of course there are a lot of lawyers out there. The law firm decided to institute a "Feed a CPA Day" on which a local catering firm would deliver a beautifully prepared and wrapped lunch to three CPAs chosen at random.

These were not necessarily firms that the lawyers dealt with on any regular basis—the point was to create a news story, not to thank anyone in particular. What it did do was put the law firm into the news story, and show that they recognized the contribution accountants make to the law business, and indeed to the world at large.

The idea can be extended to almost any business—everybody relies on some other category of supplier. Accountants are a good one, because their work receives so little recognition in the normal course of events.

In practice

- Do make sure the idea is well publicized in advance, otherwise the recipients of your largesse will be very suspicious indeed.
- Be random—giving a free lunch to your accountant is not news: giving a free lunch to a firm you don't know is news.
- Remember it's the news value you are interested in, not finding some new business associates. Don't follow up on the recipients—they will contact you if they want to (and usually they will, if only to say thank you).

STRATEGY
CLUSTERING
Jeremy Kourdi

By SETTING UP in "industry centers" where similar businesses are clustered together, firms gain instant access to a large and varied range of benefits.

The idea
The idea of clustering seems counter-intuitive. It suggests that firms should pay high real estate prices to be positioned close to their competitors. Although there are many businesses that prefer cheaper real estate further from the threat of competitors, clustering is surprisingly common in many industries. From the shops of Oxford Street in London to the technology companies of Silicon Valley, clustering has a far-reaching appeal.

The benefits of clustering are particularly relevant to new businesses. It affords easy access to an already established network of customers, suppliers, and information. It can also help build reputation—it encourages customers to associate your organization with the other respected and long-established businesses in the area.

Clustering is also a blessing for the firm in a highly competitive industry, like selling cars. While it remains easier for customers to choose your rival over you when it is positioned next-door, a company with a truly superior, competitive offering has little to fear from this.

One of the most famous examples of clustering is the entertainment industry of Hollywood, where freelancers and small firms prospered by locating near the studios. Further north there is the example of Silicon Valley—a cluster of technology companies benefiting from the pool of talent in nearby universities.

Although clustering raises a number of challenges for any business to overcome, an innovative, efficient, and dynamic company will be able to turn these challenges into unrivaled advantages.

In practice

- There are often a number of industry centers for a particular product; use careful research to decide which one best suits your business.
- Ensure your customer offering is truly competitive—the direct contrast with rival companies provided by clustering will only benefit companies with genuinely superior products.
- Highlight where you are and emphasize how your products are superior.
- Take advantage of the increased access to cutting-edge industry information—this can range from regional publications to "neighborhood gossip."
- Remember that clustering is not suitable for all companies—consider your overall business plan and the nature of your business before deciding where to locate.

MARKETING
WHET THE CUSTOMER'S APPETITE
Jim Blythe

GIVING PEOPLE A free sample or a free trial is an old ploy, but in some cases it is difficult to do without giving away a great deal more than was intended: for example, offering a free trial of a credit rating service might give the potential customer everything he or she wanted to know, without the need to subscribe permanently to the service.

Finding a way of making people want the product without at the same time giving away the main advantage is a difficult tightrope act to carry out.

The idea

When Oasis (the pop band) wanted to promote their *Heathen Chemistry* album, they followed the usual route of seeking airtime on radio, of advertising in music enthusiast magazines, and so forth: obviously these routes are used by every other band, so they needed something else to attract the attention of their target audience.

The band arranged to give away encrypted CDs with four tracks from the album, attached to the *Sunday Times* newspaper. The CDs could only be played four times before they automatically wiped themselves clean, so the recipients could not replay the tracks without buying the whole album. From the sale of each album, 50p was donated to the Prince's Trust, a charity for helping young people.

This unique approach enables people to try the album without gaining possession of its key benefits, thus compelling them to make a full purchase.

In practice

- Ensure that the freebie you are offering does not contain the main benefits that the customer would want to own.
- At the same time, ensure that it contains enough benefits for people to judge the quality of what is on offer.
- As always, try to ensure that only your target customers are given the free sample, otherwise you are wasting your samples.

PRICING

CHARGE WHAT THE SERVICE IS WORTH
Jim Blythe

IT'S VERY EASY to think that competing on price is the most effective way to go. In fact, competing on price only cuts profit margins, especially since there is always somebody else who will be prepared to undercut you—even if they go broke in the process. It is generally much better, more profitable, and safer to compete on some other aspect, for example on service level.

In many cases, customers are prepared to pay a great deal to be given a top-class service, and nowhere is this truer than in business-to-business markets, where a service failure can be extremely costly.

The idea

Merchant ships are expensive items. They cost a great deal to build, a great deal to run, and a great deal to park in harbors. Having capital tied up is expensive—the ships are only really making money when they are at sea. Having the ship waiting around in harbor while customs officials clear the cargo documentation adds greatly to the cost of operating a shipping line—a fact that three friends (Adrian Dalsey, Larry Hillblom, and Robert Lynn) noticed.

In 1969, the three friends set up a courier service, delivering ships' documentation by air from San Francisco to Honolulu. The difference was that one of the founders traveled with the documentation, taking it by hand from the shipping company offices direct to the agents' offices in Honolulu before the ships arrived. In this way, customs officials could clear the cargoes before the ships docked. Dalsey, Hillblom, and Lynn became (of course) DHL and rapidly expanded their personal delivery service worldwide.

At first sight, the cost of sending a courier door to door with documents is prohibitively expensive, especially when compared with the postal service, which would deliver documents for less than one-hundredth of the price the fledgling DHL company charged. However, the service being supplied far outweighed the cost, especially once the courier was in the position of carrying documents for 20 or 30 clients. The cost of having documents arrive late, or documents being lost altogether, would be colossal: the 100 percent reliability of the service was worth paying for.

Nowadays we have become used to the idea of courier services. They are extremely common (especially in major cities where same-day delivery can be achieved) and often compete on price. However, DHL would not exist at all if its founders had tried to compete against the postal services on price!

In practice

- Think about what you are providing, not what competitors are charging.
- Think about what your service is worth to the customer, not what it is costing you to provide.
- Ensure that what you provide will meet customer expectations.
- Don't be afraid to look expensive (and high quality) rather than cheap (and low quality).

MARKETING
CATCH YOUR CELEBRITY EARLY
Jim Blythe

CELEBRITY ENDORSEMENT CAN be a major boost to PR activities, but at the same time it can be expensive—someone famous is likely to want to cash in as quickly as possible, because today's celebrity is tomorrow's has-been.

Celebrity endorsement also carries risks of another kind: the celebrity might do something disreputable (cheat on their partner, take drugs, etc.) and this might tarnish the product or company image.

The idea

Cole & Mason manufacture various kitchen products, but they are probably best known for their pepper and salt mills. These are upmarket, state-of-the-art utensils (inasmuch as a pepper mill can be) and Cole & Mason wanted to promote them effectively on a small budget.

Food shows are perennially popular on TV, partly because they are relatively cheap to make, partly because the viewers like to see good food presented well, and partly because they are effective programs for selling advertising to supermarkets. Cole & Mason decided to recruit a celebrity chef to promote their products.

The clever part was that they didn't recruit someone who was already famous: they identified a newcomer to the celebrity chef scene, and signed him up while he was still relatively unknown. They got him to use the mills on the show, and to pose for photo shoots with the mills: the photos were sent to magazines with covering stories and, where appropriate, recipes.

Lunches hosted by the chef for journalists, cooking demonstrations at exhibitions, master classes run by the chef for competition winners, and a series of postcards featuring him and his quotes about the benefits of Cole & Mason mills all followed on in a two-year campaign. In effect, the celebrity chef was the glue that held together the components of a big campaign, but it was all done relatively cheaply by signing up the chef early in his career.

In practice

- Be a talent spotter—you need to be fairly sure that your chosen celebrity will rise in fame.
- Have a bulletproof contract. As your celebrity becomes more famous, he or she will get other offers, and may very well be tempted.
- Have a wide-ranging program of events for your celebrity to be involved in.
- Try to ensure a long tail—keep the rights to all the photos, endorsements, quotes, recipes, etc.

LEADERSHIP
COMMUNICATE SIMPLY
Jonathan Gifford

COMMUNICATING RELATIVELY COMPLEX ideas to a large number of people is a daunting task. The audience will listen attentively, but they will take away, at best, a few fragments of what was actually said. A leader's vision and core strategy should be reduced to a few simple and powerful statements.

The idea

John F. Kennedy, 35th President of the United States, was elected in 1961. In his Presidential Nomination Acceptance speech, made a year earlier, he set out a bold vision of an America that could come together to solve the problems of the age, just as the pioneers of the previous century had overcome the problems of the great expansion into western territories.

"For I stand tonight facing west on what was once the last frontier. From the lands that stretch three thousand miles behind me, the pioneers of old gave up their safety, their comfort and sometimes their own lives to build a new world here in the West ... Their motto was not 'every man for himself' but 'all for the common cause'. ... Today some would say that those struggles are all over—that all the horizons have been explored—that all the battles have been won—that there is no longer an American frontier ... But I tell you the New Frontier is here, whether we seek it or not. Beyond that frontier are the uncharted areas of science and space, unsolved problems of peace and war, unconquered pockets of ignorance and prejudice, unanswered questions of poverty and surplus."

"The New Frontier" came to be a powerful phrase that encapsulated the aims of the Kennedy administration, including complex issues of labor, housing and civil rights reform.

In the same way, the very best corporate visions can be instantly grasped, at an instinctive level, by the whole organization and even by the public at large. In the 1960s, when the car rental firm Avis addressed the fact that they were second in the market to the leader, Hertz, they adopted the memorable slogan, "We try harder". The message that Avis would try harder to please customers because they were not the market leader, was instantly understood by the public and has become an iconic statement of a company's fundamental values. It was introduced by Robert Townsend, whose tenure as CEO of Avis saw the company move from loss-making to profitability, and who led the company to become a giant in the worldwide car rental market.

In practice

- Condense your vision and key strategy into very simple statements. If you can't express them simply, they are not right.
- If you can, turn the simple statement of the core strategy into a memorable slogan. Get this right, and you will be famous.

MARKET RESEARCH

WATCH HOW PEOPLE ACTUALLY USE YOUR PRODUCTS

Jim Blythe

AMAZINGLY, MANY FIRMS have little or no idea of what happens to their products after they leave the factory. Yet such information is clearly vital in developing new products, and in knowing what the key benefits are of the old products. After all, if a baker found out that the main use for his rye bread was as doorstops he might consider changing the recipe.

The idea

Fisher-Price is among the world's largest toy manufacturers, especially in the toddler and younger child markets. The company, which is based in Chicago, hit on the idea of running a free crèche for pre-school children. The toys are all made by Fisher-Price: some are established in the market, others are prototypes.

What the children neither know nor care about is that they are research subjects. Trained observers watch the children to see which toys are the most popular, which are ignored, which are played with for a few minutes and then rejected, which are clung to fiercely at the end of the day, and exactly how children play with the toys.

This observational research is invaluable in developing new products and modifying old ones.

In practice

- You need to observe over a long period of time.
- If you can, video record the behavior rather than rely on memory or note taking.
- Have more than one observer—you may find that each of you interprets what you see differently.
- Observing people without their knowledge or consent is unethical, and could even land you in legal trouble—ensure people know what you are doing.

SALES
SUPPORT THEIR CHARITY
Patrick Forsyth

THERE ARE PARTS of the world where bribes are the norm, but for the most part it is not a good idea to bribe your prospect, and certainly that is not one of the ideas listed here. However, there are ways to please people that cannot be categorized as bribes. One is to support a charity favored by a prospect or customer.

The idea

From an Australian professional body ...

I came across this at the time of the Boxing Day tsunami in Southeast Asia. On a visit to Australia I was keen to put my time to profitable use, and suggested to a number of local bodies that I gave a talk or seminar during my visit. One organization that took up the offer was involved in raising money for tsunami victims, and it was agreed that some of the money from the event would go to that cause. I supported this charity particularly because I had been on holiday in Thailand in the aftermath of the event, so I was happy to do this. It made a favorable impression even before I had met anyone from the association.

Other possibilities can utilize the same principle. For example a financial adviser might invite people to a day's golf (yes, some business really is done on the golf course), but to play in a competition that is designed to raise money for a good cause. This gives people an additional reason to agree, and gives the adviser the chance for a leisurely chat with them.

Such activity has little to do with selling the product, and it is certainly not the solution to every sales problem (or charity fundraising problem). But there are circumstances where it is an excellent way of establishing or building relationships. Increasing the opportunity to talk to people in this way could lead to something more tangible. It might be used on a one-off or an ongoing basis.

In practice
- If you pursue this idea, remember that the cause or charity should appeal to the customer (and not be your pet area).
- Do not overuse this technique, or it might quickly be resented.

CLEAR INTENTIONS

Patrick Forsyth

A PRESENTATION THAT does not know where it is going is never going to get there, and an audience is always going to be unsatisfied with one that is such. This is surely axiomatic and there are numerous implications. Here is very much the first.

The idea

Be very clear about what you are going to do. This demands some broad thinking about intentions. Do you want your presentation to:

- Inform
- Explain or instruct
- Motivate
- Persuade
- Prompt debate
- Demonstrate
- Build on past messages or dialogue with members of the audience?

In practice

- The intentions on such a list (and by all means, add to it) are not mutually exclusive. You may want to do some or all of these, or to add other intentions to the list. The point here is that, however many things of this sort there are to do, it makes preparation and delivery easier if you are clear about them all at the outset. You certainly do not want to be busy informing people and then suddenly think, *I really should be enthusing them a bit too*. It is difficult to suddenly start to try to address a newly thought of intention halfway through a talk. So, think this through at the beginning and prepare and deliver accordingly.

SALES
THE BUYER'S CYCLE
Jeremy Kourdi

To UNDERSTAND HOW to influence someone or to sell an idea, it is essential to know how people buy. The buyer's cycle provides a clear picture of the stages that need to be influenced to make a successful sale.

The idea
One of the factors behind the success of businesses such as Dell is their ability to understand their customers. This firm (and others) ensures that its approach is as flexible as possible and as informed as it can be. Understanding buyers' attitudes will enable you to influence behavior more easily and effectively.

Buying attitudes are determined by the buyer's perception of the immediate business situation, how your proposal is likely to change that situation, and the extent to which that change will close a gap between the current reality and future goal.

In practice
Focus on each of the stages in the buyer's cycle. Consider what you can do to influence your customers at each stage:

1. *Increase awareness.* The first challenge is to develop awareness of your business or new product among potential clients. This provides a feeling of familiarity, comfort, or intrigue. This awareness can then be used to lead customers into the next stage: information. The potential market size at this stage is 100 percent.
2. *Provide information.* This stage is when specific details are provided to the customer. Their interest may vary from a passing willingness to find out more, to a passionate need to explore the offer. Whatever the customer's motives or situation, the information needs to be clear, useful, and specific. Inevitably, the market size will have shrunk as some "aware" customers fail to pick up the information, through either choice or circumstance.

3. *Help customers prioritize.* Customers weigh up the benefits and then prioritize their expenditure. For example, they may consider whether this is something they want to buy now, at this price, and in this form. They may also evaluate alternatives. Clearly, some people will not make the move from having the information to making a purchase.

4. *Help customers purchase.* Having decided to buy, the next step for the customer is to complete the transaction. It is important to enable the buyer to move as easily as possible through the process. Purchasing should be easy and satisfactory—even enjoyable.

5. *Support the customer's use of the product.* This is a stage that is often forgotten, hidden in the shadow of the purchase. A sale is not the end of the process, because customers have to use and value their purchase. If they don't, then the product may be returned, customers may stay away in future, and the resultant poor publicity and a declining reputation are likely to adversely affect future sales.

6. *Promote reuse.* This is when the product or service (or one of its components) is bought again. This generates additional revenue at a higher margin (without the cost of customer acquisition) and highlights customer loyalty to the product, resulting in a stronger sales process.

7. *Encourage advocacy.* This stage is highly prized by sellers: it occurs when customers are so impressed with their purchase that they tell others about it (Harley-Davidson is an excellent example of this). Advocacy increases awareness of the product or business and feeds back to the first stage of the process.

STRATEGY
TAILOR YOUR PRODUCTS
Jim Blythe

IT IS AN axiom of marketing that we need to identify the needs of specific groups of people. Segmenting the market correctly is the first stage in planning any marketing activities, in order to offer a product that will meet the needs of the segment and will thus have a market.

In some cases, though, it is possible to take things further and actually tailor the product to the exact needs of an individual. The drawback is, of course, cost: a tailor-made suit costs a great deal more than an off-the-peg suit, simply because it requires a much greater amount of work from the tailor. In some cases, though, tailoring the product can be relatively simple—which will provide a powerful USP for the company.

The idea

In the 1980s the PC revolution was taking off, with many people buying computers for home use. A computer is a fairly complex piece of equipment, but is in fact built from a series of modules: it is not all that difficult to plug in different modules to the basic system in order to create a tailor-made product.

A 19-year-old student figured out how to sell tailored computers directly to customers, using modular assembly in a subcontracted factory. Customers could specify exactly what they needed, with advice from the company if necessary, and the machines could be assembled and dispatched within days.

The 19-year-old student was Michael Dell. Nowadays, Dell computers are sold online as well as by telephone and mail order, and they constitute one of the three largest suppliers of home computers. Dell is able to supply laptops and PCs, custom-built to the client's exact specifications.

In practice

- Technical support and advice is crucial to this idea. People know what they need, but often do not know what they want.
- Quick turnaround is important: customers might well be prepared to accept a less well-tailored product rather than wait weeks for perfection.
- People will pay more for a tailored product, but not a lot more: make sure the extra cost of tailoring is more than covered by the premium people will pay, or by the extra business that results.

MARKETING
INTEGRATE COMMUNICATIONS
Jim Blythe

IN RECENT YEARS, the hot topic in marketing has been integrated marketing communications. Marketers try to ensure that every message coming from the company is (at least broadly) telling the same story. This is extremely difficult to achieve in practice—salespeople say whatever they need to say to make the sale, different media give different slants on the message, and of course the company's employees talk to friends and relatives about the company and its products sometimes with devastating effect.

One way of coordinating the messages is to use them to direct people to the corporate website: here the real messages can be set up.

The idea
Nine West Shoes needed a cheap and simple way to direct potential customers to the company's website. Getting people to visit a website about shoes is not easy at the best of times—shoes are not always the most exciting products, and people are unlikely to go out of their way to find a site about them.

What Nine West did was to mold the web address into the soles of the shoes. Thus, when someone wearing Nine West shoes left a footprint (after stepping in a puddle, for example), the print promoted the shoes.

Using one medium, especially an innovative one, to direct people to another one is not new—"As Seen on TV" used to be a popular message on point-of-sale materials in retail stores. What Nine West have done is create an innovative way of promoting their website.

In practice
- You must integrate the message at all levels in the company, from managing director to tea lady.

- All communications should have common visual standards.
- Your marketing communications strategy needs to be clear to everybody.
- Always start with a zero budget—add to it as you see what needs to be done.
- Marketing communications have to be built around buyer behavior and customer contact points.
- Build relationships with customers, and build brand values.
- Ensure you have a good marketing information system so that you can monitor the process fully.
- Ensure that you always use the same artwork.
- Be prepared to change if it isn't working.

ONLINE MARKETING
GET YOUR NETIQUETTE RIGHT
Jim Blythe

THE INTERNET IS a great source of information—some say too great—and journalists have not been slow to get involved. Researching a story used to mean wearing out shoe leather and telephones getting interviews and comments from company officers. Nowadays, there is little need to go out in the cold, since most information can be gleaned from corporate websites: journalists can be safe in assuming that companies will not complain about the accuracy of the information, either.

In the absence of good information on a company website, journalists may have to look further afield, using sites such as Wikipedia to provide information, or even going to "McNitemares" or "suck sites" that have been set up by disgruntled customers or former employees. In these cases, the information will have to be verified and the company concerned given a chance to respond—but this will put the company on the back foot.

The idea

Set up a special section on your website for journalists. You can put all your latest press releases on there, as well as being proactive in sending them out to periodicals: this will help fill in any gaps in your distribution, and also provides an archive for journalists. You can include your corporate history, the CVs of your top management, case studies from satisfied customers, in fact everything a journalist might need to construct a story.

Provide as much corporate information as possible on your website—and don't be afraid to provide a "warts and all" picture, because the internet means that people will find that stuff anyway. Better that it comes from you than from your enemies.

You should also provide contact details for anyone relevant to the press release or story—don't just refer everybody to the press office. This will enable interested reporters to verify facts and fill in any gaps in the story.

In practice

- Ensure your "press room" or "press page" is easy to find on your site.
- Provide links to other sites that may be relevant—your trade association, for example.
- Provide contact details for as many of your people as you can, but make sure they are willing (and able) to handle cold calls from journalists.

LEADERSHIP
DEVOLVE DECISION MAKING
Jonathan Gifford

LEADERS SHOULD GO beyond delegating tasks and devolve actual decision making. Organizations in which key decisions are made by a few individuals at the top of the hierarchy rely entirely on the experience and judgement of those few people, on their ability to absorb what information is fed to them and on the quality of that information.

Devolving decision making to the level that is closest to the customer accesses the most accurate knowledge.

The idea

Irene Rosenfeld, CEO and chairman of Kraft Food Inc, talks about how the food giant achieved success, especially in China, with its Oreo sandwich cookie—a billion dollar product in the USA—when they devolved key decisions to local managers.

"We began by giving the responsibility of making some of those decisions back to our local managers. In the past, we would have mandated what an Oreo looked like around the world from Northfield, Illinois. And that wasn't necessarily consistent with what consumers in the local markets were eating. So what we found was sandwich cookies as a format is just not appealing to Chinese consumers but wafer formats are what they are eating. And so all we did was take the flavoring and the strong cocoa taste of our Oreo together with some of the fabulous marketing that we've done around the world, and brought it to the Chinese consumer. And we are pleased to see that it is the fastest growing biscuit in China right now."

John Mackey is the co-founder and CEO of Whole Foods Market, the American retailer of natural and organic products.

The company has always believed in devolving as much decision-making power as possible. Each store is staffed by approximately eight teams of colleagues, which work as relatively independent units. Teams are free to buy locally and to choose which products they stock, following strict standards set by the centre. This gives each Whole Foods store a unique mix of products that suit local tastes and reflect local suppliers. Even recruitment decisions are devolved: new recruits join teams for a four-week trial period, after which the team votes as to whether they are taken on—a two-thirds majority is needed. The profit-per-labor-hour of every team is calculated every four weeks, and bonuses are awarded on these figures. Whole Foods teams have a good reason to accept only industrious new recruits.

In practice

- Set objectives and allow the organization to propose the best means to achieve those objectives.
- Devolve decision making as far as possible to the level nearest to the consumer.
- Give teams the power to make their own decisions about things that affect performance and results. Give them the information they need to monitor their own performance, and reward them on the basis of results, in terms of both money and recognition.

SALES
BRAG, BUT DO SO CONVINCINGLY
Patrick Forsyth

CUSTOMERS WANT TO know that you are competent, knowledgeable, and generally "know your stuff." Only then do they feel able to deal with you with confidence. You need to tell them, but out-and-out bragging can not only sound unsuitable—"He's just a braggart"— but also risks your not being believed. For example, if I was selling you my training services, and said to you, "I've been involved in sales training for more than 20 years, there's really nothing about it that I don't know, and that's a promise," you would be entitled, indeed sensible, to take it with a pinch of salt, and wonder about my communications skills.

The idea
From the world of professional services ...

If, on the other hand, I gave you reasons why I considered myself an expert, it might well be more credible. Perhaps I would say to you,

"When I first joined a training company I spent a long time sitting in on courses and talking to those leading them about why they were conducted in the way they were, before my then boss would let me anywhere near fronting an event. It was drummed into me that I would spend the rest of my time in training continuing to learn about the process. More than 20 years on, I know that's true—but I've now had a great deal of experience."

Something along these lines is much more an explanation than a boast. It contains reasons for you to believe me, and makes it seem that my current state of expertise is both hard won (it was!) and useful. This is often done well by people in professional services (accountants, lawyers, architects, and more). These are areas of business that came late to marketing, but are now operating in very competitive markets.

In practice

- This principle is useful for anyone, especially if you need to project an element of experience and (perhaps technical) expertise.
- It needs some conscious thought to avoid the reflex of just blurting out how good you think you are.

PERFORMANCE
AUDACITY
Jeremy Kourdi

How DO YOU instill a bold, adventurous approach in employees? The most successful businesses are often those that are prepared to go further and take careful, calculated risks. This spirit of audacity can be developed, with insightful leadership.

The idea

"As South Africans, we weren't really frightened of emerging markets compared to the things that we were going through at home," commented Graham Mackay, SABMiller's chief executive. Difficult trading and environmental conditions instilled determination and resilience in managers at SABMiller, one of the world's largest brewers. Having built SAB in their domestic market, they were keen to compete and succeed abroad following the end of apartheid. They were ingenious, flexible, determined, and prepared not to follow convention. For example, SAB entered markets that (in the mid-1990s) were unfashionable, in Latin America, China, and Central Europe. Although these developing economies represent attractive growth markets now, the fact that SAB had a culture of taking on challenges meant that it could go there first and achieve considerable success.

SABMiller has a bold approach to business and has become a global giant in little over ten years.

In practice

- *Find the dangerous edge.* This is the point where the greatest risks lie. Understanding where this point is will increase confidence and your ability to avoid disaster. This enables you to understand what you do not know.
- *Be supportive.* This means building a supportive environment and being specific about what will happen in any situation. Start by accepting and explaining the risk, but finish by emphasizing strengths and visualizing success.
- *Build a confidence frame.* Gradually build confidence in steady increments.
- *Develop ancillary skills.* Being good at a wide range of relevant tasks will help build confidence, especially in complex situations, and promote success.
- *Recognize that moving into a "danger zone" has positive psychological benefits.* These include heightened awareness and concentration.

DISCOURAGE THE UNDESIRABLES
Jim Blythe

MOST FIRMS SPEND most of their time trying to attract and retain customers. Most of the time, this is exactly what should be happening—but most managers (especially in service industries) are aware that some customers simply are not worth keeping. How much better would it be if they were discouraged in the first place? After all, finding out that they are not good customers involves making some effort.

The idea

Frizzell Insurance specializes in insuring people such as teachers, civil servants, and local authority workers—people who, by their career choice, show that they prefer a safe, quiet life. As motorists, these people are like gold dust, of course. Frizzell, in common with many other insurance companies, operates online and through a call center, but it is a small company and cannot handle a large influx of calls: the company therefore wanted to discourage unsuitable callers, i.e., high-risk drivers.

Frizzell's TV campaign showed couples who had insured through Frizzell for many years. The couples were shown as they are now, and as they were when they first started insuring with Frizzell, with music from that period playing. The advertising was tested with both the target audience and with the "undesirables": the target audience thought the ads were charming and engaging, whereas the undesirables thought them boring, banal, and condescending.

Frizzel experienced its biggest-ever annual growth in business, outstripping arch-rival and market leader Direct Line.

In practice

- Identify the factors that will be most likely to repel the undesirables.

- Test any advertising carefully with both the target audience and the undesirables.
- Make sure that the factors that repel undesirables do not also repel the target audience!

MANAGING TIME
GOOD, BETTER, BEST ... ACCEPTABLE
Patrick Forsyth

IT IS OFTEN the case that time management goes hand in hand with perfectionism. I would certainly not advocate that anyone adopts a shoddy approach to their work, whatever it may be. There is, however, a dichotomy here, one well summed up in a quotation from Robert Heimleur, who said (perhaps despairingly): "They didn't want it good, they wanted it on Wednesday." The fact is it takes time to achieve perfection, and in any case perfection may not always be strictly necessary. Things may need to be undertaken carefully, thoroughly, comprehensively, but we may not need to spend time getting every tiny detail perfect. This comes hard to those who are naturally perfectionists, and it is a trait that many people have, at least about some things.

The idea
It is necessary to strike a balance. There is always a trade-off here, and it is not always the easiest thing to achieve. Often a real compromise has to be made. You have to make decisions about how to do things based on quality, cost, ... and time.

In practice
- Cost is often crucial in this. It would be easy to achieve the quality of output you want in many things, but only if cost were no object. And in most jobs budget considerations rank high. It is useful to get into the way of thinking about things in these terms, and doing so realistically so that you consider what is

necessary as well as (or instead of?) what is simply desirable or ideal. In doing this, there is one key factor that needs to be built in: the significant, and sometimes the largest, cost of your time.

- Consider all the costs of your working on something; the resultant figure may surprise you. Let me repeat: make sure by all means that what must be done to perfection is done in a way that achieves just that. Otherwise make sure you always keep in mind the balance to be struck between quality, cost, and time; if you do not over-engineer quality, seeking a standard that is not in some instances necessary or desirable, then you will surely save time.

STRATEGY
BALANCING CORE AND THE CONTEXT
Jeremy Kourdi

CORE ACTIVITIES ARE the unique skills that differentiate an organization from its competitors and persuade customers of its superiority. Context activities are the processes needed to meet the industry standard, without surpassing it. Getting the balance right between the two is essential for keeping focused on the right things—it is surprisingly tricky.

The idea

Core activities are known as *business idea factors*, while context activities refer to *hygiene factors*. For example, a core activity for Microsoft might be its ability to develop new software, whereas context (hygiene) factors include its ability to process orders and dispatch products. Both are vital, but only one (the core) is where the real value of the business lies.

Shareholders typically want to concentrate on core activities, as these tend to raise share prices. Also, it is possible for businesses to become too involved in the hassle of context activities and lose focus on what differentiates them. Catering to context activities is vital for remaining in a market, while focusing on core activities grows business and increases competitive advantage.

Business strategist Geoffrey Moore recommends balancing core and context by outsourcing or automating context activities. In this way, you can ensure context activities are being handled competently, are cost-effective, and are enjoying the economies of scale of a specialist company. Another benefit is the ability to devote increased investment to gaining a competitive edge within your market.

Many companies, including Cisco, Dell, General Motors, IBM, and Kodak, have outsourced their context processes to allow their organizations to cope with both core and context demands. Sabrix, a leading provider of software for managing taxation, outsourced context processes, with company president and CEO Steve Adams stating: "Outsourcing human resources and parts of our financial IT system has allowed us to keep the right people focused on the right things—things that differentiate our company." Instead of devoting key employees to working in IT and HR infrastructure, Sabrix was able to focus talented employees on reaching new levels in tax research, software development, and customer support: the core activities for Sabrix.

In practice

- Be clear about what is core and what is context. Recognize that some of these activities might be dynamic, moving between categories.
- Be prepared to overcome possible resistance to outsourcing initiatives and the rearranging of managerial responsibility.
- Delegate core activities from top management to middle management, as they will have a better view of market trends. By delegating responsibility to different parties, you can ensure that no level within the organization becomes overwhelmed.
- Encourage top-level support to outsourcing and managing context activities.

MAKE CUSTOMERS RESPECT YOU
Patrick Forsyth

IF A CUSTOMER sees you as professional, they will be more likely to trust you, to listen to your advice—and to buy from you.

Sometimes what can engender this respect comes through general manner and how you are with people, rather than from something that is inherently part of the sales approach. In this respect sales and service are often closely related, especially in a service business. Show signs of exemplary service and selling almost automatically becomes easier.

The idea
At a hotel in the Marriott chain ...

During a recent stay of mine in a hotel the following occurred. Checking in, the system was that a uniformed member of staff came out from Reception, handled the paperwork quickly and efficiently as you sat in a comfortable seating area, then escorted you to your room. The women who did this for me did it efficiently and charmingly. When I was crossing Reception to check out two or three days later, the same person approached me offering help. Told I was checking out, she said, "Please let me handle this for you. It's Room 234, Mr Forsyth, isn't it?" Amazed at her memory I asked how many rooms there were in the hotel (nearly 500, she told me) and asked, "Do you remember everyone's room number?" She smiled and replied, "Yes, most of them." I believed her, and loved the fact that she so clearly enjoyed being able to say that. I immediately saw her differently.

She had the responsibility of looking after guests in a more complete manner than is usual—seeing to the whole check-in process for instance, and more no doubt besides. She is doubtless part of what persuades many guests to return, even without engaging in overt sales activity.

In practice

- Never forget how sales and service overlap, and never fail to see, and use, the service aspect as a way to provide a foundation for successful selling. That's especially true if what makes a mark can be done as delightfully as this.

BUSINESS SKILLS
THINK LATERALLY
Jonathan Gifford

LEADERS NEED CONSTANTLY to challenge perceived wisdom; they need to think about whether there is a different and better way of doing things, and they need to encourage the whole organization to think in this way. Unfortunately, our brains are programmed to assume that the future will be like the past.

The idea

Frans Johansson, author of *The Medici Effect*, writes about our inbuilt tendency to assume that the future will be like the past. Our minds (for very practical reasons) tend to create what Johansson calls "associative barriers". Any one idea sets off an associative chain of other ideas that we are familiar with: we jump to conclusions.

"We are more likely to make assumptions ... than maintain a mind that is open to all possibilities ... The effect is subtle, but very powerful ... By simply hearing a word or seeing an image, the mind unlocks a whole string of associated ideas, each one connecting to another." These chains of association are efficient—they help us to assess situations quickly and to take appropriate action—but they also carry costs. "They inhibit our ability to think broadly. We do not question assumptions as readily; we jump to conclusions faster and create barriers to alternate ways of thinking about a particular situation."

Johansson suggests some techniques that can help to break down these automatic assumptions and to help to see all of the possibilities in any given situation. One way of trying to break away from familiar associations is to explore "reverse" scenarios: maybe a restaurant should have no menus, not charge money for food or not serve food at all. (Perhaps the chef creates individual dishes to order from the ingredients that he has that day; perhaps food is free, but people pay for time spent in the restaurant; perhaps people bring their own food but pay for the location.)

This process does not necessarily result in a workable new idea, but it makes us challenge our pre-conceptions about what a restaurant should be. Similarly, Johansson suggests that we make a reverse assumption and then think how to make it happen: high street banks want to attract customers; assume that they do not; what should they do actively to drive customers away?

In practice

- We all tend to make unconscious chains of association, on the assumption that what has worked in the past will work in the future.
- Question assumptions and received wisdom and keep an open mind. Challenge colleagues to try and see things differently and to imagine radical new scenarios.
- Some mental exercises, like reverse thinking, can help us to break out of entrenched ways of seeing things.

PUBLIC RELATIONS
GO AGAINST THE FLOW
Jim Blythe

DURING THE DOT.COM boom there were many companies starting up on the internet, and most of them trumpeted their cutting-edge technology. Most of their customers found this a little hard to follow: the "look at our amazing technology" opening line was usually followed by an over-excited delivery of a string of technical jargon, incomprehensible to anybody but a committed computer nerd.

Creating an exciting PR campaign was the aim of these firms, but all they succeeded in doing was dazzling the potential customers and investors.

The idea

Sourceree Solutions was founded in 2000, and is a supplier of solutions for supply-chain event management. In other words, the company helps firms locate supplies and confirm their origin online.

Sourceree needed to make an impact both with potential clients and with potential investors (the firm was hoping for an injection of venture capital at the time). When the company started out, there were already many others offering online solutions for all kinds of problems, and in most cases promoting their wonderfully clever software. Sourceree decided to be different—after all, supply-chain solutions is a fairly mundane business to be in, and trying to make it exciting was probably never going to work.

The company's PR campaign emphasized their experience of the supply-chain event management market, and their knowledge of how a large number of businesses were now using the internet to solve supply-chain problems in ways that would have been impossible only a few years earlier. The campaign also highlighted instances where research showed the level of losses being incurred by companies whose supply-chain management was inefficient.

The campaign worked out fine. People appreciated the focus on customer problems rather than on the "look how clever we are" boasting of other dot.coms, and venture capital flowed in. The company has gone from strength to strength ever since.

In practice

- Focus on what interests and benefits customers, not on banging on about how clever you are.
- Be different—you can't stand out unless you are unusual.
- If you're in a boring business, it doesn't always hurt to admit that in your PR!

ONLINE COPY THAT GROWS YOUR BUSINESS

Andy Maslen

AH, SPRING. AND a young man's thoughts turn to ... his garden. Yes, once again I found myself shopping around on the internet for garden stuff. And because it looked like we'd be facing a hosepipe ban that summer, I was after irrigation and water retention solutions. Oops—did I say that? I mean water butts.

I ended up on the Crocus website and, boy, do these guys know how to write well for the web. So well, in fact, that I want to devote this idea to a mini-case study of their copy.

The idea
From Crocus, a gardening website
Crocus have nailed the tone of voice and style that their customers respond to.

Example 1—about plants

> Whatever your garden size or taste, we have put together a style guide to help you to achieve the garden of your dreams, including plants and accessories. Mediterranean, romantic, tropical, child-friendly, scented, take your pick ...

Lots of "you"s and "your"s there to make the reader feel engaged. And look at those natural, conversational phrases: "Whatever your garden size or taste," "the garden of your dreams," "take your pick."

Example 2—Processing your order

> We know it's an internet tradition but we thought it would be a bit daft to have a shopping trolley in the middle of a gardening site. That's why we've gone for a wheelbarrow. If you see anything you fancy, just click it into the wheelbarrow.

That way you don't have to go back and find it when you want to sort out your order.

Again, they let you find out about the buying process at your own pace, rather than trying to hustle you into buying before you feel comfortable. And notice that effortless tone of voice and playful use of gardening metaphors.

Example 3—Keeping shoppers happy

> At crocus.co.uk we guarantee only to send you top notch plants, products, and gifts and will inspect everything carefully before it leaves us to make sure it's in tip top condition. We also do our utmost to package and protect everything so that it doesn't get damaged on its way. However, if you do have a problem, here is what to do:

This copy is from the About Us section of the site. Even though it's addressing a potential negative—a complaint—it manages to sound straightforward and upbeat without being glib.

In practice
- Listen to the people who talk to your customers directly. The good ones, that is. Now write down what they say.
- When you're writing web copy, strive to put as much personality into your copy as possible. Make sure every page sounds like you. Even the privacy policy. *Especially* the privacy policy.

SALES
BENCHMARK YOURSELF
Patrick Forsyth

YOU MAY BE pretty good at selling (even though you say so yourself), but do you know how you compare with others, not just in your own organization, but also more widely?

The idea
From consultants Miller Heiman ...

This company specializes in the sales area. It does regular research, and one survey, conducted in conjunction with Quest Media Ltd, and published in the journal *Winning Business*, reviewed current practice and looked to the future. It examined the changing sales role, customer expectations and beliefs, and the whole way sales teams are organized, staffed, rewarded, and managed.

Key findings indicated that:

- Customers are becoming better informed and more organized, demanding, and sharp in their dealings with salespeople (with the internet being used to a significant extent for pre-buying research).
- Technology is having, and will continue to have, an effect on sales activity. Most dramatically it is replacing salespeople with electronic, impersonal buying, although this is not affecting large numbers of business areas. The dynamic nature of this area is evidenced by the uncertainty respondents reflected in their forecasts of what other influences are becoming important.
- Recruitment is a perpetual challenge, as is retention.
- CRM is becoming a more widespread basis for many customer interactions, and creating a more formal basis for them.
- Training remains a constant need (and more of it is being done, and the range of ways in which it is done are also increasing), as the level of competency of salespeople is seen as key to success.
- Reporting takes a high proportion of working time, reducing salespeople's time spent face to face with customers. This is despite the increasing computerization of data collection and reporting systems.

In practice
- Such an examination is likely to be useful to any organization wondering whether its sales operation is maximizing opportunities. (Maybe one day it will be updated.)
- Any opportunity to examine and learn about how other people

operate should be taken; such information is likely to be useful to any organization or any individual.

- At best one fact that emerges, as with the ideas here, could be adopted or adapted, and change your own practice for the better.

LEADERSHIP

SERVANT LEADERSHIP
Jonathan Gifford

THE MODERN CONCEPT of servant-leadership was introduced by Robert K. Greenleaf in an essay written in 1970. Its central philosophy is that a leader's primary purpose is to serve the organization that they lead.

The idea

Robert Greenleaf was inspired by *Journey to the East,* written by the mystical novelist Herman Hesse, author of *Steppenwolf, Siddartha* and *The Glass Bead Game.* Hesse himself was heavily influenced by Eastern philosophy; the concept of servant-leadership appears in early Indian Hindu texts, in Chinese Taoism and in Christianity.

As Greenleaf wrote: "The servant-leader is servant first ... It begins with the natural feeling that one wants to serve, to serve first. Then conscious choice brings one to aspire to lead. That person is sharply different from one who is leader first, perhaps because of the need to assuage an unusual power-drive or to acquire material possession ... The leader-first and the servant-first are two extreme types. Between them there are shadings and blends that are part of the infinite variety of human nature."

Colleen Barrett, former president of the USA's Southwest Airlines, has featured frequently in Forbe's list of the 100 Most Powerful Women. She has always described her leadership style as "servant-leadership". Customer service is her main priority, and she addresses this by ensuring that the organization delivers great service to its own workforce, on the assumption that a well-supported and highly motivated workforce will supply the best level of service to the company's customers. Barrett estimates that she spends 85% of her time working on staff and customer issues.

"When we have employees who have a problem—or have employees who see a passenger having a problem—we adopt them, and we really work hard to try to make something optimistic come out of whatever the situation is, to try to make people feel good whatever the dilemma is that they're dealing with."

In practice

- The servant-leadership approach believes that a leader's primary concern should be to supply the organization with everything it needs in order to best carry out its purpose.
- Servant-leaders must ensure the organization understands that its primary purpose is to serve customers, and that every part of the team is focused on this.
- This is not an easy option for employees, despite the focus on staff support: the focus on the ultimate goal of excellent client service demands exceptional effort from every employee.

STRATEGY

TURNING THE SUPPLY CHAIN INTO A REVENUE CHAIN

Jeremy Kourdi

AGREEING TO SHARE sales revenue with suppliers allows companies to purchase goods for a lower price, increase revenue, and cope with fluctuations in customer demand.

The idea

In the 1990s, the leader of the video rental market, Blockbuster, found itself frustrated by never having enough copies of popular movies in stock to satisfy demand at peak times. The problem was that Hollywood studios charged $60 per video, while demand typically fell sharply a few weeks after release. Consequently, Blockbuster could not justify purchasing more than ten copies of a movie, leaving many customers frustrated at being unable to rent the latest videos.

To solve this dilemma, Blockbuster proposed giving movie companies a share of the revenue from rental sales to secure a lower upfront price for videos. Blockbuster was able to break even on a video more quickly, and able to purchase more copies to satisfy demand—ensuring high standards of convenience for customers. The movie studios also benefited from increased tape sales and added revenue streams. By turning a supply chain into a revenue chain, Blockbuster had satisfied the movie companies, the customer base, and its own bottom line.

In practice

- For this idea to work for your company, the incremental revenue generated by additional units must be less than the cost of producing them.
- Administrative costs should be low so they do not use up the increased profits from the scheme.
- If there is a high degree of price elasticity in your market, the lower upfront purchasing costs negotiated through revenue sharing should be used to lower prices, to stimulate demand.
- Use sharp negotiating skills when deciding how much revenue to share with the supplier. If production costs are low, a supplier may accept a lower revenue share than you anticipate.
- Employ reliable market research to gauge consumer demand when deciding how many units to purchase, following a revenue-sharing agreement. The new lower price can make it tempting to over-purchase.

PUBLIC RELATIONS
BE HUMOROUS
Jim Blythe

HUMOR HAS ALWAYS been a good way to get people to feel positive about the organization. Many companies produce humorous advertisements, but there is no reason why PR should not also operate with a sense of fun.

Sponsorship has always been a popular tool of PR: it generates word of mouth and creates a good impression of the firm. Some firms have even managed to make sponsorship fun by backing something humorous.

The idea

Hamlet cigars have always taken a humorous approach to their promotion. The adverts were so well liked that they were released on video—no small achievement in the advertising world. When tobacco advertising was banned throughout Europe, most tobacco companies scrambled to sponsor sporting events, arts events, and indeed anything that was not advertising. The brand managers for Hamlet decided to continue with their humorous approach, and sought out something jokey to sponsor.

Thus was born the Bad Sex Award. Hamlet sponsored a prize by the *Literary Review* for the most badly written sex scenes in new literature. The 2004 award went to famous American author Tom Wolfe, who is reputed to be the only author who did not turn up to claim his prize.

Sponsorship has now also been banned for tobacco companies, which has left a void in the funding of many organizations: however, for a time the Bad Sex Award offered Hamlet a great way to promote itself.

In practice
- Look for something that your target audience likes.

- Tap into their sense of humor: this may or may not be the same as your own.
- Help the people you sponsor to publicize themselves.

BUSINESS SKILLS
THE WONDERS OF "B"
Patrick Forsyth

ANY SPEAKER MUST hold an audience's attention and this means avoiding any distractions. There are moments when what a presenter is saying is the most important thing and the audience focus should be on them and them alone. It therefore follows that even when slides are an important part of a presentation, they should not dominate.

Yet how often do presenters switch on the projector at the beginning of a presentation and simply leave it on, with a slide on screen, until the end? Do you? Be honest. Think too of how far you get beyond one slide, in terms of topic and talk, before you get to another and bring that up on screen. It is not uncommon for people to talk for ten minutes or more with the slide on the screen behind them having ceased to have anything to do with what is being said.

This leads us to the next idea.

The idea
Only allow a slide to be seen while it is relevant to and fits with what is being said. Do not allow slides to show throughout the duration of a presentation.

How do you do this? It's easy (yet with groups I meet on training courses I am amazed how many people do not know this). You press the B key on the computer. B = Blank. The screen goes dark and will return to exactly the same place in your presentation when you press the same key again.

In practice

- Making this change alone, rather than having a slide on all the time, will improve many a presentation and allow those elements of what you need to say to shine through and be put across to maximum effect. Try it and you will see how it moves the audience's attention. Switch it on and eyes, and attention, go to the screen. Switch it off and they focus on the presenter, for a while at least.

- An alternative, if you really must have something there, is to have a "filler" slide: that's something with few or (preferably) no words but some element of design and color that is relevant but not distracting. Several copies of this can be inserted into a presentation wherever you need a pause in specific visual images so that attention is solely on you.

- So, let us be clear. PowerPoint is a wonderful thing (and perhaps it should be acknowledged here that there are other similar systems). But it can present hazards. If it is ill-used, or simply used without sufficient thought—the automatic pilot approach—it can and will damage a presentation; at worst it can render a presentation ineffective and risk a presenter failing in whatever intention they had in making the presentation. This is included here as an overall point, one to plan for; other aspects of using PowerPoint slides are dealt with in Part Four.

MARKETING

WORK WITH THE NEGATIVE ASPECTS OF YOUR PRODUCT

Jim Blythe

THIS MAY SEEM perverse: after all, everyone promotes their product's positive aspects and plays down the negatives. However, people are still aware of the negatives—ignoring this elephant in the family room is likely to cause problems if you do not address it. No amount of positive promotion will overcome a serious negative, because people will assess your promotion in the light of what they already know—and if what they know about you is bad, they will simply not accept your positive messages.

The idea

When diesel fuel was first used for road vehicles, it was almost exclusively used for commercial vehicles such as buses, lorries, and some taxis. Diesel was regarded as the fuel for smelly, noisy, low-performance workhorses: the oil crisis of the 1970s changed that, with the development of high-performance diesels for cars. The greater fuel efficiency, cheaper fuel, and lower emissions meant that Continental drivers switched to diesel in their millions, but in Britain the advantages were less obvious—a small, crowded country with urban driving being the norm meant that diesel was slower to catch on.

Volkswagen saw this as a golden opportunity. VW began a campaign designed to overcome the "workhorse" image of diesel. The campaign was humorous, showing people forgetting that their high-performance VW ran on diesel—leaving notes on their own windscreens, pulling up at the wrong pump, tying knots in their handkerchiefs.

These adverts generated much higher than average recall, and VW's diesel sales rose 40 percent, making it the market leader and displacing Peugeot; 43 percent of VW's new cars sold in Britain in 2002 were diesels. The campaign was repeated in 2003 and 2004, with equally dramatic results.

In practice

- Find out what people DON'T like about your product (or about your company, for that matter).
- If you have a negative USP (unique selling proposition), try to think of a humorous way of promoting it.
- Be prepared to promote heavily.
- Don't expect instant results—it takes time to change opinions.

USE COMPLAINTS AS A SPRINGBOARD

Patrick Forsyth

EVEN THE BEST-RUN companies get some complaints. It may be to do with the product, the service that goes with it, or such matters as delivery or technical support. The first way in which to see complaints is as a source of information. They constitute feedback that must be noted: lessons must be learned, and action taken to stop the situation from recurring. Sometimes a complaint is a one-off, and only affects one customer (although it may be nonetheless annoying or costly for them because of that). Sometimes too, complaints make the news: in one instance, batteries supplied for laptop computers were allegedly causing the machines to catch fire. The cost was likely to have been tens, perhaps hundreds, of millions of pounds.

While we would all rather no complaints occurred, when they do they must be handled constructively, and the best made of the situation.

The idea

From motor manufacturer Mercedes Benz ...

I pick an example here that is safely in the past of the company involved. Satisfactorily behind them is perhaps a better way of putting it. After the Mercedes small model A car first appeared, its early models were recalled. This was not because it had an annoying squeak or a wonky door. It was because when it was driven around a corner—it fell over! (OK, I probably exaggerate, but I want an example of a serious fault.) Yet now this company's reputation for excellence seems wholly unblemished. In the immediate aftermath a good many complaints must have been fielded effectively. This is not the place to review complaint-handling techniques in detail: what I want to stress is that the response should be done openly, address the problem head on, and sort it out. With the car example, the company did not make excuses or blame others; it said, in effect, we got it wrong, we're sorry, and here's how we will sort it out.

In practice

- Too often the instinct, particularly among salespeople fielding complaints that are no fault of their own, is to instantly avoid blame: a response that often begins, "Ah, but ..." Avoid this.

- Be open, apologize, and do so personally: "I am so sorry," not, "It's those idiots in dispatch again." Provided the problem is sorted out, you can move on to sell again, and do so successfully.

CUSTOMERS
GO TO THE SOURCE OF CUSTOMERS
Jim Blythe

CUSTOMERS DO NOT just magically appear. Often they develop their specific needs over a period of time—perhaps as a result of a training program, or as a result of growing older, or simply because needs develop.

In some cases it is possible to recognize a point at which someone will become a potential customer, and help the process along. In other cases it is simply a matter of identifying a cusp and being there at the right time.

The idea

The Ikarus C42 is an ultralight aircraft with a difference—it looks and flies exactly like a light aircraft. It has a cabin heater, is more spacious than a Cessna, and can be flown on an ultralight pilot's license (which requires less stringent medical examinations and less regulation generally).

The problem is the price. The Ikarus sells for over £50,000 fully equipped, so it is not an aircraft the cash-strapped ultralight community will flock to buy. The British distributors, Aerosport, hit on the idea of selling the aircraft at a discount to flying schools so that pupils would learn on the C42. They appointed the schools as regional dealerships, so that as pupils got their licenses it would be easy for them to carry on flying the C42, either by buying one outright or by forming syndicates with other graduating pilots to buy shares in one.

Some schools set up their own share schemes, in one case offering one-twentieth shares in the aircraft, bringing the cost down below £3,000 for the would-be pilots—well within the budgets of even the poorest ultralighter.

In practice
* Identify the point at which the need will appear.
* Do whatever you need to do to be at that point when it happens—in this case, supply the training aircraft.
* Make it easy for your customers to buy from you.

PERFORMANCE
PRACTICE DEMOCRACY
Jonathan Gifford

FEW MODERN ORGANIZATIONS are run in a democratic way. Democratic process in organizations is not about the ballot box or making decisions by referendum, it is about harnessing the energies and creativity of the organization: creating an environment that favors change and adaptation, and that empowers and encourages colleagues to make a contribution.

The idea
Gary Hamel, business author and research fellow at Harvard Business School, reminds us of a number of generally accepted truths about the modern world: the power of free markets and their

ability to solve even the most complex allocation problems; the need for diversity within any ecosystem so that it can adapt to a changing environment; the need for individuals to work because they are motivated to improve their lives and not because they have been instructed to do so. These immensely powerful forces are still only imperfectly harnessed in modern organizations.

Hamel makes the point that there are very few perfect leaders, and that the great strength of democratic processes is that they compensate for this by leveraging the "everyday genius of ordinary citizens".

The real challenge for leaders is not so much to seek for perfection as leaders, but to set up structures that allow the organization to thrive with their less-than-perfect leadership. The key strength of democratic institutions is their capacity to adapt and evolve.

This, says Hamel, offers us some design rules for modern organizations: "Leaders must be truly accountable to the front lines; employees must feel free to express the right of dissent; policy-making must be as decentralized as possible: activism must be encouraged and honored."

In practice

- Democracy in organizations is not about deciding everything via the ballot box, it is about allowing the intelligence of the organization as a whole to influence the organization's future.
- Free markets and democratic institutions are infinitely adaptable. History demonstrates that attempts to run everything by central control fail disastrously.
- Leaders should not feel threatened by the process of democratization. The organization should be guided by the leader, not controlled.
- Colleagues must be invited to contribute and even to voice dissent, but nobody has the right to obstruct.
- Colleagues will feel empowered as their opinions are sought and incorporated into the organization's behavior.
- The organization, properly guided, will adapt to its environment in the most efficient way.

MARKETING
FORM A CLUB
Jim Blythe

PEOPLE LIKE TO associate themselves with the products they buy, and very often people have a great deal in common with other people who use the same products. Motorcyclists have a strong fellow feeling for other bikers, private pilots often meet up to swap stories and share experiences, and even rail commuters form associations to campaign for better service from the railroad.

Such groups are powerful—from a marketing viewpoint, they can create strong loyalties among their members (such as the Harley Owners Group, or HOG, for owners of Harley-Davidson motorbikes) or they can become a real thorn in the company's flesh, like the aforementioned rail commuters' groups.

The idea
Huggies is a Kimberly-Clark brand of disposable diapers that, as well as the basic version, offers variants such as swimming versions and Pull-Ups (used for potty training). The brand is successful in a competitive market, but one element in the marketing that gives Huggies a distinct edge is the Huggies Club.

The Huggies Club is open to expectant and new mothers, and offers discussion forums, advice from other new mothers, and the opportunity to provide feedback about Huggies products. The site avoids the patronizing "this is how to do it" approach common to many other sites—the site genuinely belongs to the mothers, and they are free to discuss anything and everything to do with having a baby and looking after it, whether it is related to Huggies or not.

Much of the site is available to new mothers without logging in, but those who want to post comments or access all of the site need to provide some basic information to register. The mothers are asked about the expected delivery date of the baby, which supermarket they usually shop in, and their names and addresses. In return, they are sent a £4 voucher to redeem against Huggies products. The information allows Huggies brand managers to tailor their marketing approach, and of course populate a database. Feedback from the site helps in tailoring new products, identifying recurring problems, and identifying new market opportunities.

Childbirth is a worrying time for most women—the excitement of having a baby is tempered by fears of not being able to cope, fears about the changing relationship between the parents, and so forth: since so many women now live far away from their mothers, aunts, and grandmothers any support and advice is welcome. Huggies have filled a gap, and at the same time developed loyalty and greater insights into their products.

In practice
- Don't be tempted to take over the site to plug the product. If you do this, you'll frighten people away.
- Use the members' personal information carefully. Don't abuse their trust.
- Give a small reward for providing the information—it's cheap at the price!
- Recruit some women to start the forums rolling. New visitors will not post to a blank site, but once it gets moving it will be self-sustaining.
- Publicize the club somewhere other than online.

INNOVATION
REINVENTION
Jeremy Kourdi

BY REVIEWING, RETHINKING, and adding flair to existing services, it is possible to develop successful aspects of a business idea while replacing others with dramatic new enhancements. In this way, old services can be reinvented, and consumers can be kept longer and sold more.

The idea

Innovation doesn't have to be all about invention. A healthy dose of reinvention can drastically alter a market and change customers' expectations. By analyzing familiar operations and experimenting with and improving the formula, it is possible to radically alter key areas of the business model while still maintaining core aspects of the formula's original appeal.

This spirit of reinvention is evident in a project by the Vauxhall-sponsored group of experts in style, design, and technology—known as the VX Collective. The creative collective is aiming to create the "service station of the future"—a roadside stop that provides environmentally friendly fuels, gourmet food, and attractive interior design. This marks a clear departure from traditional UK roadside service stations, visited mainly for their "greasy spoon" food outlets and restroom facilities. While the VX Collective is taking a distinctly fresh look at this formula and aiming at a broad customer base, it is maintaining the key aspects of the business model: occupying a busy roadside location to provide refreshment and fuel to travelers.

Although this project is still in its early stages with many practical hurdles to overcome, it highlights the idea that a new approach and new style can breathe new life into an old and long-established formula.

In practice

- Decide exactly which aspects to keep and what you want to change.
- Decide whether you wish to alter the formula to appeal to a new target market, or whether you wish to simply make it more attractive to the existing market.
- Put careful thought into why you are making a particular change and how it will appeal to its target market.

- Market research can be a rich source of ideas for reinvention. What do customers dislike about the existing services available to them, and what alterations would they most want to see?
- Be clear about the business impact and benefits, as well as understanding what needs to be done to ensure success.

PUBLIC RELATIONS
BRING IN THE SCIENTISTS
Jim Blythe

McVITIE'S IS THE leading British biscuit manufacturer, producing a wide range of sweet and savory biscuits. The company has, for some years, run an annual "Dunking Day" as a way of promoting the biscuits via the well-known habit many people have of dipping their biscuits into hot tea or coffee (dunking). The intention behind Dunking Day was to encourage tea and coffee drinkers to accompany each cup with a biscuit.

The problem was that Dunking Day had become a fairly run-of-the-mill event with little news value. Once was humorous, twice was mildly interesting, three times was pretty meaningless: the event was relegated to "special interest day" one-liners.

The idea
McVitie's PR consultants realized that they needed a story that Britain (and, as it turned out, the world) would want to hear. The consultants put forward the idea that McVitie's should commission academic research into the science of dunking, so the company engaged Dr. Len Fisher of Bristol University to investigate the physics of dunking biscuits into hot drinks.

It turned out that dunking releases the flavor of the biscuits. Photos of Dr. Fisher and his team experimenting with the biscuits were released to TV and the press, and a scientific report was produced.

The result was remarkable—the story was picked up internationally, and whatever it did for Dr. Fisher's scientific reputation, it certainly put McVitie's Dunking Day back on the news map.

In practice

- Commissioning research from universities is not cheap, but it certainly has news value.
- Make it fun—the success of the McVitie's research came from the juxtaposition of heavyweight scientific research and the lightweight subject of dunking biscuits.
- Take plenty of pictures and videos of the research being conducted.
- Ensure that the scientists you use will look good on TV and can handle such an appearance: most university scientists are used to speaking to lecture rooms full of students, so this is unlikely to be a big problem.

SALES

BE AFRAID, BE VERY AFRAID

Patrick Forsyth

ONE TECHNIQUE THAT is essential to salespeople is closing. You can do everything else right, but closing badly or failing to close can scupper all the good work that has been put in. So no apologies for including a couple of good closes here. The first one was used on me by a small travel agent on faraway New Zealand's North Island.

The idea

From a New Zealand travel agent ...

I travel regularly for work and holidays (indeed the first proposal for this book was written at 30,000 feet). So I deal regularly with travel agents, and I am often not particularly impressed. Should I have to spell out where Seoul is, for goodness sake? Sorry, I digress.

Anyway I was in touch with a firm in Auckland, since I had discovered that it was likely to be cheaper to book a trip onward from there than to do so from Britain. Because it was a long way to travel, and the project was cost-sensitive, I made the original inquiry well ahead of the time I expected to be traveling. I got a quote and acknowledged it, saying "decision later." Thereafter I got a series of reminders by email. These used the classic fear close: in this case a plea to book early, as the time at which I intended to travel was "peak season."

So far so normal, but what I felt made the follow-up contacts unusual was that they continued other parts of the sales pitch, and enhanced them too. The staff didn't just add a couple of lines saying hi: they took some time to refer to sights to be seen and things to be done, to mention particular places to go and to stay. Their chatty nature began to make me feel there was a relationship being built, and the chances of my using them increased steadily over some months. The frequency was not overdone, and it will be interesting to see what happens next if I leave the decision much longer. So far, so well done.

In practice
- This is both a nice variant on a classic method of closing, and a good example of persistence—surely an inherent characteristic of good salespeople.
- Making follow-up contacts interesting and thus more likely to be retained and acted upon is always going to work better than a routine "Anything I can do?" call.

STRATEGY
BUILD A NEW DISTRIBUTION CHANNEL
Jim Blythe

SOMETIMES DISTRIBUTION CHANNELS are so tied up by existing companies it is difficult (even impossible) to get a product to market.

Even when retailers can be identified, often part of the chain is contracted to some major supplier who blocks the distribution at the wholesale stage.

For small companies in particular, finding a route to market can present a major challenge: often the big boys are not interested unless there is a fairly substantial financial commitment in terms of renting shelf space or supplying large amounts of product on extended credit.

The idea

When Red Bull was first launched in Britain, it was an attempt to create the energy drinks market from scratch. The company was founded in Austria in 1984, but only started selling the drink in 1987.

Breaking into the British market proved difficult. The company wanted to target a young audience, partly because they would have the longest usage life and partly because young people often participate in sports or need to stay up late, either to party or to study. Red Bull therefore began by recruiting students to act as part-time salespeople, visiting nightclubs and sports centers to promote the drink. Since the nightclub owners were seeking to attract a young audience, the student salespeople represented a powerful influence.

Eventually Red Bull established its own warehousing and distribution, but again ran these using students as part-time workers. Apart from keeping costs down, this ensured that the entire workforce matched the brand values, and (perhaps even more importantly) were able to act as influencers, telling their friends about the product.

Today, Red Bull has reached the point where it sells 3 billion cans of the drink a year.

In practice

- Decide where you really want to sell your product, and focus on just those outlets.

- Decide who would be your best advocates for the product in those outlets.
- Follow up with a continued commitment to the distribution chain, even when other channels open up.

MARKETING
THINK SMALL
Jim Blythe

MOST RETAILERS LIKE the idea of being big. Big stores run more efficiently, operate with fewer staff, and can carry a wider range of merchandise. Stock can be bought in larger quantities, which of course makes purchasing more efficient, and it's easier to make an impact on the customers.

However, as with many other aspects of marketing, it often pays to swim against the tide and do something that other people aren't expecting.

The idea
There are many locations in the country where small premises are available. Rail and bus stations often have kiosk-sized locations, and many High Streets have small store units. In some cities, there are arcades containing small units, and many shopping malls have hole-in-the-wall space for rent. Often these can be picked up cheaply—but what retailer would be interested?

During the 1980s several companies began to locate specialist retail outlets in these tiny store spaces. One of the most successful was Tie Rack. Tie Rack opened in 1981, specializing in ties (of course), which are small, high-value items. Although Tie Rack outlets were tiny, they could still carry a much wider range of ties than mainstream retailers such as department stores: Tie Rack were able to compete very effectively in high-footfall areas such as rail stations.

Doing something the others aren't doing is basic to marketing strategy.

In practice

- Think outside the box.
- Look for a potential resource that is currently being underused or ignored altogether.
- Specialize—only very large firms can try to be all things to all people.
- Don't compete head-on with the big boys.

LEADERSHIP

MARCH TOWARDS THE SOUND OF THE GUNS

Jonathan Gifford

IN CORPORATE AFFAIRS it is essential to know where the main action is taking place, and to turn the organization in that direction. The organization must understand that this action is of vital importance to everybody and that jobs and the organization's entire future are potentially at risk; it needs to march towards the sound of the guns.

The idea

In any battle, even with modern communications, events become confused. It may not be clear where the main action is or whether you are in the right position. A long-established piece of military advice has been to "march towards the sound of the guns". The gunfire clearly signals where an engagement is taking place; in the absence of any command to hold your position elsewhere, it is likely that you will be able to help by turning up at the scene of the fighting.

This advice holds true in business. Leaders often need to remind organizations that the action is not inside the comfortable corporate headquarters but outside somewhere, wherever customers are drifting away and competitors are stealing ground.

When Louis Gerstner was charged with turning around IBM in the 1990s, he felt that the company's long-established market dominance had taken the edge off its competitive spirit. He wanted his senior team to feel personally aggrieved about the damage that competitors in the burgeoning personal computer market were doing to IBM. He made a controversial speech to IBM's top management, pointing out that IBM's share of the market had halved at a time when the industry was rapidly expanding, and that customer satisfaction with IBM was dropping.

"I summarized those two snapshots of our collective performance by saying: 'We're getting our butts kicked in the marketplace. So I want us to start kicking some butts, namely, of our competitors ... We've got to create some collective anger here about what our competitors say about us, about what they're doing to us in the marketplace ... One hundred and twenty-five thousand IBM-ers are gone. They lost their jobs. Who did it to them? Was it an act of God? These guys came in and they beat us. They took that market share away and caused the pain in this company. It wasn't caused by anybody but the people plotting very carefully to rip away our business." Many IBM staffers were unhappy about the tone of this speech, but Gerstner was making a key point: organizations have to fight to survive.

In practice

- Market changes are impersonal. The competition, on the other hand, actively wants to kill you. Both forces are equally deadly.
- This is not an academic exercise—jobs, livelihoods and even the future of the organization are at stake.
- Like armies, organizations must march towards the action: the battlefield is out there in the real world, not inside the organization.

MAKE YOUR CUSTOMERS LAUGH
Jim Blythe

MAKING PEOPLE LAUGH has always been a good way of getting them to like you. The same is equally true of companies—humor is often used in advertising, especially for "fun" items such as toys or beer.

For some products, humor is less often used but can still be very powerful. Jokes aimed at an educated, better-off audience can often be subtle—and in particular can generate some positive word of mouth as the jokes are passed on.

The idea
BMW manufactures upmarket cars for wealthier drivers. Normally, car advertising is serious—it usually emphasizes the emotional aspects of ownership (the style, the comfort, the feeling of power) but sometimes discusses technical, practical aspects of ownership such as fuel economy, emissions, maintenance scheduling, and so forth.

Each year, on April 1st, BMW runs a spoof advertisement, usually talking about some major new technical breakthrough in the design of the cars. For example, one year the company advertised that new European Union regulations banning right-hand-drive cars from Continental Europe had caused BMW to invent a car with no steering wheel, directed by the driver's head movements. The ad warned against turning around to talk to back-seat passengers, and flagged up the dangers of looking at passers-by or interesting views. Another year the company announced the invention of a windshield coating that caused flies to bounce off, and in yet another year they announced a car that would automatically give the owner's microwave oven a call so that dinner would be ready on arrival home.

These adverts certainly created an impact at a relatively low cost, but more importantly they generated word of mouth and great memorability. People showed the adverts to their friends—something that would be very unlikely to happen with any other approach.

In practice
- If your product is upmarket, don't be afraid to be subtle.
- Press advertising is relatively cheap and offers a semi-permanent medium so that people can show their friends the joke—at the same time, joke adverts for the press are easy to produce.
- Be sure to make it clear at the end of the advert that it is a joke—also, try to ensure that someone who actually believes it would not be hurt by the misunderstanding.

BRANDING
LIFESTYLE BRANDS
Jeremy Kourdi

BY MAKING YOUR brand synonymous with the hobbies and aspirations of a particular cultural movement, you can massively increase the appeal of your product.

The idea
It is one thing to have a well-respected brand. It is another thing entirely to have a brand that encapsulates an entire culture, identity, and lifestyle. Brands that achieve this are known as "lifestyle brands."

Used by customers to show membership of a particular cultural movement, lifestyle brands can be a form of wordless communication within society. They can also reinforce consumers' esteem and perception of themselves.

Two areas that lifestyle brands draw on are national identity and subcultures. Lingerie retailer Victoria's Secret sought in its early marketing campaigns to evoke the British upper class. Likewise, successful luxury lifestyle brand Louis Vuitton draws on the opulent image of the French aristocracy.

Subcultures—particularly in music and sport—lend themselves well to lifestyle brands. Surf and sport brand Quiksilver embodies the modern lifestyle brand. Retailing clothes, wetsuits, surfwear, and sunglasses, it has created sponsorship deals with 500 board sport professionals. To promote its presence in the surfing lifestyle, it sponsors the annual elite Quiksilver Pro tournament. All of this effort has paid off: it is a market leader in the surfing industry, a trendy fashion label for surfers and non-surfers, and a member of the Fortune 1000. When customers buy Quiksilver apparel, they are buying a lifestyle of sun, sea, and surf, without the worry of having to brave any killer waves. Your product need not be sold just for its functional use: it can be marketed as an entry fee to the life your customers desire.

In practice
* Provide sponsorship deals, to show you are aligned with the culture you wish your brand to embody.
* Placement of marketing is vital. Make your brand's presence known at appropriate festivals, tournaments, meetings, parties, and cultural hotspots.
* Sell a range of products involved with the culture—this will broaden your appeal and increase credibility.
* Subcultures are a good target for lifestyle brands, as they often feel a strong need to assert their group identity.
* Elite cultures are also suited to lifestyle brands.
* One factor is often overlooked when creating a lifestyle brand: ensure your product offering is compatible with the "lifestyle" you are promoting. If you want to market your organization as an elite sporting brand, remember to actually sell quality sporting equipment that matches the needs and perceptions of the target market.

MARKETING
KEEP THEM WAITING
Jim Blythe

THE RECEIVED WISDOM in business is that people want what they want when they want it, and if you don't supply them they will go elsewhere. This is true in 99 percent of cases—most people will move on rather than wait.

There may be a case, though, for developing a unique selling proposition based on having a long waiting list. Some restaurants do this (Rick Stein springs to mind) and some hotels (many paradores in Spain have waiting lists, especially for festival times). This works if you have something that nobody else has—a unique design, an upmarket restaurant, or (of course) the only hotel inside the Alhambra Palace in Granada.

The idea
The Morgan Motor Company is a tiny car manufacturer based in Malvern, Worcestershire. The company makes sports cars with a distinct retro feel—the flagship car, the 4/4, has been manufactured since 1936 (although it has obviously been modified and updated many times in the intervening years). It is, without a doubt, the car's looks that sell it.

Morgan maintain a waiting list of around two years for the 4/4: the car sells, new, for around £27,000 (a very reasonable price for a hand-built sports car), but one that is immediately available would fetch around £32,000. In other words, someone who agrees to buy a Morgan can sell it the day after delivery for £5,000 more than the manufacturer's price.

At first sight, this seems crazy—if the factory simply produced enough to meet demand, they could charge an extra £5,000 per car. Making people wait, though, gives the Morgan its unique selling proposition—Morgans don't depreciate.

All other cars lose value as soon as they leave the showroom, but a reasonably maintained Morgan will fetch at least its price when new, and sometimes more: Morgans from the 1930s sell for around £8,000, much more than they cost at the time. This gives the company something that no other motor manufacturer has—a product that is an investment.

In practice

- This only works if you have a clear and definite advantage over competitors already.
- The wait needs to be long enough to excite the customers, not so long that they give up.
- The product or service should be upmarket and prestigious.
- You are relying on conspicuousness—people need to be able to show off their new acquisition to their friends.

SALES
DON'T WASTE CUSTOMERS' TIME
Patrick Forsyth

WE ALL KNOW people are busy these days. Customers normally take what they consider an appropriate amount of time to make a decision. So it makes sense not to try to sidestep that, by either rushing them or spinning out the sale. That's especially true if they don't see the extra time taken as useful, and it's worse if they see the process as unnecessarily and uncaringly lengthy.

The idea

From book publishers Bantam Press ...

Sometimes the time a salesperson is allowed must be agreed upfront, and sometimes too it needs to be negotiated. A salesperson must try to get time to make the planned pitch, and a customer must accept that if they want to make an informed decision, they must listen to key information about the product or service. The key point here is to respect the time customers have available, then actively work on descriptions, indeed your whole pitch, to ensure that you can make a powerful case in the time available.

In some industries people are under more time pressure than in others, and the unremitting nature of that pressure means that salespeople have to consider this or they simply cannot do the job. One example is publishing. Large publishers not only have hundreds or thousands of titles in print, they add dozens of new ones every month. A salesperson selling to retail bookshops has to find a way of being strikingly succinct. Some titles may be dealt with in a minute or less. Some years ago when Stephen Hawking's surprise bestseller *A Brief History of Time* was selling in its millions, I asked salespeople on a publishing industry sales training course to pick a title to describe, first without time pressure, then with a tight cut-off time. When we came to the succinct version, a representative from Bantam Press simply held up Hawking's book and gave a four-word sales pitch: "It's now in paperback."

Sometimes circumstances make this easy, but even when they don't, the principle stands. You must not risk wasting customers' time. Working out truly succinct, yet powerful, descriptions is a certain aid to sales success.

In practice

- It can be easy to spend longer with customers than they find ideal, because they might not tell you so.
- So ask about timing. It will be regarded as a courtesy. Then you can fit your pitch to their timescale and get their full attention throughout.

PUBLIC RELATIONS
DO GOOD BY STEALTH
Jim Blythe

MANY FIRMS MAKE a big song-and-dance about their charity work, promoting their generosity in sponsoring this or that good cause. This is all well and good, but can easily backfire: a firm that continually harps on about its good corporate citizenship makes people wonder whether it is only contributing to charity in order to look good—in the same way as a rich person suddenly becomes overwhelmingly generous as death approaches, the suspicion is that the firm (like the person) is simply trying to buy its way into heaven.

The alternative is to keep fairly quiet about charitable behavior—but how can this benefit the company?

The idea

Body Shop is world renowned for its unusual approach to the cosmetics business, and indeed to business in general. Founder Anita Roddick famously said that she didn't believe in marketing, but in fact she was eminently good at doing it: she was equally good at public relations, and elevated Body Shop in many ways.

One of the most important aspects of the Body Shop organization is that each store is encouraged to carry out charity work within the local community. Staff can choose which projects they want to become involved in, and can decide their own way of contributing, with the support of the firm.

This means that local Body Shop branches might be involved in creating a children's playgroup, in supporting a local hospice, in fundraising for a kidney machine for the local hospital, or in any one of hundreds of different ways. Staff sometimes volunteer their time to help, sometimes collect money, sometimes lobby local councils to act. Body Shop allows them time off work to do this, but many staff members carry on in their own time as well.

The result of this approach is that staff feel part of the local community, they feel that they are working for an ethical employer, and they feel more like part of a team. In the local area, word soon gets around that Body Shop is helping: the publicity arises through word of mouth, rather than as the result of press releases or advertising. This is surely the most powerful way of generating interest.

In practice
* Involve your staff—in fact for preference put them in charge of the project.
* Support your staff effort. If you can't give them time off, let them use company facilities or provide them with funding—perhaps by matching any money they raise.
* Do not be tempted to publicize what they are doing. This is likely to damage the word-of-mouth effect and dilute the impact of the exercise.
* Accept that results may be a long time in coming, and there will be problems along the way as staff make errors or choose inappropriate projects. Don't be afraid to let them learn.

MANAGING TIME
AIM AT INFLUENCING PARTICULAR RESULT AREAS
Patrick Forsyth

EVERYTHING YOU DO in time management terms is designed to effect efficiency, effectiveness, and productivity; to enable you to do more and to do everything better than would otherwise be the case, so as to achieve the results your job demands. But there are advantages to be gained en route to these ends, and these are useful in their own right.

The idea
Considering and keeping specific advantages in mind can help you adopt some of the methodology necessary to an organized

way of working and make the whole process easier. Such advantages include:

- Having a clear plan, knowing and having an overview of what must be done—the first step to successfully completing the tasks on your list. Such clarity will make adequate preparation more likely and this can reflect directly on achievement.
- Having a clear link between things to do and overall objectives, which is a sound recipe for keeping on track.
- Being better organized (e.g., not wasting time looking for things).
- Your memory coping better with what you actually need to remember (the systems take care of some of this for you, and it is not necessary to keep everything in your head).
- Being better able to identify and concentrate on the essentials.
- Wasting less energy on irrelevancies.
- Making better decisions about how things should be done (and better business decisions generally).
- Better coordination of tasks (progressing certain things in parallel saves time).
- Having a greater ability to cope with or remove distractions and interruptions.
- Cultivating the habit of greater self-discipline about time matters, which makes consistency of action progressively easier.
- A greater ability to cope with the unexpected and emergency elements of any job.

Any of these are useful, but some may be more useful to you than others, at least at a particular moment.

In practice

- It may be useful to look for the particular advantage you want: wasting less energy on irrelevancies or, more specifically, attending fewer meetings, for example. Or you may wish to adopt methods that suit you precisely. This is not to say that all those listed above do not have a good general effect on productivity. They do. Focusing what you do carefully will enable you to achieve more, and get greater satisfaction from the results you do achieve.
- Additionally, you may have more time to develop what you do and how you do it, and motivate yourself (and staff you may

have), all of which can potentially improve things still further. All this may also remove some of the things that create the feeling that a job is "hard work." "Working hard" is nearly always a prerequisite of success, but you do not want tasks to constantly be like trying to nail jam to the wall when a little organization will ensure they go smoothly.

MANAGING
GIVE THE TEAM THE TOOLS TO DO THE JOB
Jonathan Gifford

ONE OF THE most important functions of leadership is to ensure that the team has the tools to do the job. This is a very wide-ranging responsibility that includes not only ensuring that the team has the most efficient and up-to-date kit that they need to function effectively, but also that team members are kept informed about the most recent developments in the organization.

The idea
Fred Smith, founder, chairman, president and CEO of FedEx, believes that one of the main functions of the company's top management is to support the "frontline folks" by enabling them to deliver FedEx's "purple promise": a deceptively simple-sounding vision: "To make every customer experience outstanding".

Advances in technology have allowed the company to give more control to these frontline folks, and the company's management see their main function as keeping their team as well-equipped as possible.

"I mean, the power that we are putting in the hands of our pick-up and delivery people, in our airplanes and our trucks and our sortation equipment; it's fantastic compared to what was possible just a few years ago ... The most important element in the FedEx system are the people that are out there, the frontline folks that are delivering what we call our 'purple promise', and the frontline management equally so. So we've always looked at it that the top management of the organization's job is to try to make their job easy … give them the best tools, give them the best service, give them the best methodology."

Business and management consultant and writer Marshall Goldsmith reminds us that there are important ways in which we can fail to give teams the tools to do the job: "withholding information" is a good example. Withholding information, says Goldsmith, is often unintentional but it is nevertheless effectively a power-play, and one that has a pernicious effect. "We do this when we are too busy to get back to someone with valuable information. We do this when we forget to include someone in our discussions or meetings. We do this when we delegate a task to our subordinates but don't take the time to show them exactly how we want the task done."

In practice

- Ensuring that the team has the right tools to do the job includes physical kit, back-up, efficient methodologies and operating systems.
- Having confidence that the management team is well-equipped to deal with any new problems that may arise, and that there is a system in place to deal with these, is another form of back-up for the team.
- Some things that leaders do—even unintentionally—prevent the team from having everything they need to do the job. Withholding information is a good example.

DIRECT MARKETING
IT CAME FROM OUTER SPACE
Andy Maslen

USUALLY, MARKETEERS WHO don't, or won't, overprint envelopes say it's because "Then they'll know it's direct mail." I'm sorry to disappoint these wide-eyed hopefuls, but your reader *already* knows it's direct mail. Unless you're handwriting every envelope and using postage stamps, there are enough clues to give the game away to even the most simple-minded recipient.

Instead, why not try to show them that it's *relevant* direct mail. *interesting* direct mail. Direct mail that could change their lives. You do this with copy. And maybe graphics too. Just as with email subject lines, the outer copy entices you to open it. It arouses your curiosity. It promises some benefit or other.

The idea
From *Radio Times*, a TV and radio listings magazine

The outer envelope for this mailpack covers all the bases. The copy reads, "Your guide to the TV and radio you'll love." There's also a montage of covers. And a flash reading, "Get 12 issues for £1." It's a really powerful come-on to open the envelope. Which is all we need at this stage.

Here's a little example I put together to show you why envelopes are so important.

Suppose you're selling a £130 product by direct mail. You mail 10,000 pieces at a cost per piece of 50 pence. Your total marketing cost is £5,000.

Let's also suppose that you get a 1 percent response rate, i.e., 100 orders. But if we also assume that only 20 percent of people—2,000— actually open your envelope, that's where all 100 orders come from. And your effective response rate is in fact 5 percent. Let's call that your conversion rate.

If it costs you £75 to fulfill each order, your total fulfillment costs are £7,500. So your total costs are £12,500. Your total revenues are £13,000 and your profit is £500.

Now, imagine you find some way of getting 25 percent more people to open your envelope, giving you 2,500 potential buyers. Without increasing your conversion rate, you now have 125 orders.

Your marketing cost is the same: £5,000. Your fulfillment cost has risen to £9,375, making a total of £14,375. Your total revenues are £16,250 and your profit has jumped to £1,875. A 275 percent increase.

. And guess how you get more people to open your envelope. That's right! You give them a *reason* to.

In practice

- If you are trying to get renewals for any kind of relationship-based service, use a line of copy that says something like "Important news about your membership."
- Use a photo that dramatizes the fundamental product benefit. If you offer a premium when people become customers or take a free trial, show that with a line promising details of how to get hold of it inside.

STRATEGY
VENDOR LOCK-IN
Jeremy Kourdi

DEVELOPING PRODUCTS THAT are only compatible with other products in your range shuts out competitors and ensures repeat business from customers.

The idea

Being able to devise a foolproof strategy for retaining customers and maintaining a steady, reliable stream of revenues is the dream of many corporate executives. By using vendor lock-in—ensuring customers are dependent on your products and unable to move to another vendor without substantial switching costs—you can achieve this.

Gillette's razor-sharp business acumen exploits vendor lock-in. Its razor blade handles are only compatible with its brand of razor blades; consequently, its razor blades are the primary source of income. Manufacturer of electronic toothbrushes Philips Sonicare also uses vendor lock-in. Its toothbrushes have an electronic base that requires a Sonicare replacement toothbrush head, ensuring customers will return to Sonicare and preventing them from switching to another manufacturer. Switching cost is the cost a consumer incurs when purchasing from a new company and is a key aspect of vendor lock-in. The higher the switching cost, the less likely a customer is to switch.

This concept is not new. Many businesses do this: printer manufacturers like Hewlett-Packard, camera companies such as Canon, coffee retailers such as Nespresso, all provide proprietary, reusable components for their products. These businesses ensure success by planning the reusable component of their products from the start. Where many attempts at vendor lock-in fail is viewing the reusable component as just an add-on. It isn't. It is the product, the benefit for the customer, and the profit for the business.

In practice
- Consider selling the original product for a low, eye-catching price to stimulate sales of the add-on components.
- Alternatively, consider making the "base product" expensive to persuade customers they have made an investment in your brand and deter them from switching to another company. The choice depends on your product, your market, and your customers. What would they value most?
- Offer a range of add-ons compatible with the base unit. This element of choice helps overcome consumers' fears that they are "stuck" with something of diminishing utility.
- Be aware that demand for your products will be interrelated— if demand for one decreases, demand for the partner product will decline.
- Switching cost is not always real—it can just be imagined by the customer. It can be enough simply to persuade your customers that it will be inconvenient or costly to switch to a new vendor.
- Plan your vendor lock-in strategy from the start. Clearly, this strategy works best for products that need to be regularly replaced.

PUBLIC RELATIONS
DO SOMETHING INCONGRUOUS
Jim Blythe

DOING THE UNUSUAL is the essence of good, eye-catching PR. Doing something incongruous takes things a step further—the juxtaposition of wildly differing images is what is striking here.

The idea

The Lowry at Salford Quays, Greater Manchester, is a major arts complex. It houses the Lowry Gallery, two theaters, bars, restaurants, and several smaller art galleries, but it tends to be perceived as being solely concerned with the work of artist L. S. Lowry.

For the PR consultants involved, publicizing the complex presented numerous problems. Although it was named after Salford's most famous artist, the message needed to get across that it was a center for the performing arts as well as for paintings and sculpture: in addition, the brand itself was unknown. The PR people needed to communicate the Lowry's significance as a performing arts venue for the whole Northwest, and also needed to encourage people to buy tickets well ahead of the official opening date.

Spin Media, the PR consultancy involved, staged a "Ballerina on a Building Site" event in which ballerinas in leotards and hard hats danced on the construction site itself. This proved to be an irresistible photo opportunity for the press and TV. An opera singer sang from *The Barber of Seville* while shaving comedian Johnny Vegas's chest hair, and DJ Mark Radcliffe reported on the progress of the building during radio interviews, thus involving a younger audience.

Over the three days following the event, the box office received over 1,000 phone calls. In the first two weeks it accepted bookings for almost £20,000 worth of tickets, and the mailing list grew by 1,000 people a week.

In practice

- Something incongruous should also be something relevant to what you are trying to publicize.
- The incongruity should be visual if at all possible—you are looking for striking pictures.
- As with all stunts, you need to prepare well beforehand, and prime your journalists.

BUSINESS SKILLS
BREAKING THE ICE
Patrick Forsyth

TRAINERS USE THE word "ice-breaker" to describe something that at once engages people and prompts thought and participation. It is not only training sessions that can benefit from such a device.

The idea

When appropriate, involve people instantly through some sort of ice-breaker. This can even be done ahead of an introduction of any sort—that can follow at a stage where people have been put more in the mood.

Most often something the audience work together on will suit. For example, on giving a talk about time management (the subject of another book in this series, *100 Great Time Management Ideas*), I might ask people to compare with someone sitting alongside what they find the worst time-wasting interruption, and usually their answers are things that can easily be linked to the topic.

Or alternatively if appropriate, you can give people a task to be done individually. This can even be set—instructions on screen, perhaps—to keep people busy as the group assembles. Sometimes when I run courses on business writing I show a slide with this task on, just to create the necessary focus on language:

As you scan this short paragraph, try to spot what is unusual about it. Half an hour is normal for many to find a solution that is both logical and satisfactory to its originator. I do not say that anything is "wrong" about it, simply that it is unusual. You may want to study its grammatical construction to find a solution, but that is not a basis of its abnormality, nor is its lack of any information, logical points or conclusion. If you work in communications you may find that an aid to solving this particular conundrum. It is not about anagrams, synonyms, or antonyms but it is unusual. So, what about it is unusual?

Note: if you want to digress for a moment and think about this, the answer is shown below.

In practice

- Choose something that fits the occasion, the topic and the audience; it may appear odd if it is solely to engage the audience.
- Spell out the rules but keep it very simple: "Take two minutes and discuss with your neighbour..."
- Putting the brief on the screen if you are using slides may help those who failed to listen.
- After the exercise has concluded, thank people and make a clear link with the business in hand as you continue.

The answer to the conundrum is that the text does not contain the letter "e". It is unusual because it's the most commonly occurring letter in the English language.

PERFORMANCE
DEVELOPING A SALES CULTURE
Jeremy Kourdi

"PUTTING CUSTOMERS FIRST" is a frequently heard business mantra, but what does it mean and how can it be achieved in practice?

The idea

The argument is simple. If you can get everyone in your organization to view their work from the point of view of the consumer, your business will be more effective and likely to succeed. This sounds obvious but can be hard to achieve. The challenge is to overcome the inertia of previous attitudes and to instill a new sense of energy and a focus on the customer.

In practice

HSBC is a financial services business that since 1992 has achieved a compound annual growth rate of 17 percent. It has become one of the world's 20 largest corporations, and since 2004 has been striving to achieve organic growth, largely by focusing on current and potential customers (rather than through acquisitions or improving business processes). Shifting the approach of a large, venerable, and long-standing bank that employs over 300,000 people in 80 countries is no mean feat. Several factors are prominent in its move to a greater sales focus:

- *Proactively manage performance.* Get the right people working at their best, and make sure everyone knows that success is determined by the customer. Help individuals to achieve their potential; if you need to change the people you have in the business, do so.
- *Ensure you have the right management information.* It informs decision making and shows people the indicators and issues that they need to focus on.
- *Establish a robust sales process.* This will ensure the basics are being covered, while emphasizing what matters and providing a framework for action.
- *Value relationships.* Relationship management is central to a sales culture because it leads to greater understanding of customers. Thinking of customers in terms of your relationship together takes them from being a statistic to being something that is more significant and valuable.
- *Segment your customers.* This leads to greater clarity, insight, and success. This is important in competitive, fast-moving markets, and ensures offers are more likely to appeal because they are matched with the right customers.

- *Avoid complacency and develop an entrepreneurial approach.* This is hard to achieve because it relies on the other stages being accomplished first. With the other measures in place, the culture and focus of the business will inevitably change and strengthen.
- *Display strong leadership.* This includes the need to communicate, to act as a role model for the values that you believe are important, to inspire trust, and to be personally effective.

SALES
AVOID GIVING A DISCOUNT
Patrick Forsyth

EVERYONE LIKES A bargain. What is more, customers have been led to expect that prices vary. Take airfares: go to a dozen websites and travel agents, and you will find yourself looking at a dozen different prices. Many of them are likely to be for exactly the same flight, airline, and so on. In this environment shopping around is the norm, and so too is asking for a discount. How do you either stop the question being asked, or resist the suggestion when it comes?

The idea
From among others a menswear shop ...

This is a problem area, and not one that is addressed by any one magic formula (is anything?). But this idea works well in certain circumstances. Wherever price varies in the way it does in, say, a car showroom—each car gets you from A to B, but different models and specifications cost different amounts—you need to check what the customer is thinking about price. Asking "What's your budget?" is likely to cause people to clam up (they know that declaring their hand makes negotiation more difficult). So as the customer investigates, asks questions, and comes toward a choice, there is another tactic to use. It works too in areas where a number of different products are being selected together. Perhaps the customer is buying an outfit: suit, shirt, tie, shoes, and suchlike.

Once the prospect is considering an option, price it in terms of an estimate. "That specification would cost around £1,200: how does that sound?" You may get good information in return. If the answer is an out-and-out "Way too expensive," you could turn them to look at a less expensive option. If it's "Sounds about right" or the like, you can use it to avoid getting into negotiation over discounts. That's particularly true when you've rounded up the estimate, so the final price is less than has already been agreed as acceptable in principle.

In practice

* Pick your moment for asking this kind of question. The customer needs to be in the process of decision making.
* It is also important to use the right sequence here. Agree the estimate, then use that agreement to avoid debate about a final price. "That's a little less than what you looked at/agreed to earlier" makes a positive point.

BRANDING

HAVE A STARTLING BRAND

Jim Blythe

MAKING YOUR BRAND name stand out from all the others is an obvious thing to do—yet many firms (especially small businesses) have brand names that are based on the founder's surname, or house name, or favorite pet's name. This is a classic wasted opportunity.

On the other hand, many firms try to develop memorable brand names, and often have expert help in doing so. Cutting through the clutter of short, memorable, zingy brand names is difficult to say the least.

One answer is to make the brand name controversial—but to do so without getting it banned altogether.

The idea

Controversial marketing is nothing new—Benetton's advertising campaigns show that—but getting a brand name that is controversial is more risky: an ad that oversteps the mark could be banned by the advertising authorities, which would mean losing the cost of producing the ad, but a brand name that oversteps the mark and is banned could lose the company its identity.

Enter French Connection United Kingdom. French Connection was founded in 1972 as a fashion chain, and although it did well the brand name did not exactly stand out from the many other slick names retailers were using. In 1997, though, the company hit on the idea of calling itself French Connection United Kingdom, and using the lower-case acronym "fcuk" on its goods. The effect was electric. The company produced T-shirts with slogans such as "fcuk fashion," "hot as fcuk," and (in Australia) "no fcukin worries." The company was successful in claiming that fcuk is simply the company's name rather than a misspelled Anglo-Saxon word, but young people still bought the T-shirts.

The new brand appealed to rebellious teenagers who had not even been born when the company was founded—and when some people in authority failed to see the joke and banned the company's advertising, sales went up even further (and with reduced promotional costs as a sweetener). Being banned in Boston was a major boost to the company's American interests: in 2001, the company hung a poster saying "San Francisco's First fcuk" outside their first store in that city.

Being controversial carries risks—but in this case it certainly carried rewards as well.

In practice

- Try to be funny as well as controversial.
- Don't go too far—you might get banned altogether!
- If possible, link the controversial brand to your company's name. This will help you in defending against banning charges.

- The main appeal of controversial brand names is to younger people. This idea would not work for an older audience, or in a "serious" context such as financial services.

TEAMWORK
CREATE FOLLOWERS
Jonathan Gifford

LEADERS NEED TEAMS that will do something because it is the right thing to do for the organization, rather than because they have been told to do it.

To achieve this, leaders should avoid directing people to do specific things and, instead, try to create "followers"—people who have chosen to follow your direction.

The idea
Anne Mulcahy of Xerox Corporation talks about the need for colleagues to "believe in a story" about the direction in which the organization is moving, so that they can embrace that direction with real commitment.

"We talk a lot about execution and the importance of it. But I actually think it's a lot more about followership—that your employees are volunteers and they can choose to wait things out if they don't believe. And that can be very damaging in a big company. So it is absolutely this essence of creating followership that becomes the most important thing that you can do as a leader ... People really have to begin to believe in a story to get passionate about the direction the company is going in ... There's nothing quite as powerful as people feeling they can have impact and make a difference. When you've got that going for you, I think it's a very powerful way to implement change."

W.L. Gore & Associates, manufacturers of the waterproof and breathable fabric Gore-tex and of many other polymer products used in a wide variety of industries, have always encouraged a work environment where employees commit to projects that they want to get involved with.

The company follows a policy where "all commitments are self-commitments". Employees must choose which projects they want to contribute to and accept the responsibilities that come with those choices. Commitments are binding, and reward is based on the contribution made to each team, so that there is both the incentive to take on more tasks and a self-regulating concern about over-commitment. An individual's contribution to a project is assessed in annual reviews by 20 peers; everyone is ranked against the rest of the business unit in terms of contribution. Gore employees have signed up for everything that they are expected to deliver.

In practice

- Leaders need to create followers; they must present compelling reasons why people should want to follow a chosen direction.
- When colleagues have embraced a particular idea and have themselves become passionate about it and when they understand exactly what contribution they personally can make, then the organization is capable of achieving powerful change.
- People are most engaged when they have chosen the projects to which they commit themselves; personal commitment is far more powerful than enforced compliance.
- If rewards genuinely follow delivery against these commitments, the system becomes self-motivating.

SALES COPY

WRITE MORE AND DOUBLE YOUR PROFITS

Andy Maslen

OUR HOUSE IS stuffed with story books. Some we can read in a few minutes, others take an hour or two. Guess which ones my children prefer? This preference for engagement runs deep in the human psyche. And it may go part of the way to explaining why long copy tends to work better than short copy. In fact, it's been shown that the best copy can double your profits.

Now, many otherwise sane and rational people (you know, marketeers, business owners, people like that) get all huffy when advised that longer copy works better. Yet these are the same sane and rational people who want maximum profits. Hmm.

The idea
From a successful mail order and internet marketing business

Here's another great example of a highly successful business that appears to break the rules about web copywriting. I say "appears" because the "rules" he's breaking aren't rules at all—just myths. I looked at the website of a very successful American marketing consultant and found dozens of long pages including one, picked at random, with 3,072 words of copy.

He's not doing this because he *likes* doing it. He's doing it because it *works*.

Long copy is, in general, more responsive than short copy. This applies to web pages. Sales letters. Emails. Ads. Whatever. Some of the world's most profitable mail-order businesses have tested relentlessly, and ended up with 12-, 24-, or even 32-page sales letters. For fun? Yeah right! No, for *profit*. "But people don't read that much copy," the cry goes up.

Well, here's the kicker. Maybe they do read it and maybe they don't. Nobody knows. But what we do know is that they *respond*.

Here's my analysis of what's happening. Let's say you have an eight-screen email sales letter. On every screen you include three cross-heads, each one encapsulating, in some way, a benefit. That's 24 benefits-driven headlines. Your reader may well not be reading word for word. But even if they just skim and scan, they are picking up a couple of dozen reasons to buy.

Or you could send them a one-screen email. With three heads. They might not read this one either (a fact often overlooked by the naysayers), preferring to skim and scan. But now they're getting three reasons to buy instead of 24.

That's an 88 percent REDUCTION in selling power.

In practice
- First you have to find out as much as possible about the target reader for the copy. Then you have to dismantle the product until you have a gut understanding not of what it *is*, but of what it *does*.
- Finally you must create a proposition for buying that is so irresistible that once they're hooked, your reader will happily keep reading until you've finished with them.

PUBLIC RELATIONS
MOVE FROM THE GENERAL TO THE PARTICULAR
Jim Blythe

COMPANIES, AND MARKETERS in particular, are prone to lumping people together in categories. Marketers are great at talking about "the consumer" as if it is one person, finance people talk about "the shareholders" or "the creditors," and (crucially) HR people talk about "the staff." Obviously we need to do this much of the time, if only because it makes conversation easier, but it pays to remember that each of these people thinks of themselves as an individual.

Sometimes it is possible to emphasize this in PR, even though most PR operates through mass media.

The idea
BUPA (the British United Provident Association) is Britain's leading provider of private medical care. Founded in 1947, just ahead of the

introduction of the National Health Service, it remains a vital part of Britain's healthcare infrastructure, filling in gaps in NHS provision.

BUPA wanted to improve its internal culture by creating greater employee involvement in the brand. The aim was to improve service levels and reduce customer complaints, as well as provide employees with a feeling of belonging and team spirit.

BUPA's PR people came up with the concept of "One Life." This was built on the power of one, the concept that a single person can change things. Staff with unusual talents or hobbies were invited to audition to take part in the program of events, and a video was commissioned showing interviews with customers explaining how their experience of dealing with BUPA staff had changed their lives for the better.

This approach moves well beyond the "employee of the month" award (which is often nothing more than a huge embarrassment to the recipient anyway). It celebrates individuality, and expands people out from being considered simply in their role in the organization.

In practice

- Find interesting individuals within your workforce, and celebrate them.
- Give everyone a chance to demonstrate their own individuality.
- Involve customers in talking about the contribution of individual employees.

CUSTOMERS
EMPOWERING YOUR CUSTOMERS
Jeremy Kourdi

THE IMPORTANCE OF providing information to the client should not be underestimated. Information encourages customers to buy and to get the maximum out of the service being provided. Conversely, businesses should be eager to accept information from the consumer in the form of customer satisfaction and feedback surveys.

The idea

From 1989 to 1991, Ryder—the largest truck-leasing business in the world—suffered a steady decline in its business and slipped to second place in its core American market. To address this problem, Ryder recognized the need to use information more effectively to serve customers. Its approach highlighted three key influences affecting current and potential customers:

1. *The need to help customers buy*: for example, by producing a brochure explicitly explaining why they should buy Ryder's insurance, as well as providing another brochure offering other supplies and accessories. Ryder recognized that customers would want to compare products with those of competitors, so it produced a truck comparison chart, highlighting its competitiveness and reassuring potential customers.
2. *The need to help customers use the service*: Ryder provided a free guide to moving to every customer and potential customer, published in Spanish and English.
3. *The need to help customers to continuously adapt their usage*: as well as ensuring that each outlet was well ordered, displaying a strong sense of corporate identity and commitment to customer service, Ryder ensured that there were additional products and services available at its outlets. These included information about the advantages of using Ryder's towing equipment and details of longer-term discount rates.

The benefit of these measures to customers was closely monitored with a customer satisfaction survey, prominently placed in each truck cab. Apart from checking customer satisfaction, they highlighted Ryder's renewed commitment to service, enhancing future sales prospects. This approach contributed to Ryder's ability to turn around its business.

In practice

- Ensure that existing and potential customers have easily available information about the various services and benefits your company offers.
- Collect feedback from clients to ensure their satisfaction and to present an image of your company as customer focused.
- Enable customers to use your product—provide them with instructional information, ideas, online guides, people to talk with—anything that will empower the customer and help them adapt your product to their needs.

SALES

SHOW TO SELL

Patrick Forsyth

SOMETIMES, WITH SOME products, you do better not to talk about something, but to show it—demonstrate it—working. Whether it is a photocopier or a car in which you offer prospects a test drive, the principles are similar.

The idea

Many people do less than a good job of demonstrating. But here I have in mind Panasonic, and a perfectly conducted demo of theirs I once attended ...

What are the key factors if a demonstration is to work and boost the chances of sales success? Many of the basic rules of selling apply here. You must focus on needs, maintain interest (maybe not every aspect of your offering will be of the same level of interest to your customers, and a comprehensive run-through of features may be neither necessary nor appreciated), go through matters following a pre-explained structure and sequence, and above all, talk benefits. The job is to get people to imagine something in use. So remember:

- Set up fast. Make sure you get everything ready. Have you got the key and is the electricity switched on?
- Make it understandable. This is vital. Demonstrations can be spoiled by jargon, gobbledegook, and confusion. Sometimes they consist of an over-lengthy discussion about irrelevant details. Everything must be spelled out so that it is crystal clear. If your prospect finds it easy to understand, that is a good sign. Prompts to imagination can quickly build up a powerful picture.
- It must work! If anything fails to work as you say it should, then from the customer's point of view you have a problem, and quite right too. The experience must be smooth as silk.
- Make them feel how it could be. Everything must be done not just so they "get a feeling for something" in a general sense, but also so they can truly imagine how it would be to own and use the product.
- Project what you want—and what the customer wants. If the customer has asked you to demonstrate something specific, make sure you show how your offering will meet their needs.

In practice

- Throughout the process of demonstrating, the main emphasis is on proof. You are not just talking about your offering, you can show it, and the prospect can try it—and seeing is believing.
- You must work to ensure everything is exactly as you want. There are very few second chances in selling, and in few parts of the process is this truer than when you demonstrate something in this way.
- Time spent beforehand to make sure that you get it right is time very well spent.

MAKE USE OF CHECKLISTS

Patrick Forsyth

EVEN ROUTINE TASKS can give pause for thought. If you do something wrong or incompletely in respect of some detail, how much time does that waste?

The idea

To avoid those pauses for thought—*How does this go?*—and, more important, to remove the necessity to do something again or the cost or inconvenience of not having it complete, consider the role of checklists.

Even a tiny number of cases of uncertainty may make more checklists something that will save time.

In practice

- Consider an example: many companies have a form that is completed when a sales inquiry is received. Completing such a form does not only create a record and act as a prompt to further action; it can also act as a checklist, for instance reminding someone to:
  - Check the inquirer's job title as well as name.
  - Ask how they heard of the company or product.
  - Refer to an account number.
- There might be many such items involved. Many such routine tasks are not both routine and predictable, just as the conversation with the customer may take all sorts of routes and it is easy to forget those questions that might be considered optional, or at least of lesser importance. So a checklist helps. This can be either a form designed to be completed and acting in this way as the completion proceeds, or as a point of reference, literally just a note of what should be done. They can be originated by an individual or department or be an overall organization standing instruction.

All sorts of things lend themselves to this sort of approach; you may like to make a mental note to look, in particular, at things that provide assistance outside your own area of expertise. For instance, if you are a dunce with figures, but occasionally have to undertake some marginal costing, keep the "crib sheet" that helps you do it safely to hand.

LEADERSHIP
QUICK WINS
Jonathan Gifford

MAKING A FEW quick fixes helps to establish a new leader's credentials. However, the search for quick wins should not be obsessive, and it should not be at the expense of colleagues. Most quick wins should be a collective effort.

The idea

When Alan Leighton became chairman of the UK's Royal Mail, the national postal service had recently been renamed Consignia as part of management changes that had attempted to revitalize the organization. The changes had not worked, and the Consignia name—which was widely disliked—was also associated with failure. Leighton changed the name back to the "Royal Mail" (with quick royal permission gained via Charles, Prince of Wales, with whom Leighton had worked in connection with the Prince's Trust, a charity aimed at creating opportunities for young people).

"The Royal Mail was all about its heritage," said Leighton, "which was royal and British, a fact reflected in its uniform and red livery. The core idea was that it was much more than just a company. I knew it would also give me a quick win on taking the chair to reverse the unpopular change and ditch the Consignia name for good; and a quick win is very useful for any new boy. It would help to prove to critics, fed up with lacklustre service, that we really meant business."

On the other hand, Mark E. Van Buren and Todd Safferstone of The Corporate Executive Board Company have written about the "Quick Wins Paradox". Their research demonstrated that an excessive focus on quick wins can lead to insensitive behavior that damages leaders' relationships with their new teams.

As a Harvard Business Review article by the authors reports, "In a study of more than 5,400 new leaders, the authors found that struggling leaders tended to exhibit five behaviors characteristic of people overly intent on securing a quick win. They focused too much on details, reacted negatively to criticism, intimidated others, jumped to conclusions, and micromanaged their direct reports. Some managed to eke out a win anyway, but the fallout was often toxic. The leaders who were thriving in their new roles, by contrast, shared not only a strong focus on results—necessary for early successes— but also excellent change-management skills. They communicated a clear vision, developed constructive relationships, and built team capabilities ... Collective quick wins established credibility and prepared them to lead their teams to harder-won victories."

In practice

- Early quick wins are valuable for any leader. They establish your presence and prove that you have the ability to make things happen. They can impress the organization and the outside world.
- The search for quick wins should not become obsessive and it must not be achieved by railroading changes past your new colleagues.
- Establishing good team relationships and achieving collective quick wins early on will set the scene for the concerted team effort that will be required to tackle more fundamental problems.

PUBLIC RELATIONS
WRITE A REVERSE PYRAMID
Jim Blythe

PRESS RELEASES ARE the mainstay of public relations, yet many firms do not handle them well. Many press releases are simply thinly disguised advertisements, and of course periodicals will not print these for free: they expect to get paid for running advertisements.

Press releases have the big advantage that periodicals do publish them for free. They also have an even bigger advantage—people read them, even when they have skipped past the advertisements.

The key to getting a press release published is to make it as easy as possible for the journalists and editors to use the release as it stands, without having to rewrite it. Newspapers have a lot of space to fill, every day of the week, and going out to research news stories is both time-consuming and expensive. Like any of us, journalists are more than happy to save time and effort—so a well-written press release can be a godsend on a day when news is slack and the paper needs to be filled.

The idea
A press release is a news story about your company. The point here is it should be news—something that is out of the ordinary, and that will be interesting to the newspaper's readers. A story about your latest sales promotion is not interesting unless there is something very unusual about the promotion, but a story about your new factory creating 250 new jobs in a depressed area is interesting.

The story needs to be written in a way that journalists and editors relate to. Journalists are trained to write in a "reverse pyramid" style. The whole story is contained in the headline, then each paragraph offers a little more detail: the intention is that the story can be cut from the bottom by a subeditor to fit the available space. The best way to get the idea of how to do this is to read some newspaper stories: it is easy to see how the story is complete at each paragraph.

Press releases should also be written for the specific periodical. A story about a breakthrough in engineering techniques might be interesting to an engineering trade journal, but would not be interesting to *Cosmopolitan*: an article about your new female chief engineer would have the reverse characteristics.

In practice

- Write in the style of the journal you are aiming for.
- The press release must be news—not just a thinly disguised advertisement.
- Make things easy for the journalists by writing in a reverse pyramid style.
- Cultivate your local newspaper—get friendly with the journalist who is most likely to be interested in what you have to say, then when you have a story it will be more likely to be used.

BUSINESS SKILLS
THE SOUND OF SILENCE
Patrick Forsyth

OF COURSE WHAT you say and how you say it are of prime importance to the success of your presentation, but so too is what you don't say. A good presentation will contain some pauses. The dramatic pause is a well known device, well used by politicians and actors, but many presenters are wary of the pause and a prime symptom of nerves or lack of experience is to speak too quickly and pause hardly at all; even on some occasions forgetting to breathe.

The idea

Slow your pace and learn to pause—the effect on the variety of your verbal presentation and the power it can add to emphasis is worthwhile and useful.

In practice

- You need to get used to how long a pause is or should be. When people dry up it worries them, but often the pause seems much longer to the presenter than to the audience. Try counting to yourself and decide what makes an appropriate pause, then you can do this as you present when a real pause is necessary.

- In a pause that does—inadvertently—get out of hand, divide it in two to render it unnoticeable. Thus if you do fumble trying to think what comes next say something—"There's another point I wanted to make here, ah yes..."—it gives you a moment to think, halves the pause and is hardly evident.

- Try a pause between main points. Round off one point with a powerful statement, give it a few seconds to sink in and then proceed. The combination of a powerful sign off from one point, a pause and a change of tone as you move on contributes to a lively approach.

- Use this with repetition. A dramatic pause is... A dramatic pause is... A dramatic pause is... For some things, repeating three times like this works well.

- Let a few moments of silence add positively to your presentations and it will soon become a habit that is easy to apply.

BUSINESS SKILLS
FOLLOW YOUR INSTINCTS
Jonathan Gifford

LEADERS ACQUIRE VERY good business instincts. These instincts represent the distillation of many years of experience, but they are often experienced as a kind of emotional reaction; a "gut feeling" that a decision is right.

Scientific evidence strongly suggests that we are right to trust these instincts: our emotional response system can be faster to make a "decision" than our conscious mind.

The idea

Neuroscientists Antonio Damasio and Antoine Becher devised an ingenious experiment known as the Iowa Gambling Task. Volunteers were asked to pick cards from four separate piles; the cards awarded money prizes or exacted penalties but were rigged so that two of the stacks of cards offered relatively higher payouts but also occasional heavy fines. These piles of cards were the ones to avoid; playing the other stacks of cards produced a better overall result. The researchers wired up the volunteers to detect signs of stress and anxiety in the electrical conductance of their skin.

After only 10 cards had been drawn, volunteers showed signs of unconscious anxiety when they reached for cards from the "bad" packs. It took 50 cards before volunteers began consistently to draw cards only from the "good" packs; it took 80 cards before the average volunteer could explain why they were favoring the good packs. Our emotions can be faster to react than our conscious minds.

Richard Branson, chairman of Virgin Group, encourages leaders to engage their emotions at work: "Your instincts and emotions are there to help you. They are there to make things easier. For me, business is a 'gut feeling', and if it ever ceased to be so, I think I would give it up tomorrow. By 'gut feeling', I mean that I've developed a natural aptitude, tempered by huge amounts of experience, that tends to point me in the right direction rather than the wrong one. As a result, it gives me the confidence to make better decisions."

Anita Roddick, founder of the Body Shop, built the success of her cosmetics and body-care retail chain largely on her ground-breaking championship of social issues. The company struggled when it attempted to move into the USA market, and Roddick says that she failed to follow her gut instincts.

"Some people might say I interfere too much, but in America I felt I let myself be persuaded by others ... When sales began falling, we brought in a whole group of marketing people and product development people and they just looked around at what was going on in the marketplace and said we should do the same. I should have stepped in and told them that if that's the way the market is going, we should go in the opposite direction."

In practice

- Our emotions, based on our experiences, are faster to react than our conscious minds; we feel scared or nervous before we can explain why, but for what turn out to be good reasons.
- Leaders should engage with their emotions at work: it is a mistake to believe that "cool, detached rationality" is the best way to approach every decision.
- You understand your organization better than nearly anyone else. Expert advice will be based on current realities, whereas your hunch about the future may very well be correct.

SALES
FOLLOW UP ON CUSTOMERS LATER
Jim Blythe

FOLLOWING UP ON customers after a sale is something few companies practice in any serious way, and when they do it is usually through a half-hearted "courtesy call" a few days after the purchase, in the course of which the caller makes a clumsy attempt to sell the customer something else. Car dealers rarely call their customers (say) two years after the sale with the idea of seeing if the customer is ready for a trade-in: yet this seems like an obvious thing to do, since the dealer already knows the customer's car, and will have a fair idea of its worth. This is, of course, one of the basic tenets of relationship marketing—but few companies do it.

Giving people time to recover from the experience of making a major purchase is also important—following up too quickly can seem over-eager. The typical reaction from a customer might be "I just spent £800 with you, what more do you want?"

The idea

The Futon Shop follow up on sales approximately one year later, offering add-on products such as drawers to fit under the futon, covers, cleaning, and so forth. After a year the customer has become used to the futon being around, and is ready for extras in a way that he or she was not at the time of purchase (obviously, or they would have bought the extras at the time of buying the original product). The customers have also had the chance to recover from the initial investment.

In general, customers welcome the approach, because they are ready to spend again and find the approach reassuring rather than threatening.

In practice

- You need to keep very good records, and diarize things well.
- You need something of real value to offer the customers.
- Calculating the appropriate time gap is a matter of considering the value of the initial purchase, and the type of add-on you are offering.
- Try to avoid calling it a "courtesy call"—people are wise to it, and it is bad to start off by lying to your customers.

CUSTOMERS
MASS CUSTOMIZATION
Jeremy Kourdi

LARGE-SCALE INFORMATION gathering and storing enables the provision of a high-quality, personalized service for each client. By adding value to your product, you can shut out competitors and ensure repeat business.

The idea

By applying information technology effectively, and training all of its employees to use information, the Ritz-Carlton hotel chain has, over the last 15 years, developed into one of the most successful luxury hotel chains in the world, providing customers with a highly personalized service. The Ritz-Carlton strategy was quite simple: to differentiate itself from its competitors by offering distinctive service and customer value at a competitive price.

What was uncommon, however, was the emphasis on several key principles, which were underpinned by a blend of strong leadership and the successful management and application of technology. These principles included:

- A vision of an efficient, personalized service. It was important to ensure employees were committed to providing a quality service. IT systems were standardized throughout the business, and an organizational culture was developed that emphasized the need to capture and disseminate useful information about each individual customer.
- The desire to ensure hotels operated error-free and to retain customers through a precision marketing strategy. To achieve this, Ritz-Carlton spent years accumulating in-depth knowledge about its work processes, then combined technology with individual skills and innovation, which has enabled Ritz-Carlton to track individual customer preferences.

For instance, employees observe guests, record their preferences, and store the data on a company-wide information network. This enables other employees to reuse the information and provide the most personalized service available, leveraging their contact with the customer to shut out competitors. When customers check in, they receive the room and location they prefer, and throughout their stay Ritz-Carlton supervisors scrutinize relevant details for each customer so that they can personalize service, providing extra pillows, favorite beverages, preferred newspapers, and so forth.

The Ritz-Carlton approach is a great example of the power of mass customization—the ability to deliver rapidly, efficiently, and profitably a range of products and services satisfying each individual customer.

In practice

- Utilize employees at every level within your company, as well as the benefits of technology, to listen to your market at a uniquely advanced level.
- Store information on clients in an easily accessible way, to ensure that a distinguished level of personalized quality is provided.
- Swiftly reorganize people, information, and processes when necessary in order to deliver the benefits of a highly customized and attentive service.

BUSINESS SKILLS
OVER TO YOU
Patrick Forsyth

FOR MANAGERS, IF a task must be done, but you cannot get to it, then the best way to give yourself more time is to delegate it to someone else. This is eminently desirable and yet, for some, curiously difficult.

So let's look at the difficulties. Delegating is a risk. Something may go wrong and, what is more, as the manager, you may be blamed. So, despite the fact that the risk can be minimized, there is temptation to hang on to things. This makes for two problems: you have too much to do (particularly too many routine tasks) and this keeps you from giving due attention to things that are clear priorities. And staff members do not like it, so motivation—and productivity on the things they are doing—will also be adversely affected.

An additional fear is not that the other person will not be able to cope, but that they will cope too well—being better than you. But this is not a reason that should put you off delegating—the potential rewards are too great. Besides, people are more likely to do things differently and that can help development of both individuals and methods.

The idea

So don't do it—delegate.

The amount you can do if you delegate successfully is way beyond the improvement in productivity you can hope to achieve in any other way. All that is necessary to make delegation successful is a considered and systematic approach to the process such as that detailed in Appendix 2.

In practice

What does successful delegation achieve? There are five key results:

- It creates opportunity for development and accelerated experience for those to whom matters are delegated.
- It builds morale (precisely because of the opportunity noted above) through the motivational effect of greater job satisfaction, and achievement long and short term in the job (and ultimately beyond it).
- It has broader motivational effects around a team, as well as on the individual.

In addition, there are advantages to you. As a result of the time freed up:

- Time and effort can be concentrated on those aspects of your job that are key to the achievement of objectives.
- A more considered, or creative, approach can be brought to bear, uncluttered by matters that may distract or prevent a broad-brush or longer-term perspective.

PUBLIC RELATIONS
161 DEVELOP YOUR NEWS SENSITIVITY
Jim Blythe

NEWS HAPPENS ALL the time, and many PR firms concentrate on creating it rather than on latching onto it. However, there are only so many news stories that can come from a firm—and really very few that are all that riveting for the average audience.

On the other hand, though, there may be many news stories out there that have a bearing on your industry and on which you could comment for the news.

The idea

Amnesty International made good use of the 1999 visit of Jiang Zemin to Britain. Obviously the news media were eager to report the visit, so a week before the arrival of the Chinese President, Amnesty issued a press release detailing China's human rights violations and offering to provide a spokesperson during the visit. This moved human rights onto the news agenda, and also provided the press with a more newsworthy scenario—simply showing the President meeting the Prime Minister or the Queen is one thing, but having a controversy and, more importantly, having a few pointed questions to ask him was invaluable.

During the visit Amnesty's head of press, Richard Bunting, appeared on Channel 5 News, BBC's *Newsnight*, and a live in-studio debate about human rights in China. During the President's visit, protesters appeared wherever he made a public appearance: the Metropolitan Police's efforts to protect him from embarrassing encounters backfired in PR terms because it created even more possibilities for TV news crews to collect dramatic footage of the apparent suppression of peaceful protest in Britain.

In practice

- Monitor the news for any upcoming story that might have resonance for you.
- Prepare beforehand—in particular, flag up the issue to the press.
- Controversy is good. It can only help your situation.

PERFORMANCE
ENCOURAGE DIVERSITY
Jonathan Gifford

Diversity in any ecosystem is essential to its survival: the different adaptations of various organisms within the system allow some to flourish when changing conditions condemn others to decline.

Organizations must encourage diversity, in terms of the people that they employ and the systems that they operate, to help them to adapt to increasingly rapid rates of change.

The idea
When the intelligence centre at Bletchley Park was set up in the UK during World War II to decode enemy ciphers, it recruited people from a wide range of backgrounds, including mathematicians, chess champions, linguists and crossword puzzle solvers.

The different mental disciplines and abilities that each member of the team brought to the task enabled the dramatic breakthroughs that a team composed only of mathematicians, for example, might not have achieved.

As Gary Hamel, research fellow at Harvard Business School, highlights: "The diversity of any system determines its ability to adapt. Greater diversity—of thought, skills, attitudes and capabilities—equals a greater range of adaptive responses. The risk in a fast-changing world is that a company becomes over-adapted to a particular ecological niche ... As change accelerates, investing in diversity is not a luxury, it's a survival strategy."

Stuart Miller, former CEO and chairman of the energy exploration and marketing group, Royal Dutch Shell, talks of the benefits that come from working with a multi-national and multi-ethnic group of colleagues.

"You begin to find that you get some really neat ideas generated from creating a culture where people of different ethnicities, cultures, backgrounds [and] countries ... come together. Invariably, you find that the best ideas come from this mosaic of players working together in a team on a project. They will come up with an answer that is different from what any one of them would have come up with individually."

In practice

- Organizations that are very homogeneous are badly equipped to deal with change: the skills and mental attitudes that have become entrenched in the organization are unlikely to deal well with changing situations and environments.
- There is an ingrained tendency to recruit people who will fit into the organization's existing culture: people who are "like us". Build teams of people with different attitudes, skills and experiences.
- Encourage the team to continue to broaden their experience whenever possible; create chances for them to learn about areas outside of their own specialization.
- Companies whose employees come from a wide variety of cultural and ethnic backgrounds provide the organization with a competitive advantage; a rich cultural mix tends to generate innovative approaches, and safeguards the organization against parochialism.

MARKETING
TAP INTO COUNTRY-OF-ORIGIN EFFECT
Jim Blythe

IF YOU HAVE a product that can be exported (and who doesn't?) you might be able to use country-of-origin effect to your advantage. Country-of-origin effect is the phenomenon by which products and brands are colored by consumers' opinions about the country the product comes from—and for many firms it can work greatly to their advantage.

For example, we tend to believe that Germans are good engineers, that the French produce great food, the Belgians make good chocolate, and the Americans are good at fast food. There are, no doubt, bad German engineers, incompetent French chefs, poor-quality Belgian chocolatiers, and very slow American restaurants, but the overall impression remains.

The idea

Cachaca is a Brazilian spirit made from sugar, rather like a white rum. Until recently, cachaca was virtually unknown outside Brazil, since only about 2 percent of cachaca production is exported. This all changed, however, when Sagatiba was launched onto the British drinks market in 2005.

The company's advertising agency, Saatchi & Saatchi, decided to use a Brazilian theme. The most famous icon of Brazil is, of course, the statue of Christ the Redeemer that stands on the Corcovado in Rio de Janeiro. Saatchi & Saatchi was aiming for a young audience, so it began by (controversially) hiring graffiti artists to spray images of Christ the Redeemer on walls all over the East End of London. It also commissioned an image of a pool player resting his arms on a cue balanced across his shoulders—imitating the pose of the statue.

Ultimately, Sagatiba seeks to tap into British perceptions of Brazil— hence the use of Christ the Redeemer. The British advertising bears no relationship to the way the product is marketed in Brazil (where the slogan "O que e Sagatiba?" or "What is Sagatiba?" is used in adverts showing jungle tribespeople worshiping the god Sagatiba, a Japanese monster movie with Sagatiba as the name of the monster, and even a naked man whose girlfriend says "Sagatiba" in a sultry voice). Sagatiba has also tapped into other Brazilian icons, soccer and samba drumming, but these have not played as well as the Christ the Redeemer icon.

In practice

- Ensure that the perception you tap into is the one that the target audience has of your country—this is likely to be different from your own perception.

- Test the alternatives. There may be more than one icon that you could use, but only one will be the most effective one.
- Never, ever, simply translate your existing advertising into a foreign language. Cultural differences go well beyond language.
- Always check with people who live in the country you are targeting. They may sometimes be wrong, but as a foreigner you will almost always be wrong if you try to guess how consumers will react.

SALES
GET THE COMPETITION INTO THE DISCUSSION
Patrick Forsyth

IT IS AXIOMATIC that decrying the competition is not a good idea. If you say to a customer that company X is rubbish, it always turns out that the person deals with them, likes them, or their brother-in-law works for them. Rather than giving you an edge, it can easily be self-defeating: it makes you sound defensive, arrogant, or just plain spiteful. None are attractive characteristics, or likely to help create rapport or a good relationship. But dealing with the question of the competition may be unavoidable in a conversation.

The idea
From many a different industry ...

If a customer brings a competitor into the conversation, especially if they ask your opinion of it—"How do you compare with X?"—the best tactic may be to praise your rival. Indeed it may well work best to lay it on with a trowel: "From what I hear the company has a good reputation, makes excellent products, and always seems to deliver on time." Such a statement may well prompt a response that pulls back a bit. "We've done some business with them, and they're fine," your customer might reply, "but I wouldn't go that far. We did have one delivery problem." This has brought you into a conversation that helps you position the customer's relationship with competitors and attitude to them, and this should make what comes next easier. Even if the customer agrees with you, the exchange might be useful. At the least, it might help you decide such a relationship is impossible to challenge, and save you time as you simply go on to another prospect.

As a secondary tactic, just asking can cast doubt. Say, "What do you think of their service?" You're not knocking your rival, but it sounds just a little as if you know it isn't perfect. The reply might help you identify chinks in the relationship that you can use to strengthen your own case.

In practice
- Certainly this is an area in which to take care. Your instinct may be to rubbish the competition (especially if you know you can make a stronger case), but it's wiser to take a more considered approach.

PUBLIC RELATIONS
CREATE A PHOTO OPPORTUNITY
Jim Blythe

THEY SAY THAT a picture is worth a thousand words. For most newspapers and magazines a striking picture can take up more space than a thousand words, and takes a great deal less effort to produce. Getting the photographers along to your media event will make the story a great deal more publishable, and will also create a great deal more interest among your publics.

For this to happen, the story must be visually exciting as well as newsworthy, of course. Finding something that will make a good news photograph is a challenge, but it is a challenge that can be met, with a little creative thinking.

The idea

A razor manufacturer that had a new type of blade to promote offered a £1,000 charity donation on behalf of bearded celebrities who were prepared to have their beards shaved off publicly. The company contacted a rock star, an MP, and a comedy actor, all of whom agreed to take part. The company set up a barber's chair in Parliament Square in Central London, and invited the press to send photographers along.

The resultant pictures were widely used, and of course the company was mentioned in many of the stories (although the blade itself wasn't). The company capitalized on the event by using its own photographs of the occasion in its advertising, so readers made the connection between the company and the stunt.

In practice

- Ensure that you have something photogenic: celebrities are always good, but other possibilities might suggest themselves.
- Don't forget to invite television news crews as well. Good photo opportunities are also good video opportunities.
- You will need to back up the story with other communications, e.g., advertising, if readers are going to make the connection.

MANAGING MEETINGS
CANCELLATION AS A TIME SAVER
Patrick Forsyth

THIS IS A brief point, and links to the topic of meetings, which crops up in more than one section. There is an issue here that can waste large amounts of time. It is surprising and curious how meetings that are scheduled for a good reason still run even when not only has the good reason gone but everyone knows it has gone. It is difficult to understand. Perhaps someone thinks it is too late to cancel (I would rather hear two minutes before the meeting that it is canceled than turn up and waste time), or they think that it will still be useful as minor matters can be dealt with "as the people are coming together anyway."

The idea

Usually the thinking above is wrong. It is better to cancel the meeting, or postpone it if the main reason for it has not gone away forever. The idea here is simply to do this and not be sidetracked into allowing time to be wasted.

In practice

- This principle is especially true of regular series of meetings. The example of ten meetings being held through a year is the kind of thing where it is often better to schedule ten knowing you are in fact likely only to need eight or nine. The disruption of one dropped is very much less than pulling an extra one together at short notice, and this should become the habit. Never go ahead just because it is "the regular meeting" or you will waste time.
- There is even a case for refusing to use words such as weekly or monthly in the title of a meeting; it can end up prompting meetings that prove useless.

BUSINESS SKILLS
BE AUTHENTIC
Jonathan Gifford

IT IS OFTEN believed that leaders need to control their emotions and to be able to present a "front" to their team which does not reflect their inner feelings. This has led to discussion about "the masks of leadership" and debate as to whether leaders can afford to be truly authentic.

The idea

The concept of the "masks of leadership" belongs to a bygone age.

Leaders must be authentic. People need to see the human process that has led a leader to their current position; only then can they genuinely believe in, and be inspired by, the leader's conviction.

Bill George, former chairman and CEO of Medtronics and co-author with Peter Sims of *True North: Discover your authentic leadership*, sets out five dimensions of authentic leadership.

1. Pursuing purpose with passion: a leader's passions demonstrate the true purpose of their leadership.
2. Practising solid values: integrity is required of every authentic leader.
3. Leading with the heart: authentic leaders lead with their hearts as well as their head.
4. Establishing enduring relationships: people demand a personal relationship with their leaders as a guarantee of trust and commitment.
5. Demonstrating self-discipline: authentic leaders set high standards for themselves and expect the same from others.

Dieter Zetsche, Chairman of Daimler AG and Head of Mercedes Benz Cars, puts the point succinctly: "You have to be the real deal. Don't pretend to be John Wayne if that description doesn't fit you. And if you are John Wayne, don't pretend to be Woody Allen."

In practice
* Be guided by your passion: what you really care about is what you really want to do.
* Show integrity in all that you do; establish the organization's core values, promulgate them and live by them.
* Be prepared to share your human doubts, fears and uncertainties with your team; empathize with your colleagues; make decisions with your heart as well as your head.
* Allow colleagues to see you as a person and not only as a figurehead; leaders need to engage with people at an emotional level to be able to inspire trust and gain commitment.
* Be self-disciplined. Take responsibility and hold others accountable for their own decisions.

STRATEGY
SCENARIO PLANNING
Jeremy Kourdi

SCENARIO PLANNING ENABLES organizations to rehearse the future, to walk the battlefield before battle commences so that they are better prepared. Scenarios are not about predicting future events. Their value lies in helping businesses understand the forces that are shaping the future. They challenge our assumptions.

The idea

In the 1960s, Pierre Wack, Royal Dutch/Shell's head of group planning, asked executives to imagine tomorrow. This promoted sophisticated and responsive strategic thinking about the current situation, by enabling them to detect and understand changes. Pierre Wack wanted to know whether there were other factors in the supply of oil, besides technical availability, that might be uncertain in the future. He listed stakeholders and questioned the position of governments in oil-producing countries: would they continue increasing production year on year? By exploring the possible changes to government policy, it became apparent that these governments were unlikely to remain amenable to Shell's activities. Many oil-producing countries did not need an increase in income. They had the upper hand, and the overwhelming logic for the oil-producing countries was to reduce supply, increase prices, and conserve their reserves.

When the 1973 Arab–Israeli War limited the supply of oil, prices rose fivefold. Fortunately for Shell, Wack's scenario work meant Shell was better prepared than its competitors to adapt to the new situation—saving billions of dollars, it climbed from seventh to second place in the industry's profitability league table. It knew which governments to lobby, how to approach them, where to diversify, and what action to take with each OPEC member.

Scenario planning enables leaders to manage uncertainty and

risk. Above all, scenarios help firms to understand the dynamics of the business environment, recognize new opportunities, assess strategic options, and take long-term decisions.

In practice

- Scenarios are not predictions: they are used to understand the forces shaping the future. What matters is not knowing exactly what the future will look like, but understanding the general direction in which it is moving—and why.
- Plan and structure the scenario process: for example, by agreeing who will be involved.
- Discuss possible futures (usually by working back from a possible view of the future).
- Develop the scenarios in greater detail.
- Analyze the scenarios: why they might occur, what you would do if they did.
- Use the scenarios to shape decisions and priorities.

CUSTOMERS
169 LOVE YOUR CUSTOMERS, LOVE WHAT THEY LOVE
Jim Blythe

GETTING CLOSE TO the customers is a no-brainer. The better we understand them, the better we can serve them and the more likely they are to come back. However, most firms tend to think of "the customer" as being someone very different from "the staff."

Yet in many cases the people running the business have very similar interests to the people who come to spend their money there. This is especially true in retail—people working in clothes stores have an interest in fashion, people working in music stores are usually keen musicians, people who become chefs have an interest in good food, and so forth. The question is, how do we turn our love of these things into a love of the customers?

The idea

Tim Waterstone opened his first bookstore in 1982: he needed a job, having just been fired by W. H. Smith. From the start he aimed to share his own love of books. Customers were encouraged to browse, to the extent that Waterstone provided seating so that people could read the books for a while if they wanted to. There is nothing to stop someone sitting all morning reading, but in practice few people do this—they might read a few pages, or even a chapter, but (since they are obviously book lovers) most of them buy the book to read it at home. Staff are chosen for their love of books, and for their knowledge of specific types of book—they are expected to be able to talk to customers on an equal level.

Senior management appear on the corporate website almost hidden behind their favorite books: each has made a list of the books that have shaped their lives. Waterstone's staff are always helpful, always knowledgeable, not because they have been through a customer relations training course but because they enjoy sharing their love of books with like-minded people.

In practice

* Decide why you wanted to work in the industry you work in.
* Think about your customers—do they have the same interest?
* Decide what you can do to encourage their interest and help them enjoy your mutual enthusiasm.
* Now find out whether your staff and colleagues feel the same.

BUSINESS SKILLS
GAINING ACCEPTANCE
Patrick Forsyth

THERE IS MORE to be achieved than just putting across the content of your presentation. Here we consider that you may well want people to agree with your ideas.

The idea

If you want to get people's agreement to something, you have to do more than just inform and impress them; you must incorporate some additional techniques into what you do—you must make your message persuasive and credible.

In practice

- Acceptance can be prompted in a number of ways, specifically by:
  - Relating to the specific group: general points and arguments may not be as readily accepted as those carefully tailored to the nature and experience of a specific audience (with some topics, this is best interpreted as describing how things will affect them or what they will do for them).
  - Provide proof: certainly if you want to achieve acceptance, you need to offer something other than your word—as the speaker you may very well be seen as having a vested interest in your own ideas. Thus adding opinion, references or quoting test results from elsewhere and preferably from a respected and/ or comparable source strengthens your case. This is evidenced by our experience in something like buying a car: are you most likely to believe the salesman who says, "This model will do more than fifty miles per gallon," or the one who says, "Tests done by the magazine *What Car?* showed that this model does 52 miles per gallon."? Most of us will be more convinced by the latter.
- It is particularly important not to forget feedback during this important stage:
  - Watch for signs (nodding, fidgeting, whispered conversation, and expressions) as to how your message is going down—try to scan the whole audience (you need in any case to maintain good eye contact around the group).
  - Listen too for signs—a restless audience, for example, actually has its own unmistakable sound.
  - Ask for feedback. There are certainly many presentations where asking questions of the group is perfectly acceptable and it may be expected—even a brief show of hands may assist you.

- Aim to build in answers to any objections that you may feel will be in the mind of members of the audience, either mentioning the fact: "I know what you are thinking; it can't be done in the time. Well, I believe it can. Let me tell you how..." Or by not making a specific mention, but simply building in information intended to remove fears.
- Even if you build in answers to likely disagreement, some may still surface, so you have always to be ready to expand your proof as you go.

ONLINE MARKETING
CHECK OUT THE BLOGS
Jim Blythe

THERE ARE MANY weblogs and forums out there, some of which are dedicated to sharing experiences of dealing with local businesses. For example, TripAdvisor carries customer reviews of hotels throughout the world.

The problem for the businesses is that the comments tend to be derogatory. People are much more likely to vent their spleen on a website than they are to be complimentary, although sometimes people feel moved to be nice about somewhere. Monitoring the blogs is therefore an important PR activity—as is ensuring that people say nice things about you.

The idea
Check the blogs regularly. Most of them offer the businesses a right to reply—and you should seize the opportunity. Often you will be able to identify the person making the complaint, and can contact them to make amends—if you make this offer on the blog itself, it will go a long way toward repairing the damage.

Straight refutation of the complaint, or (worse) self-justification, can be seriously counterproductive. You need to state your case, sure, but you can be a little humble about it!

Don't be tempted to get a friend to post a glowing recommendation on the blog. They rarely read true, and the blog master will take exception to it if you are found out.

In practice

- Be prepared to admit it if things went wrong and it was your fault.
- Learn from the comments.
- Don't be afraid to contact people who complained. Only good things can come of it—and people are less likely to be vitriolic if they are dealing with a real person rather than a weblog.

MANAGING
TRANSFORM THE TEAM
Jonathan Gifford

EFFECTIVE LEADERS DO not direct the team from "outside". They join the team and motivate people by establishing goals and directions with which people genuinely identify. The purpose of the organization becomes a common purpose, and people start to take ownership of their work.

The idea

Leadership authority James MacGregor Burns introduced the concept of Transformational Leadership. He contrasts this with Transactional Leadership, in which leaders essentially "do a deal" with the people they lead, exchanging one thing of value for another—giving people money for their labor being the obvious example of such a transaction.

Transformational Leadership is different. This happens, Burns argues, when "one or more persons engage with others in such a way that leaders and followers raise one another to higher levels of motivation". This kind of leadership is a "transformation" not an "exchange". It is a mutual process in which leaders and followers are all part of the same endeavor; people encourage and support each other; they engage with the purpose of the organization and take ownership of their work. Transformational leaders must lead by example; they will need to earn their colleagues' trust, admiration, loyalty and respect.

Jarvis Snook, CEO of UK building group Rok, recalls his experience as a works manager with a local building firm earlier in his career. He talks about the workforce: "They were paid the minimum the industry could get away with, and no one asked them their view or opinion. Their main reason for coming in to work was to have a chat with their mates. I talked to them about customer service—'If Mrs Jones wants her back bedroom decorated in time for Christmas, then stay on an hour extra in the evening and we'll pay you the overtime.' The company hadn't done that before; it was steeped in process— the workforce was just a tool." Performance improved and Snook was appointed to the board of the company. "It took me a while to work out what I'd done, but I'd changed the workers' perception of themselves; they became a valued part of the company, not a tool. They were more energized about what they were delivering for the business."

In practice
- Effective leaders work as part of the team. They motivate and inspire people as part of a group effort.
- Transformational Leadership requires impressive personal characteristics; the successful leader will need to earn people's trust, admiration, loyalty and respect.
- Successful transformation begins to support itself; colleagues encourage each other; leaders are themselves motivated and supported by their teams.
- People take ownership of their work and are personally rewarded by the organization's success.

COMPETITION
DON'T COMPETE
Jim Blythe

MOST OF THE jargon of business strategy is derived from warfare. Campaigns, guerrilla attacks, capturing markets, and so forth make us think in terms of killing off the opposition, seizing their territory, and establishing a new regime with ourselves as leaders. There is no reason why business should be a battleground, however. It is perfectly possible to cooperate rather than compete—provided you stay within the law.

Cooperation with non-competitors has been a common marketing ploy for many years: takeaway food outlets cooperating with video rental stores, for example, and tourist attractions cooperating with local hoteliers are obvious partners. Increasingly, though, there is a trend for competitors in the same industry to look for joint projects as a way of cutting development costs—car manufacturers cooperating on design (the Ford Galaxy, VW Sharan, and Seat Alhambra are essentially the same car). This idea can be extended considerably, however.

The idea
When Communism ended in most of Eastern Europe in 1989, Western manufacturers soon realized that there would be a relaxation of trade restrictions between East and West, and the West would be flooded with shoddy, but extremely cheap, Eastern European products. Skoda was already establishing itself in the West, and was actually producing some half-decent cars (even if the designs were somewhat old-fashioned). Their reputation for clunky reliability made them a threat, but rather than compete head-on with them, and perhaps risking entering a price war if Skoda engineers could recapture their former days of glory, VW decided to cooperate.

Investment by VW in Skoda was not just financial. VW took over Skoda in 1991 and redesigned the plant, re-educated the engineers, and cooperated with them in developing new vehicles. Unlike many West German companies, who simply bought out Eastern competitors and closed them down, VW went the cooperative route, allowing Skoda to build its own brand and ultimately to take over all aspects of car marketing, from design through to showrooms. Most other Eastern European car manufacturers have sunk without trace, while Skoda has been able to take advantage of Eastern Europe's low overheads and salaries and VW's technical assistance to flatten the opposition.

Skoda operates independently of VW, but is a means of increasing VW's customer base and shutting out possible competitors from low-cost countries. As an investment, that has to be better than competing.

In practice

- The cooperation must have benefits for both parties—make sure you're bringing something to the party.
- It should not attract the attention of monopolies regulators—you can't collude to carve up markets!
- Competitive synergies need to be apparent so that you don't simply cannibalize each other's existing markets. You should be cooperating in order to compete better against other firms.
- You don't need to buy out the competitor. You can often cooperate effectively in other ways.

SALES COPY
WHAT DO YOU MEAN "IF"?
Andy Maslen

GET PEOPLE CRAVING or longing for your product (or, to be more precise, feeling that your product can deliver whatever it is they're truly longing for or craving) and you're almost home. But there's still one hurdle you have to leap before you've made the sale. Every sales representative worth their salt knows all about it. Even though it's hard to do. Ready?

You have to ask for the order. So let's talk about the call to action (again). Whatever you're writing, from press releases to Google Adwords, emails to sales letters, you have a commercial goal in mind. That translates into an action your reader must take.

The idea
From a furniture retailer

When you're asking for the order, the trick is getting your reader to take the action using all the word power you can muster. Here's what not to write (from a mail-order furniture retailer) ...

If you would like to order ...

If? IF??? What do you mean "If"?

You've just spent a day, a week, or a month planning, empathizing with your reader, researching your subject, structuring your sales copy, writing the damn stuff, then editing, polishing, and proofreading and you mean to tell me you're allowing them to imagine there's a possibility they won't buy? No. This is no place for the conditional mood. Instead, *command* them to buy. That means using the imperative mood. Like this:

Order today.

Better yet,

Order today and you also receive this package of extra goodies worth £29.99.

Or,

Subscribe now and save 30% off the full rate.

Or,

Register now and bring a colleague along for half-price.

Using the mood of command doesn't mean your reader *will* place that order. But it will push the waverers off the fence, some onto your side. You could go further than the straightforward statement of the product or service being ordered and recap your main benefit and offer. When you're writing your call to action, here's a checklist of language attributes. Your call to action should be:

- Clear.
- Short.
- Simple.
- Direct.
- Urgent.
- Irresistible.

If nobody never asked for nothing, nobody would never buy nothing. [*Er, what?—Ed.*] Oh, all right. In Plain English, if you don't ask, you don't get. Don't be afraid to be specific in asking your reader for what you want. You might be pleasantly surprised.

In practice

- Don't ask for the order, *tell* them to order.
- If you find an errant "If you would like to place an order ..." at the start of your call to action, delete it and replace with "Order today and you will ..."

LEADERSHIP
HERDING CATS
Jonathan Gifford

ONE OF THE hardest leadership tasks is leading without the usual implied back-up of "command". People who are leading any kind of federation of equals do not have the same levers of power that are available to other leaders. It is more like "herding cats".

The idea

Harvard Business School professor Allen Grossman spent six years as president and CEO of Outward Bound USA. His abiding interest is in the creation of high-performance non-profit organizations:

"Someone described the task of running a federation as herding cats. The people in the organization were wonderful, but they had a deeply held cultural orientation for independence on the local level. I was the national CEO. I had to build consensus and convince local groups to agree that organizational change was not only in Outward Bound's best interest, but in their own self-interest as well. It was a really overwhelming and, at times, daunting challenge."

Narayana Murthy, co-founder and CEO of India's Infosys Technologies Ltd, helped to pioneer the Infosys concept of a Global Delivery System, optimizing costs and allowing around-the-clock project input from different time zones. Murthy describes a leader's role in bringing together many disparate elements of a loosely-bound organization as "telling a story" and "creating hope".

"The leader has to create hope. He has to create a plausible story about a better future for the organization: everyone should be able to see the rainbow and catch a part of it. This requires creating trust in people. And to create trust, the leader has to subscribe to a value system: a protocol for behavior that enhances the confidence, commitment and enthusiasm of the people. Compliance to a value system creates the environment for people to have high aspirations, self esteem, belief in fundamental values, confidence in the future and the enthusiasm necessary to take up apparently difficult tasks."

In practice
- Some leadership tasks do not have the usual elements of direct management. Teams and individuals may not report directly to the leader, who therefore has no scope to influence behavior by means of the usual rewards and sanctions.
- In these circumstances, a leader relies on diplomacy and consensus-building and on agreement that success for the group as a whole results in success for the individual members of the group.
- This becomes challenging when the leader needs to instigate change at an organizational level in order to achieve greater success for the organization as a whole.

- Creating an overall value system, and a group "story" that people can engage with on a fundamental level, leads people to willingly take on tasks that move the organization towards its expressed goal.

SELF-HELP
LET THE PLANT GROW
Patrick Forsyth

CONCENTRATING ON PRIORITIES is a key factor in good time management. These need deciding, and also in the light of changing circumstances they may need ongoing review and adjustment.

That said, some people use up hours of valuable time thereafter reviewing their decisions again and again to double-check them. In effect it is like digging up a plant to look at the roots to see if it is growing well. Some people seem to seek constant reassurance about their decisions, and this can just waste time and is also, in my view, a certain route to stress.

The idea

Trust your decisions about priorities. Having considered their selection thoroughly, you make a decision. There is no reason at that point to doubt that it is other than a good one. And, in any case, no amount of further review will change the fact that you can do only one thing at a time, and, however illogical, it is this that a long list of things to do sometimes prompts us to look to change. It does not matter whether the first thing to be done is followed on the list by ten more or a hundred more: something has to be done first. Action must follow.

So make the decision, stick to it, and get on with the task. The quicker you do that, the sooner you will be able to move on down the list.

In practice

Stress is seemingly a common problem, yet stress is a reaction to circumstances rather than the circumstances themselves. You should be able to say that you:

- Know your priorities.
- Have made work-planning decisions sensibly, basing them on reasonable and thorough consideration of all the facts.
- Are sure there is no more, for the moment, you can do to make things easier.

Knowing you have made good decisions, and are now proceeding to implement them, should allow you to be comfortable about the process, and to reject any tendency to stress. Just worrying about things, and worrying at them, when you should be getting on and taking action is a sure recipe for stress. Keep calm by keeping organized and you will be better placed to maintain and increase your effectiveness.

PROBLEM-SOLVING
SIX-HAT THINKING
Jeremy Kourdi

"SIX THINKING HATS" is a powerful technique created by Edward de Bono. It is used to look at decisions from a number of perspectives, helping you to think differently and acquire a rounded view of a situation.

The idea

Many successful people think from a rational, positive viewpoint. However, if they do not look at a problem from an emotional, creative, or negative viewpoint, they can underestimate resistance to plans, fail to make creative leaps, and overlook the importance of contingency plans. Conversely, pessimists can be excessively defensive, while emotional people can fail to look at decisions calmly and rationally. Each of these "thinking hats" is a different style of thinking, and the "six thinking hats" technique will help you assess problems from many angles, enabling decisions to combine ambition, effectiveness, sensitivity, and creativity.

In practice

Adopt a different hat based on your situation and priorities.

1. *White hat.* Focus on the data available. Look at the information you have and see what you can learn from it. Look for gaps in your knowledge and either try to fill them or take account of them, by analyzing past trends and extrapolating from data.
2. *Red hat.* Look at problems using intuition, gut reaction, and emotion. Try to think how other people will react emotionally, and try to understand the responses of people who do not know your reasoning.
3. *Black hat.* Look at all the bad points of the issue, trying to see why it might not work. This highlights the weak points in a plan, allowing you to eliminate or alter them or to prepare contingency plans for them. This helps to make plans more resilient. It is one of the real benefits of this technique, as problems can be anticipated and countered.
4. *Yellow hat.* This requires thinking positively and optimistically, helping you to see the benefits of the decision. It helps you to keep going when everything looks difficult.
5. *Green hat.* This involves developing creative solutions. It is a freewheeling way of thinking, in which there is little criticism of ideas.
6. *Blue hat.* This emphasizes process control, and is exhibited by people chairing meetings. When ideas are running dry, it can be useful to use green-hat thinking, as the creative approach can stimulate fresh ideas.

PUBLIC RELATIONS
SET AN AMBUSH
Jim Blythe

AMBUSH PR IS about riding on the back of someone else's expenditure, and it happens frequently when companies sponsor events. Although being an official sponsor of a major event such as the football World Cup or the Wimbledon tennis tournament carries a great deal of publicity value, it does cost a lot of money as well, and often the sponsors are lost among a welter of other organizations so that the payoff becomes hard to identify.

The idea

During the 1998 soccer World Cup, held in France, Nike and adidas were clear rivals. The major advantage of soccer from a PR viewpoint is its ability to attract world TV audiences, so for global brands such as Nike and adidas the attraction is obvious.

The organizers of the World Cup, FIFA, only allow one main sponsor in each business category, so Nike and adidas could not both sponsor the event. adidas "won the toss" and became the official sponsor, even though some of the competing teams were sponsored by Nike: the sponsorship fee was reputed to be £20 million, but Nike was able to ambush the event for a great deal less.

Nike set up a "football village" among the startling buildings at La Défense, on the northern edge of Paris. Entry was free, and the company laid on a number of "fun" events aimed at young soccer fans. Nike was not allowed to use the World Cup logo, or even refer to the event directly, but most people visiting the Nike village were blissfully unaware of this. The company even set up a "road show" to tour France, giving schoolchildren the chance to play against a Nigerian under-17 international team. Nike's expenditure on the village was only £4.2 million, much less than adidas's investment, for very similar results.

Ambushing adidas's efforts not only gave Nike an unearned advantage: it also detracted from the impact of adidas's PR exercise. adidas were not quick enough off the mark in countering Nike, but it is hard to see what they might have done to prevent Nike's actions.

In practice
- Find an event that links to your product in a fairly direct way.
- Carry out your own activities in as close a proximity to the main event as you are able.
- Do not make any direct statements linking your firm to the event—let your actions speak for themselves.
- Expect retaliation.

BUSINESS SKILLS
ENGAGING WITH THE AUDIENCE
Patrick Forsyth

EVERYTHING YOU DO can contribute to the effectiveness of a presentation, and does so at every stage, although the beginning is especially important to get you off to a good start. Certainly the audience begin to judge how things are going early on, so if they:

- Feel it is beginning to be accurately directed at them
- Feel their specific needs are being considered and respected
- Feel the speaker is engaging
- Begin to identify with what is being said

Then you will have them with you and can proceed through the main part of the presentation—and can do so with confidence that a good reaction at the start can be a firm foundation for continuing success.

The idea
The creation of rapport is not subsidiary to gaining interest; it is surely inextricably bound up with it and creating rapport must be

addressed as an intention in its own right. So, you need to think of anything you can build in that will foster group feeling.

In practice

Numbers of approaches contribute here. The following provides some examples:

- Be careful of personal pronouns. There are moments to refer to you and others as "we" (and sometimes fewer as "I"). Thus, "We should consider ..." may well be better than "You must ..." or, "I think you should..."
- Use a (careful) compliment or two: "As experienced people you will..."
- Use words that reinforce your position or competence (not to boast, but to imply you belong to the group): "Like you, I have to travel a great deal. I know the problems it makes with the continuity during an absence ..."
- Be enthusiastic, but always genuinely so (this reminds me of the awful American expression that, if you can fake the sincerity, then everything else is easy; not so—back to enthusiasm). Real enthusiasm implies sincerity and both may be needed. Expressing enthusiasm tends to automatically make you more animated, so remember another old saying: enthusiasm is the only good thing that is infectious.

LEADERSHIP
SEE THE BIGGER PICTURE
Jonathan Gifford

ONE SIGNIFICANT CHARACTERISTIC of really successful leaders is their ability to see the bigger picture. A leader who can successfully predict significant movements of markets or of society as a whole is at a huge advantage.

The other sense of "seeing the bigger picture" is to see one's organization from the broadest possible perspective, in terms of its relationship with employees, stakeholders and with society as a whole.

The idea

Bill Gates, ex-CEO of Microsoft, was one of the first people in the world to see that computers might become a universal household product. A fellow undergraduate at Harvard University remembers:

"Bill was one of the first people I ever knew who really had this concept of computers being everywhere ... He saw that as being the future ... He also talked to me about the concept of everyone being able to discard all the books and paper materials and access everything they wanted to know by computer—to do all communication by computers."

The student also recalls that Gates imagined personal computers would be omnipresent in people's homes, but not in offices.

Harvard Business School professor and author Michael Beer made a study of the leaders of what he calls "High Commitment High Performance" organizations; companies that had held a position in the top half of their industry for 10 years or more, and within which what Beer calls a "high commitment" culture had been created.

"The CEOs were quite different in personality, background, and leadership style. But they were similar in what they saw as the purpose of the firm. They shared the view that a firm has a larger purpose than simply profit and increasing stock price, although they were all laser-focused on profitability and saw it as essential to achieving their larger purpose for the firm. They had a multi-stakeholder view of the firm as opposed to a shareholder view. The purpose was to add value to employees, customers, community, and society—not just shareholders. These CEOs operate from deep beliefs and values. Their purpose is to leave a legacy of a great firm."

In practice

- Leaders who see the bigger picture in terms of movements of markets and of society as a whole have a huge advantage over the competition.
- The most successful corporate leaders have a habit of seeing the organization as a whole; taking into consideration employees, consumers and every other stakeholder, as well as shareholders.
- These leaders consider the organization's relationship with society and are concerned with the larger purpose of the organization.

DESIGN

MAKE THE PRODUCT EASY TO DEMONSTRATE
Jim Blythe

SHOWING PEOPLE HOW to use a product can be easy, or it can be hard. If the product is itself a complex one, and especially if it is one that might need specialist training to operate, the demonstration needs to be as simple as possible. Complexity of use is a major barrier to adoption—so it is worth ensuring that the product looks easy to use.

This may even need to be included as part of your product design.

The idea

When Remington first introduced the typewriter, they realized that most people would consider it to be a big investment, considering that a pen or a pencil seemed to be doing the same job perfectly adequately. The company needed to demonstrate the speed and efficiency gains that a typewriter could provide—if it could not write faster than someone with a pen, it was a pointless exercise buying the machine and learning to use it.

The company therefore laid out the top line of the machine as QWERTYUIOP so that its demonstrators could type the word TYPEWRITER extremely quickly. The rest of the keyboard was arranged to minimize the keys jamming in use, even though this slowed down the operation (the later DVORAK keyboard is much easier to use).

Remington's keyboard layout was so successful in marketing the new technology that the QWERTY keyboard survives to this day, despite being relatively inefficient: the alternative might have been that typewriters might never have been adopted.

In practice

- This works best for complex products.
- Don't be afraid to redesign the product to make the demonstrations more striking.
- The easier something looks to operate, the more likely it will be adopted.

MANAGING
KNOW WHEN TO LEAVE WELL ALONE
Patrick Forsyth

SOMEONE MANAGING A team has to give members of that team space to complete the tasks they are engaged in, whether these are work that simply has been allocated or jobs that have been delegated. There is a temptation, perhaps particularly when a job is first delegated and you worry whether it will be done right, not only to check up but to do so on a frequent and ad hoc basis. Because this is offputting to those who may be at some midpoint on a job—a point at which things are not finished and look that way—it can actually end up delaying completion and perhaps giving you a false impression of their capabilities. Checking up takes time and may set back the way things are going rather than help. Certainly too overt an approach does nothing for motivation.

The idea

Do not hover. If something needs checking, and it may well do, then such checks should be discussed and agreed at the start of the work. Then the people concerned know what to expect. They can plan for any checks at particular—known—moments, and such checks will, as a result, be more likely to be constructive—or, indeed, unnecessary, as those concerned will work to make sure that when the monitoring process arrives all will be on schedule.

In practice

- If you work to make such checks an agreed part of the plan, if you make them constructive, then you will not have to spend very much time on them at all. The team working well, with minimal supervision, is a great asset to any manager wanting to conserve their own time.

- A manager who hovers unnecessarily is resented, and any resulting element of poor relations with staff tends to be time-consuming.

MANAGING
GIVE PEOPLE AUTONOMY
Jonathan Gifford

SUCCESSFUL LEADERS OFFER substantial autonomy to members of the team and to parts of the business. Individuals are empowered and respond to this; decision making is de-centralized, bringing more opinion and experience into the process; whole units can be allowed to take control of their own destiny while remaining "part of the family".

The idea

Harsh Mariwala, chairman and MD of Indian health and beauty group Marico Ltd, promotes a culture of autonomy and argues that decision making should always be decentralized, with leaders contributing only where they can "add value".

"My trust level in people is very high. For example, in my company, my colleagues can make their own decisions, including in financial matters. I have never regretted this culture ... I don't make any day-to-day decisions. It is all left to my team. In that sense, leadership should be based on decentralized decision making. Leaders should be involved only if they add value to any decision, not otherwise."

William Weldon, Chief Executive Officer of Johnson & Johnson, thinks that his company is "the reference company for being decentralized" in the way that it delegates responsibility for local markets to local teams.

"The men and women who run our businesses around the world usually are people who grew up in those markets, understand those markets and develop themselves in those markets. They can relate to the needs of the customer, whoever that customer may be ... the problem with centralization is if one person makes one mistake, it can cripple the whole organization. This way, you've got wonderful people running businesses. You have to have confidence in them, but you let them run it—and you don't have to worry about making that one big mistake."

Reynold Levy, president of the Lincoln Center for the Performing Arts in New York City, says: "Our growth has been organic growth. You know, the Chamber Music Society of Lincoln Center, the Film Society of Lincoln Center, Jazz at Lincoln Center were originally concerts produced by Lincoln Center and then they found their own audience and their own support and they became their own institutions. So, our approach has not been to acquire arts institutions but to grow them naturally ... One of the functions of the organization I run is to find new audiences for different art forms, create institutions and then spin them off. They remain part of the family, but they have their own independence and autonomy."

In practice
- Trust colleagues and give them as much scope for independent action as possible.

- Decentralize decision making so that many opinions and wide experience influence the organization's decisions. This reduces risk.
- Move decision making closer to the consumer. Intervene only when you are certain that you have a unique contribution to make.
- Consider giving a high degree of autonomy to devolved operations; give them overall objectives and allow them to deliver results within these parameters.

SALES
USE YOUR CUSTOMERS' TIMING
Patrick Forsyth

SOMETIMES IT IS difficult to know the best time to do something. This is true of anything in life: when should you apply for a new job, move to the country, or just broach the subject of what color the living room should be painted with your partner? With customers we always seem to have a sense of urgency. We not only want an order, we want it soon, or even right now. This may be understandable, but it reflects a focus on us, not on them.

Information is the key to choosing the right time. An early boss of mine once made a light-hearted comment to the effect that he had got himself a pay rise by saying it was a leap year and he had to work harder. I stored the remark away for two years until another leap year came along, then reminded him of it. I got a laugh and a small extra rise. With customers the information you glean and act on may be different, but the effect can be similar.

The idea
This from a company selling office furniture ...

It is often helpful to customer relations if you involve yourself to some degree in your customers' lives. You need to think about whether it is useful to send them a Christmas card or something on their birthday, whether to mention a work-related anniversary you know about (maybe they have been at the organization for ten years, or it is 100 years since the business was started). It may be useful to note other things that come up in conversation too. It's nice to be able to ask at the next meeting, "How did your son do in that exam?" or "Did you have a good holiday in Crete?"

But one event in your customers' lives is key to sales success. It is the timing of their financial year and the budgeting that goes with it. Find out when this is (and perhaps something of how the budgeting process works), and it can help your timing very specifically. You can then consider: is a purchase best suggested ahead of the new year, to mop up funds in this year's budget, or once the new budget is in place? Mention your thinking, and you'll be seen as fitting your suggestions to the realities of your customer's situation, rather than just pushing for an order now.

In practice
- The starting point of all such things is questions. Do not forget to ask.
- Keep clear notes. Sometimes information may not prove useful for some weeks or months, but you want to remember and not waste the opportunity it presents.

MANAGING
AGE-SENSITIVE MANAGEMENT
Jeremy Kourdi

UNDERSTANDING THE TRAITS and desires of the different age groups present in the workplace will allow you to provide them with the incentives and motivation they truly value, improving overall corporate performance and morale.

The idea

Tesco, one of Britain's most successful retailers, employs people of different age groups so that their workforce is more representative of society as a whole. This enables Tesco to relate well to all its customers, who have a wide range of ages.

The contemporary workplace contains four age groups:

- Silent veterans over 64 years old
- Baby boomers aged 45–63
- Generation Xers aged 30–44.
- Generation Y aged 29 years and under.

Age-sensitive management suggests that these different groups have different expectations, and therefore require different management techniques and performance-based incentives.

Although it is not foolproof, it can provide a general guide to possible differences in the expectations of young and old employees. With an aging workforce and shifting demographics, the manager who can motivate regardless of age has a significant advantage.

In practice

The value of age-sensitive management is that employees are more motivated and customers are better served. The key is certainly not to discriminate on the basis of age, but rather to be sensitive to the attitudes of all your employees. What one group favors may not encourage or motivate another group of people of a different age.

- *Silent veterans* tend to have the most traditional ideas of interaction, favoring formal contact and face-to-face meetings. They typically value recognition of their skills and abilities.
- When managing *baby boomers*, clearly define goals and break down the process into a series of individual targets. Place an emphasis on teamwork and motivational talks. Rewards should be public, with noticeable displays of recognition.
- Allow *Generation Xers* slightly more freedom to achieve their targets: tell them what to do, but allow them to decide how to

achieve the goal. Keep channels of communication open to allow ideas, opinions, and feedback to be discussed in a candid and honest way. Practical rewards, such as days off or monetary bonuses, are welcomed.

- *Generation Y* should be given plenty of opportunities to build their skills and experience—view yourself as both an instructive guide and a boss. Find out their personal goals, and make broader company targets relevant to those individual goals. Communication should be informal and positive.

SELF-HELP
SOLDIERING ON
Patrick Forsyth

THERE IS AN important but simply stated point to be made here about health, something that can all too easily be neglected because of pressure of work. Long-term health is one thing (and beyond our scope here—except to say that reducing pressure should avoid ongoing stress in the negative sense), but your day-to-day state of health has some essentially practical implications. Deadlines and the projects that have them are important. But no one is indispensable (it may be a sobering thought, but it is true). If you were not there, then other arrangements would have to be made; a few, perhaps lesser, priorities might suffer, but things would for the most part work out. Yet, if illness threatens (and I mean minor illnesses rather than being rushed into hospital), there is a great temptation to struggle on, and this tendency is more pronounced when an important deadline is looming.

The idea
Don't soldier on regardless. Now I am not suggesting that you take to your bed at the first sign of every tiny sniffle, but this is worth thinking about logically in a way that balances short- and long-term considerations and the time implications of both.

In practice

- If a couple of days struggling on ends with you being away from the office for a week once you have to give in to whatever bug you may have picked up, and a day off right at the beginning would have caught the thing in the bud, then this is not the most time-effective way of dealing with it.

- Obviously, it may be difficult to predict the course of minor ailments, but it is worth a moment's thought, and certainly it is often the case that the instant "I am invaluable and must struggle on" response is not always best. Quite apart from anything else, you do not want to sneeze all over everyone for several days, then take to your bed and, on your return, find that the whole department has caught the bug from you so that everyone is off sick and the impact on time has escalated.

PUBLIC RELATIONS
CREATE A FEATURE
Jim Blythe

THE MEDIA, AND especially television companies, are always on the lookout for good, interesting ideas for documentaries. They need shows with strong human interest, and preferably ideas that are unusual takes on topical subjects.

Any TV show has to be of interest to as wide an audience as possible, of course: humor, human interest, tragedy, or topicality are clear factors in the interest value of a documentary. Bringing these factors to bear is not always easy. Also, TV documentary makers are not going to produce a half-hour- or hour-long plug for the company and its products, so any expectation that they will do so is doomed to disappointment.

The idea

A company specializing in recruiting Australian teachers contacted a TV company with an idea for a documentary. The documentary makers were offered the chance to follow two Australian teachers as they experienced working in Britain: the show highlighted the differences between teaching in Australia and teaching in Britain, the discipline problems in British schools, the much higher level of bureaucracy in Britain, and the difficulties the Australians experienced in fitting into life in a new country.

As a fly-on-the-wall documentary the show was a great success: it had human interest (people being placed in a difficult and challenging situation), personal interest for the audience (seeing what actually happens in schools, and how it might be different elsewhere), and elements of humor and tragedy as the Australians met with triumph and disaster. An extra advantage for the TV company was that the show could be sold for broadcast in Australia.

Of course, the recruitment company got very few mentions during the show, but any interested parties would have had little difficulty in recognizing the firm, and since the show was broadcast in Australia as well as Britain it went out to exactly the right target audiences.

In practice
- Think through the whole idea from the viewpoint of the TV company. What will they gain from it? What spinoffs might there be?
- Accept that you will get a lot of coverage, but very few direct mentions. Consider the implications of this.
- Be prepared to put a lot of time and effort in, since you will be expected to act as a general dogsbody for the production company.

CRISIS MANAGEMENT
SURVIVING A DOWNTURN
Jeremy Kourdi

SEVERAL CLEAR PRINCIPLES and techniques can help turn a business around from the brink of disaster.

The idea

By the end of 1999, significant problems emerged at US technology giant Xerox. There was too much change, too fast; new, opportunistic competitors emerged; economic growth was slowing; key decisions were flawed. These issues combined with regulatory and liquidity challenges to bring about a massive decline in revenues, the departure of customers and employees, and debts of $19 billion.

Despite this, Xerox, led by CEO Anne Mulcahy, survived the downturn and staged a remarkable comeback. The business had doubled its share price by 2006, reduced costs by $2 billion, and achieved profits of $1 billion in 2005.

The foundation for a revival in Xerox came from a strong brand with a loyal customer base, talented employees, recognition of the need to listen carefully to customers, and greater responsiveness. The key was to win back market share with a competitive range of new products.

In practice

Several factors underpinned Xerox's resurgence, outlining the key areas to address:

- Listen to customers, employees, and people who know the business. Create a culture of good critics, and be aware that managers can become out of touch, even within their own organization.
- Learn Six Sigma—it can improve costs and service for customers, by providing a disciplined way to make process improvements.
- Recognize the need to be "problem curious," constantly looking for ways to differentiate and improve.
- Provide a clear, exciting, compelling vision of what the future will look like. People value a guiding light, as it provides certainty.
- Invest in the future and innovate. In 2005, two-thirds of Xerox's revenues came from products launched within the previous two years.
- Be entrepreneurial—find ways to sell products and control costs.
- Manage cash.

* Remember that strong leadership is essential. A business relies on its people—and people need to be aligned around a common set of goals and plans.

ZERO TOLERANCE AND THE STAFF KITCHEN
Jonathan Gifford

IF THE TAP in the staff kitchen is broken and nobody mends it, colleagues begin to feel that the leadership does not care. Like fixing broken windows in a housing estate, mending small things that are broken helps to keep the sense of communal pride that people normally have in their environment.

The idea
In a famous paper called "Broken Windows", the academics and political scientists, James Q. Wilson and George L. Kelling set out the idea that failure to mend small things in communal areas sends out a signal that nobody cares. Even normally well-behaved and law-abiding members of the community may join in destructive behavior as things begin to degenerate.

"Social psychologists and police officers tend to agree that if a window in a building is broken and is left unrepaired, all of the rest of the windows will soon be broken. This is as true in nice neighborhoods as in run-down ones. Window-breaking does not necessarily occur on a large scale because some areas are inhabited by determined window-breakers whereas others are populated by window-lovers; rather, one unrepaired broken window is a signal that no-one cares, and so breaking more windows costs nothing ... Untended property becomes fair game for people out for fun or plunder, and even for people who ordinarily would not dream of doing such things and who probably consider themselves law-abiding." BBC Director General Greg Dyke put this kind of thinking into action when he decided to visit BBC offices outside London that were often overlooked by management.

"I went to BBC offices that no Director-General had visited in decades. I found that some of our staff were working in buildings that should have been condemned years earlier. I remember visiting our building in Leicester, the home of BBC Leicester and the Asian Network, and saying to people afterwards how awful it was. I was told that if I thought it was bad I should wait until I went to Stoke. When I finally visited Stoke I was pleasantly surprised; it wasn't that terrible. But over the next four years BBC Radio Stoke moved to a better building. We also moved to a new building in Sheffield and started work on replacement premises in Birmingham, Leeds, Hull, Liverpool, Glasgow, and finally Leicester. We also renovated buildings right across the country."

In practice

- Small things matter. Colleagues will not be able to embrace new strategies or initiatives if some minor but significant aspect of their day-to-day working life convinces them that they are not valued.
- Letting small things go unfixed has surprising repercussions: previously well-behaved people begin to treat things with less respect, or even to indulge in minor acts of vandalism.
- Fixing the small things also has a disproportionate effect. A small amount of effort and expenditure convinces people that the leadership does, in fact, care.

SALES
ENHANCING CUSTOMERS' RECALL OF YOU
Patrick Forsyth

HERE IS A card trick that creates a positive, and lasting, impression. A smart business card is part of the basic kit of anyone selling. In some markets (in the East for instance, where the Japanese even have plastic waterproof cards to exchange by the pool), their existence and use is especially important, and they may have a translation of the information on the back.

But cards can all look much the same. Just glance at your store of those from other people—better still, put yours among them and see if it stands out. So something that is truly distinctive may be worthwhile. One tactic used by some organizations is for people to have their photograph on their card. (It can be color or black and white, and is in some cases a line drawing—I have seen cartoons and caricatures too.) Here is a different idea.

The idea
From FMC Southeast Asia Pte Ltd (a firm in the undersea technologies sector) ...

One manager with this company always gives people two cards. They are printed on a card of a shape you may be familiar with as an example of an optical illusion (see opposite). When two cards are put down one above the other, one seems clearly to be the larger. Put them one on top of another and it is clear they are identical in size. It is of no significance other than as a bit of fun; but it is memorable.

I have another card, a tiny 6 × 4 cm, which has only a picture of someone on the front, the words CALL ME, and a telephone number. On the reverse side it says, "The lack of business from you has made this economy-sized card necessary." That idea is maybe not for everyone, but why not have several different cards if they are useful?

In practice
- Review any sort of standard printed material regularly. Do not think of it as fixed and unalterable.
- Then find formats that work for you and your customers.

191
TO MEET OR NOT TO MEET ...
Patrick Forsyth

How OFTEN HAVE you come out of a meeting and not only been dissatisfied but wondered what you were doing there or even why the meeting had been held at all? If you answer "never," then you must work for an extraordinary organization, and if it is "often" you are in good company.

The idea

The idea here is simple—avoid unnecessary meetings. That said, there are two situations we must consider here: your meetings and others to which you are invited.

In practice

Consider two kinds of meeting:

* *Your meetings*: Before you open your mouth to say, "Let's schedule a meeting," pause, think—and think of the alternatives. Ask questions: is the proposed topic a matter for debate or consultation, or can you make a decision without that? Can any information that will be disseminated at the meeting be circulated any other way? If brief conversation is necessary, is it enough to have a word on the telephone, in the corridor, or over a working lunch? Often the answer suggests an alternative, and a briefer one than a meeting. If so, make a telephone call, send a note, or take whatever action may be called for to achieve what you want. Remember to consider the time spent by everyone at the meeting. It is right to think of six people meeting for an hour as representing the equivalent of six hours' work: more, in fact, because people have to prepare, to get there—and someone must set up all the arrangements. It is an important part of any meeting convener's responsibility to think carefully about who should attend, remembering that every time another name is added to the list, not only will this take up that person's time but it will extend the duration of the meeting.

- *Others' meetings*: With these, while there will be some you must attend, the same applies: think first before you agree to participate. You may find there are things you attend for the wrong reasons (just to keep in touch, or just in case something important crops up, perhaps). Maybe the minutes are sufficient to accommodate this. Or maybe, if you are a manager, it is important for your section to be represented, but you can delegate someone else to attend and report back to you. This may take some resolve. There may be aspects of the meeting you enjoy, topics on which your contribution allows you to shine, but it may still not be a priority to attend.

In either case, whatever the meeting is about, make sure it is essential, and that there is no alternative.

COMMUNICATION
ENCOURAGE REAL DEBATE
Jonathan Gifford

EVERYONE WANTS TO please the boss, who runs the risk that he or she will be the last person to know that the organization has a problem.

The idea
Dieter Zetsche, chairman of Daimler AG and head of Mercedes Benz Cars, says: "The higher you climb up the ladder, the more people will tell you what a great guy you are. The worst trap you can fall into is believing them. It's important to encourage people to give you feedback and to disagree if they have a different opinion. It depends on your reaction. Otherwise you are totally alone. You will lose touch and ultimately make decisions which are really dumb."

Alan Mulally, president and CEO of Ford Motor Company, introduced a weekly leadership meeting at which every department was represented in order to review key indicators for each project, which were represented by "stop light" color codes: red, orange or green, to represent the project's status. "I remember the first couple of weeks, we got the process going, everybody was kind of getting familiar with it, and it seemed like it was OK. And then all the stop light charts started to get filled in and everything was green, and I stopped the meeting and I said, 'Fellas and ladies, we just lost $12 billion! And everything is green? Aren't there just a few things that need special attention?' And in the next week ... because you've got to make it safe because the minute that you're intimidating, the minute that it's not comfortable to show you how it is, everything will be green, right? So the next week, boom. Up comes a bright red." Mulally applauded the red light and asked the project manager what he needed to fix the problem. A launch was behind schedule; more technical and manufacturing support was needed to get the vehicles out on time. The team discussed the issues and volunteered their departments' assistance. Three weeks later the project was on "orange" and in another two weeks it was "green".

After this experience, the team members were more prepared to be honest in their assessments and to flag up issues.

In practice

- People tend to present leaders with good news and will tend to put the best gloss on the situation rather than to flag up a genuine problem.
- Only when problems have been acknowledged can help be supplied and a solution found. Teams must be encouraged to recognize real problems honestly and to debate them frankly.
- Leaders can block this process by reacting negatively to bad news and by shouting at the messenger.
- Open and non-judgemental debate must be encouraged to bring problems into the open so that the team can find a solution.

I REALLY MUST APOLOGIZE ...
Patrick Forsyth

IT ALWAYS AMAZES me how many people either begin their presentation with an apology or include one, or more, within the introduction. There is inevitably something of a negative feel to this, and audiences do not like it. This gives us one of our more simple ideas.

The idea
Do not start with an apology.

Rather, if something might be mentioned this way and must be, then make that mention positive in tone. All sorts of things come into this category. People are sorry that:

- We only have twenty minutes
- It is late in the day
- Everyone is not present
- The meeting was called at short notice
- They have no slides—or so many

It is best either to ignore these, not mentioning them at all, or turn them around, stressing benefits. I like to remember an old saying in this context: Given oranges the job is to make marmalade. You should not be excusing your performance, or blaming the audience but getting on with the job. Do not agree to make a twenty minute presentation if you really cannot do justice to something in the time—if you take it on, it may need explanation but not apology.

In practice
- Accentuate the positive, for example don't say, "I am so sorry that we only have twenty minutes. It's going to be difficult to do justice to this in that time," rather say, "We only have twenty minutes, not long so what I will do is ..." some details may have to follow.

- Do not add an apology to a negative just to make it more palatable. Some things are best dealt with factually. For example, do not say, "I am sorry, that question would take me beyond my brief," rather say, "I'll have to leave that one as it takes us beyond our brief" but perhaps add, "do have a word with me later if that helps."
- If an apology really is necessary (rather than a kind of protective reflex) then make it clearly, sincerely and do not labor the point, instead move on promptly to positive matters.

STRATEGY
BUILT-IN OBSOLESCENCE
Jeremy Kourdi

BEFORE YOU RELEASE a product, create a plan for when and how it will become obsolete. This allows you to control change in the market, prepare for it, and use it to your advantage.

The idea
The theory of "built-in obsolescence" can be described as "instilling in the buyer the desire to own something a little newer, a little better, a little sooner than is necessary." This definition highlights the underlying nature of planned obsolescence.

Obsolescence is the point where a product has become useless—from being out of fashion, outmoded, incompatible with other operating systems, or simply expired. Two types of obsolescence exist: stylistic obsolescence and functional obsolescence. These two types are not mutually exclusive—they are often interrelated and lead to each other. By planning the point at which your product becomes obsolete, you can begin developing a replacement and an accompanying marketing campaign. It is also possible to trigger obsolescence to stimulate sales and ensure you remain ahead of competitors.

The majority of products are destined to become obsolete—in some markets, such as fashion and technology, obsolescence is fast-paced and woven into the fabric of the industry. Technology firm Apple provides an impressive example of this; it frequently develops new MP3 players that are upgraded in both style and technical features, making its older products stylistically and technically obsolete.

It is possible to use this strategy to make your competitors' products obsolete. For example, by releasing a popular new computer chip you can trigger the obsolescence of your competitors' operating systems.

Obsolescence is inevitable—use it to your advantage.

In practice
- Avoid triggering the obsolescence of products too frequently, as this is often an unnecessary investment and may cause a consumer backlash.
- Base the engineering of a product on your "obsolescence strategy"—a product will not need to last for ten years if it will be obsolete after two.
- Offer long-term warranties on products that will soon become obsolete—this will reassure customers and it is unlikely the guarantees will be claimed.
- Do not make built-in obsolescence obvious to the consumer— this will lead to frustration and unwillingness to purchase.

COMMUNICATION
WRITE A LETTER
Jim Blythe

LETTERS COLUMNS OF newspapers often offer an easy way to get your story across. Of course, you have to have a good letter to write, and preferably one that is newsworthy in itself.

Writing an open letter to a business rival can be a very effective ploy, especially if the rival has said unkind things about you—this is your chance to reply in public!

The idea

Sir Richard Branson is one of the world's great self-publicists. He has a talent for promoting himself and his companies in controversial and exciting ways, none more so than his various airlines. When he launched Virgin Blue in Australia, the boss of rival airline Qantas, Bob Dixon, made a number of statements to the effect that Virgin Blue would never succeed. Three years later he made a further comment to the effect that Virgin Atlantic would never be allowed to land in Australia, at which point Branson put pen to paper.

In an open letter sent to newspapers throughout the world, Branson repeated back some of Dixon's statements about Virgin Blue, and showed how they had been proved wrong: he then went on to offer a wager. He said that if Virgin Atlantic were not allowed to fly into Australia within 18 months, he would personally wear a Qantas stewardess's uniform and work on Qantas' London to Sydney flight, serving their customers throughout. If, on the other hand, Virgin were allowed in, he would expect Dixon to don a Virgin uniform and work the Virgin flight. Branson attached a mock-up picture of a Virgin stewardess with Dixon's head superimposed.

Dixon turned down the offer, saying "We are running an airline, not a circus."

The result of this letter was, of course, widespread publicity: Branson came out looking like a confident, clever entrepreneur, while Dixon came out looking like a humorless curmudgeon. In the event, Virgin Atlantic was given landing rights in Australia, so Dixon would have lost the bet—but, in any case, Branson came out the winner.

In practice

- Be sure to have your facts right. Don't make any statements that might be construed as libellous.

- Be humorous rather than nasty: nobody respects someone who bad-mouths their opponents, but people are generally fairly positive about jokes.
- Make sure your opponent has plenty of opportunity to reply: the response will generate as much publicity as the original letter.

SALES
LOSE YOUR EGO
Patrick Forsyth

In many fields of selling it is more important to get the order than to get the credit or some kind of personal involvement.

The idea
A consulting firm (which must remain nameless ...

Without a doubt the best example I have ever come across of this occurred in a training consultancy. A potential project had reached a crucial stage. An inquiry had been received, meetings held, and a written proposal submitted. Everything seemed to be going well, and at his most confident, the consultant who had achieved this much believed that confirmation was imminent. Indeed he soon got a response, but it was negative.

In many bespoke businesses the next step is to try to find out why the company hasn't won the contract. If you can do so—in this case it might have involved price, method, timing, a less than favorable comparison with an alternative supplier, or many more reasons—this can be useful information for the future.

Sometimes such a discovery call can actually change things and turn a no into a yes, as happened this time. The consultant telephoned the decision maker and persuaded him to discuss why the company had said no. However he was not very forthcoming. Various reasons were floated but there was nothing substantial, nothing that seemed to be the key factor. Reading between the lines, the consultant opted for bluntness. "I think I know what the problem is," he said. "You don't like me." There was a long silence and then the prospect agreed!

This is not something most clients would want to say unprompted. But not only did the consultant find out the reason, he turned the situation around. He persuaded the client to meet a younger colleague and consider giving her the job. She got it.

In practice

- We cannot all get on with everyone to the same extent. Beyond that, the principle of checking on the reasons for a refusal is eminently worthwhile.
- So too is an approach that does not take too egocentric an approach to things.

CULTURE
MAKE IT FUN
Jonathan Gifford

THERE IS EVERY reason to try to create an atmosphere at work in which people have fun. In ventures that depend on creative talent, a working environment that encourages play brings people together, breaks down barriers and creates an atmosphere of easygoing, collaborative endeavor.

In other environments, laughter can be the essential social lubricant that reduces stress levels and keeps teams of people working together on difficult projects.

The idea

Dan Nye, CEO of the business social networking site LinkedIn from 2007 to 2009, explains how the rapidly growing company went out of its way to create an atmosphere where talented young people could come together, have fun—and work late.

"We have a big game room where there's a PlayStation 2 and the game *Guitar Hero* ... We've also got a ping pong table and a pool table. What's the idea behind all the games? It gets people from across functions interacting, communicating and playing. We're trying to build social bonds and break down barriers between groups. We also do it so people can grab something to eat or play a quick game and keep working late. It's a great business decision."

Jacqueline Novogratz is a venture philanthropist with Acumen Fund, a non-profit venture that sets out to tackle global poverty. She leads entrepreneurial local projects around the world, many of which are run by women. She talks about the importance of shared laughter and about the fact that, at the most basic level, dignity is a more important driver than money.

"The real lesson for me was how that dignity is so much more important to the human spirit than wealth. And that what these women, as all of us, needed was to know that we could cover basic needs, but to have the power of being able to say no to things that we didn't want, that we didn't want to do. And so leadership as a way of inspiring, listening, and letting people, you know, grow themselves in their own way. And it was a small experience in some ways, and yet one that I think about all the time that taught me so much about listening and dignity—and laughter as a really, really key component. The more stressed I got, the less anything worked; and the more we could laugh, the more we got done."

In practice
- If you want people to enjoy themselves at work, try to make work a more fun place to be.
- Having fun at work breaks down barriers and creates informal groups that cross established hierarchies.
- When there is fun at work, people are less keen to leave.
- In difficult human enterprises, shared laughter can be the vital element that keeps the endeavor alive.

COST CUTTING
STARING INTO SPACE
Anne Hawkins

SPACE COSTS MONEY.

If you own it you've got capital locked up in it that is costing you interest. If you don't own it you've got rent to pay.

In either case you have rates, maintenance costs, heating bills ...

But that's not all.

What about the opportunity cost? What else could you do with some freed-up space?

The idea

Think creatively about floorspace.

Don't just accept the 'We've got 5 years left on the lease so we can't down-size until then' argument.

If you're stuck with existing floorspace costs, take the opportunity to do more with it... any space you can free is effectively exactly that, free!

Get organised!

How often do you hear people wish that they could 'start again' on a greenfield site so that they organise their processes such that products flowed better through the business? If only there were some free space ...

Are people working in a muddle because there isn't space to organise workspaces properly? If only there were some free space...

This company was reluctant to accept that there was a great reason to organise floorspace more efficiently. They seemed to have completely forgotten about the £20,000 per annum in rent they were paying for a unit at a trading estate a few miles away, in which they were storing redundant tooling. By reorganising layouts, they were able to accommodate the stores on-site (and at the same time were encouraged to re-think which tooling really had to be kept).

Find a partner!
This coffee-shop re-organised its seating so that a local newspaper retailer could rent vending space.

Another manufacturer used surplus space on the shopfloor to sub-let to a supplier who could then move his products directly on to the manufacturing line as and when required.

Flaunt it!
And if you've no immediate use for the space, report on it separately as an 'enabler' to highlight the opportunity on offer.

By ruthlessly clearing unnecessary occupied floorspace and cordoning off the resulting vacated area of the factory, this other manufacturing unit was excellently placed for winning the contract to build the new product.

In practice
- Motivate people to use floorspace efficiently by charging out a cost for space as part of departmental expenses.
- When any floorspace is released, remove the charge for it from departmental spend and report on it separately as the cost of unutilised space to focus everyone's attention on possible profitable uses.

TIPS FOR POWERFUL EMAILS
Andy Maslen

HERE ARE A few of the challenges we face when writing emails. First of all, your recipient can get rid of this intrusion into her working day without lifting a finger. Oh, OK, she does have to lift a finger, but only by four millimeters, before stabbing the mouse button and trashing your promo.

All she needs to do is check out your From field and subject line before deciding that, yep, this is junk mail. (Let's just hope she doesn't consider it the s-word and permanently block emails from you.) If she uses a preview pane, boy have you got a hurdle to jump. As she pages down through her emails, she can see a big chunk of yours without opening it.

The idea
From Which?, a consumer organization
When I registered with Which? Online I received a welcome email, as you do. And although this should be a simple thing to get right, few organizations do. Which? nailed it. The opening's so simple I am always amazed when people forget how to do it:

> Dear Andy
> Thank you for registering with www.which.co.uk.

Then there are a few paras outlining how I log in to the site, what to look out for, how to get in touch if I have a query, and so on. They even tell me to add them to my whitelist so their emails get through. Finally, there's a nice personal sign-off:

> Regards
> Malcolm Coles
> Editor, www.which.co.uk

Yes! Signed by a real person.

Here are a few more thoughts on how to write more powerful, engaging emails. Start strong. Give your reader an instant reason to keep reading. What is the huge wow-factor difference your product can make to your reader's life? Give them that. Straight away.

Aim for the most conversational style and tone of voice you can manage without alienating your reader. An email is no place for using "purchase" instead of "buy." And your language needs to be less formal because people are used to the informality of email as a communications medium.

Break up overlong paragraphs. That means virtually all of them. Where do you break them? Wherever it feels OK to do so.

Keep it ultra personal. In direct mail letters, some copywriters feel it's OK to talk about "subscribers," "our customers," or "executives." (They're wrong.) But in an email, which someone might be reading on their BlackBerry or cellphone, you *must* use a personal style to hook them.

In practice
- Remember that email is a personal medium. Strive to replicate the tone and style of the emails your prospects *want* to open. Try using "you" rather than "customers."
- Give your reader lots of chances to order or respond. Not just one at the end.

LEADERSHIP
COMMUNICATE THE VISION
Jonathan Gifford

THE VISION THAT a leader has chosen for the organization is the single most important thing that must be communicated to the team. It needs to be repeated on every possible occasion, in clear and memorable terms.

The idea

Bob Iger is the president and CEO of the Walt Disney Company and the sixth person to hold this role since the company was founded by Walt Disney in 1923. Disney's grand vision is "To make people happy". Iger sets out what he describes as his strategic vision: "To use technology to reach more people, more often, in more convenient ways".

This strategic vision led Iger to make some of Disney's most valuable properties available for streaming online; a highly controversial decision. Iger stresses the importance of putting in place the fundamental structures that will enable people to carry out the vision.

Most importantly, he emphasizes the need to communicate the vision: "One of the things that becomes very, very important for a CEO to accomplish is a strategic vision, and then to enable people by creating the right environment to carry it out. And it becomes also important to articulate that vision often because it won't get carried out unless it's both clear and well-spoken."

John Ryan, president of the Center for Creative Leadership, reminds us that it is not enough to communicate the vision to the top team: leaders must find time to communicate to the whole organization.

"The sheer time demands of serving in a leadership role can undermine our overall effectiveness as leaders. Moreover, when we do turn our attention as executives to communication, we sometimes make things even worse. In my own experience, which includes observing clients all over the world, it's clear that most organizations are very uneven in their communications. They're often good at the top. Their executive and senior management teams understand the CEO's vision and strategy. But the deeper you dive into the organization, the more muddled things get.

Middle managers and frontline employees often have no idea how to connect their daily work to the larger strategy. Frequently they don't even know what the strategy is. Does that sound familiar? We shouldn't blame them for disregarding our occasional memos about 'adding value' and 'synergies' and 'thinking outside the box.' It's our fault as leaders when we don't communicate in meaningful terms that make sense throughout the entire organization."

In practice

- A leader's vision for the organization is his or her most important contribution. Leaders must communicate that vision and create an environment that enables people to accomplish the vision.
- Communicating the vision on a few occasions at "set-piece" events will never be enough. Leaders must communicate their vision as often as possible and to as many audiences as possible, at all levels of the organization.
- The vision must be clearly presented. It must be easy to understand and it needs to appeal to achievements that people can genuinely relate to: people cannot be inspired by jargon.

PUBLIC RELATIONS
RUN A SURVEY
Jim Blythe

NEWS MEDIA EXIST to disseminate facts, and also to entertain their readers and viewers. While it is often difficult to access news media (especially television) with a straight news story, it can be relatively easy to do so with an entertaining piece.

Newspapers and TV news often run stories about amusing surveys that have been conducted, and surveys have the advantage of appearing factual (even if they have not been conducted very scientifically). In many cases, a survey does provide genuinely useful information, of course.

The idea

Nescafé is Britain's best-selling coffee brand. For many years, the company ran a series of advertisements centered on a burgeoning love affair between two neighbors who join each other for a coffee, in different circumstances. The romantic and indeed sexual connotations of sharing a coffee have become well established in the culture.

In Britain, as in many other countries, inviting someone in for a coffee after a night out often has other connotations—it may just be an invitation to finish off the evening with a friendly coffee, or it may be an invitation of a more intimate nature. Nescafé ran a survey that asked people whether they thought the line "Do you want to come in for a coffee?" after a date was an offer of a refreshing cup of coffee, or whether it was actually an invitation to move the relationship on to the next stage. The results were amusing, and the topic itself was of course one that many people found relevant: it is certainly a situation that almost all single people encounter on a regular basis.

The survey was widely quoted on TV news, and also sparked a number of magazine articles—all good PR for Nescafé.

In practice

- Run the survey as conscientiously as possible. If you can, get a market research agency to run it for you—this will give it much greater credibility. The agency may give you a cheap price, since they will also gain PR value from the exercise.
- Choose something that will resonate with a lot of people, even if your product has a limited market. Otherwise the news media will not be interested.
- Be controversial if possible. This is true for all stories, of course, but surveys can be tedious otherwise.

MARKETING
REDEFINE YOUR AUDIENCE
Jeremy Kourdi

FINDING NEW AUDIENCES for your product can allow you to broaden your sales potential and escape crowded markets.

The idea

Do you think you know who the best people are to target with your marketing? Think again. Reconsidering who may be interested in your products opens up a new world of potential customers, for the company intrepid enough to find a new audience for its advertising.

The Polish division of the brewing firm Carlsberg decided to create a beer to be marketed primarily to women. Karmi, a beer with a low alcohol content and high emphasis on flavor, was colorfully packaged and launched on International Women's Day. This was a bold move in an industry that typically focuses on selling to a male clientele, with advertising campaigns usually centering around sports sponsorship deals and scantily clad models.

This strategy of redefining your audience was also followed by British clothing retailer Marks & Spencer, after its reputation for catering to older female clientele became insufficient to sustain its business. Marks & Spencer decided to expand into a younger, more style-focused market, and launched Per Una, a new range of clothes designed to appeal to women in their twenties and thirties. While it had traditionally emphasized comfort over style, the decision to present a fashion-forward image helped Marks & Spencer broaden its appeal—and turn around its flagging sales.

In practice

- Seek an external view of your market—for example, by talking to customers, by benchmarking with other businesses, or by appointing new employees from outside the business.

- Focus on how you could adjust your product to appeal to a new audience.
- Maintain the core principles of your product—while you should add new selling points to appeal to new audiences, do not discard your original ones.
- Do not neglect your old market—maintain committed relationships with all your intended audiences.
- Remember that it can be difficult to move into a new market, especially if that market is crowded. Choose your new audience wisely.

ARE YOU STANDING COMFORTABLY?
Patrick Forsyth

BOTH ARMS AND hands give rise to one of the most asked questions from presenters: What do I do with my hands? Awkwardness about what to do with them can be a distraction to the speaker. And if they are awkward then they become a distraction to the audience. They should be an asset to the speaker and make a positive impression on the members of the audience; so too should gestures. Beware:

- Too static a pose is awkward and distracting (and may look too formal or imply nerves).
- Some static positions look protective (implying fear of the audience). This is true of standing with arms folded or clasped in front of the body.
- Too much arm waving seems nervous and is equated with fidgeting (this is especially so of arm waving and hand gestures that do not seem to relate to what is being said—the Magnus Pyke school of presentation).

The idea
Adopt a position and manner that appears natural and comfortable.

Doing so can play a part in adding interest, enthusiasm and emphasis, and gives an impression of confidence and thus expertise.

In practice

- The most obvious natural position is simply standing with both hands hanging loosely by the sides. The problem here is that many people find that the more they think about it the harder it is to be natural. The only route is thus to think about it first, to decide on a number of positions that can be adopted as bases from which a period of greater animation can commence, then forget about it. Remember that for men in a business suit, one hand in a pocket may have an appropriate appearance; two never does, it just looks slovenly. One useful alternative to arms by the sides is to give your hands something specific and appropriate to do, for example:
  - Hold some suitable item (perhaps a pen).
  - Hold onto something (perhaps a corner of a lectern)—one hand is best here, using two can make it look as if you are hanging on for protection, so even with one hand, avoid white knuckles!
- This is certainly an area that can benefit from some thought; however, what works best is a fluid transition between these things. A natural pose, then shifting to another, then making a gesture and moving back again works well. Rest assured it comes with practice and try to avoid becoming hyper-conscious of it. If you relax and forget about it, you will adopt a natural pose and manner; one which will look right.

PERFORMANCE

AVOID DUPLICATING INFORMATION UNNECESSARILY

Patrick Forsyth

MAINTAINING ANY INFORMATIOIN system takes time, and this is multiplied if the information is being recorded in identical or similar form in several different places.

The idea

This is worth a check, and there is a quick check you can run in a few moments. The job you do will give rise to the areas of information with which you are concerned, but, whatever it is, a simple matrix of information shown alongside places where it is filed or stored will quickly show if duplication is occurring.

Such an analysis will also quickly show the extent of any kind of duplication—and the sheer extent of the recording going on. If you then think about where information is most often sought, you may well find that only a minority of places are in fact necessary. Cuts—perhaps recording something once instead of four or five times—will then save work and time.

In practice

Sometimes tasks seem important and then something happens to show that this was not true at all, or perhaps not true any more. This is often the case with information. Something is asked for, is provided regularly, and can continue to be provided long after it has ceased to be useful; it becomes an unquestioning routine.

You should make it a rule that whenever you are asked or need to provide any information to anyone (with copies to whomever else), you make a diary note to check at some time in the future—in six or 12 months perhaps—whether it is still necessary. Find out whether it still needs to be sent:

- On the same frequency (would quarterly be as good as monthly?).
- To all the people originally listed.
- In as much detail (would some sort of summary do?).

Any change that will save time is worth while and you may find that it is simply not necessary to provide the information any more. Very few people will request that information stops coming to them, but if asked may well admit that they can happily do without it. Be wary of this sort of thing, or it is quite possible that all around your organization, action of this sort is being repeated unnecessarily.

SALES
USE A SPOKEN LOGO
Patrick Forsyth

THERE ARE MANY circumstances when it is advantageous to be able to describe to people what you do and what you sell briefly in a sentence. One common occasion is when you meet someone at a conference and they ask, "What do you do?" If you waffle at such a moment you lose any chance of creating interest, and maybe a specific opportunity to do business.

The idea

This idea comes from the book *Why Entrepreneurs Should Eat Bananas* by Simon Tupman (Cyan/Marshall Cavendish Books), a valuable selection of ideas for "growing your business and yourself." Simon Tupman, who runs Simon Tupman Presentations, is a motivational speaker and author.

He coined the phrase "spoken logo" as an antidote to perhaps unwittingly bland and bald descriptions such as "I am a lawyer," "We make electronic equipment," and "We conduct market research." Simon quotes one of his customers, an accountant, who replies to this question with, "I take the hassle out of keeping books and records up to date for busy people who have better things to do." This is a good example because it gets straight to the point, focuses on the benefit for clients rather than the service provided, and encapsulates a good deal very succinctly.

Along the same lines, that lawyer (if he or she works in conveyancing) might say, "I take the hassle out of buying and selling a house, and make sure there are no hidden surprises." The market researcher might say, "I reduce the risk in people's businesses, and help identify market opportunities that can boost profit." Such statements are designed to prompt a useful exchange rather than a simple conversation-stopping remark like "Oh really." They also convey sufficient information that if there is any common ground that could lead to a business opportunity, they'll help to identify it.

In practice

◦ Finding a phrase like this off the top of your head is difficult, so give it some prior thought. Think about your business, and develop (and keep updated) a clear spoken logo. It will stand you in good stead in a variety of networking and other situations. It can be a route into a more detailed conversation that allows some real selling.

PERFORMANCE
LEARNING TOGETHER
Jeremy Kourdi

RESPONDING TO CHANGES in business markets is best achieved with a willingness to learn and develop ideas as part of a group, creating an "intensive learning culture."

The idea

Nokia, the world-renowned cellphone technology company, was, in the late 1980s, a nearly defunct diversified conglomerate, mostly known for its rubber and tissue products. The decision to put all the energy and remaining resources behind a minuscule (by industry standards) telecommunications activity, more specifically an emerging cellphone technology sector, triggered an intensive learning culture and period of business growth.

By the end of 1996 Nokia Group was the global market leader in digital cellphones, and one of the two largest suppliers of GSM networks. In just a few years, this resilient Finnish business had learned enough to become the trendsetter in cellphone design, making its product a high-tech lifestyle attribute that many fashion products could envy.

On the cellular network side, Nokia was also setting the pace with solution-oriented customer services, thus raising the competitive threshold.

Most companies, having achieved this level of success in such a short time, could be expected to miss the next industry turn if there ever was one—and there was: the rise of the internet. However, Nokia kept pace with this change, creating phones that were internet-ready, and helped create the now ubiquitous mobile information culture.

Commenting on Nokia's "thinking process," CEO Jorma Ollila noted:

> Of course, we get masses of information, but what is important is that we discuss it a lot among ourselves, kicking it around, looking at it from different perspectives. It is a collective learning process and the key point is whom we should discuss a new piece of information with, to augment it and give it more meaning than it had originally. Then, we make some choices, try them out, listen to the feedback and redirect as needed. With this collective learning process we are all on the same wavelength and we can act very fast when needed.

Nokia has certainly suffered its share of setbacks, but to successfully make a journey from near disaster to world domination in less than ten years shows a sustained flexibility and desire to learn at all levels. Clearly this is vital for a business in an industry as new and fast moving as cellphone technology, but the Nokia approach—applied throughout the business—highlights the value of moving from information to knowledge.

In practice
- Capture, disseminate, share, analyze, and discuss information and insights.
- Hold regular discussion groups consisting of people working at all levels inside the company as well as external experts.
- Discuss the significance of developments in the market, as well as possible future trends and scenarios.
- If it is decided that the company should bring in new policies or move in a different direction, then brainstorm the workability and practicality of these changes. Decide who will implement them, and how.

PUBLIC RELATIONS
WRITE A FEATURE
Jim Blythe

A LARGE AMOUNT of PR is conducted through press releases—so much so that some people think PR stands for "press release." However, it is perfectly feasible to write a much longer piece if there is something useful for you to say.

As always, a feature cannot be merely a long advertisement for your brand or company. It should be something that is of general interest to a large number of people, and you cannot merely plug your own services.

The idea

A firm of lawyers in London was looking to increase its conveyancing business, so one of the partners wrote an article on ways of cutting the cost of moving home. The article examined every aspect of moving—legal fees, estate agents' fees, removals costs, insurance, and surveying costs, and explained how to make savings in each area.

The article was published many times throughout Britain, and although the firm was not directly plugging its own services the article was always clearly identified as having been written by one of the firm's partners. Every time it appeared, the firm got more inquiries for conveyancing, even though the article was often cut or even edited heavily by the periodicals it appeared in.

Articles like this can run and run, and will always make the writer look like an expert—they also generate a feeling of trust, since the writer is clearly trusting the readers with some useful information, and perhaps cutting themselves out of a fee. Readers will think of the author as someone who is genuinely out to help them—which immediately opens the door to an open and honest relationship.

In practice

- Don't mention your firm until you're well into the article—if at all. It will only be edited out.
- Give good value in the article. If it's interesting and useful to the readers, it will be published and read.
- Include pictures if at all possible. This is especially important for magazines.

SELF-HELP
THINKING AHEAD
Patrick Forsyth

THIS MIGHT APPROPRIATELY be called the opposite of the "if only . . ." school of ineffective time management. Too often managers find themselves in a crisis that would be all too easily resolved if they could wind the clocks back. We surely all know the feeling. "If only we had done so and so earlier," we say as we contemplate a messy and time-consuming process of unscrambling. In all honesty, though the unexpected can happen sometimes, crisis management is all too common ... and often all too unnecessary. Coping well with crises that are, for whatever reason, upon us saves time; certainly if the alternative is panic.

The idea

If you can acquire the habit of thinking ahead and take a systematic view of things, then you are that much more likely to see when a start really needs to be made on something. If things are left late or ill thought out (and the two can often go together), then time is used up in a hasty attempt to sort things out at short notice. This tends to make any task more difficult and is compounded by whatever day-to-day responsibilities are current at the time.

In practice

- Some people find that to "see" the pattern of future work and tasks in their mind's eye can be difficult. One invaluable aid to this is the planning or wall chart.

• Whatever you do to document things, however, the key is to get into the habit of thinking ahead—at the same time and without disrupting the current day's workload. Anticipating problems and spotting opportunities can make a real difference to the way you work in the short term.

MANAGING
ALLOW CHOICE TO DRIVE DECISIONS
Jonathan Gifford

LEADERS MUST SET the broad direction of an organization—the core vision—but the collective intelligence of the organization can help decide how best to achieve that vision. The more broadly this collective decision making is based, the better.

This is a form of market-driven decision: letting the market (in this case, the organization's collective talent) dictate where the organization should direct its efforts.

The idea

Mukesh Ambani is the chairman and managing director of Reliance Industries, India's largest private sector corporation. His father, Dhirubhai Ambani, founded the company, trading in spices and then textiles, later taking the company public and diversifying into petrochemicals, telecommunications, food, power, life-sciences and other sectors.

In 2006 the company was divided into two new organizations, each headed by Dhirubhai's two sons, Mukesh and Anil. Mukesh says that he gets most satisfaction from seeing the company blazing new trails and challenging the status quo.

Reliance Industries allows its junior managers to select the areas in which they would most like to work, via a competitive process, after a six-month induction process to "teach them the Reliance way". Each Reliance business makes a presentation to the newcomers, who are then invited to choose the field in which they want to work.

"In the 1990s," says Mukesh, "finance and treasury was the in thing. Then it was marketing. In the last two years, most bright young people want to work in rural areas. This is a big mindset change … Young people want to go to Punjab and stay there for a month to figure out what works. In telecom, when we said we would go into [rural areas], a lot of our friends thought it [was] all talk. Even the regulator was sceptical … In retailing, they are saying, we don't want to do merchandising; we want to create those rural markets. In that sense, it is great fun. I always tell my young guys, we are going on an expedition together. When you do that, we need to support each other because we can get lost quickly … Today it is rural areas that are making more money. I have noticed that talent is automatically motivated by larger goals and some of the brightest people want to do things that are different."

In practice

- Leaders set the overall compass bearing but should not attempt to describe every stage of the journey.
- A well-run organization is full of intelligent people who understand the world around them. Their instincts about future trends and profitable avenues are probably correct.
- Try to create internal markets that allow colleagues to choose paths that most interest them: these paths are likely to be successful.
- Make sure that resources follow people's choices so that the organization is changed by colleagues' decisions.

COST CUTTING
BE RESOURCEFUL!
Anne Hawkins

MAKE THE MOST of what you've got. If you use your materials more efficiently you'll also have less to dispose of—and in some instances that can be a costly business.

The idea
Getting value for money from your materials isn't just a question of the price you've paid for them. You need to minimise waste and look for cost-effective solutions to dispose of what's left. [Even if you've managed to obtain your materials free of charge (see below), you're going to want to use them as effectively as you can.]

Don't feed the skip
With expensive materials it can pay to invest to save. This business uses computer software to assist with bedding parts more effectively and, with laser cutters allowing parts to be positioned closer together, there is even less material in the off-cut bin.

With aluminium plate being more expensive than aluminium bar, this manufacturer switched from cutting parts out of plate to machining the shapes from bar on a CNC machine and then slicing the bar to size.

If you're using your materials more efficiently you'll also have less to dispose of—and in some instances that can be a costly business.

Finding a use for those slow-moving items in stores will divert them away from their gradual progression towards the skip.

Reductions in the amount of scrap you produce will also stop those skips filling quite so quickly.

Sell it on!

But despite everything you've done, you're almost inevitably left with materials and other items to get rid of.

Look creatively at how you could either sell unwanted items, or at least have them picked up and disposed of free of charge.

Make sure that there are procedures in place (and that they are adhered to) for segregating materials to maximise their value... and that your problem doesn't just disappear overnight! Scrap metal can be valuable if sorted and stored appropriately.

Recycle

Make arrangements for free of charge collections for items that can be recycled; such as paper, plastic bottles and plastic coffee cups.

Site the recycling points appropriately and conveniently.

In the canteen, place recycling containers alongside collection points for trays so that everyone clears these items from trays as they finish their meals. This not only promotes recycling, but saves time for catering staff as trays can be stacked and cleared more efficiently. (Asking your diners to scrape their leftover food into receptacles for the local pig-farmers might prove a step too far for those with a delicate disposition ... and an unwanted reminder of school dinners ... although it might prove a useful motivator for reducing waste.)

Have a recycling point next to the coffee machine as you can track down contractors who will collect plastic coffee cups (and even pay you something for them) if they are slotted into a purpose-designed receptacle.

Don't have individual bins in offices but have central recycling points. Not only will this help you reduce your cost for garbage removal, but it should also help you make savings on your cleaning contract costs!

Find your ideal partner.
There are agencies out there (including those funded by the government) desperate to match you with businesses who want your unwanted items—or, on the flipside, who could supply you with products you could use either at a knock-down price, or, in some instances for free. Successful 'marriages' might include using materials from demolished buildings for groundworks on new housing estates, using your 'rubbish' as a source of power or forming an alliance with a scrapstore. (Scrapstores typically collect tons of business waste each year at no cost to the donor and pass it on to groups to be used for art or educational purposes.)

In practice
- Look at the flow of materials and other products through your business.
- Consider whether there are cost improvement opportunities by re-engineering what you do to use someone else's waste.
- Question whether you use your resources as effectively as possible and whether for example, you re-use off-cuts whenever practicable.
- Find out how much you spend on waste collection. Delve through the skips and see what's in there... and then think creatively!

VALUES
BUILDING TRUST
Jeremy Kourdi

TRUST IS AN essential aspect of business, notably when leading people, selling to customers, or building the long-term reputation and value of an enterprise. Trust is easily taken for granted, hard to define, and easy to undermine or destroy—but how can it be built?

The idea
Trust matters in business, underpinning issues as diverse as sales,

financial management, and leadership, as well as affecting job satisfaction and career prospects. However, increased profitability is not the most compelling reason to build trust. People value trust, but what is overlooked is that its absence results not in a neutral situation but in something worse. As businesses have discovered, when trust is undermined, there is a high cost to pay.

The Innocent Drinks Company epitomizes many of the characteristics of a high-trust organization. It produces high-quality fruit drinks and smoothies with a passion, professionalism, and good humor that invite trust. This tone is set from the top. Like many trusted leaders, the executives at Innocent Drinks do not spend much time focusing on trust. Instead, they simply display the energy and skills that people (employees and customers) value— and trust follows. This avoids the paradox of trust, where the more it is discussed, the weaker it becomes.

In practice

In recent research, people were asked to rate the significance of a range of attributes when deciding whether to trust someone. The most popular attributes are fairness, dependability, respect, openness, courage, unselfishness, competence, supportiveness, empathy, compassion, and passion. These drivers of trust need to be understood and delivered, if trust is to be developed.

There are several practical steps to developing trust, but the most fundamental one is to be genuine: you have to mean what you say and be sincere in your approach. Consider the following actions:

- Deliver what you say you will, and be true to your word.
- Create an atmosphere and expectation of trust by trusting others.
- Keep team members informed by asking what information would be most helpful, explaining issues carefully, and sharing available information.
- Give constructive feedback by clearly identifying the behavior that you are giving feedback on (focus on the behavior, not the person).

- Act with integrity and sincerity.
- Treat others as you would wish to be treated yourself.
- Understand who you are dealing with, taking time to find out how they work and what motivates them.
- Be dutiful, diligent, and consistent.
- Recognize success and reward good performance.

CRISIS MANAGEMENT
LET YOUR ENEMIES TALK
Jim Blythe

BEING ATTACKED IS not pleasant—most of us feel resentful, especially when we feel we are being wrongly accused. So a typical response from a company under attack is to try to silence the opposition—perhaps by taking out a lawsuit (as McDonald's has been known to do) or by denying access to the media (perhaps by threatening to withdraw advertising).

Although this type of behavior is very human, it is also very counterproductive—there are simply too many ways in which a protester can make his or her voice heard. The internet, the gutter press, even satirical magazines all offer access for someone to bad-mouth you.

The idea
Many major companies have "save" reps who are paid to handle complaints. The "save" reps are trained to allow irate customers to vent their anger—shouting at the rep is tolerated, up to a point, because the reps know that the customer is angry with the situation, rather than the company (and certainly not with the rep). Once the customer has ranted for a while, he or she usually calms down and a reasonable dialog can be conducted.

Translating this idea into the wider context, allowing your enemies to rant in public only gives them the opportunity to make themselves look foolish. Someone who loses their temper is likely to say things that are ill-advised: often they will overstate the case and look ridiculous to the observer, and meanwhile you can compose your response.

A good rule is to avoid being intimidated by a silence. Many people feel that they have to say something once the other person has stopped speaking—but if you wait a few moments, they will often go on to say something entirely ridiculous. This tactic also gives you time to think of a good response.

In practice

- Allow your enemy to state their case in full.
- Don't get emotional yourself—this is just business!
- Remember that the person who loses their temper is usually the one who loses a lot more.
- Don't be tempted to retaliate by suppressing your enemies—you will invariably come across as a bully, and people will assume that you have something to hide.

PUBLIC RELATIONS
GIVE A GIFT THAT REALLY DOES SOMETHING
Jim Blythe

CORPORATE GIFT-GIVING is a well-established PR activity. Thanking your most loyal customers by giving them something nice, rewarding staff with freebies, or handing out company calendars to your most efficient suppliers is common practice in many firms.

However, as we all know, having 15 company calendars and six from the local takeaway, plus eight diaries and 23 desk sets does little for your well-being: probably most corporate gifts of this type end up in the bin. This does nothing for your reputation, and still less does it do anything for the recipients of the gifts.

The idea

Choose either a gift that is unique or one that will still be appreciated even if it is duplicated. For example, the House of Commons has Scotch whisky bottled and labeled for MPs and others to buy as gifts for colleagues, constituents, staff, and so forth. Even if someone were to receive several bottles, this would not be a problem, and having a bottle of whisky with the House of Commons crest on it is a good conversation-starter at parties or at Christmas.

Hiring a cartoonist to draw a caricature of the recipient can be a lot less expensive than you might think. One corporate party organizer arranged for a cartoonist to mingle with the guests, drawing each one: the cartoonist charged £300 for the evening, and drew more than 50 cartoons. Paying £6 a time for an original caricature is extremely reasonable, and it makes a memorable gift for anyone.

Promotional clothing can be good in the right circumstances: if you are in a business where special clothing is needed (for example, if you are a motorbike training school) you might want to consider having coveralls printed with your logo. Discreet is better than obvious, of course.

In practice

- Think about your gift: would someone be happy to get three or four of them?
- If possible, give something that is personal to the recipient: it is more likely to be kept if it is personal.
- Try to avoid the obvious, and do ensure that your gift relates to your business.

BUSINESS SKILLS
THE LAST WORD
Patrick Forsyth

MOST PRESENTATIONS MAY well be followed by questions; indeed you may wish to prompt them to create discussion or debate, or simply to avoid an embarrassing gap at the end of the session. A common danger of a question session is that it tails away at the end and thus, especially if someone else is in the chair, the final word is taken away from you. What can happen is that, after a few questions, they are slower coming, the last one is somewhat insubstantial perhaps and the chair then ends the meeting abruptly: "Well there seem to be no more questions, let's leave it there and thank our speaker..."

The idea

One important point is relevant here. You will often do best to keep the last word of the whole session for yourself; so organize to do so.

In practice

- If you are in charge, you must keep an eye on the time, accommodating a question session but allowing time for a final word of summary or perhaps an injunction to act (how you finish clearly depends on the sort of presentation it is).
- A useful route for when you must work with a chairman can be to introduce question time in a way that reserves the right of the speaker to have the final word. This can be done specifically through the chair: "Right, Mr Chairman, perhaps we should see if there are any questions. Then perhaps I could reserve two minutes to summarize before we close." In effect you organize the chair into working your way (and seeing it as sensible so to do). Few people taking the chair will take exception to this approach, still less so if everything is going well.

MANAGING PROJECTS
ALLOW FOR THE UNEXPECTED
Patrick Forsyth

WHATEVER YOUR JOB, some tasks are likely straightforward. They consist essentially of one thing, and all that matters is deciding when to complete them and getting them done. But many tasks are made up of a number of stages that may be different things you do yourself or do with other people. In addition, some stages may be conducted in different locations and the whole process may take days, weeks, or months. All of which makes it important to schedule such multistage things in the right way if all priority tasks are to be completed on time. What can happen is that you take on a project and begin by feeling it is straightforward, but then find that it is rather more complex.

Consider an example: you are to produce some sort of newsletter. Let us say this is done in four stages: deciding the content, writing it, designing it, and printing it. You complete stage one and stage two, but at this point it has taken somewhat longer than you thought. You hasten into stage three, but halfway through it becomes clear that the complete job will not be finished on time. At that point it may be possible to speed things up, but other priorities could suffer, or the only way to hit the deadline may then be to use additional help, spend additional money, or both.

The idea

What needs to be done is to approach scheduling from the end of the cycle. Start with the deadline, estimate the time spent on each stage, make sure that the total job fits into the total time available, and *allow sufficient time for contingencies*—things cannot always be expected to go exactly according to plan.

In practice

- Furthermore, do not look at one thing in isolation: see how something will fit in with or affect other current projects and responsibilities. It may be that you need to adjust the way stages work to fit with other matters that are in progress. For example, perhaps one part can be delegated so that this is ready to enable you to pick up the project and take it through to the end.
- A variety of options may be possible early on, whereas once you are partway through a task the options may well decline in number and the likelihood of other things being affected increases. All that is necessary here is that sufficient planning

time precedes the project, and that in thinking it through you see the overall picture rather than judging whatever it is as a whole and oversimplifying it by just saying "No problem" as you take something on.

BUSINESS SKILLS
LEARN FROM FAILURE
Jonathan Gifford

NOBODY WINS ALL of the time—and the only sure way never to fail is never to take a risk, which is not an option for leaders.

The trick is to try to avoid "betting the company" on any one decision, and for the leader and the organization to learn from the inevitable failures that strew the path to success.

The idea
John Chen, president and CEO of USA software services company Sybase Inc., says that leaders need to embrace failures: what is important is that we learn from the process.

"In some strange way you have to enjoy the negative outcome. The ball bounces both ways. Sometimes it bounces your way and sometimes it doesn't. You can only work hard enough to maximize the chances in your favor ... I think 90 percent of high achievers agree it's not just the results that are important. The path is equally, if not more, important to me. It's like playing a game. If you play a game and lose but did the best you could, you don't feel bad. Sometimes, however, you lose a game because you didn't try, and you feel really lousy. So I think the willingness to keep trying is a big part of achievement. It's actually fun to review some of the failures and what you have learned from them. It helped me tremendously. On long plane rides, I always think about the failures that hurt and what I learned from them."

Eric Schmidt, chairman and CEO of Google, says that leaders need a degree of "arrogance" to be able to believe that they can hope to instigate change, but that they must accept that there will be failures and mistakes.

"Arrogance is needed as a leadership model because you have to believe that you could actually change the world in order to attempt it, otherwise you would never try. You would just sit around and say, 'Oh woe is me'. So we temper it by the reality that we are not perfect, that we make mistakes. We've had a series of business failures, and not large ones but small ones, which we talk a lot about so we can understand the errors that we've made. So while we are not perfect, we are consensus-driven as a company. That's the reason why I spend a lot of time talking and learning from mistakes that we've made."

In practice
* Nobody can bring about change without making mistakes and experiencing failures.
* Sometimes even your best efforts will not be rewarded with success.
* Failures are a huge resource of valuable information: learn from failures; ensure that the organization has learned the same lessons; move on.

PUBLIC RELATIONS
PIGGYBACK YOUR STORY
Jim Blythe

MUCH OF WHAT appears in the news is PR. Often major companies expend a great deal of money and effort to get their stories into print, and to alert the news media to what they are doing.

For the astute PR person, this can provide an opportunity to hijack the publicity and piggyback a PR campaign on the strength of it.

The idea

A large American cellphone company arranged a major PR campaign to publicize its launch of what was then the world's smallest cellphone. A chain of restaurants cashed in on this by announcing a ban on all cellphones in its establishments, on the grounds that they annoy other customers.

The press picked up both stories, and asked the cellphone company to comment on the ban: stupidly, they refused to do so, and the press therefore ran with the story of the ban without mentioning the new telephone at all. This was a PR disaster for the cellphone company, but a triumph for the restaurateurs—the lesson being twofold: first, grabbing an opportunity can often pay off beyond expectations, and, second, if you have a PR campaign you must ALWAYS be prepared to talk to the press!

In practice

- Be prepared to grab opportunities as they arise.
- Always talk to the press if they ask you to—only bad things can happen if you brush them off.
- Move fast—delay will mean the other company's story goes in first.

SELF-HELP
AVOIDING A COMMON CONFUSION
Patrick Forsyth

MOST PEOPLE ARE in agreement about their work situation. In a word, you are busy. There are so many things to do and insufficient time in which to do them all. Furthermore, the picture changes as you watch. Just as you get one thing done and dusted, others join the queue. The mail arrives, you open your email, someone comes up to your desk and asks a favor, the boss says, "This is urgent" ...

Yet realistically not everything is of the same import. As this book makes clear, we are all struggling with a plethora of interruptions, admin assumes monstrous proportions, and the processes we must go through make a labyrinth look like a walk in the park. But some things are core tasks, and at the end of the day it is those things that contribute directly to achieving the results we are charged with that must be put first.

The idea
The principle here is trite, a cliché, but it is also a truism. The right approach here is itself a major contributor to personal productivity. It is simply that you should:

Never confuse activity with achievement.

Recognizing that there is a difference between what is urgent and what is important must become a reflex for the effective time manager. Diversions, distractions, and peripheral activity of all sorts must be recognized and kept in their place.

In practice
* This must be a permanent state of mind; in effect it is one of the guiding principles that help ensure a productive approach.
* Not only must the positive aspect of this be kept in mind; so must the tendency to rationalize the wrong things for the wrong reason, categorizing something as important when it is not.

Priorities, dealt with elsewhere, must be just that—and the measure of what is a priority must always include the measure: does this link to planned results? One might also ask: will it take you forward? You may be busy, but "being busy" is never an end in itself.

TALENT
EMPLOYEE VALUE PROPOSITION
Jeremy Kourdi

THE STRUGGLE TO attract bright, talented workers is increasingly challenging. Firms must devise a comprehensive, appealing perception of their organizations—and it must be genuine, delivering what it promises, or those bright employees will leave.

The idea

The balance of power has shifted from employers to employees. Daniel Pink, former chief speech writer for Al Gore, attributed this shift to "Karl Marx's revenge," with the means of production now in the hands of the workers. The internet has made it easier for potential employees to search for jobs, check expected salary levels, and find out what it is like to work within a particular organization.

While the power of employees has grown, many organizations have lost their appeal to job-seekers. They no longer provide financial stability, with many firms unwilling or unable to offer job security.

In light of these shifting conditions and following research into 90 companies, the Corporate Executive Board (CEB) suggested formulating an employee value proposition (EVP) to attract the best workers. An EVP is the benefits an employee can expect to gain from working with an organization. The CEB found firms that effectively managed EVP could expect to increase their pool of potential workers by 20 percent. Surprisingly, they were also able to decrease the amount they paid to employees—organizations with successful EVPs paid 10 percent less.

With the workplace changing and the number of "free agents" growing, it is increasingly important to develop a strategy for attracting the best. Remember, talented people need organizations less than organizations need talented people.

In practice

- Developing a successful EVP is important to organizations wishing to attract younger workers or technologically skilled workers.
- Emphasize the stimulation and value of the work your organization does, as well as the rewards and opportunities.
- Provide opportunities for employees to engage in informal training and to advance their skills.

- Encourage current and former employees to champion your organization. Many people now put more trust in word of mouth than in advertising.
- Fine-tune your EVP for different sections of the job market.
- Change key aspects of the EVP for different areas of the world.

BUSINESS SKILLS
ANYONE HAVE ANYTHING TO SAY?
Patrick Forsyth

WITH THE FORMAL presentation complete, there is often time for questions and/or comments. Often this presents no problem; the only difficulty is dealing with them, but sometimes a yawning silence is embarrassing and unwanted. What do you do then?

The idea
Resolve to create—prompt—questions or comment if necessary. You need to take the initiative, but must do so in the right way to make it acceptable and effective.

In practice
- There are several ways of directing questions and prompting comments. You can use:
  - Overhead questions: these are questions put to the group generally, and useful for opening up a subject (if there is no response, then you can move on to the next method)—"Right, what do you think the key issue here is? Anyone?"
  - Overhead and then directed at an individual: this method is useful to make the whole group think before looking for an answer from one person—"Right, what do you think the key issues here are? Anyone? John, what do you think?"
  - Direct to individual: this is useful for obtaining individual responses, and testing for understanding—"John, what do you think...?"

- Non-response/rhetorical questions: this is useful where you want to make a point to one or more persons in the group without concentrating on anyone in particular, or for raising a question you would expect to be in the group's mind and then answering it yourself—"What's the key issue? Well, perhaps it's..."

All these methods represent very controlled discussion: dialogue that goes from speaker to group member to speaker and then to another group member (or more), and finally... back to the speaker.

- In addition, bear in mind two further types of questions, the use of which can help to open up a discussion:
  - Re-directed questions, useful to prompt discussion and involvement in the group and answer questions posed to you: "That's a good point John. What do you think the answer is, Mary?" This makes people think and creates involvement, rather than simply providing an answer by the speaker directed at one individual. Choose people thoughtfully; it may often be appropriate to say why you have selected someone—"With your recent involvement in XX, what do you think, Mary?"
  - Developmental questioning, where you take the answer to a previous question and move it around the audience, building on it and asking further questions—"Having established that, how about...?"

SALES
GUARANTEE AS MUCH AS YOU CAN
Patrick Forsyth

ANY PURCHASE PUTS the customer in the position of taking a risk. This is very clear with anything mechanical—the customer wonders whether it will go wrong, and if it does, how things will be handled and what it will cost in time and money. Given that customers have this worry, can you take advantage of it?

The idea

From the motor manufacturer Hyundai ...

Cars are certainly a product for which people worry about reliability. A failed car can not only cost you time and money; it can leave you stranded, risking other things like your reputation at work, or ability to visit someone in hospital. So customers want a guarantee. Over the years the length of the guarantees offered has increased—a year, two years, more—and they do provide confidence and make a sale more likely.

As I write this, Hyundai is offering a full five-year guarantee, and certain aspects of the car are covered for longer than that. Given that this is not the most famous make of car, I suspect that this must help sales success significantly, not just because of the length of coverage but also because of what it implies about Hyundai's confidence in its products, and how it compares with some larger and better-known manufacturers. Five years is longer than many people keep a car, so the guarantee is likely to impress.

This is part of the risk-reversal process referred to elsewhere. The device is here being used as a major sales aid by making the time covered by the warranty extra-long, perhaps unexpectedly long.

In practice

- There is a principle here that can be used in many businesses where, because of their nature, customers worry about reliability and the consequences of something causing problems.

PRICING

SET THE PRICE, EVEN ON THINGS YOU ARE GIVING AWAY

Jim Blythe

IT'S AN INTERESTING facet of the human psyche that we don't value things that we get for nothing. There was the famous example of the man trying to give away £5 notes on the street—and no one accepted them, suspecting a catch.

Many organizations have free newsletters or house magazines that they send out to staff and other stakeholders, knowing that (probably) most of them end up in the bin. On the other hand, who would pay for a newsletter or a brochure from a company?

The idea

The Marketer is the Chartered Institute of Marketing's magazine. It is sent out free to all members, and although there is a mechanism for non-members to subscribe, virtually all the readers get the magazine for free. This is fairly obvious, since the circulation of the magazine is around 37,000 copies per month, and CIM has a worldwide membership of 47,000.

However, it does have a cover price on it of £10 (which is in itself enough to deter any would-be non-member subscribers). The purpose of putting a price on the cover of a free magazine is twofold: first, it gives an impression of quality that is absent from a free magazine. Second, it gives the recipients the impression that they have been given something of real value, not simply something that is cheap and disposable. For Institute members, the cost of the magazines (at £10 a time) is just over half the annual membership fee, so *The Marketer* offers a clear, tangible, and indeed monthly benefit of membership.

People are far more likely to read something that has a price tag attached, even if they did not actually pay the price—the value is clearly there.

In practice

- Don't go over the top on the cover price—it should be realistic, considering the quality and content of the magazine.
- Make sure the price looks "natural," as if it is about right for the magazine, and is no more obtrusive than it would be on a paid-for publication.

- If possible, include a subscription service telephone number. You never know—someone might actually want to subscribe, but in any case it increases the credibility of the cover price.
- This principle applies to other give-aways—free gifts with a purchase should carry a price tag.

CULTURE
GOOD ENOUGH
Jonathan Gifford

LEADERS SHOULD PURSUE excellence but be wary of perfectionism. It is more important to get a product out into the market in a timely way than it is to wait until that product or service is "perfected".

The benefits of the last refinements are likely to be greatly outweighed by failing to release something when the market is ready and before the competition can move in.

The idea
Sir John Harvey-Jones, ex-chairman of ICI, makes the point very well: "Remember that the best is a relative not an absolute measure. The standards of the best are set by the competition and one's aim is always to exceed them. However, as in many other aspects of business management the best, if sought in absolute terms, is the enemy of the good."

Business authors Mike Southon and Chris West have written about the need for companies to adopt more of the attitudes and techniques of entrepreneurs. They warn of the tendency (amongst entrepreneurs, as well as others) towards perfectionism: "Many entrepreneurs are passionate custodians of 'brand value'. While they are right up to a point to be so, beyond this point they are wrong: waiting for perfection can cause fatal delay ... A mentality develops—'Just wait until we've fixed the X problem'—which puts the rest of the business into paralysis."

In the 1990s, the giant mainframe computer manufacturer IBM, was in trouble. The new personal computer was revolutionizing the market, and IBM was seen as being large, bureaucratic and slow to react. The company was obsessed with perfecting its products before release, to the detriment of successful marketing. An insider joke at the time was: "Products aren't launched at IBM. They escape."

IBM staffers John Patrick and David Grossman played a fundamental role in introducing IBM to the potential benefits of the emerging world wide web. They built what was then the world's biggest website for the 1996 Summer Olympics, in the face of considerable resistance from some of their senior colleagues, who were institutionally resistant to "trying something out" in public. But with the Internet, problems could be fixed in real time on the server. Patrick and Grossman introduced a set of new principles for the growing community of IBM web developers, which included: Start simple, grow fast; Just don't inhale (the stale air of orthodoxy); Take risks, make mistakes quickly, fix them fast; Just enough is good enough; Don't get pinned down (to any one way of thinking).

In practice

- Organizations must release products and services at the right moment that are good enough to attract customers.
- Leaders should encourage a culture that embraces change and experiment: "perfectionist" cultures see change and experiment as risks to an idealized brand.
- Products can be developed and improved over time; the search for perfection before launch can be at the expense of the ideal window of opportunity.
- The pursuit of excellence must not be allowed to prevent experimentation or to slow the organization down.

COMMUNICATION
WRITE A NEWSLETTER
Jim Blythe

INTERNAL PUBLICS CAN sometimes be forgotten in the drive to create a top-class external reputation. Yet employees are extremely important—apart from the need to motivate them to work effectively, employees talk to people when they go home. They are the ambassadors of goodwill for the company: if they bad-mouth their employer, they will be believed by their families and friends.

People devote a great deal of their lives to working, and not just for money. If we were motivated just by money, we'd all be pornographers and drug dealers, because that's where the money is. As things stand, we all try to do work we find agreeable for employers who treat us with respect.

There are many ways in which employees can be brought on board: a newsletter is one of them. It provides a non-threatening communications link between management and staff, and (perhaps more importantly) among staff. It also helps to generate a feeling of belonging, which is good for morale.

The idea
Newsletters are simply a brief outline of the latest developments in the firm. They can be produced in hard copy, with or without illustrations (desktop publishing makes it easy to include photos or cartoons), or can be produced electronically. The choice depends on whether employees are all on email or not.

Employees should be encouraged to contribute their own news. Knowing that Jane in Accounts is expecting a baby, or that Eric is moving house this weekend, may seem irrelevant to the management but it helps to create a sense of community. In larger firms, staff might be encouraged to tell the newsletter when they have pulled off a successful deal or had a breakthrough in developing a new product. This can be an important source of information for senior management, since it indicates what people are most proud of in their work.

News from management should be about things the staff will be interested in, such as a big new order, a successful new product launch, or somebody getting a promotion. Negative news should be avoided.

In practice

- Publish regularly—once a week or at least once a month.
- Don't let the newsletter become a propaganda device for management.
- Encourage staff to contribute. At first the contributions will be poor—let them get used to having a newsletter, and the quality will improve.
- Only include positives in the newsletter. There are other places to discuss negatives.

 SALES
TBA—TO BE AVOIDED
Anne Hawkins

IN THE CHASE for additional business, salespeople can occasionally overlook minor details—such as agreeing how much the customer is going to pay.

(If so, what is the likelihood that they'll also remember to negotiate other critical details, such as *when* the customer is going to pay!)

The idea

While no doubt most of your customers are honourable people, this is not a position in which you want to put yourself. TBAs (orders with prices To Be Agreed) should not be an acceptable basis for authorising work to commence as it leaves you vulnerable to having taken on loss-making work (without this being a conscious decision) or, at worst, with no recovery of your costs at all.

You can get caught at an unguarded moment. A valued customer (or one you'd love to get on your books) calls you frantic for help. They need you to make a rush order (or drop everything to carry out a service) to get them out of a fix. With the comment, "Don't worry we'll sort out the paperwork later," they're gone.

Disaster in the making

This disaster-recovery business fell victim to a TBA and needed a little help themselves. A prestigious organisation, about to open a landmark facility, was making arrangements for the forthcoming opening ceremony when it started to rain. Through the roof of the VIP box. In the ensuing panic the disaster-recovery business was contacted and employees, contractors and materials were rushed to the site. Working against the clock, temporary repairs were carried out and by the time the scissors were raised to cut the ribbon, it was sunny smiles all round. The recovery team even returned after the ceremony for another couple of days' work to carry out a permanent fix. The organisation was delighted with the service they had received and the quality of the work carried out and were generous in their offers to recommend the company to others.

They were not so generous, however, in paying the bill!

Apparently unable to pay until they had recovered the cost from their insurers, the recovery business was told it would have to wait. With no contractual payment terms in place there was little they could do but bide their time and learn their lesson.

And the boot can be on the other foot.

It can be very easy when under pressure to rush to find a solution to a predicament without waiting long enough to negotiate and agree terms. If the machine has broken down and you can't get the customer's order out ...

You could end up with a bill you'd never bargained for!

In practice

- Insist on the customer placing an order before you start work—in an emergency it can be faxed over to you or given to you on your arrival at the site. Don't forget to check those terms and conditions!
- If you are in a business where the nature of the work makes it difficult to set a final price, agree on the core price (preferably with formalised stage payments) and the basis (and timescale) on which 'extras' are to be agreed, invoiced ... and paid!

SELF-HELP
RESOLVE TO "BLITZ THE BITS"
Patrick Forsyth

NOTHING IS PERFECT and it is inevitable that as you plan and sort and spend most time on priorities some of the small miscellaneous tasks may mount up. If this is realistically what happens—and for many people it is—then it is no good ignoring it and pretending that it does not occur. Rather, you need to recognize it and decide on a way of dealing with it.

The idea

Make the miscellaneous a priority. Actually, let me rephrase that: make the miscellaneous a priority *occasionally*.

The best way is simply to program an occasional blitz on the bits and pieces. Not because the individual things to do in this category are vital, but because clearing any backlog of this sort will act disproportionately to clear paper from your desk and systems. (Remember 80 percent of the paper that crosses your desk is less important than the rest.)

In practice

- So, just occasionally, clear a few minutes, or an hour if that is what it takes, and go through any outstanding bits and pieces. Write that name in your address book, answer that long outstanding email, phone back those people whom you wish to keep in touch with but who have not qualified recently as priorities to contact, fill in that analysis form from accounts, and do all the other kinds of thing you know tend to get left out and mount up.

- Ideally there should be no bits and pieces. If you operate truly effectively, then this sort of thing will not get left out; it will be dealt with as you go. Really? Pigs might fly. If you are realistic, then, like me, you will find this kind of "catch-up" useful. Be sure it does not happen too often, but when it does, you can take some satisfaction from the fact that a session to "blitz on the bits" clears the decks and puts you back on top of things again. It makes you more able to deal with the key tasks without nagging distractions.

SALES

USE VISUAL AIDS EVEN WHEN YOU CANNOT

Patrick Forsyth

EVERY SALESPERSON KNOWS the truth of the old saying that a picture is worth a thousand words. Visual aids (everything from a graph to the product itself) have to be used in the right way. You must let them speak for themselves, and that means keeping quiet once they have been introduced and shown. (This is typically not something that salespeople find easy to do, but people cannot concentrate on taking in what they see and listening at the same time, so if you talk, they might miss a point and your case will be diluted.)

The idea

This comes from the world of mining ...

The way to make the best of visual aids is not simply to see what is available and use it, whether it's appropriate or not. It is to see what *could* be useful and organize whatever is necessary to make it available. A salesperson selling mining equipment made this point strongly to me. He sold machines like a Black & Decker drill but the size of a small car. It was not practical to bring a machine along to someone's office, and it was difficult to get potential buyers to go and look at machines until he had generated some interest.

This salesperson carried a large and very heavy pilot's case to his first meetings with prospects. Inside was a piece of granite. (He had a nice story about how it was formed millions of years ago and came from the Grampian Mountains in Scotland.) One side of it had been cut by the machine, as easily as a knife would go through butter, judging by how flat and shiny it was. It provided dramatic evidence of the power and precision of the equipment, and was doubly effective in making its point because, given the nature of the machinery, prospects were not expecting to see anything.

In practice

- If necessary you must contrive or invent something that will do the visual job you want, that will stimulate a prospect's imagination. Of course, the first task is to decide what role the visual can usefully play.
- Even when what is sold is not very visual, the same principle applies. For example, I saw an accountancy firm increase the sales of audits to small/medium-sized businesses by producing a double-sized set of accounts. This could then be shown to prospects with a commentary about what they could do with the information they contained (for example, better manage their cash flow).

INNOVATION

INNOVATIONS IN DAY-TO-DAY CONVENIENCE

Jeremy Kourdi

EVERYDAY LIFE PROVIDES people with a large number of small challenges. By considering potential solutions to these challenges, it is possible to develop a new product that will be used regularly by many people.

The idea

Creating innovative products for day-to-day convenience combines the financial benefits of being a first mover with the reward of creating a product that is used every day by many people.

An example of an innovation in day-to-day convenience occurred in 1938, when Lazlo Biro, while working as a journalist, noticed that the ink used in newspaper printing dried quickly. He worked with his brother, the chemist Georg Biro, to produce a pen with a rotating socket that picked up ink as it moved. The BIC version of this innovation is now a ubiquitous possession, with 14 million pens sold *every day*.

Another example of the drive for everyday convenience is the BlackBerry device. The BlackBerry first made headway into the mobile communications market by concentrating on a portable email device, but now incorporates text messaging, cellphone, web browsing, and other wireless services. An impressive participant in the all-in-one convenience trend in modern technology, the BlackBerry is now a common reference in popular culture and a favorite of businesspeople across the world. However, it is possible that BlackBerry did not innovate as far as it could have, with a storm of legal controversy surrounding originality. Regardless of this, both Biro and BlackBerry provide an important lesson: push creativity to its limits and find a way to provide simple, ubiquitous convenience.

In practice

- Try to design products with a focus on ease of use.
- Focus on the time-saving potential of the idea.
- Consider using deep-dive prototyping to develop, improve, and test the product.
- Don't view things as impossible—consider how you can achieve things, not whether you can.
- Consider your everyday life—what products would you most like to see enter the market?
- Observe existing products and decide how they can be more convenient and user-friendly.
- Ensure you patent your inventions as soon as possible.

PUBLIC RELATIONS
BECOME SUSTAINABLE
Jim Blythe

BEING PHILANTHROPIC IS one thing—doing things that also help the business is something else. Using your employees to clean up a local beauty spot is a wonderful PR exercise, because it leads to news coverage and it also motivates your staff—they feel they are working for a caring organization. However, it does virtually nothing for the longer-term benefit of the business.

Moving from a purely publicity-oriented approach to a business-oriented approach requires a certain amount of creative thought and long-term commitment—but then PR is a long-term process, as is running a business.

The idea

Microsoft give away computers to schools. This is an example of philanthropy—the schools benefit from the free computers, and Microsoft creates a feel-good factor with the parents, teachers, and children.

However, the real pay-off is that the computers (of course) are loaded with Microsoft software. The children therefore grow up with Microsoft, the teachers have to learn to use it, and even the parents are likely to use it if they have a computer at home, simply because they need their children to be able to transfer easily between home and school.

Equally, Procter & Gamble have the problem of trying to do business with people in the developing world who live on less than a dollar a day. The company therefore invests in projects that use P&G products to create a higher level of earnings. This is very much a long-term strategy—it may be 40 years before the programs show results—but for P&G this is not a problem. In the meantime, they are still getting all the benefits of being philanthropic.

Becoming sustainable in this way adds value to your philanthropy and creates a long-term benefit for your company.

In practice
- Think long-term. What you give today may not pay dividends for years—but it will pay off eventually.
- Be philanthropic by all means, but keep an eye on the long-term sustainable benefits.
- Don't waste time, effort, and money on doing anything that doesn't connect directly to your business in the longer term.

PROFITABILITY
MILK THOSE COWS!
Anne Hawkins

PRODUCTS OR SERVICES that have gone through the development stage, have been introduced into the market, and for which there is now relatively stable demand are known as 'cows'—or more importantly, as 'cash cows'. As it says on the label, if you get it right, you can milk the 'cow' and cash should pour back into the business.

The idea

Nurture your 'cows' to ensure a high cash yield through their ability to earn decent margins on reducing investment.

There are two reasons why you should be earning decent margins on your products. Firstly, if you've aligned your business correctly and understood what your customer wants, the price he is currently paying 'rewards' you not just for the ongoing costs you are incurring, but also for the investment you've already made in the earlier development and 'star' stages of the cycle. Secondly, as you've tackled a lot of those teething problems (e.g. with tooling) that had previously been adding to your costs, your margins improve.

Not only do margins look good, investment in Working Capital should also be decreasing as you can reduce buffer stock as sales volumes and lead times become more predictable and your supply chain and quality more reliable.

However, businesses have a strange habit of killing off their cows.

It's often the fault of the costing system. Absorption costing systems tend to over-cost products at the 'cow' stage of the cycle.

Does this matter? It does if people unwittingly use the costing system for decision-making. Operations are moved to sub-contractors as the 'make-buy' decision gets distorted; products are moved to 'low-cost' economies that aren't; and if prices start to fall due to increased competition, the decision is taken to axe products that are in reality still highly profitable.

Job lot

This sub-contractor offered two capabilities—high-tech machining and manual assembly—but unfortunately had only one internal cost rate. The effect of this was to substantially under-cost what were cost-intensive machining jobs and over-cost assembly work. At a strategic review, they looked at the financials and decided to ditch their assembly work on which they appeared to be making little if any margin and canvass for loads more apparently highly-profitable machining work. The result? Disastrous. It became all too clear that the assembly work was their cash cow and that without it the business, from a financial standpoint, began to grind to a halt. The company did survive but had a tough time with huge amounts of debt to service while it reversed its strategy and focused on what actually proved to be not only its cash cow, but also its core competence—manual assembly.

In practice

- Manage your products through each stage of their life-cycle—you may need to squeeze every drop you can out of your 'cows' if you're going to be able to find the cash to bring those new products to fruition.
- Treat the information from your costing system with scepticism!

MARKETING

DO YOU DISSOLVE YOUR WORRIES IN A SOLUTION?

Andy Maslen

I WAS TAKING my children to school this morning and we saw a lovely big truck, on the side of which was emblazoned a picture of a window frame and the immortal line "joinery solutions." Son Number Two tugged on my hand and said, "Daddy, why doesn't he just say 'Handmade hardwood window frames'?" (My son is very advanced for his age.)

"Perhaps," I said, "he's worried that if he says that, people won't take him seriously." "Yes, Daddy," he said. "But now they don't know what makes him special." "Well then," I continued, a little nonplussed at this cross-examination, "maybe he thinks 'joinery solutions' is a modern thing to say." "But that's what everyone says now, Daddy. Thank goodness at school we have milk in the morning, not 'liquid dairy solutions.'"

The idea
From just about everyone
In just one week I have seen the following:

- "Delivering solutions globally."
- "Drinking water solutions."
- "Image solutions."
- "Customer relationship management solutions."

And best of all, by some considerable margin, in an advert for the lingerie section of a local department store:

- "Bra solutions."

This is what's known in the copywriting business as me-too-itis. The funny thing is, nobody who actually *buys* any of this stuff actually gives an expletive solution for "solution." Householders who want new wooden window frames generally call them just that. And, having checked with a couple of my female acquaintances, I can confidently assert that women go shopping for a new bra—not a new bra solution.

So what's going on? I suspect it has something to do with bored marketing executives wishing their products were more "exciting" and trying to jazz them up by hitching them to the s-word. Either that or imagining their customers will somehow feel cheated at being offered just a spade instead of an "excavation solution." This is just laziness. If you don't think "spade" is sufficient to sell spades, then do your research and be creative. Truly creative. Call it an "old-style, drop-forged spade with ash haft and non-blister grip." More people will buy it and you'll make more money.

In practice
- Of course you want your products to get customers salivating. But that means thinking about what they're *really* looking for, rather than just copying somebody else's lame copywriting idea.
- And yes, of course they want a solution to a problem of some kind, but what they *don't* want—or ever think of asking for—is a blah blah blah solution. Avoid.

LEADERSHIP
KEEP A SENSE OF BURNING URGENCY
Jonathan Gifford

LEADERS NEED TO transmit their own sense of urgency to their colleagues. There is a great deal to achieve and a limited amount of time; it is essential that leaders impress their sense of urgency on the team from day one.

The idea

Ex-chairman and CEO of Schering-Plough, Fred Hassan, took over the pharmaceutical company when it was facing significant legal and financial problems.

"I've been facing a lot of challenges in my career. This one was the biggest I've ever seen. So I set up a roadmap as quickly as I could. I had to move forward with imperfect data, and that's where experience and insights help ... It was a very simple roadmap of five different phases ... we had to break the problem down into bite-size pieces that we could deal with, and we still had to look forward to a period when there was going to be a lot of good hope for the company. If people can see the hope—the light at the end of the tunnel—then they do build up that sense of purpose that I was trying to build ... Then also there is a sense of urgency. Once you've built up a sense of direction in terms of where you're going, you have to build up a sense of urgency. And if you can show that you can generate energy inside yourself and generate energy around you, the whole system starts to generate energy around that sense of direction, and then one gets about doing some very purposeful things."

Microsoft founder Bill Gates is famous for his energy and his drive to be the best. Interviewed in his office looking out on the huge new "Microsoft campus" in Seattle after the company had established itself as the world's leading software corporation, Gates was still hungry for more.

"We have a vision of where we are trying to go, and we're a long ways away from it ... We are not top of the networking heap, or the spreadsheet heap, or the word processing heap. Computers are not very easy to use. We don't have information at our fingertips. There is one thing that is fun—I look out there and see fun people to work with, who are learning a lot ... [But] staring out the window and saying, 'Isn't this great,' is not the solution to pushing things forward ... You've got to keep driving hard."

In practice

- Leaders must convey their sense of burning urgency to their colleagues.
- The team needs to understand what needs to be done; the benefits of doing it and the need to do it quickly. The leader's own energy can then begin to spread through the organization.
- The sense of urgency must stay in place after the first objectives have been met. There is a real danger of allowing the organization to relax. There are always new challenges.

PUBLIC RELATIONS
WRITE A CASE STUDY
Jim Blythe

IN THE BUSINESS-to-business environment, and even in many consumer industries, there are times when simply talking about yourself becomes tedious for the readers. If you're in consultancy, training, education, or anything where you are helping clients, you could gain a lot by talking about your clients rather than yourself.

Companies such as trainers and consultants often have trouble establishing credibility with new customers. After all, you are expecting people to commit to you before they know whether you're any good—and that takes a great deal of faith.

The idea

What many firms do is write case studies about their clients. Obviously the clients have to be happy for this to happen, and you won't be able to put anything in there that is confidential, but in many cases the clients themselves are more than happy to have some extra PR at no cost or effort to themselves apart from approving the copy.

The case studies can go on your website, or if they are newsworthy enough they could even be sent to trade magazines. A good case study need only be a couple of hundred words long, but it's a triple-win situation. You get publicity and improve your own credibility, your client gets extra coverage with third-party endorsement from you, and the journals get good, interesting copy that fills a space. Another plus is that case studies have a long life—they are less time-sensitive than news stories.

Almost any consumer service industry can produce case studies. A flying school could run profiles of successful students, talking about their background and reasons for learning to fly: a hair salon could produce a write-up about a client who has appeared on TV or been voted Woman of the Year, and so forth.

As always, the key is to be alert for opportunities.

In practice

- Always check with your customer before using them as a case study.
- Give as much detail as you can—if you can quote figures for improved business, for example, then do so (even if you only say "Our client's turnover increased 23 percent in a single year").
- Use the human factor as much as you can. Quotes from your contact at the client firm will always go down well: pictures are even better.

MANAGING TIME
GIVE YOURSELF SOME TIME RULES
Patrick Forsyth

WHEN THINGS GET left, as they can easily do, then it can cause problems, and those problems can waste more time. Something is late. Someone chases. You respond (with excuses?). Moving into firefighting mode, you clear a gap, maybe affecting other matters, and then the omission is made good.

The idea
There is a whole category of things where a simple rule will avoid them being overlooked and causing the sequence of events described above: give yourself an "action now" time rule that prompts to get something out of the way and helps make doing so a habit.

In practice
- You can choose the time extent. You might select two minutes. If something appears needing action and you reckon it can be done in a couple of minutes—do it at once and get it out of the way.
- The time needs to fit your work and activity. For some people it might be two minutes, or ten or something in between, but the assessment you make and how you act because of it can keep what may be a significant percentage of your tasks on the move in a way that prevents them being likely to get delayed or cause problems.

This is an example of a wholly self-imposed discipline, but one that can work well and add to your time management effectiveness just a little more.

MANAGING
BE FIRM
Jonathan Gifford

LEADERS NEED TO take firm action when standards have been allowed to slip, or when groups of colleagues attempt to get exceptional treatment by using their power or influence.

Leaders who are not firm will be perceived as being weak. People are resentful when a colleague's poor performance or exceptional treatment is overlooked. The organization begins to suffer.

The idea

When Douglas Conant took over as president and chairman of Campbell Soups, the company was in trouble. Conant joined the company in 2001, after it had lost half its market value and been the worst-performing food company in the world for the previous four years.

"If you can imagine being in a troubled work environment for four years as an employee, seeing it go from bad to worse ... We had lost a lot of our best people and we needed to replace them." Conant took firm action. "I'm known around here as being very tough on standards but being tender with people. We had a level of activity and competence that was required to do the job, to dig ourselves out of the hole. People needed to get up to that—to that level of competence. If they couldn't, we'd help them find a role in the organization or outside the organization where they could succeed."

When television executive, Greg Dyke, became managing director of the British television franchise, LWT, he found that established union agreements were making it unaffordable to make programmes in-house. Greg told the team that unless the existing arrangements were changed, all future programmes would have to be made by independent producers. He reduced the standing workforce from 1,500 to 800, and embarked on a programme of discussions with groups of 20 colleagues at a time to explain why the changes were necessary for the company's survival. He offered generous redundancy terms to people who decided not to stay on under the new regime.

"One day I went to the leaving party of some videotape engineers who had earned fortunes in their time at LWT but who didn't want to stay on in the new world when their wages, and particularly their overtime, would be cut dramatically. They had decided to take redundancy instead. One of them summed up the past when he said quite openly to me, 'You can't blame us, governor. If the management were fools enough to give it, we were going to take it.' Who can disagree?"

In practice

- No organization can be run without firm direction.
- Leaders should establish clear standards and benchmarks of behavior that must be seen to apply to every group and individual.
- If any group or individual is benefitting unfairly from a position of power or influence, every other member of the team feels disadvantaged.
- Practices that have become established may no longer be in the organization's best interests. People will want to continue as they have always done; it is a leader's job to be firm.

SALES
MAKE YOUR CUSTOMER IMPROVE YOUR PRODUCTIVITY
Patrick Forsyth

FOR ANYONE SELLING, and certainly for a full-time salesperson, sales productivity is vital. Only when you are face to face with a customer or prospect will you produce business, yet there is so much more to be done. Tasks ranging from administration to traveling (and details like finding somewhere to park) take up time and, if unchecked, reduce your productivity.

The idea
From a financial adviser based in the City of London ...

I regularly receive telephone calls from financial advisers (don't we all?), and one sticks very much in my mind. He was interesting and personable, and I listened for longer than I might have done with someone less good. I already had an adviser I was happy with, however, and did not want to pursue matters with him. But I did ask him what would happen next should I be interested. "You come and see me," he said. This surprised me. Most such people cannot wait to come to my home or office, so I queried it. "Don't you mean *you* come and see *me*?" When he confirmed that I must visit him, I explained my interest, and asked him why he used this tactic.

He explained that, first, he was concerned to maximize his productivity. "I spend time on the telephone and I spend time with prospects and clients," he said, "but I spend no time traveling, parking or sitting in other people's reception areas." Second, he was concerned to identify the best prospects. "Only those with real interest will take the time and trouble to visit me." In addition, he found that the tactic differentiated him from other advisers. "Even before I meet people they have an impression of me that helps me. They are intrigued and interested, and arrive prepared to listen," he commented.

He added that it was partly because he was based in central London and dealing with clients within easy reach of his office that this system worked well for him. He had been top salesperson in the company three years running. Of course, some prospects will have no truck with this, but enough liked it to make his approach effective—and his productivity, and thus his sales results, high.

In practice
- Never fear trying radically different ideas (although you may sensibly test them first).
- Assisting customers' productivity always goes down well, but keep tight control of your own productivity too.

BUSINESS SKILLS
INTELLIGENT NEGOTIATING
Jeremy Kourdi

By LEARNING WHERE the pitfalls lie in negotiations, it is possible to sidestep them and ensure satisfying results that last for all involved.

The idea

Harvard Business School (HBS) professor James Sebenius specializes in the field of complex negotiations. In 1993, HBS made negotiation a required course in its MBA program, and created a negotiation department within the school.

Sebenius identified six mistakes responsible for the failure of many negotiations. By avoiding them you can negotiate your way to success. These pitfalls, outlined in *Harvard Business Review*, are:

- *Neglecting the other side's problems.* If you do not understand the problems your negotiation partner is trying to overcome, you will not be able to offer the best solution.
- *Letting price bulldoze other interests.* It is easy to focus exclusively on price. Make sure you do not ignore other important factors—such as creating a positive working relationship, goodwill, a social contract between both sides, and a deal-making process that is respectful and fair to everyone.
- *Letting positions drive out interests.* Despite the existence of opposing positions, there may be compatible interests. Rather than trying to persuade someone to abandon a particular position, it can be more productive to develop a deal that satisfies a diverse range of interests.
- *Searching too hard for common ground.* Common ground can help negotiations, but different interests can allow both sides to get something out of the deal.
- *Neglecting BATNA.* This refers to the "best alternative to a negotiated agreement": the options you will be faced with if the deal falls through. By analyzing your prospects—and

your partner's prospects—you can decide what to offer in the negotiation and when to offer it.

- *Failing to correct for skewed vision.* Two types of bias can affect negotiations—*role bias* and *partisan perceptions.* Role bias (the confirming evidence trap) is the tendency to interpret information in self-serving ways, overestimating your chances of success, while partisan perceptions (the over-confidence trap) is the propensity to glorify your own position while vilifying opponents. You can overcome these biases by placing yourself in the position of your "opponent."

In practice

- An understanding of others' desires and perspective is crucial to being able to persuade them why they should agree to your proposal. Explore their position with them.
- Research an individual or company before negotiation. Do not limit research to information immediately relevant to the deal—a broad knowledge of the industry, company goals, and market conditions the organization faces will give you extra weight in negotiations.
- Do not feel the need to be overly aggressive. Show that you are a firm negotiator, but remember that mutual understanding and establishing rapport will yield large rewards.
- Conduct a full analysis of potential agreements that allow both sides to win, without either party having to accept a loss.

238 BUSINESS SKILLS
BITE-SIZED AND MANAGEABLE
Patrick Forsyth

SOMEONE TELEPHONED ME recently selling mobile phones. Because such were on my mind (I knew my contract was nearly up)—perhaps rashly—I asked for some details. The flood gates opened and I found myself swept along by a torrent of figures. It was far too much to keep in mind; I was being asked to compare this with that ... and that and that and that. I rapidly decided this was not going to be a useful review and discontinued the call.

The problem of getting information across in a way that keeps it manageable is common to presenting. Any mechanism that helps achieve this is worth a moment's thought.

The idea

The idea here is to use what has become known as "chunking". I had not heard the term until recently, so let me explain:

If you want to order additional copies of this book you should telephone 02074218120, but you will not see this number printed like that anywhere else; all telephone numbers are chunked. This one to: (0)20 7421 8120. It is much more difficult to remember—or even read—a string of 11 undifferentiated numbers than 3 sets: one of 3, one of 4, and then one of 4 again. Even in these days of speed dialling, think how many numbers you know in your head. If you want even small children to remember your mobile number (in case they get lost), you break it down still more, perhaps linking it to words or a story.

In practice

- This principle applies to anything that we need to explain, from the chapters in a book to the size of "information units" we use when making a presentation. Any information that goes on and on—losing itself in its own complexities—can usefully be divided into bite-sized chunks.
- This is particularly useful for explaining numbers: telephone numbers, sales figures, projections, forecasts, accounts, etc.
- And it is especially useful for explaining large numbers. As a huge example, there are some seven thousand million, million, million, million atoms in a human body. Unimaginable, but perhaps the sheer size is better explained by saying it is a number 7—followed by 27 zeros.
- So, whenever an explanation is getting out of hand, stop, think and divide it into logically arranged bite-sized pieces.

COST CUTTING

MAKE SURE YOU'RE NOT INADVERTENTLY INCREASING COSTS!

Anne Hawkins

How INTEGRATED IS the management of your business? Do you have 'joined up' thinking by your management team? Or are metrics (or measures of performance) departmentalised with scant regard as to whether great performance in one area has struck a blow elsewhere?

You get what you measure—so make sure it's what you want.

The idea

Look carefully at proposals to improve costs as not all of them will have the desired effect.

Purchasing savings

Keep your purchasing staff close to their customers—that is, everyone else in the business. Be cautious of making price savings the key performance target for buyers as this might prove to be a very costly improvement initiative! What matters isn't price but value, so you need to monitor usage to see if you're really saving money. Whenever buyers change the source or specification of products not only should they review the impact on usage, but they should also check with their internal customers for feedback on other cost impacts.

For example, if you change your supply of materials you need to consider not just the effect on usage but also issues such as whether machines jam more frequently, assembly takes longer, or if there are increases in warranty claims. Purchasing cheaper paper for your printer may not just mean you can no longer duplex print, but the dust produced may mean more frequent service call-outs ...

Total acquisition costs

Side-stepping suppliers approved by headoffice for cheaper alternatives might result in the overall loss to the group of retrospective purchasing discounts.

Buying more expensive (but more energy-efficient) equipment may prove the cheaper option. And don't overlook other types of running cost—for example, the lower-priced printer might require expensive print cartridges.

Personnel
The total acquisition cost of your most valuable assets—your people, is phenomenal. Just think payroll into perpetuity! So it might pay to re-think what constitutes cost-effective when it comes to the selection and remuneration of employees.

And of course there are those decisions taken to 'save money' by sub-contracting work out—where you end up paying the supplier's costs as well as your own.

And investing in tooling to save time making your products only to find that you haven't actually saved any money ... in fact, you've added to your costs by buying the tooling.

'Make do and mend' may be costing you a fortune.

It's not that straight-forward is it?

In practice
- Talk through the wider implications of cost improvement proposals with all parties before implementation—then monitor and review to pick up on any unintended consequences. These might not always be negative!

CULTURE
MAKE SMALL IMPROVEMENTS
Jonathan Gifford

LEADERS WHO RELY on remarkable and spectacular successes as the route towards their goal are likely to be disappointed.

Steady, incremental improvements are more achievable and more reliable.

The idea

Reuben Mark, former chairman and CEO of Colgate-Palmolive, led his company for a remarkably long period, serving 23 years as CEO and 22 years as chairman. He suggests that any company's progress should be targetted at small, incremental gains.

Using the analogy of the game of baseball, he argues that leaders should not rely on a spectacular but unlikely succession of dramatic successes—"home runs"; but on the steady accumulation of less spectacular results—"singles and doubles".

"The essence of leadership is the idea of continuous improvement. No matter what, you can always coach people to do a little better, and if everyone does that, the whole organization moves up ... It's not romantic and not revolutionary or headline-getting, but over time, that's what generates success."

Vikas Kedia is an India-born Internet entrepreneur who founded InterNext Technologies, based in Nevada, USA. After the unsuccessful launch of a software company to detect click fraud in online advertising, Kedia ran out of money. He found a job as a software designer, paid off his debts, and had the idea for developing an online community site that would allow people to share advice and information about their own financial problems online, in real time. Kedia highlights small improvements as one of the key means to achieving the successful new venture's monthly, tactical goals.

"We have strategic goals with us on what we are doing and why we are doing this. But we optimize our tactical goals on a monthly basis ... Within the organization, if we recognize that we can make small improvements we will do these. The idea is there is no one big thing that will get us where we want to get. There are actually a lot of small things that will help us to get where we want to get. So we keep on making the small improvements, keeping in mind the broader strategy."

In practice

- Once the vision is established, it is more likely to be achieved by a series of small advancements than by dramatic leaps forward.
- Keep looking for any big breakthroughs that might be achievable, but look on a daily basis for small improvements that will move you towards your goals.
- Encourage an attitude and a spirit within the team that makes people feel that they have not had a successful day unless they have made some improvement to their part of the operation.

PUBLIC RELATIONS
SPONSOR SOMETHING IN B2B
Jim Blythe

MOST SPONSORSHIP IS aimed at encouraging business-to-consumer relationships, but there is really nothing to stop business-to-business companies sponsoring appropriate events. Typically, business-to-business markets are characterized by having relatively few customers, so those you have are worth impressing.

We tend to think that business buyers are not affected by emotional considerations, so a business buyer who supports Manchester United will not increase his purchase of left-handed sproggletackets just because their manufacturer sponsors the team. This is far from being the case—industrial buyers are still human beings, and are as affected by emotional considerations as are the rest of us.

Of course, they need to justify their decisions—after all, if we as consumers decide to buy something, we don't have to justify it to the boss!

The idea

Inmarsat is a company that provides cellphone communications services to ships, aircraft, and workers in remote parts of the world. In effect, the company provides cellphone services where everybody else is out of signal, because its systems work direct to satellites without the need for a network of ground stations. Obviously, this service comes at a price, so Inmarsat deals mainly with corporations such as shipping lines, oil exploration companies, mining companies, and airlines.

Inmarsat sponsored the World Rally Championship for several years. The rally emphasizes driving in remote and inhospitable parts of the world—precisely the locations where Inmarsat can provide service—and so it matches exactly with the company's image of reliability and tenacity in the face of challenging environments.

In exchange for the sponsorship, Inmarsat got TV exposure in more than 200 countries. Each of the 14 stages of the rally provides an opportunity for corporate hospitality, and Inmarsat technology is used to relay information to the TV stations that give updates on the progress of the rally. Without this technical input, TV stations would be very limited in their ability to report progress on the rally, so of course they are happy to acknowledge the source of the information. This in itself provides a dramatic demonstration of the company's technical capabilities.

Participative sponsorship, in which the relationship goes beyond a mere exchange of money for publicity, is a growing area. Inmarsat has certainly created an impact with its innovative approach.

In practice

- Find something that demonstrates your capabilities.
- Look for the spinoffs: the corporate hospitality possibilities, the TV link-ups, the news value.
- Ensure that your B2B customers know what you're doing.

PERFORMANCE
DO A SWAP
Patrick Forsyth

EVERYONE HAS DIFFERENT skills and also different things they get done most quickly and easily. Some of the things you find laborious a colleague may think to be small beer. You can use this fact to save time.

The idea

As pretty much everyone is in this position, it makes sense to swap some tasks. For example, in sales someone has to analyse, document, and circulate sales results in various forms (to show sales progress, salesmen's targets, results by territory, etc.). If one person is very good at the analysis—crunching the numbers— and another is good at presenting the information graphically— something needing expertise in the right computer program— then perhaps they can collaborate. All the analysis can be done by one, while all the graphic representation is done by the other. The entire job might then be completed more easily and faster— leaving more time to apply to other tasks, primarily dealing with customers.

If such a deal works well, the gain can be considerable. You may want to be on the lookout for suitable swap situations that will help you.

In practice

- Swapping is something that can be done in all sorts of ways around groups of people working together (even in different departments). There is only one possible snag to watch out for and that is any developmental role that is part of a job having been allocated to someone in the first place. If a manager expects you to become familiar with a task and build up some sort of expertise in it, then you are not likely to do that by letting someone else do the work.

- Swap arrangements must turn out to be fairly balanced, of course—if one party finds themselves with far more work than the other, then the arrangement will not last, as someone will end up unhappy. More complex swaps—for example, two smaller tasks for one larger one—may achieve a suitable balance. Choose well and you may evolve a number of such arrangements all around the organization, each of which saves you time. As long as the network does not become too complicated (it must continue to work when you are away for a while, and deadlines must be compatible), then it is one more useful way of saving time on a regular basis.

SALES
THE RIGHT WEIGHT OF CASE
Patrick Forsyth

A DIFFICULTY SOME salespeople have is in deciding how much to say about their product or service. Realistically comprehensiveness is often not one of the options: more and more buyers lay down time restraints in one way or another. You might sensibly regard such a time limit as negotiable, but once you have agreed it there is merit in sticking to it, unless the prospect is so interested that they extend it, either formally or informally. Beyond that pragmatic view, however, how do you judge how much to say?

The idea
From research done by m62 visualcommunications ltd ...

Most of the ideas suggested here are based as much as anything on observation, but this one is based on research. This company specializes in helping create business-winning presentations (deciding on the message and creating the visual aids to convey it). In this capacity its staff must judge carefully how much to suggest is said, not least because they can be paid in part on results. So they did some research into the "weight of a case."

The answer was clear. The greatest chance of a positive reaction is given by five key points stated in benefit form. Do not take that too literally: you may do well by using four or six, or even seven points. But outside these parameters you risk a negative reaction. Too few points, and the case will sound insubstantial; too many, and it will become tedious and people will lose interest. Of course, quantity is not everything. Naturally it matters what you say and how you say it, and what priority you give to different points. But there is guidance here, and it is worth thinking in this way about the core of your message—the case you want to present. Although the research was directed primarily at "big-ticket" selling, and situations where a formal pitch and presentation is necessary, common sense suggests that it is a good general point to bear in mind.

Note: the research is described in Nick Oulton's *Killer Presentations* (How To Books), which also outlines the best methodology you could wish for in creating persuasive PowerPoint presentations.

In practice
- The case you make easily becomes repetitive if you don't give it thought. So analyze what you say, and make sure it has sufficient "weight" in the kind of way described above.

MANAGING MEETINGS
NEVER COMPETE WITH INTERRUPTIONS
Patrick Forsyth

MEETINGS, EVEN THOSE that are well planned, are vulnerable to distractions. A variety of time-wasting things can and do take place during meetings. Prevention is clearly best, but you may have to deal (and so does the chair) with everything from tea and coffee being noisily delivered, to people being handed, or leaving to collect or deal with, messages—"Sorry, but I just must attend to this one"— and the ubiquitous cellphone. So, what to do?

The idea

In all cases the best rule is to act so as not to allow the distraction to spoil things.

In practice

- So you should acknowledge the distraction, then wait until it has passed. Take a natural break while the tea and coffee are poured, for instance. A two-minute "stretch" break every now and then will anyway help keep people alert in a long meeting, and prevent individuals causing a disturbance as they have to excuse themselves for a moment.
- If interruptions are managed well, then time wasted will be kept to the minimum and key elements of the meeting—a presentation of some important plan, perhaps—will not lose effectiveness and impact by being only half heard or understood. Thus you will avoid the need for recapping and further explanation, which extends the time still more.
- A good chair will think of such things in advance, time the refreshments to coincide with a natural break (and, ideally, the conclusion of an item on the agenda), make sure that cellphones and bleeping reminder systems are switched off, and see that suitable instructions have been left outside the meeting room about messages.

MARKETING
EXPERIENTIAL MARKETING
Jeremy Kourdi

HOLDING GATHERINGS TO celebrate and promote your product can be a lively, effective way to get customers involved with and attached to your brand and services.

The idea

The idea of using themed parties to promote products challenges the assumption that potential customers are simply passive viewers of advertising. By actively involving customers in an "experiential" advertising event you differentiate your brand and build strong customer loyalty.

Holding a brand-themed party typically involves selecting a range of products to promote, and creating a way to integrate a sales pitch into a celebratory social event. Two famous examples of this tactic are Avon beauty parties and Ann Summers parties, where customers are invited to become salespeople and sell products to their friends in the context of a party. Party-goers try free samples and discuss the merits of different products. This creates a feeling of kinship and humor among customers rather than a feeling of being targeted by marketing—making them more receptive to purchasing products.

The sales tactic does not always have to be overt. Branded parties can simply be an opportunity to create awareness of your brand, create a buzz around your company, and entice people into buying at a later date. In 2006, Diageo, the company producing Baileys Irish Cream, hosted a series of "cocktail parties" in London nightclubs, where party-goers were given complimentary Baileys liquor and free recipes for using Baileys in cocktails and desserts.

Whether you are using branded parties to build an awareness of your company, or simply to sell products, they provide an enjoyable and effective marketing solution.

In practice
- Branded parties do not have to be aimed at just the "young and trendy" market—a range of events can be organized to cater to the preferences of your target customers.
- Ensure the event is as enjoyable and stress-free as possible, to allow attendees to form positive associations with your product.
- Provide free samples to introduce your product.
- Be original. Cutting-edge and daring ideas for corporate parties can gain large amounts of publicity.
- Consider the tone of the event, taking into account the desires of

the demographic group you are appealing to and the purpose of the event.

- Maintain consistency with the company's values and overall approach.

CRISIS MANAGEMENT
BE BOLD IN A CRISIS
Jim Blythe

CRISES HAPPEN WITH monotonous regularity, whatever business you're in. Obviously some industries have more newsworthy crises than others—a burst oil pipeline is more likely to hit the headlines than a failure in the ticket machines at a provincial railway station—but crises still need to be handled well, and a failure of the ticket machines on the London Underground would certainly make the headlines.

In some cases, companies need to be bold in their responses. There is no point in tickling a problem with a feather when you should be beating it with a stick.

The idea

Johnson & Johnson is a multinational healthcare company. Apart from producing baby powder, lotion, and the like, the company manufactures over-the-counter pharmaceuticals such as Tylenol, a painkiller widely used worldwide.

In 1982, seven Tylenol customers died of cyanide poisoning. The cause turned out to be deliberate sabotage, by person or persons unknown: in other words, some crackpot decided to poison people. Johnson & Johnson immediately recalled the entire stock of Tylenol then on the shelves of American stores (31 million bottles in all) for a total cost of around $100 million.

The FBI thought that this action was unnecessary, since all the cases had occurred in the Chicago area only, but the FBI are not PR experts. Johnson & Johnson's bold action was a PR triumph: although sales dropped dramatically at first, within a year they had reached their former levels and Tylenol is now the biggest-selling analgesic in America.

In this case, bold action showed that the company cares about its customers: even though there was almost no chance of anyone from outside the Chicago area being poisoned, Johnson & Johnson's action reassured people and, equally importantly, it was newsworthy. At a local level, seeing company officials removing product from shelves made the news and was highly visible for the "man in the street."

In practice

- Consider the situation from the customers' viewpoint. Their confidence needs to be restored, or sales will never recover.
- No one will buy the potentially damaged stock anyway. You lose nothing by recalling it.
- Be equally bold in publicizing what you are doing. That is, after all, the point.

CUSTOMERS
BAIT THE HOOK
Jim Blythe

OFTEN PURCHASES OF one product encourage purchases of another. A gift or loan of one product creates demand for something else that shows a profit. People sometimes need a little nudge to buy from you rather than from somebody else—and you can often arrange to give them that nudge at very little cost, if you just think about people's needs.

In some cases, providing a free service is enough to tip the balance!

The idea

Waitrose, the upmarket supermarket chain in Britain, are well aware that people like to throw the occasional party. They sell everything anyone would need, from invitations through to cleaning products, but of course so does every other supermarket chain. Waitrose's idea for nudging people was to offer a free glass hire service. If you're throwing a party, Waitrose will lend you the glasses, no strings attached, for free provided you bring them back clean. Breakages are charged at £1 a glass (although it's actually cheaper to buy a replacement glass from the store and put it in the box).

Obviously if someone is collecting the glasses from Waitrose the next step is to buy in the booze, the food, the napkins, the paper plates, and so forth. Few people would borrow glasses from the store and then buy everything else in Sainsbury's: the loan of the glasses shows trust of the customer, which in turn will reflect back on the store. The advantage for Waitrose doesn't stop with the sales, either—lending people things is a way of demonstrating friendship, which creates a longer-term obligation on the part of the customer. Waitrose have even extended the scheme to cover loans of fish kettles, since most households would only occasionally need to cook a whole salmon, for example.

Waitrose have a long history of considering customer need first, then working out how to make a profit from satisfying the need. Encouraging people to have more and bigger parties is part of that ethos—and very effective it has proved as well.

In practice

- Ensure that what you are offering will not cost you too much to give. The glasses loan is actually extremely cheap, if the administrative element is disregarded.
- Don't attach any strings. If you do, the element of trust is lost.
- Accept that some people will abuse your trust.
- Ensure that the free gift or loan really does link to something that will show a profit—in the case of Waitrose, the high-margin snack foods are probably the most profitable product link.
- Be confident you can recover the loaned goods—or at least if not, that you can afford to lose them!

CULTURE
DRIVE THE CULTURE RIGHT THROUGH THE ORGANIZATION
Jonathan Gifford

ORGANIZATIONS CAN BE let down by the behavior of anyone within the organization at any level. We are all familiar with the bad impression created by poor service: an off-hand response to a complaint; an indifferent receptionist; an insensitive sales person; poor record-keeping. We do not conclude that is an unusual event and blame the individual concerned; we decide that the organization is not well managed. Leaders must drive a successful culture right through the organization.

The idea
The cultural values of successful organizations tend to be established early on. Leaders are likely to find that they need to rediscover and re-emphasize the original values of an organization from time to time and to ensure that the values—the culture—are understood by everybody.

Sir Stuart Hampson, former chairman of the John Lewis Partnership, carried out extensive research across the organization. A set of very consistent values emerged: be honest; show respect; recognize others; work together; show enterprise; achieve more.

"They were not words that I had invented," said Hampson, "they were how everyone felt." Hampson makes the point that everyone within the company, at any level, should follow the spirit of the organization's culture. "Every one of us should operate those values at all levels; whether you are the chairman or whether you come from working with a multi-national and multi-ethnic group of colleagues.

"You begin to find that you get some really neat ideas generated from creating a culture where people of different ethnicities, cultures, backgrounds [and] countries ... come together. Invariably, you find that the best ideas come from this mosaic of players working together in a team on a project. They will come up with an answer that is different from what any one of them would have come up with individually."

In practice

- Organizations that are very homogeneous are badly equipped to deal with change: the skills and mental attitudes that have become entrenched in the organization are unlikely to deal well with changing situations and environments.
- There is an ingrained tendency to recruit people who will fit into the organization's existing culture: people who are "like us". Build teams of people with different attitudes, skills and experiences.
- Encourage the team to continue to broaden their experience whenever possible; create chances for them to learn about areas outside of their own specialization.
- Companies whose employees come from a wide variety of cultural and ethnic backgrounds provide the organization with a competitive advantage; a rich cultural mix tends to generate innovative approaches, and safeguards the organization against parochialism.

MARKETING
HOLD A COMPETITION
Jim Blythe

COMPETITIONS, LOTTERIES, CONTESTS of any sort always attract attention, but some are more newsworthy than others. Competitors remember the firm, and often talk about the competition, but the best outcome is, of course, if the competition makes the news in some way.

Some types of competition are better than others for this.

The idea

In 1958, the mayor's office in a small Spanish fishing village made a major strategic decision. They decided that the village should try to attract more foreign tourists. The village itself was picturesque, it was near to a new international airport, and package holidays by air were just beginning to become available. The mayor envisaged a town with a few small hotels, attracting well-off northern Europeans to inject some cash into the local economy, which was suffering greatly under Franco's dictatorship.

The mayor's office decided to organize a song contest. Songwriters and performers were invited to the village, and a series of performances were organized: the song contest was intended to be newsworthy, and to attract the kind of middle-class audience the village was trying to cultivate. A recording deal was on offer for the winner (and of course recording studios were very happy to sign up any promising losers as well).

In the event, the winning song became a major hit, not only in Spain but throughout the Spanish-speaking world. The village itself gained dramatically from the publicity, and although the mayor's original concept for the village disappeared, it disappeared under a colossal injection of investment: the original fishing village was overwhelmed by the mass of concrete hotels that now characterize the town it has become—it is, of course, Benidorm.

Whatever we might think of Benidorm, it is certainly a prosperous place and a lot of money has been made: and it all started with a song contest.

In practice

- Choose a competition topic that is newsworthy.
- Invite specific contestants if at all possible—if not, ensure that your pre-publicity is targeted at contestants who will generate publicity themselves.
- Ensure that the competition is strongly branded.

SALES
NEVER TELL OBVIOUS LIES
Patrick Forsyth

It may be that selling involves some exaggeration, and occasionally a little white lie, but more than that runs risks. Tell someone that the battery life of some gizmo is twice what it actually is, and this description may help clinch the sale, but it may also mean the customer is back promptly to return the goods, and resolves never to buy from you again.

Yet despite the logic of this, some salespeople not only tell lies, they compound the damage by telling obvious lies, in some cases making statements that are both cliché and spotted as doubtful at ten paces. My least favorite, and a common one, is the salesperson seeking an appointment who says something like, "What about Tuesday morning at 10 am? I will be in your area then." Now, not only do I not believe this for a single second (the person will be in my area only if I agree to a meeting), strangely I do not see helping the person to reduce their travel time as a priority at this early stage in our relationship. Certainly it is not a reason to see them. Such a line simply fails to reflect the realities of the relationship.

The idea
For all salespeople overrating their own convenience ...

Do not say this, or indeed any other permutation of it. Not ever. Certainly do not offer it baldly as a reason that someone should see you. If a prospect agrees to a meeting, if you have persuaded them to take an initial interest, then by all means try to make meeting them productive. If you want to offer a time that is easy for you (rather than asking them what suits them best), at least be honest about it, and position it as helping you. They may well be helpful: having agreed to see you, they may well not want to appear awkward. But express the thought too early and in the wrong way, and you create the reverse of the impression you want.

In practice

- Nothing creates negative feelings in a customer about a salesperson faster than this sort of thing.
- Avoid it.

MANAGING
BE DEMANDING
Jonathan Gifford

TEAMS EXPECT leaders to be demanding. If the leader is not demanding, the team assumes that there is no urgency and that they need not put themselves out too much. A leader who is not demanding more of his or her team than they can comfortably deliver is not really leading.

The idea

In the early days of Microsoft Corporation, Bill Gates was a famously hard taskmaster. Early employees at Microsoft Corporation worked incredibly long hours, in a chaotic but creative environment. Late-night pizzas at the office were the norm, followed by even more work into the early hours of the morning.

At the same time, the working atmosphere was extremely casual: there was no dress code; people worked the hours that they wanted to work and would sometimes take a break to see a movie, play electric guitar or set up a competitive sports session in the corridor and then get back to work.

Bill Gates himself would often sleep at the office. One programmer from these early days said, "Bill was always pushing. We'd do something I thought was really clever, and he would say, 'Why didn't you do this, or why didn't you do that two days ago?' That would get frustrating sometimes." But as another early programmer, Steve Wood, also said, "We'd often be there 24 hours a day, trying to meet a deadline or ... getting a new product out. We noticed the long hours, but it wasn't a burden. It was fun. We weren't doing it because someone was standing over us with a whip saying, 'You guys have got to do this.' We were doing it because we had stuff to do and we had to get it done."

These "Microsoft Kids" felt that they were working at the edge of a technological revolution. They were excited by their work and uncomplaining about the demands on their time, energy and creativity.

In practice

- The leader sets the tone for the organization; if the leader is not demanding, nobody else will be.
- Being demanding is not the same as being an impossible taskmaster or an unreasonable employer. People can only work exceptionally hard on a voluntary basis and for a limited time.
- People like to be challenged at work; to feel that they are part of something important and challenging. When people are involved in this way, they will work exceptionally hard without complaint.
- Encourage this kind of environment but do not abuse people's commitment: an exceptional commitment of time and energy should be temporary.
- During these intense spells, give colleagues the opportunity to let off steam. Allow them some indulgences to reward their exceptional contribution.
- Create ways for people to have fun in the office, especially "after hours".

ONLINE MARKETING
PUT YOURSELF ON YOUR WEBSITE
Jim Blythe

WEBSITES ARE BECOMING the cornerstone of good PR as people rush to them to check out companies they are planning to sell to, buy from, or work for. Most websites cater admirably to these publics, yet few of them feature the boss.

The technology exists to put video clips on the website—so what's stopping you?

The idea

Some bosses are using their websites to explain job vacancies. Having someone talk through what the job entails and what kind of person the company is looking for has a great deal more impact than a dry advert in the Situations Vacant column of the local newspaper, and brings the whole process down to a personal level—which is, of course, what business is all about.

The idea can extend to other areas of the business. You could explain what you want your suppliers to do, explain what you can do for customers, or explain your ethical stance. Videos can be changed regularly, and they don't take long to make: you could even have a guided tour of the business, or show some satisfied clients.

Having someone senior talking on the website dramatically improves the human face of the company. Too often, people talk about "faceless" corporations: yet it is so easy to add a face.

In practice

- Don't do this unless you feel confident and relaxed in front of a camera. Many CEOs have made complete idiots of themselves by starring in their own advertising.
- Don't make the clips too long. They will take too long to download, and not everybody has a state-of-the-art computer and internet connection.
- If possible, get someone professional to make the recording. Don't be tempted to get your sister's teenage son to do it with his Christmas-present video camera.

BUSINESS SKILLS
VALUING INSTINCT
Jeremy Kourdi

PERSONAL QUALITIES SUCH as instinct, experience, and intuition can be used to defy market research and create a previously untapped niche in the market.

The idea

Market research is often hailed as the main factor that should drive decision making. However, instinct, personal experience, and intuition are just as vital, especially in difficult times.

This was recognized by Bob Lutz, who, as president of Chrysler during the late 1980s, found sales in America and abroad weakening. Critics claimed the organization was uninspired and lagging behind competitors. Bob Lutz believed the answer was to develop an innovative, exciting car. Stylish, with a powerful ten-cylinder engine and five-speed manual transmission, the Dodge Viper was given a premium price of $50,000. Many advised that no American-made car would become popular at such a high price, and that the investment would be better spent elsewhere. Lutz's idea was based on nothing more than personal instinct, without any significant market research. He had to overcome considerable internal opposition, as this approach to decision making was not typical at Chrysler. However, the Dodge Viper proved to be a massive commercial success, even appearing in a number of video games as an elite racing car. It changed the public's perception of Chrysler, halted the company's decline, and boosted morale.

Bob Lutz's belief that the radically different Dodge Viper was the right decision for Chrysler was a triumph of instinct over rationality. Arguably, though, the decision was entirely rational. When threatened with stagnating sales, a lackluster brand and competitive pressures, what else was there to do except throw the rule book away by innovating and connect with customers by "wowing" them? Bob

Lutz may have reached his decision through instinct, but it was his experience that told him which rules to apply.

In practice

- Differentiate yourself from competitors by basing decisions on personal experience and instinct rather than typical market research or other rational methods.
- Do not be afraid to undertake bold decisions when drastic action is required.
- Talk with people—colleagues, customers, commentators, and people in other industries. Explore their views and ideas.
- Ensure the idea is executed methodically and efficiently.

COMPETITION
SHOW PEOPLE THE COMPETITION
Jim Blythe

MOST OF US are a little bit afraid of our competitors. All too often, they come over and eat our lunch—we lose customers to them, and if we keep on losing customers to them, we lose our business. What is easily forgotten, though, is that they are probably just as afraid of us as we are of them. After all, we have a better product, better customer relationships, and we are all-round nicer people.

So why not be up front about it with our customers? We don't have to run our competitors down, in fact that is usually counterproductive because people feel sorry for the underdog, but there is nothing wrong with telling people what our competitors have on offer—after all, it's hardly a state secret.

The idea

When Judy Kearney was director of sales and marketing at Holiday Inn, the company lost a large corporate customer to a rival hotel chain. Kearney tried persuasion, but to no avail—the lost customer was happy with the new chain. However, the decision-makers were not the people who stayed in the hotels—the guests were actually salespeople, engineers and executives on business trips. Kearney asked them if they were happy with the new hotel chain, and found that they preferred Holiday Inn.

Kearney suggested to the management that they survey their staff themselves and find out if they were happy. She pointed out that unhappy employees are unproductive employees: the company management carried out the survey and found (to their surprise) that employees preferred Holiday Inn.

This was still not enough. The decision-makers agreed to visit Holiday Inn and see the improvements for themselves, but still insisted on seeing the competition as well: this is where Kearney showed a touch of genius, plus a penchant for risk-taking.

She arranged a tour of Holiday Inn's own hotel, but also agreed to line up all the other visits on the same day, even volunteering to drive them around to the competitors' hotels. The customers were overwhelmed by this, and gave Kearney the contract—apart from Holiday Inn scoring well against its rivals, the fact that Kearney showed such faith in her own product that she was prepared to help them see the competing products was convincing, to say the least.

In practice

- Don't ever criticize your competitors—it looks like a lack of confidence in your own product.
- Let people make their own decisions, but be prepared to guide them a little.
- Go out of your way to be helpful. This builds trust, and a sense of obligation.
- Make sure you really ARE better than the competition on the factors the customer values most.

ONE THING AT A TIME—TOGETHER

Patrick Forsyth

THE DISPARATE NATURE of the tasks most people handle makes managing them difficult. You tend to flit from one to another and need different things in place to tackle each.

The idea

Another overriding principle of good time management is to batch your tasks. Here again proprietary time management systems all have their own methodology, and it is in some cases over-complicated, certainly for my taste, but of course what works best for you is the only measure. I am inclined to believe that more important than the precise configuration of the system here is the number of categories: three to six are ideal simply because that is manageable. It does not matter too much what you call them:

- PRIORITY.
- IMPORTANT.
- ACTION NOW.
- OBTAIN MORE INFORMATION.
- READING.

These are just some of the options (and there are those who manage perfectly well with A, B, and C).

In practice

The key thing is to match the categories to the way you work, for instance:

- You may need FILE and may consider other action categories such as TELEPHONE, DICTATE, WRITE, and DOCUMENT, and similar ones that are particular to your business and your role in it such as PROPOSALS, QUOTATIONS, or the names of products, departments, or systems.

- An important area these days is things that demand you go online. If you have a variety of (genuine) tasks that need you to work in this way, time may well be saved by batching them together.
- A manageable number of batches of this sort can, if you wish, link physically to filing trays on your desk or some distinguishing mark on files themselves. (Incidentally, beware of color coding as the basis for office-wide systems, as a significant proportion of the world's population is colorblind.)

CRISIS MANAGEMENT
COMMUNICATE IN CRISIS
Jonathan Gifford

COMMUNICATION IS NEVER more important than when the organization is facing a crisis. There is a common tendency not to give out more information than is absolutely necessary. In fact, a lack of information will only make the situation worse.

If a leader can communicate that a particular course of action is essential and that it will be successful, people will come together to face the problem in a positive way.

The idea

When Andrea Jung, chairman of the board and chief executive officer of Avon Products Inc, undertook a radical restructuring of the company, she relied on her belief in "hyper communication".

"I think the honesty, the speed of communicating our plans, and doing so in person—being willing to stand there instead of sending out a memo—helped enormously in that transition phase. It was interesting that so many people came up to me after I'd spoken and said: 'I have no idea if I'm still going to be here or not, but I just want you to know that it was really unique and critical that you were so honest at this point.'"

Gerard Kleisterlee, president and CEO of Dutch electronics multinational Philips, talks about the need to communicate more intensively in times of crisis: "I don't think we have to address people differently, but probably we have to communicate with them more intensively. Particularly in difficult times, in times of uncertainty ... as a leader you have to be more visible. ... If management adopts 'salami' tactics—announcing the bad news one slice at a time—that can create a general level of uncertainty among employees ... At this point, as the CEO, I have to be clear about the position of the company: Is our strategy robust? [If you can] communicate that effectively throughout the company, then a crisis can rally people. It can awaken their fighting spirit and draw people closer together."

In practice

- When an organization is in crisis, the rest of the organization needs to know about it.
- It will be impossible to hide the truth, and any attempt to play down the crisis will allow colleagues to feel that the situation is not as bad as they feared. Releasing bad news in dribs and drabs makes the team more anxious.
- Colleagues whose jobs may be at risk deserve to know the worst possible scenario as soon as possible. Keeping them informed and involved allows them to contribute to the solution of the crisis: colleagues who are stressed and badly informed will not be able to contribute anything at all.
- Leaders must present not simply the problem but also the solution: the plan of action.
- The problem and its solutions must be presented not only internally but also externally, to all stakeholders and to the media.
- Colleagues who are reassured that the organization can survive will be motivated to do whatever they can to help.

KEEP CUSTOMERS THINKING OF YOU
Patrick Forsyth

IT IS HARDLY a new idea to keep in touch with customers. Memories are short, especially when people are busy, and exposed to numerous other messages from other people and organizations. So most salespeople do it to some degree or another, but sometimes it is regarded as a waste of time. For instance, the very nature of the business might make it inappropriate. Or does it?

The idea
From a specialist retailer ...

When repeat purchases are a possibility, most businesses make an effort to stay in touch with customers. But when they are not, further contact can seem like a waste of time. Yet one company shows that this is not always true. It is a specialist retailer selling wedding dresses. The average marriage may not always last as long as it used to do, but even so a customer is hardly likely to come in a fortnight after their wedding wanting another wedding dress.

Yet this retailer scheduled in (and budgeted for) a number of specific follow-up contacts after the dress was delivered and paid for. It sent flowers and a card on the big day to wish the couple well, an invitation to a function a month or so later, a card on their anniversary—for several years. And more. Why take this line? Why spend money and effort in this way? Because people getting married are often at a stage in life when they know others in a similar position, and with something as memorable as a wedding, the likelihood of recommendation can be high. (Maybe 50 percent of customers in such a shop are there, in whole or part, through recommendation.) If the dress was a picture, if the day was memorable, then enhancing the idea of just how helpful the provider of the dress (and perhaps other elements of the wedding arrangements too) was is highly likely to increase the number of referrals. This idea is much more straightforward and cost-effective than canvassing more widely for new business. And those who come inquiring because a friend suggested it are that much easier to sell to than colder prospects.

In practice

* Whatever the time scale, ensure that this sort of follow-up and potential recommendation is possible in your business. Even if the traditional view does not make how to do it immediately obvious, it is worth some thought to find a way.

TELL THE WHOLE STORY
Jim Blythe

OFTEN FIRMS WILL issue a press release about an exciting new product, but, unless there is really something very interesting about the product, the journals will simply spike the story.

Stories about new products are almost always going to look like thinly disguised advertisements. Newspapers do not exist to publish free advertising—they charge for space—but they will publish something interesting.

The idea

When James Dyson launched his new upright vacuum cleaner, he simply did not have the resources to run the kind of advertising campaign the product warranted. The cleaner's innovative design made it stand out in the showrooms, but it cost around double the price of a conventional vacuum cleaner and the advantages were certainly not immediately obvious. Dyson decided to engage the potential customers by hanging a tag on each machine that explained the difficulties he had encountered in designing the vacuum cleaner and getting it onto the market.

The tags were an immediate success. People enjoyed reading the Dyson story, so Dyson went one step further and gave interviews to selected reporters (rather than issue a press release). The thrust of the stories was Dyson's life experiences rather than the features and benefits of the vacuum cleaner, but the stories and the tags enabled potential consumers to become involved with the whole Dyson story: people's natural tendency to admire the lone inventor, struggling to get his ideas to market, helped develop a lot of goodwill toward Dyson.

Telling the whole story made Dyson a success, where other lone inventors (Sir Clive Sinclair is one) failed to catch the imagination of their markets.

In practice
- Tell the whole story—hold nothing back.
- This idea works best if there is a human interest element to the story of your new product.
- Back up the story with some point-of-sale reminders.
- Engage your audience.

PROFITABILITY
A TAXING QUESTION
Anne Hawkins

FEW PEOPLE WANT to pay more tax than is necessary.

Tax takes away some of the business' hard-won profits (and more importantly cash) that you would have loved to keep for other purposes.

The idea
Always remember the important difference between tax avoidance and tax evasion. The first one is a legitimate activity carried out to minimise the cost of tax to the business. If you carry out the second one, you are likely to end up behind bars.

Minimising your liability to the taxman can be greatly aided by getting yourself a good accountant.

If you get it right you may well be able to more than cover the cost with savings in your tax bill—especially if you're constantly getting fined for late submissions and late payments.

Ask around. Get recommendations from others in a similar kind of business to you and operating on a similar scale—accountants tend to specialise.

Then negotiate.

While accountants may charge astonishingly high hourly rates, you can minimise your bill by making the work they're going to do for you as straightforward as possible.

Professional rates for professional work
Don't get caught for the cost of the accountant having to carry out the duties required to salvage a situation he will kindly (but expensively) refer to as 'Incomplete Records'.

If there's clerical work to be done, pay a clerk—at a fraction of the amount your accountant will charge you.

This creative entrepreneur pays an accountant to prepare her accounts. Having recently dropped a large box full of assorted paperwork on her accountant's desk she light-heartedly related how her accountant had gone pale and protested that 'this wasn't included in the agreed fee'.

How pale will the entrepreneur's face be when she sees her accountant's bill?

You could start by ...
- Being organised. Agree with your accountant (or your auditors) what records you're going to keep and the format in which you're going to keep them. Then do it.

260
AVOID PURPOSELESS MEETINGS
Patrick Forsyth

WHEN DID YOU last lose patience in a meeting? Meetings are held every day without real—or clear—objectives, and take longer and become muddled as a result. And "objectives" does not mean meeting to:

- Start the planning process.
- Discuss cost savings.
- Review training needs.
- Streamline administration.
- Explore time saving measures.

The idea

All meetings should have clear objectives and these should be specific. So saying you will discuss how you might save 10 percent on the advertising budget over the next six months is clear. Better still if that is a figure picked as achievable and it is something currently necessary (despite the effects it might have). At the end of the meeting we should be able to see if what the meeting was convened to achieve has really happened, or is likely to, for such an objective might take more than one short meeting to finalize.

So a specific statement of objectives—which should be in writing in many cases and circulated to all those due to participate—will have a number of effects:

- People will be clear why the meeting is being held.
- They will be better able, and perhaps more inclined, to prepare.
- Discussion will be easier to control, as people will focus more on the topic and the meeting will be more likely to achieve the desired result and to do so in less time than would be the case with a vague description.

In practice

- So, if you ever go to meetings where the objectives do not seem to be clear, ask what they are. Others may well agree that they are not clear, and a few minutes spent early in the meeting clarifying this may be time well spent rather than launching into discussion and finding that the meeting grinds to a halt in confusion half an hour later. Better still, ask before you attend. A clear objective is a real necessity; no meeting without this is likely to conclude its business either promptly or satisfactorily.

SALES

ASK FOR REFERRALS

Patrick Forsyth

SOMETIMES WE ARE reluctant to ask for referrals, yet if you are recommended to a prospect by someone who already buys from you (and is satisfied), that's likely to give you a small head start. So why is there a reluctance to ask? Is it embarrassment perhaps, or fear of rejection or failure? It is not likely that an existing and happy customer (obviously don't ask any dissatisfied ones!) will be angry or upset at your asking. They might see it as inappropriate in some way, but if so they are most likely to decline politely, not shout at you.

The idea

Many people do this, but I'll credit my thinking of it here to the guy who drives me to the airport ...

Steve runs a taxi company. Actually that description does his operation a disservice: he runs a "luxury car service," and specializes in weddings and events, runs to the airport and longer journeys. He charges just a little bit more than the Mondeo cowboys who frequent the various taxi companies in the town. (Actually I must not malign them all, but some are perhaps just a touch unreliable.)

Steve always turns up on time, wears a suit, and drives a rather nice Mercedes. In the car are newspapers, something to drink, and interesting conversation if you want it. On the customer service front you cannot find anything to criticize, and that is always a good foundation for selling.

Steve has learned that referral is a good way to build a business, and always asks if there is anyone he can contact or to whom you can pass on his details. The business card he hands over alongside this request is of good quality, and he can provide a more detailed postcard-sized information card too (which mentions for example that he has a six-seater vehicle as well as regular cars). This is the sort of idea that is so simple, so routine, and yet often neglected. Steve makes it a priority, and each time I book to travel with him he seems to be busier. See you on the 22nd, Steve.

In practice
- First, if you do this kind of thing you need to support it with the right material.
- Then it needs to be made a firm habit.

STRATEGY
CANNIBALIZING
Jeremy Kourdi

INSTEAD OF ALLOWING other companies to eat into your market, consider bringing in new products to compete with your existing ones. This may sound like suicide, but handled expertly it allows you to remain on the cutting edge and ahead of the competition.

The idea
When there is a limited market for a particular product or service, any new competitors may consume the market. A possible response to counter this is cannibalization—bringing in new products

to compete with your existing offering. This is a tactic used by a surprisingly large number of businesses, from the café franchise Starbucks to the technology manufacturer Intel.

Starbucks' well-known tendency to open branches within minutes of each other represents a fierce desire to keep competition at bay. Even though these branches will be competing with each other for a limited number of clients, Starbucks has recognized that this is preferable to competing with other potential market leaders, such as Costa Coffee and Caffè Nero.

Manufacturers of computer hardware and software, such as Apple, Intel, and Microsoft, are other well-known examples of cannibalization. By regularly bringing out upgraded versions of their products (ie faster computers or more virus-resistant software) they not only remain at the cutting edge of the industry; they also persuade customers to purchase new products, and allow less room for competitors to encroach into their market. This works well in fickle markets with limited loyalty (for example, Starbucks may feel that people wanting a coffee may be prepared to get it from anywhere). It also works when people want, for whatever reason, to keep up to date—for example, with the latest technological developments.

In practice
- Judge market conditions in order to decide precisely when to cannibalize a particular product. Developing a product often takes time and money—if the existing product is highly profitable and not at risk from competitors, postpone the introduction of a new offering to a time when it is necessary or desirable.
- Cannibalize when it is anticipated that a competitor will introduce a potentially popular new product.
- When sales are stagnating, cannibalizing your older products with more cutting-edge offerings can radically stimulate overall sales.
- Do not be afraid of competing with yourself. Although it may seem daunting at first to risk cutting off the market for your older products, it should be recognized as a positive way to

handle the cut-throat, dynamic nature of modern business. Also it will force you to innovate and overcome complacency.

MARKETING
FOCUS ON THE KEY ISSUE FOR YOUR CUSTOMER
Jim Blythe

PEOPLE JUDGE WHAT we do by their own criteria—not by ours. Knowing what the critical factors are is a key element in marketing success—and it isn't always easy to spot.

Retailers often focus on the virtual price war—the battle to persuade customers that they are cheaper than anyone else. However, this is not always the most relevant issue from the customer's viewpoint—there are many other factors involved in choosing which retailer to favor with our business.

The idea
Tesco supermarkets have many good ideas for gaining a competitive edge. Price is only one of the elements in their approach—like all the other major grocery retailers, they have to keep their prices keen, but this does not in itself provide a competitive advantage.

One of the elements that customers find important in supermarkets is the length of time spent queuing. Queuing up to pay for goods is frustrating because the customer wants to take actual possession of the shopping—not to mention move on to the next of the day's tasks.

Tesco guarantee that they will open more checkouts if there is more than one person ahead of you in the queue, until such time as all the checkouts are open. The system is monitored at Tesco headquarters: every 15 minutes, every till in the country freezes until the checkout operator enters the number of people in his or her queue. If there are more than two people in the queues for more than 5 percent of the time, the store manager is asked for an explanation. Managers are expected to be able to estimate the demand at the tills by monitoring the number of people in-store at any time.

This type of thinking is what has propelled Tesco to being the number-one British supermarket chain. Caring about what CUSTOMERS find important is the key.

In practice
- Find out what your customers think is important—if necessary, ask them.
- Pay attention to customer grumbling. There may be a solution to the problem that neither you nor they are aware of.
- Don't assume. Ask.
- Sometimes the solution is easily attained—but if not, you should calculate the cost–benefit trade-off and if necessary look for a cheaper solution.
- Pleasing your customers can only be a good thing.

SELF-HELP
BEST TIME FOR APPOINTMENTS
Patrick Forsyth

APPOINTMENTS—INTERACTIONS WITH other people—take up a major amount of many executives' time. Many of these occur on a planned basis: they are scheduled appointments.

The idea
Recognize that exactly when you program appointments makes a real difference to your productivity and think carefully about their scheduling. Allow sufficient time; one appointment running into another always causes problems. And always schedule a period of time—in other words, a finishing time as well as a start time. It is impossible to do this with 100 percent accuracy, but it helps to aim for what's ideal.

In practice

Think about:

- The potential for interruptions: an early meeting, before the office switchboard opens, may take less time because there are fewer interruptions.
- The location: where it is geographically makes a difference, and a meeting room may be better than your office, especially if you need to clear the decks and move what you are working on just before it starts.
- Timing that makes it inevitable that it continues into lunch or a drink at the end of the day.
- Timing that restricts your ability to schedule other appointments, in the sense that something mid-morning could mean there is not sufficient time to fit in another meeting before it, or after it and before lunch.

And take especial care with gatherings that involve more than one other person. You have to be accommodating here, but do not always consider others' convenience before your own—it is you who will suffer. Record appointments clearly in the diary and consider separately the various aspects of meetings commented on in a number of other sections.

BUSINESS SKILLS
KNOW THE DETAIL
Jonathan Gifford

EFFECTIVE LEADERS KNOW their organization in detail. A good grasp of detail informs all decisions and allows leaders to ask penetrating questions and give meaningful direction to their teams.

The idea

Alan Sugar, entrepreneur and founder of the UK electronics

company Amstrad, said, "I know where every screw, nut and bolt is in my company."

Dr Ram Charan, business advisor and author, talks about the need for leaders to have a "deep immersion" in their business, especially in today's fast-moving business environment.

"I define management intensity as a deep immersion in the business's operational details and the day-to-day competitive climate the business is facing, along with hands-on involvement and follow-through. It's so important now because of the accelerating speed at which things are changing. Surviving a volatile environment requires frequent operational adjustments ... It's not enough to sit in your office and read reports and issue directives. You've got to know what's happening daily, and adjust plans and processes accordingly. Big-picture strategic thinking is still important, but it must take a back seat to this operational immersion—leaders need to be involved and visible, and communicating all the time."

Frank Zhou, general manager of pharmaceutical company Abbott International China, believes that being able to pass on detail is essential; that it is not enough to "offer some directions and then walk away".

"Many people in professional management in China are pretty young ... Some people become directors or managers at a very young age and they have not had extensive experience compared to their counterparts in Western markets. So, how can you impart discipline and professional skills to these young, ambitious and sometimes impatient people? That's the key. The way I do this is by being vigorous in terms of follow-up, in terms of details. If you just give [colleagues] a speech, or some directions, and then walk away, this may work in the US or Japan, but it may not work in China. So, in China, you have to be more determined, more focused on details, and spend more effort."

In practice

- Few leadership actions are more impressive than demonstrating that the leader knows more about the enterprise than even an expert colleague. Leaders must understand the detail of their organization and demonstrate this to the team.

- As the speed of business change increases, leaders need to be immersed in the detail of their business in order to react quickly.
- Colleagues, especially less-experienced colleagues, need detailed instructions and follow-up to be able to perform effectively.

PUBLIC RELATIONS
STIMULATE DEBATE
Jim Blythe

PRESSURE GROUPS ARE great for creating negative stories about products and companies, and no pressure groups are more adept at this than the environmentalists. The environmental lobby sees itself as campaigning for a crucial issue—the saving of the only planet on which humanity lives—and in view of the importance of the issue one can hardly blame them for being extremely determined in their approach.

This does, of course, leave firms with a lot of firefighting to do, and many of them immediately become adversarial in their behavior. Direct attacks on the environmentalists are unlikely to do anything other than fan the flames—but entering into an honest debate might well be more successful.

The idea
During the 1980s, research by the British Antarctic Survey revealed that there was a massive hole in the ozone layer, centered over the Antarctic. The ozone layer is what protects us from excessive ultraviolet light and damaging cosmic rays, so it is of considerable importance. The British Antarctic Survey research indicated that the hole was caused by the use of CFCs (a gas) as a propellant for aerosol sprays.

The British Aerosol Manufacturers' Association wanted at first to produce press releases showing how important aerosols are to business and consumers. This was intended to counteract the negative publicity generated by the environmentalists. However, the BAMA's PR consultants, Grayling PR, realized that telling people how convenient it is to have aerosol hairspray would be unlikely to carry much weight against the Doomsday scenario coming out of the Antarctic.

Grayling advised highlighting exactly what the industry was doing, and would do in future, to remove CFCs from their products. Grayling were able to point out that the BAMA had set a deadline for removal of CFCs well ahead of the international deadline, and invited debate from the environmental lobby to help meet the requirements even sooner. By showing that the industry was reacting responsibly to the issue, the BAMA took the sting out of the argument and allowed its positive messages to get through.

In practice
- Meet issues head-on: don't try to skirt around them.
- If the issue being presented by your opponents is more important than anything you can bring to bear, you have no chance of fighting it.
- If you are under attack from someone more powerful than you, you have to show that you are responding to their claims.

CUSTOMERS
UNDERSTAND HOW YOU ARE JUDGED
Jim Blythe

IN SERVICE INDUSTRIES it is easy to imagine that we are being judged on our core product. Hairdressers think they are being judged on the hairstyle, restaurants think they are being judged on the food, and so on. Often the customers have a different viewpoint, however, and as with everything else in marketing we need to consider our customers' viewpoint ahead of our own.

Finding out how people judge us is not always straightforward, but sometimes we can get a very good idea from reading the kind of advice people are being given.

The idea

Restaurant critic The *Artful* Diner suggests that people examine the restrooms of the restaurant. If the restrooms are dirty, it is extremely unlikely that the kitchens will be clean—after all, the restrooms are the part of the restaurant you are allowed to see, so how much worse will be the parts they are not allowing you to see?

A survey carried out by London Eats found that 29.4 percent of Londoners thought that the cuisine was the most important factor in choosing a restaurant; 20.8 percent thought that recommendation was the most important, 18.3 percent thought price, 10.7 percent thought ambience, 10.7 percent thought service was most important, and only 10.2 percent thought location was most important.

In practice

- Read newspapers and magazines that carry reports about your industry, for an idea of what your customers are being advised.
- Ask customers what they like about you. If you can, ask your competitors' customers what they like about your competitors.
- Work out ways of improving people's perception of you.
- Whatever they regard as important is what you have to get right—other factors are less important, no matter how much you might regard them as essential.

PROFITABILITY
KEEPING YOUR DOGS UNDER CONTROL
Anne Hawkins

WHEN DEMAND FOR your product starts to fall as it reaches the last stage of its demand life-cycle, it is referred to as a 'dog'. If you've avoided being a lemming, you've predicted the cliff-edge and controlled your stock levels by keeping in pace with customer demand. You've now got to realign the way you manage this product or service through your business to control the costs.

The idea

What may have been the best process for making the product in an earlier stage may not be so appropriate now that as a 'dog', it is demanded less frequently and/or in smaller quantities.

Round them up

A manufacturer of small but relatively high-value products segregated manufacture between two sites. One site dealt with the high-volume repeaters in the 'cow' stage of life while the other produced the 'strangers and aliens' associated with the 'dog' stage. Equipment was aligned to needs with the emphasis on cost-effective high volume machinery for the former and equipment enabling fast changeovers for the latter.

When customers came to 'help them take cost out of their products' it was important to plan the visit to make sure that they steered the customer firmly towards the 'dogs' and away from the 'cows'.

Selective breeding

Another manufacturer looked at not only how he could realign the type of equipment used to make his product, but also how he could merge orders by standardising the product wherever possible and leaving the differentiated packaging as far downstream the process as he could.

Sting in the tail

When checking out the condition of your 'dogs', remember that your costing system might not pick up on those additional 'hassle' costs brought about by the complexity of producing small quantities of a large range of items.

In practice

- Look critically at the condition of your 'dogs' and be selective about which ones you keep.
- Manage the demise of those to be discontinued to avoid being left with obsolete stock on the shelf.

LEADERSHIP
BE ACCOUNTABLE
Jonathan Gifford

A LEADER HAS TO accept responsibility for the actions of their team. In difficult circumstances, stakeholders in the company and the general public will expect to see the leader, in person, addressing issues directly and demonstrating clear accountability.

The idea

When American car giant Chrysler encountered financial difficulties in the 1980s, its recovery was led by Lee Iacocca, who led a drastic programme of restructuring and cost-cutting, selling the company's loss-making European operation to Peugeot.

He also revitalized Chrysler's product line and, critically, successfully lobbied the United States Congress to guarantee loans that would enable the company to stay afloat. The first press advertisements attempted to win over public and government opinion for the loan guarantee scheme, under the headline *"Would America be better off without Chrysler?"* The ads carried Iacocca's signature.

Iacocca said, "We wanted to show the public that a new era had begun. After all, a chief executive of a company that's going broke has to reassure people. He has to say: 'I'm here, I'm real, and I'm responsible for this company. And to show that I mean it, I'm signing on the dotted line'. At long last, we would be able to convey that there was some genuine accountability at Chrysler. By putting my signature on these ads, we were inviting the public to write to me with their complaints and their questions. We were announcing that this large, complex company was now being run by a human being who was putting his name and his reputation on the line."

As the company's finances began to recover, Iacocca launched a consumer advertising campaign in which he himself appeared, promoting his company's products. Using the slogan *"The pride is back"*, the advertisements also featured what was to become Iacocca's trademark catch phrase: *"If you can find a better car, buy it."* Consumer confidence in Chrysler rapidly recovered.

In practice

- A leader is accountable for everything that happens in the organization. When things go wrong, the leader must be seen to be accountable, and to be available to the public via the media.
- Organizations where no leader can be identified as responsible are seen as being rudderless and without direction. There is no alternative to accountability.
- When leaders succeed in identifying themselves with an organization, consumers and stakeholders are reassured to see that there is a visible figurehead; a person who has made himself or herself accountable for the whole organization.

ONLINE MARKETING
GET YOUR OWN DOMAIN NAME
Jim Blythe

EVERYBODY USES EMAIL, in fact it's amazing that the Post Office still has anything to deliver. What many of us in small businesses do is use something such as Hotmail or Gmail for our email address, because it's cheap or free.

This gives a poor impression to customers, though: it looks as if you are not serious about your business.

The idea

Major companies have their own domain names, and there is nothing to prevent you from doing the same. Acquiring a domain name is not difficult, and it isn't expensive either: companies such as GetDotted.com will sell domain names from as little as £2.99 a year. This gives unlimited email, and a website, all in your own name.

The PR advantages are obvious. With your own domain name, you look serious about what you're doing. You are easier to find online because search engines will often go directly to your site. Your brand name or company name goes out on every email you send.

With your own domain name your staff can also have dedicated email addresses, which increases the exposure of your brand name, especially if you are in a business where a lot of emails are sent out.

In practice

* Choose a name carefully—you will have it for a long time.
* Remember that you have to keep paying for the name or you lose it.
* If necessary, buy up similar names to prevent your competitors hijacking them and redirecting inquiries to their own sites.

INNOVATION

INNOVATION CULTURE

Jeremy Kourdi

ENCOURAGING PEOPLE IN your organization to see things differently attracts the best employees and increases the distinctiveness and value of your business.

The idea

A British innovation company, ?What If!, shows clients how to make their organizations more innovative. Their processes challenge people to see things differently by stepping out of their comfort zones and risking ideas that may seem to make little sense. Two key, but separate, processes are needed for innovation:

- Idea building, where people propose ideas and then develop and nurture them.
- Idea analysis, where these ideas are assessed.

Companies that struggle to be innovative often do so because ideas get stifled in their infancy by an excessive rush to judgment and analysis.

Having the right kind of processes for idea generation and innovation is important, but processes are not enough. Innovative organizations also have a general environment and culture that values and fosters innovation.

In practice

Research by the Talent Foundation identified five catalysts for successful innovation:

1. *Consciousness.* Each person knows the goals of the organization and believes they can play a part in achieving them.
2. *Multiplicity.* Teams and groups contain a wide and creative mix of skills, experiences, backgrounds, and ideas.
3. *Connectivity.* Relationships are strong and trusting, and are actively encouraged and supported within and across teams and functions.
4. *Accessibility.* Doors and minds are open; everyone in the organization has access to resources, time, and decision makers.
5. *Consistency.* Commitment to innovation runs throughout the organization and is built into processes and leadership style.

SALES
PROMISES, PROMISES
Patrick Forsyth

WE ALL LIKE it when someone makes and keeps a promise. We expect them to keep it, and it is, well, nice when they do. In selling and doing business with customers many promises are made: to deliver on a particular day, allow time for payment, give an extra discount. Some of them are large and significant promises. You have to keep them, and usually you do. If the company fails to deliver on anything like this, for instance not producing the goods on a particular day when the customer needs them, it matters, and you will find yourself with a complaint to handle; and quite right too.

You can also use promises that are not so major to help you sell successfully.

The idea
This thought is prompted by rather fewer good experiences than might be hoped for ...

A promise kept does not just satisfy the customer on the particular matter to which it relates; it also sends out signals. While the major things tend to be accepted as givens—delivery promised for the 25th and made on the 25th—little things are viewed differently. Yet "smaller" things can have a big impact, and many small things quickly mount up. Promise to ring back by 2:30pm, and you must do just that. Promise to have an email in the customer's in-box within an hour and it must be there. Yet it is precisely such "little" things that can be missed. Something happens, and it's 2:45 when you ring. But somehow you figure you meant "about" 2:30, and you don't even apologize, telling yourself there's no harm done.

Customers regard such things as a sign that goes way beyond the import of the particular matter. First, they want to deal with someone who is reliable. The effect is cumulative: if you keep many small promises, it gives a good, positive impression. It enhances your profile, and makes trust and agreement more likely. And vice versa, of course. Furthermore, failures in such small matters are seen as a sign—an unwelcome sign—of likely future inattention to detail. Let a customer down on one thing, and they are entitled to say, "What else don't they bother about?"

In practice

- Resolve to take this issue seriously, and it will work effectively for you. Go on—promise yourself you will.

BUSINESS SKILLS
STAY ALERT
Jonathan Gifford

LEADERS MUST STAY alert to changes in the business environment; to the responses of customers and stakeholders; to the needs and reactions of colleagues.

Luckily, alertness is our natural response to fear, and leaders have plenty to be fearful about. Fear is a healthy response to new and challenging circumstances; it keeps us alert.

The idea

John Sculley became CEO of Apple Computer in 1983, having previously been president of PepsiCo. Change and risk make us naturally fearful, says Sculley, but this is what keeps us alert.

"Anyone who is successful in business today must be able to deal in a risk environment, and I can't imagine they don't feel some fear in the process. Learning how to cope with your fear doesn't mean the fear goes away. It just means you learn how to succeed anyway, with it. That's probably positive in the sense that you remain alert, because in today's environment, things change so quickly—they can change day to day. What you thought were the ground rules for your industry one day can dramatically change the next because a competitor introduces a new product or the pricing structure shifts in the industry or scarce commodities suddenly become more scarce. These things happen instantaneously, so I think learning to live with fear and managing it is actually an important attribute to success. It's not something to be embarrassed about."

Jonathan Schwartz took over as CEO of Sun Microsystems when the company's co-founder, Scott McNealey, stepped down after 22 years at the helm, having helped to establish Sun in the 1980s as a major computing company and then successfully steered the company, as CEO, through the aftermath of the burst of the dot-com bubble in 2001. In an interview at the time, Schwarz acknowledged that taking over from McNealy—one of very few CEOs with a tenure of more than two decades—was difficult.

"It was terrifying. For me. Here is the guy who established a reputation and created the company that we are today, and [to] have him throw the keys to me and say, 'I'll talk to you in six months. Call me if you need me,' was pretty daunting. We have a perch in the industry, we have a presence and a reputation which I don't want to just uphold, I'd also like to amplify. Any new CEO who says he is not scared on the first day of his job is lying."

In practice

- Leaders must cope with constantly changing circumstances and make decisions that involve risks. These things are frightening.
- Fear is a natural reaction. Successful leaders, like successful soldiers, acknowledge their fear and function with it.
- Any leader who is not experiencing some degree of fear is too complacent. There is always something to be scared of.
- Fear makes us alert, which is extremely useful. Alertness is a key leadership attribute.

PUBLIC RELATIONS
THINK LOCAL
Jim Blythe

MANY FIRMS TRY to segment their markets by age, or income, or attitudes. Yet the most telling thing about someone is none of these—it is where they live. Where we choose to live says more about us than anything else, simply because we choose to live in places that we personally find conducive. People who like the countryside live in the country, people who like plenty of nightlife live downtown, people who like family life live in the suburbs, and so forth.

This is why people often develop fierce loyalty to their region, and even their neighborhood. For the astute public relations practitioner, this represents a golden opportunity.

The idea
Tesco, Britain's biggest supermarket chain, has run a Computers for Schools exercise every year since 1992. For every £10 a customer spends in store, Tesco gives the customer a voucher that can be collected by local schools and used to buy computers.

This is more than just a sales promotion, though. Note that the vouchers do not benefit the customer directly: they benefit local schools. The Tesco customer has the warm feeling of helping a good local cause, but without actually having to spend anything. Tesco has the kudos of helping a local cause, while still operating on a national basis—yet the cause is branded across the country rather than being linked to a specific area. The scheme not only has an effect on the customers, but also creates a degree of gratitude among the children who benefit from the computers—and children grow up to be grocery shoppers.

Finally, Tesco has ensured that a higher proportion of school leavers are computer-literate and therefore are likely to be useful employees—many of the children who benefited from the original 1992 scheme are now adults working for Tesco.

In practice

- Find something that taps into people's sense of community.
- Only run the scheme at times when it will create most benefit. Don't run it all year round, or it becomes part of the furniture and fades in people's consciousness.
- Let your customers pass on the goodwill. They will feel better for it, and think better of you, too.

COST CUTTING
BE VIGILANT
Anne Hawkins

ALL EXPENDITURE SHOULD be authorised.

Don't go over the top—convoluted authorisation procedures just tie up more of your time and money—but you do need to make sure there is a proper process for committing the company's money.

But even if you do have authorisation procedures in place, some types of expenditure have a habit of finding their way round the system and catching you out.

The idea

Make sure you don't end up paying for things you don't want or didn't have. Beware of:

Evergreens

These are those purchase agreements that automatically renew if you fail to take action. Companies rely on your disorganisation (or inertia)—and you'll end up paying for it. If you do decide to take on contracts set up in this way, make sure you immediately put an entry in your diary to review your needs (and shop around) well in advance of any trigger-dates. A chart of all such contracts can be a helpful visual reminder of when you need to take action. If you regularly price-check your motoring insurance you'll understand the kinds of savings to be made—either by changing supplier or by negotiating a matched price.

Scams

Don't be misled into paying for things you never ordered. A classic scam played particularly on small businesses is to invoice you for an entry in a trade directory that you never authorised. Other common scams include receiving unsolicited faxes that appear to offer you great discounts on a product but you find that faxing back for further details costs you dearly.

Look out for invoices for renewing your domain name. Is the name right—look carefully. Is it renewal time? Did the invoice come from the same place as last time? Are payments to be made to the same bank account?

Incorrect pricing

If mistakes by utility companies and some supermarkets are anything to go by, there's loads of cost improvement opportunities here!

In practice

- Run off a report of all invoices paid without a purchase order reference as these will identify instances where the normal authorisation procedures have been bypassed.
- Chart any evergreens.
- Remind everyone of the importance of checking the small print —and if they're not authorised to sign or are uncertain as to what they're signing for—don't!
- Make sure people check the invoices they receive—and that goes for your bill from the taxman as well!

A MAGIC WORD
Patrick Forsyth

EVERYONE HAS TO accept that they cannot do everything. This must probably be taken literally because there may be an almost infinite amount to do, particularly in any job that has some kind of inherent innovative or creative nature to it. Many people could just go on listing more and more things to do, not all equally important, but deserving of a place on their "to do" list nevertheless. Even if your job is not like this, you certainly have to accept that you are not going to do everything at the time you want.

The idea
For reasons of workload and priorities, you are going to have to say "no" to some things. Regularly, and with many people, you need to resolve to think before you agree, and to turn down involvements in some things even though they would be attractive to you (in effect saying "no" to yourself!). Agreeing to things you should turn down will lead you away from priorities; saying "no" is a fundamental time saver. It was well put by Charles Spurgeon: *Learn to say no; it will be more use to you than to be able to read Latin.*

In practice
For instance you may have to turn down:

- *Colleagues*: What is involved here can vary, and if there is a network of favors, with everyone helping everyone else, you do not want to let it get out of hand either way. Turn down too much and you end up losing time because people are reluctant to help you. Do everything unquestioningly and you may be seen as a soft touch and will end up doing more than your share. So balance is the keynote here. Timing is important too; you do not have to do everything you agree to instantly.
- *Subordinates*: Here they cannot tell you to do things, and, though they need support, this must not get out of hand—choose

how long you spend with them and ensure the time spent is worth while.

- *Your boss*: Working with a boss who does not have enough to do, or who expects everything to be done instantly just because they are in charge, can play havoc with the best intentions of time management. You may need to regard it as your mission to educate them and have to conduct a campaign of persuasion and negotiation to keep any unreasonable load down.

LEADERSHIP
RECOGNIZE PEOPLE
Jonathan Gifford

NOTHING BINDS PEOPLE to a leader more effectively than a personal connection; a proof that the leader recognizes individuals and values their input.

Leaders should try to get to know as many of their team as possible. Being recognized and addressed by name makes people feel valued and appreciated.

The idea
The great French general, Napoleon Bonaparte, later to become Emperor of France, inspired fanatical loyalty from his army. He was quick to reward conspicuous acts of bravery and feats of arms, often making immediate promotions and awards on the battlefield itself. It was said that he never forgot a face, and that he was often able to remember names, and even to recall on which campaign a soldier had served with him. Napoleon worked hard at this ability, however, spending time committing lists of names to his prodigious memory.

The memoirs of Madame de Rémusat, lady-in-waiting to Napoleon's wife, the Empress Josephine, provide a vivid contemporary account of Napoleon as seen through the eyes of the imperial court.

"Bonaparte's reception by the troops was nothing short of rapturous. It was well worth seeing how he talked to the soldiers, how he questioned them one after the other respecting their campaigns or their wounds, taking particular interest in the men who had accompanied him to Egypt. I have heard Madame Bonaparte say that her husband was in the constant habit of poring over the list of what are called the cadres of the army at night before he slept. He would go to sleep repeating the names of the corps, and even those of some of the individuals who composed them; he kept these names in a corner of his memory, and this habit came to his aid when he wanted to recognize a soldier and to give him the pleasure of a cheering word from his general. He spoke to the subalterns in a tone of good-fellowship, which delighted them all, as he reminded them of their common feats of arms."

In practice

- Being able to recognize members of the extended team is a great asset for any leader. It makes people feel valued and it binds them to the leader.

- There is no substitute for genuine recognition: being able to remember that you have met a person before, and in what part of the organization they work, is a start; being able to put a name to the face is best.

- This is not easy to do, even in a medium-sized organization: time spent studying staff lists would be rewarded.

- Ask colleagues to brief you about colleagues you are about to meet to help refresh your memory.

SALES

SURPRISE CUSTOMERS WITH SPEED OF RESPONSE

Patrick Forsyth

A RAPID RESPONSE used to mean a brochure sent out on the day that a request for one arrived. Now communications are different: we email and text instantly, and can look at company details in real time on the internet. At the same time technology can slow things down and annoy people. For example, who has not had a bad experience with automated telephone systems? We ring ... and we wait. We go through interminable selection of options (which always seem to put "Just let me speak to someone" at the end of a long list), and listen to music we detest, and endless statements that "Your call is important to us." Clearly little has been done to actually demonstrate that. I am getting on a hobbyhorse here, but it's still the case that it is wise not to do this, or anything like it. However, sometimes it is possible to use technology in a way that truly impresses, and provides genuinely good service.

The idea
From the subcontinent of India ...

India is an enigma. It's a huge country, with millions of poor people, as well as a burgeoning economy, and everything it takes to be a major tourist attraction. Oberoi Hotels feature on the itinerary of many visitors wanting to do things in style. As with many hotels, many overseas customers now make first contact with them by looking at the website, through which you can also send a message asking for any specific information needed.

Recently when I did just that, I did not receive a message back over the ether. Instead I received a telephone call not much more than 15 minutes later from the company's British representative. Much of the time, the time difference between the countries makes it possible to do this in working hours, and it is impressive: a virtually instantaneous response from someone that you think of as being too far off for such action.

In practice
- The salesperson who responds promptly is in a strong position. They have all the details the customer has provided, they impress with a timely response, perhaps unexpectedly so, and are ideally placed to make the most of the contact.
- Ensure that internal organization promotes this sort of thing, and never allow systems and administration to hinder it (as so often happens).

PUBLIC RELATIONS
USE TESTIMONIALS
Jim Blythe

THE BEST KIND of PR is the PR that comes from your customers (and indeed the rest of your publics). What you say about yourself is always a little suspect—people are well aware that you have a vested interest. But what your customers, staff, suppliers, and so forth say about you is far more credible.

Testimonials have, of course, been in common use since Victorian times, but the age of communications has provided us with a lot more possible ideas.

The idea
Ask members of your publics to write you a testimonial. If they don't have time to do it, write it for them and ask them to approve it—obviously you need to be fairly careful here, since people do not always like to have words put in their mouths.

Testimonials are best used on your website and in publications (such as brochures) that people ask for. Using testimonials in advertising is often regarded as suspect—this is because communications that are unsought are assumed to be biased, whereas information someone has asked for is assumed to be fairly accurate.

A good way to encourage your clients to write testimonials (at least, if you're in a business-to-business market) is to ensure that they plug their own business in the testimonial. If you're writing the testimonial for them, this is something you should do on their behalf.

In practice
- Always ask people if it's OK to publish a testimonial on their behalf.

- If people are busy, offer to write it for them—but be sure that the "too busy" statement isn't just a polite way of saying they don't want to be featured.
- Only use the testimonials in sought communications such as websites and brochures.

THE LEADERSHIP PIPELINE
Jeremy Kourdi

MAKE CLEAR TO everyone in your organization the skills they need to possess and the results they need to achieve if they are going to progress to the next level. This will help them succeed in their career, and boost your business along the way.

The idea

Many organizations only pay lip service to career planning. Yet, at a time when there is a shortage of the right people and skills, it really does pay to "grow your own" talent. One example of this working well is RBS Insurance, which makes clear to all of its employees:

- The skills that are needed at each level of management.
- The skills that need to be developed before moving up to the next level.
- The content of the role at each level and what it is that individuals do.

In their book *The Leadership Pipeline*, authors Ram Charan, Stephen Drotter and James Noel highlight six stages in the leadership journey: self-leadership, people, manager, unit (individuals responsible for the delivery of part of a business), business (individuals accountable for the results of a business), and enterprise leadership (individuals responsible for more than one business).

As individuals progress through the "leadership pipeline" they encounter different "transition challenges"—for example, moving into their first people-management role, when moving from self to people leadership. There is also a focus on specialist roles such as legal, accountancy, marketing, and finance.

The advantage of managing leadership transitions is that it provides a framework for leadership development, highlights what success looks like at each stage, and describes how to improve skills— from new employees to top executives. It also ensures consistency across the business, and, above all, explains how to prepare for career advancement.

The leadership pipeline meets three business needs. It provides clarity about what is required, it makes the right development accessible for all, and it helps to focus development activities. Individuals benefit greatly from a clear, transparent career path.

In practice

- Identify the different stages or levels of leadership within your business.
- For each level, decide: a) what skills are required, b) what activities are involved and what leaders at that level actually do, c) how a leader needs to prepare for the next level—what skills and activities are missing that will be needed at the higher level?
- Provide practical processes and tools, such as personal development planning, coaching, and development programs to help make the transition.

MARKETING
INTRODUCE A THIRD ALTERNATIVE
Jim Blythe

PEOPLE HAVE MANY ways of judging value for money, but most of us will tend to judge by comparing with other similar products. Since price is also used as a surrogate for judging quality, people often simply go for the middle price—they tend to assume that the cheapest product is probably not very good quality, and also that the most expensive one is too luxurious or not good value for money. This creates a problem for companies with two products in their range—which one will customers go for?

The idea

Continental AG is a German-based vehicle tire manufacturer. It has a very substantial share of the market for tires fitted as original equipment to BMW, Mercedes, and Volkswagen cars, as well as supplying tractor manufacturers, truck makers, and bicycle manufacturers.

For the general public, Continental supplies tires under its own name and under the Uniroyal brand for the premium end of the market, under the Semperit brand in the mid-range, and under the brand names of the companies that fit tires. The result of this is that customers will have at least three prices to choose from: few choose the highest price, and equally few choose the cheapest, so the Semperit brand has a very large share of the replacement tire market.

In practice

- Decide which of your competitors poses the most competition.
- If they are cheaper than you, introduce a more expensive version to run alongside yours—this makes theirs look like the downmarket version.
- If their product is more expensive than yours, introduce a "value" version so that theirs looks like the overpriced version.
- As always, beware of retaliation!

TALENT
ATTRACT AND ENCOURAGE TALENT
Jonathan Gifford

THE LIMITING ASSET of the 21st century may well be talent. Leaders must work hard to attract young talent, ensuring that their organization has a reputation as a place where people want to work and where there is a commitment to developing people.

The idea

Ruben Vardanian, chairman and CEO of Russia's oldest private investment bank, believes that the availability of skilled and talented people will be the defining issue for businesses in the current century.

"The question for leaders is how we can create a system to attract the best people, because the main fight of the 21st century is not about assets. The main struggle in the 19th century was about land. In the 20th century, it was about industrial assets and natural resources. In 21st century, the main fight will be for the best people. Because people need to believe they want to work for you, that they can realize themselves in your company. To attract them, we need to have the right system in place and develop them for the long-term. Many companies are not ready to do this because they hire people, but they don't spend enough time or effort in developing them. I think leaders need to be very, very committed to these types of things."

Azim Premji, chairman of Wipro, India's largest software company, highlights the need to spread the net of recruitment as widely as possible.

"For one thing, we have spread our recruitment net wider than the top five business schools in India; we now hire people from the top 25 management institutes. We have MBAs whom we have recruited from these institutes, and they rank very close in quality to people we hire from the IIMs [Indian Institutes of Management] ... In fact, last year we took in 160 people from these schools. Second, we do lots of internal training and give people major responsibilities even if they are only 60% ready. Our experience is that people are pretty elastic when you give them responsibility, and they just grow rapidly with the job."

Some successful business people have chosen to fund colleges that will supply the talented young people of the future. UK businessman Phillip Green, owner of several of the UK's largest retail operations, helped to finance the UK Fashion Retail Academy, motivated by his problems in filling vacancies at his Arcadia clothing empire.

James Dyson, industrial designer and entrepreneur, founded the Dyson School for Design and Innovation to encourage Britain's next generation of designers and inventors.

In practice

- The ability to find, attract and retain talented and skilled people may be the defining issue of 21ˢᵗ century business.
- Recruiting talent is only the first step; people must be encouraged, developed, trained and stretched.
- Organizations should develop close links with the relevant educational establishments. If these do not exist, it may be necessary to help to create them.

SALES
TELL PEOPLE YOU'VE WON AN AWARD
Patrick Forsyth

GIVEN THAT ANY salesperson needs to build a case, and that one huge reason to buy is not normally going to persuade everyone, you need to seek out a number of factors that together combine to produce a weight of a case that is irresistible. Your product may only have a certain number of benefits, and it is difficult to create more (certainly without changing the product), but credibility factors are another matter. Not only may there be many things to add here; you may be able to take action to ensure that there are more.

The idea
Lonely Planet travel guides ...

These guides are now well known and successful, but their start was not meteoric and at one time their future hung in the balance. The *Lonely Planet Guide to India* won the prestigious Thomas Cook Travel Guidebook Award. This might be called lucky, but the company did of course have to ensure that the book was good, and enter it so that it was considered for the award. One of the founders of the company, Tony Wheeler, was quoted as saying, "It took us to another level. It really opened doors and made a huge difference for us." He was saying more than that the award was announced on the cover of the book: he was surely saying it was how the company used the fact that made the difference. You can imagine the enthusiasm with which the representatives of a comparatively new and small company included this fact in their sales presentation at that time.

Of course your product most likely is no contender for this award, but the amount of awards to be won is legion. A product and a sales pitch can benefit from anything, from the firm's founder being "business person of the year" to awards for technical excellence, quality, staff, customer service, and more. Many such awards are on an industry basis, while others are national, or local to a town or county.

In practice
- Find out what awards are open to your product or service, and how to go after them. (Suggest an application to management if it needs support.) A winning story can add to a winning case and enhance the sales presentations you make.

PUBLIC RELATIONS
LET PEOPLE RIP OFF YOUR IDEAS
Jim Blythe

MOST FIRMS GET defensive about others piggybacking on their main brands. Some firms even go so far as to take legal action against anyone who dares to encroach on their territory—as has been the case with McDonald's, who have even tried to protect the "Mc" prefix. This was a forlorn hope in Britain, where the law allows anyone to operate a business under his or her own name, even when that name is already in use by someone else—with so many Scots having names beginning with "Mc" (and a fair number being called McDonald), there was no chance whatsoever of the courts upholding any such action. McDonald's just managed to make themselves look foolish and oppressive.

Contrast this with Toys "R" Us, who have never taken any action against firms such as Tiles "R" Us. Toys "R" Us know that the other firms will actually help promote the Toys "R" Us brand in a light-hearted way.

The idea
Weblogs Inc. is a company that makes weblogs commercial. It was founded in 2003, and hosts around 150 weblogs. The profit comes from advertising revenue—weblogs attract very specific audiences, and advertisers find that they have a high success rate when they advertise on a Weblogs Inc. site.

From the very beginning, Weblogs Inc. has taken a laid-back attitude to other people using the format and even the brand name. For example, a Spanish entrepreneur set up Weblogs SL to operate in the Spanish-speaking world, without permission from the American company (although he does acknowledge the American source for the idea).

The founders of the company say, correctly, that the imitators will only ever be imitators. They cannot catch up: all they are doing is making Weblogs Inc. look good to its publics by implying that it is worth imitating their business plan and brand name. As the founders say, one yacht crossing an ocean looks lost and adrift: 40 yachts look like a race.

People who adapt your brand name push you further up the ladder: those who steal your ideas completely look like thieves, and will not command respect. Suing them just makes you look bad.

Clearly the founders got it right, since Weblogs Inc. was sold to AOL in 2005 for a reputed $25 million.

In practice

- Don't sue small companies that are stealing your ideas. You will just look like a bully.
- Be positive about firms that copy you. It only makes you look better.
- Remember that thieves are unlikely to be trusted by customers— you have little to fear from this type of competition.

PERFORMANCE

BE CAREFUL WHAT YOU WISH FOR!
Anne Hawkins

YOU GET WHAT you measure—so make sure that what you measure is what you want.

The purpose of performance measures (often known as metrics or KPIs—Key Performance Indicators) is to select a small group of measures that will reveal not only how well the business is performing but also, when compared to targets, where there is need for improvement if plans are to be achieved.

It is important that the measures chosen are 'holistic' and that achieving them collectively will result in better overall business performance.

The idea
Don't single out individual metrics and improve them to the detriment of others.

Holistic health
Take the analogy of someone who decides to enter a marathon. It is sensible, when about to embark on an intensive fitness program (or an improvement regime), to go to the doctor for a check-up. Humans (like businesses) are a mass of complex processes or activities. Does the doctor (or should you) try to measure everything? No, he selects a few key measures such as blood pressure, cholesterol and body mass index to ascertain how fit our potential athlete is now and what areas he needs to work on to become even fitter (and hence more competitive) into the future. Just the same with businesses.

Let's assume the doctor tells our runner that the only thing that matters is weight-loss. At the next check-up our determined athlete has taken the doctor at his word and shed so much weight that he can hardly stand, let alone compete.

Similarly, if you tell people that the only thing that matters in the business is getting inventory levels down they'll come down.

But your customers will probably suffer.

If you tell the buyers the only thing that matters is making purchase price savings you'll get them.

But you may have to expand your stores (as a result of bulk buying), and buying cheaper items may not result in the overall cost-savings you had anticipated.

When setting measures of performance, it's important that they flow consistently from top-level objectives down to individual or team metrics and do not conflict!

Avoid mixed messages

Measured on their ability to bring in business, members of the sales team in this company spotted an opportunity to win a substantial amount of additional work if they could reduce the turnaround time on orders from the customer. It was decided that it was cost-effective to lay down additional inventory in order to achieve this. The inventory was purchased and the sales team advertised the reduced leadtime for orders and the extra business started to pour in.

As did the customer complaints when goods failed to be delivered as promised.

The reason? Nobody had talked to the team in the despatch department who were sitting on goods for several days before shipping them. Why? Because they were being measured on their performance in consolidating shipments to reduce carriage costs as part of a separate campaign to improve margins.

In practice

- Take a fresh look at where your business is going, what you need to do to achieve this, and therefore the measures you need to have in place to manage your progress.
- Make sure that your measures don't send out conflicting messages and that you get across the point that the objective is overall business performance improvement, not departmental gratification.

MANAGING MEETINGS
IN THE BEGINNING—OR NOT?
Patrick Forsyth

MEETINGS ARE POTENTIALLY time-wasting in a number of different ways. Certainly without some basic organization they can go round in ever-decreasing circles and fail to focus on essentials and get things done.

The idea

Never end a meeting with AOB. Any Other Business, or AOB, is that miscellany of bits and pieces, often the awkward topics, gripes, administrative details, and suchlike, that add tedium and time to a meeting.

Consider what happens if this is taken at the end of the meeting: as the items forming this are tabled—and others are thought of—a long, rambling session can develop that extends the time well past that intended. It also lets the meeting tail away rather than allowing the person leading the meeting to bring it to a firm and, if appropriate, punchy conclusion.

In practice

Taking Any Other Business first and dealing with it promptly should be made a habit—it is a proven time saver.

- First, whoever is in the chair should remind those present what is listed under Any Other Business. This should not include individual items that can be dealt with separately in discussion with just two or three people, and that do not need the whole group present. Any items of this sort should be firmly deferred.
- Then an amount of time should be allocated: *Let's take 15 minutes to get these items cleared up.* With the main part of the meeting still pending, it is much easier to insist that the time specified is adhered to, and that discussion does not become protracted over minor matters. Allowing the latter is a sure way to risk failing to achieve the meeting's main objective, or at least to take longer than necessary to do so.

CUSTOMERS
LET THEM SHOUT!
Jim Blythe

IRATE CUSTOMERS CAN be hard to deal with. They feel let down when their product (or more often, service) goes wrong, and they want to hit back. Of course, yelling at the only person who can help them is not good policy, but it's difficult for most people not to do this, and it's even harder for the company employee or manager to take things calmly when confronted with an irate customer.

All too often, a customer complaint ends up degenerating into a shouting match between the customer and the manager—even if an employee is empowered to disconnect from the customer (for example, by hanging up the telephone or calling Security), this does not solve the problem.

Ultimately, people solve problems for themselves. If the problem cannot be resolved by talking to the person who supplied them, the customer will go to someone who can solve the problem—usually a competitor. Not only does this lose you the customer, it also generates a large amount of negative word of mouth.

The idea

The Cellular One cellphone company has 40 "save" reps in its San Francisco call center. These people have the job of saving defecting customers wherever possible: each "save" rep takes about 50 calls a day from disaffected customers, many of which are abusive.

The first step in the save process is to allow the customer to vent their anger. The reps are trained to ignore abuse, and to understand that the customer is angry about the situation they find themselves in: they are not really angry with the company, and certainly not with the "save" rep. The next stage is to work out what the actual problem is—where the service has gone wrong, in other words. For example, a customer whose calls keep being disconnected probably has a problem with the telephone rather than with the network, so reps are empowered to send out a new telephone to see if that will fix the problem.

The next step is to follow up a few days later. This is essential—if the problem still persists, the almost-defected customer will in fact defect permanently, rather than call back again. It is easy to assume that the problem is now fixed simply because the customer doesn't call back, but it is often the case that the customer has fixed the problem themselves by going to one of your competitors!

In practice

- Let the customer vent their feelings—and don't take it personally.
- Find out calmly what the root of the problem is, and offer a solution.
- Follow up afterward to check that the problem has been solved—don't assume it's all OK just because the customer didn't come back to complain again.
- Try to ensure that the same problem doesn't happen again for another customer.

TEAMWORK
SILO BUSTING
Jeremy Kourdi

How DO YOU get people to collaborate within an organization across business divisions? The answer is to focus on the thing that should unite you most—the need to serve customers—in five practical ways.

The idea

Many businesses have either failed or not realized their potential because they were divided by rivalry and did not adequately serve customers. This matters at any time, but is particularly problematic if the firm is launching a new product or looking to sell more to existing clients and contacts.

In 2001, GE Medical Systems (now GE Healthcare) started providing consultancy services (known as Performance Solutions) to complement its sales of imaging equipment. Initial sales for consultancy services were strong, but declined by 2005 because of a lack of coordination between divisions selling equipment and consultancy. Its response was to alter its approach, to be more customer-centered, and to change the sales organization.

In practice

- *Start by increasing coordination across boundaries.* This can be done in three ways: sharing information, especially about customers; sharing people and skills; and, as far as possible, making collective decisions. The danger is that traditional silos will be replaced by customer-focused ones—yet even this is a step forward. The key is to overcome traditional divisions.

CUSTOMERS
MAXIMIZE YOUR COLLECTION OF USEFUL INFORMATION
Patrick Forsyth

INFORMATION IS POWER, as the saying has it. In selling this is certainly true, and it follows that the finding-out process—identifying customer needs—is a key one. Not least, it helps in dealing with competition. If you find out more and more thoroughly about a customer than a competitor does, then everything you have to do thereafter will be easier (and it'll be more difficult for the competitor if they have failed to discover key facts).

The idea
From residential conference center Highgate House ...

This establishment is one of the best places in Britain to hold a conference or meeting. I have visited and used it many times wearing my training hat. Successful operators in this field must offer excellent facilities and service, but also, in selling themselves, must recognize that they are not in the business of meeting rooms and tables and chairs. They are in the business of "helping people make their meetings go well." And that means finding out enough about any meeting someone is thinking of holding to sell (and deliver) the venue as the best place for it. I often arrange meetings, and although I am usually asked what kind of meeting it is, if I say "a training meeting," the only further question is, how many people will attend? The venue staff ask nothing about the topic, the people, the importance, or anything else.

To get fuller information you don't just need to ask careful questions; you also need to provide the opportunity for the customer to talk and explain. The idea here is to use silence as part of the process. On one occasion I observed one of the salespeople at Highgate House get a fuller picture of a meeting than I ever thought possible. She used five separate (open) questions, including such phrases as, "Tell me more about the delegates." After each answer she kept quiet for a moment rather than moving straight on to another question— and in each case the pause prompted the customer to fill out their answer a little more. Just a few seconds may do the job, but it needs longer than instinct normally dictates. On this occasion, she was able to use the full picture she had uncovered to get an order. Surely saying nothing to sell more is about as easy as it gets.

In practice
* Questioning is at the heart of overall sales technique, and is worth examining in context. (My book *Outsmarting Your Competitors*, Marshall Cavendish Books, reviews the whole area of sales technique.)

MANAGING
GET OUT OF THE LIMELIGHT
Jonathan Gifford

LEADERS CAN FIND it difficult to stop themselves from making a contribution to colleagues' ideas because they feel the need to offer the benefit of their own knowledge and expertise.

The benefit of giving this advice may be outweighed by colleagues' perception that they have lost ownership of the idea.

Some leaders also feel the need to demonstrate why they are the leader and to indulge in competitive behavior.

The idea

Executive coach and business author, Marshall Goldsmith, says that leaders, understandably, feel the need to demonstrate why they are the leader, and to offer the benefit of their knowledge and experience on every occasion. Goldsmith calls this "adding too much value":

"Imagine you're the CEO. I come to you with an idea that you think is very good. Rather than just pat me on the back and say, 'Great idea!' your inclination (because you have to add value) is to say, 'Good idea, but it'd be better if you tried it this way.' The problem is, you may have improved the content of my idea by five percent, but you've reduced my commitment to executing it by 50 percent, because you've taken away my ownership of the idea."

Goldsmith also identifies "winning too much" and "telling the world how smart we are" as unconscious habits that hinder a leader's relationship with the team. Leaders are competitive by nature, but they don't need to win at their colleagues' expense or to blow their own trumpets. Leaders often fail to address behavior of this kind because they see it as being part of what makes them successful: "it's just the way I am". Goldsmith identifies this as a problem in itself: "the excessive need to be me".

In practice

- We all have minor behavioral defects. In a leader, these can greatly reduce their effectiveness and the ability to inspire others.
- A lot of these behavioral patterns stem from an instinctive need to "steal the limelight"; to be seen to be the leader.
- This ineffective behavior is often seen as "just the way we are" but it reduces colleagues' levels of motivation.
- Leaders should not prove themselves by indulging in competitive behavior at colleagues' expense. Allowing colleagues to have self-confidence and to get their own share of the limelight is a key part of successful leadership.

PUBLIC RELATIONS
GO WHERE PEOPLE WILL SEE YOU
Jim Blythe

PEOPLE OFTEN FEEL that they are bombarded with messages from companies. This is not strictly true, of course—bombardment is rather a strong term for what actually happens, and of course we are surrounded by messages from family, friends, the boss, and Uncle Tom Cobley and all—we simply ignore most of them.

Among the hardest audiences to reach are young people. Often they are suspicious of the older generation, who after all represent the authority that the young people are finally finding themselves out from under. Even in the 1960s we had the slogan "Don't trust anyone over 35," and most of us didn't trust anyone over 25!

The idea
During the 1997 general election, Labour realized that one of the main planks in their campaign would be getting younger voters out. Young people tend to vote for left-wing parties, when they vote at all—many do not bother to vote, and care little about politicians and their policies.

Labour's PR people decided to take the fight to the pubs and clubs where young people congregate. They put signs up in the toilets of pubs and clubs with the slogan "Now Wash Your Hands of the Tories." This humorous and unexpected approach resonated with young people in an environment where they might be expected to talk to other young people about the message—and, of course, Labour won the election.

In practice
- Find out where your target audience can be found.
- Choose a message that links to the environment in which your target audience is found.
- Do something unusual!

SELF-HELP
A COSMIC DANGER
Patrick Forsyth

BLACK HOLES, COLLAPSED stars so massive and with such powerful gravity that they pull in everything and even light cannot escape from them, make the old expression about going down the plughole seem pretty small beer. In most offices there are corporate equivalents of this phenomenon, "black hole jobs" that suck in all the time you can think of and a bit more.

The idea

Watch out for such jobs and beware—just like real black holes, if you get too near there is no going back and an involvement means all your other plans have to be put on hold.

What kind of jobs warrant this description? They are usually projects involving a number of different tasks. They are often contentious, may involve an impossibility of pleasing everyone and can be ruinous of reputations, as well as taking up a quite disproportionate amount of time. They include a range of things from arranging the organization's twentieth anniversary party and celebrations to planning the move to new offices. Such things have to be done (you may have such things in your job description, in which case it is a different matter), but they often call for "volunteers." This can mean the managing director suggests it, in public, in a way that makes refusal risky: *It is only a suggestion, of course, but do bear in mind who's making it.* At this point others heave sighs of relief and resolve not to get involved even in a tiny support role.

In practice

- You will know, if you have any wits at all, the kind of tasks in your office that have these characteristics and should, if you value your ability to keep on top of your other tasks, plan to be well away whenever there is a danger of you getting lumbered with one. Do not say you have not been warned.

COST CUTTING
TELL PEOPLE WHAT THINGS COST
Anne Hawkins

WITH REFERENCE TO stationery and other consumables, you often hear the complaint that people wouldn't waste so much 'if it was their own money'. Perhaps one of the reasons behind the waste is lack of information rather than just a question of who's footing the bill.

The idea
If you want people to be cost-conscious, they have to be conscious of cost!

Handy information
A newly appointed manufacturing manager was concerned about the high level of spend on protective gloves. When he explained to his team how much each pair of gloves cost they were horrified. The result? Not only did gloves get treated as consumable rather than disposable items, the buyer also shopped around and sourced an alternative glove that met requirements, lasted just as long and was much cheaper.

Emergency action
A delegate on a course recommended using an old style pricing gun to put a price tag on all items in stores, stationery cupboards, consumable stations etc. He did this in an A&E unit in Waterford and, without taking any other action, saw the consumable costs come down by 15%. Apparently his greatest problem was admitting the simplicity of his idea to the Hospital Management Team!

The price is—what?
Run on similar lines to popular gameshows, as the 'warm-up' at the start of a briefing session, another company asked employees to match costs to pictures of consumable items. Interestingly, even after being given the individual prices, many were unable to rank the items by annual total spend.

In practice

- Get hold of a pricing gun!
- To grab attention and encourage people to think twice, put up visually attractive cost information at the point of use. This may have the double win of not only reducing immediate usage, but also triggering bright ideas of how to re-engineer the task to avoid using the item at all.

(And while on the subject of usage—a centralised stationery cupboard with items signed out to individuals has been known to work wonders!)

VALUES
DO THE RIGHT THING
Jonathan Gifford

ORGANIZATIONS MUST OPERATE ethically. Companies that exploit their employees or the environment, or that fail to work successfully with their local or global communities, will increasingly find themselves subject to damaging criticism. They will also find it very hard to recruit and retain talent.

The idea

Sir Christopher Gent, chairman of GlaxoSmithKline, says that trust is an organization's "licence to trade".

"The need to be valued in your community is becoming more of an issue. There has to be a level of trust, because that trust is your licence to trade. It's absolutely critical in a pharmaceutical business such as GlaxoSmithKline. After all, it's a matter of life or death for the people we care for. This perception of community value is now pretty widely accepted."

Indra Nooyi, chairman and CEO of PepsiCo, talks of the moral need to respect the environment, and about the need for companies to demonstrate ethical and sustainable practices.

"We call this 'performance with purpose', and environment sustainability is a critical part of that performance with purpose. Basically, our goal is to make sure that when it comes to water and energy, we replenish the environment and leave it in a net zero state. So across the world we have unleashed the power of our people to come up with ideas to reduce, recycle, replenish the environment— and we are making great progress by reducing how much water we use in our manufacture and the carbon footprint that we put on the environment. As a consequence, what we are seeing is an incredible investment in all these environment initiatives ... really in two ways: one is tangible financial investment; second is a huge return on investment and because new employees are usually idealistic young people who just graduated from college. They want to come to a company to work for a purpose, that is wise about the next generation. And they see PepsiCo really making a difference to an environment as a whole. They really want to work at PepsiCo because they want a company that is working on meaning rather than just taking."

In practice

- Being in business means making ethical decisions. There is a moral imperative to behave well towards the environment, the local and national communities and employees. There is also a practical imperative: organizations that behave badly may lose the "licence to trade" offered by the trust of the community in which they do business.
- People buy brands that they trust. In the modern world, "trust" has a wide context that goes beyond trusting the brand to deliver its immediate promises and includes a wide range of ethical behaviors.
- Talented people will increasingly want to work for organizations that they believe are making a positive contribution to local and global concerns and which operate in an ethical way.

DEVELOP A SEPARATE BRAND FOR EACH MARKET

Jim Blythe

BRANDS ARE THE personality of the product. They appeal to a particular segment, and what suits one segment will not suit another. Very few brands are able to cross between segments—people get to like specific brands, and (of course) dislike others.

Sometimes firms will use an overall brand to "wrap" the others—Heinz is a good example—and sometimes firms will use a single brand to cover a wide range of products (as Virgin does, very successfully), but in most cases firms use a separate brand identity for each product-segment match.

Sometimes, though, the product has to function in very much the same way as all the other products if it is to work with those other products.

The idea

Nokia is one of the largest manufacturers of cellphones in the world. As such, it has a range of cellphones at various prices to suit various pockets: within each country, and even between most countries, the function of the cellphones has to be compatible with the cellular phone infrastructure, so there can be little variation in performance.

However, as with nearly every other product, there is a segment of wealthy people who are prepared to pay more simply to have a product that is exclusive, i.e., excludes the rest of the population on the environment. As a consequence, what we are seeing is an incredible investment in all these environment initiatives ... really in two ways: one is tangible financial investment; second is a huge return on investment and because new employees are usually idealistic young people who just graduated from college. They want to come to a company to work for a purpose, that is wise about the next generation. And they see PepsiCo really making a difference to an environment as a whole. They really want to work at PepsiCo because they want a company that is working on meaning rather than just taking."

In practice

- Being in business means making ethical decisions. There is a moral imperative to behave well towards the environment, the local and national communities and employees. There is also a practical imperative: organizations that behave badly may lose the "licence to trade" offered by the trust of the community in which they do business.
- People buy brands that they trust. In the modern world, "trust" has a wide context that goes beyond trusting the brand to deliver its immediate promises and includes a wide range of ethical behaviors.
- Talented people will increasingly want to work for organizations that they believe are making a positive contribution to local and global concerns and which operate in an ethical way.

MANAGING

MANAGING BY WANDERING ABOUT (MBWA)

Jeremy Kourdi

IT SOUNDS IMMENSELY trivial, but participating with employees and observing their day-to-day activities in a friendly manner can help you to discover and solve problems, gather knowledge, and form valuable relationships.

The idea

A personable and hands-on style of management, MBWA advocates walking around departments, talking with employees, and casually observing the process of work. In this way, valuable relationships can be formed with employees and knowledge can be shared. While it normally accompanies an "open door" management approach,

MBWA involves many more proactive elements, such as seeking problems through casual observation and discussion rather than waiting for employees to report them. An organization where the manager is fully integrated with their team, and aware of their attitudes and the challenges they face, will become more robust and adept at spotting potential problems ahead of competitors.

MBWA revolutionized the "ivory tower" approach of many managers and was soon adopted as part of the Hewlett-Packard (HP) Way—the open management style of successful technology business Hewlett-Packard. The HP Way soon became widely respected and mimicked by global corporations.

Care should be taken to ensure that employees do not view efforts at increased socialization and observation as an attempt to "spy on" or pick fault with their work. If they do, this will increase barriers and stress levels rather than reduce them. The solution is simple: be genuine in your interest and involvement. When done in a friendly, non-threatening manner, MBWA can carry an organization through difficult times and help managers to develop a business plan with an intimate knowledge of the people and resources that will be enacting it.

Blindingly obvious common sense? Yes. Important? Yes. Frequently overlooked and neglected? Yes.

In practice

- Be prepared to learn from employees—they are one of the most valuable sources of insight and ideas in your organization.
- Take advantage of natural opportunities to socialize, such as in communal office spaces and over drinks.
- Talk to, and build relationships with, a range of individuals with different responsibilities within your department.
- Provide practical support and be dependable, fulfilling any promises. Listen to what people say, and consider how and why they are saying it.
- Use MBWA as an opportunity to communicate, explain, encourage, discuss, and decide.

- Understand the personal requirements of team members. They are responsible for enacting company policy and it is important to be aware of their strengths and weaknesses when deciding on company strategy.

PUBLIC RELATIONS
COME FLY WITH ME
Jim Blythe

THOSE OF US who travel internationally are familiar with in-flight magazines. These are found on most airlines in the seat pocket in front of you, and are aimed at the wealthier members of society (which is, of course, anyone who can afford to buy an airline ticket).

In-flight magazines are a neglected resource: since they don't appear on news stands and don't have a wide circulation, they don't feature in most guides to the media. That means they are below the radar for many PR people, and yet they offer many opportunities to reach a well-off, semi-captive audience.

The idea

In-flight magazines have the same need for interesting articles and news stories as any other periodical. So, for example, if you are running an event that is open to the general public, contact the editors of in-flight magazines for airlines serving your city and see if they will include you in the What's On column.

Writing articles for in-flight magazines can also generate publicity. Editors get far too many travelogues (the "what I did on my weekend away in Athens" type of story) and far too much material that is completely misdirected. An article about business trends in your country or city, especially if it is accompanied by some good photographs, might work much better. For example, an estate agent might write about property trends, a restaurateur might contribute some traditional recipes from the local cuisine, or a clothes store might contribute an article on fashion trends.

The possibilities are endless!

In practice
- As in any other magazine, you must target well.
- Remember that many people on the flight are not on holiday—they are traveling for work, and are probably not interested in your article on travel.
- Be authoritative. Only write about what you know.
- Remember that a lot of people on the flight will have English as a second or third language—keep it simple, and don't use slang or obscure idioms.

STRATEGY
KEEP YOUR EGGS IN ONE BASKET
Jim Blythe

MARK TWAIN SAID that the wise man keeps all his eggs in one basket—then watches that basket. This can be good advice for the smaller firm: spreading the resources too thin, or trying to please everybody, is likely to end in tears since larger firms can do this effortlessly.

Specializing means cutting out competition—large firms have real trouble in specializing, not because they lack the resources but because they cannot convey a specialist brand message easily: no one will believe that they can specialize in everything.

The idea
Young's Home Brew is a specialist wholesaler dealing only in products for people who brew their own wines and beer. Young's has a website that has a section for retailers (Young's customers)

and a section for consumers offering advice and information about home brewing. This provides information that may not be easily available elsewhere—for example, special yeasts are now available that will survive in alcohol strengths as high as 40 percent, creating the possibility of brewing full-strength spirits at home.

Young's has managed to establish a reputation second to none in terms of specializing in home brew. They have become the first port of call for any retailers, and the consumer site encourages more people to ask for Young's products when setting up their own home brew operation.

In practice

- Resist the temptation to try to please everybody—this will blur your brand values.
- Make sure you really ARE the expert in your chosen specialism.
- Convey your specialist status to all interested parties—intermediaries, suppliers, consumers, everyone.
- Use the internet, but not exclusively: why not contact your local TV, radio, and press to tell them you are available as an expert commentator?
- Being a specialist means you are not going head-on against the big firms. You would have to be very drunk to pick a fight with the bouncers—so why do it in business?

BUSINESS SKILLS
LISTEN, LEARN AND ACT
Jonathan Gifford

LEADERS NEED TO listen to what colleagues, customers and any other interested party is saying, and to learn from what they hear. It is essential to understand the other person's point of view. Showing team members that you have listened, understood and acted is very motivating.

The idea

Wu Xiaobing, president and MD of pharmaceutical company Wyeth China, has worked in different countries and different cultures. He believes in the need to "listen, adapt, understand and learn".

"Everyone has challenges. I had a lot of challenges and they are still coming continuously. If you look at my experience ... I have worked in various countries and grown up in a different cultural background ... The biggest thing is that you have to listen, adapt, understand and learn constantly; don't take it for granted that you are necessarily right. You need to listen to others sincerely, to understand why he says things differently. When someone challenges your argument, he has his own reasoning. You have to understand his reasons."

Alan Mulally, president and CEO of Ford Motor Company, talks about how listening and taking action as a result is immensely energizing for the team. Ford's senior management hold weekly business-plan review meetings that cover the company's global operations.

"And it's very interesting because we invite guests every week to the business-plan review ... They could be in assembly. They could be in finance. They're from all across Ford worldwide. Then we invite them in as guests. We introduce them as guests of the leadership team ... And then at the end of the meeting we go back around through the guests and we ask the guests for their feedback for what they thought. I know it is the most incredible experience, it makes your eyes water ... We had, I think, on one of those meetings about the launch of that vehicle, we had one of the assembly workers that was going through that process and she said, 'You know, this is so exciting because what you are looking at here with that red is exactly where I am and it is red [Mulally had introduced a "traffic light" system for the review meetings that would flag up progress on any project as red, amber or green], but I know that we are getting help now because you know it, we know it; you listened to us.'

In practice

- Listen to what anyone has to say; understand his or her point of view; learn and adapt.
- Create situations that prove you are listening: set up systems that flag up potential problems; invite colleagues to senior meetings; show that you are aware of the issues; make help available.
- Show the team that they are allowed to have problems and that the organization will supply them with the necessary help and support.
- This open attitude will create a "can-do" problem-solving atmosphere.

PUBLIC RELATIONS
JOIN A TRADE ORGANIZATION
Jim Blythe

ROTARY CLUBS, CHAMBERS of commerce, and the like have a long history. They provide networking opportunities for businesspeople, and can often be a source of new business. Local and regional business opportunities abound, but developing a good relationship with other local businesses is a worthy aim in itself.

Many such organizations themselves need PR assistance, but rarely have anyone professional to help out.

The idea

After joining the organization, volunteer to become its press officer. This will put you in the driving seat: you will be the first to hear about new developments, you will make yourself popular with other members, and you will establish more and better contacts with journalists.

Being a press officer for the organization itself does not mean, of course, handling PR for the members. They will have to fend for themselves. What it does mean is contributing something tangible at a fairly low cost in time and effort, and simultaneously widening the reputation of your firm and yourself.

Don't worry too much if you aren't very experienced in PR. Nobody else will be either, unless they have someone experienced already—in which case the job will not be available (although it could be extremely productive to volunteer as deputy, since you will have the opportunity to pick up a lot of tips).

In practice

- Join a suitably effective organization—ensure the people you should be associating with are also members.
- Volunteer for things. If you put yourself about, only good things will happen.
- Be proactive in asking for roles, producing articles, and dealing with the press.

SALES
REMOVE FEAR OF RISK
Patrick Forsyth

MANY BUYERS ARE fearful of the decision you ask them to take. They feel insecure, they lack knowledge, they lack experience, they are conscious of acting for others—what will my boss say?—and all these feelings and more amount to the same thing: they are fearful of failure. They worry about the consequences if the product does not work, does not perform as expected, or any sort of shortfall appears after purchase. The good salesperson is aware of this, and sets out to diminish this fear during a sales meeting. But is there more you can do?

The idea

When Phoebe was six years old ...

She wanted a kitten. This reminds me of a remark I saw on the internet, attributed to Annabel (also aged six): if you want a guinea pig, start by asking for a pony. Never have I come across a clearer indication of the nature of negotiation: ten more years and she will be a force to be reckoned with. Sorry, I digress. Imagine that Phoebe's parents went through the first stage and agreed to her having the kitten. They checked out various sources, and soon found that this was a difficult purchase. What was the right time for a kitten to leave its parents? Had it been inoculated, was it healthy? The last thing they wanted was for Phoebe to be upset by her new kitten falling sick, or, worse, dying.

One breeder suggested that they choose a kitten and take it home. (He threw in some free food for the first few weeks.) Then he would contact them in four weeks' time to check that the kitten was fit and well. Only at that stage would they pay for the kitten, and any signs of trouble would mean they could choose a new one. It was not a guarantee (the kitten might still be sick), but it displayed great confidence. If he could make that kind of offer, it was unlikely that he had not really inoculated the little cat.

In practice

- Consider not just diminishing the risk, but reversing it (as above). Here it means the risk is with the breeder, not the customer. That's attractive.
- See if you can find ways of reversing any risk your customers may feel they are being asked to take. If you can, they will like it.

COST CUTTING
BUYER AWARE!
Anne Hawkins

You've DECIDED THE exact specification of what you need—how do you make sure you're getting the best value for money?

How do you make the best use of every £1 in your budget?

Use your specialists in the purchasing department.

The idea

All non-payroll expenditure should go through the purchasing department, where there is expertise in identifying alternative sources of supply and negotiating the best deal (not just in respect of price but also with regard to payment terms).

Does this always happen in your business?

It can be very frustrating to find that the buyers have been avidly scrutinising every penny spent on materials and consumables and negotiating every bit of credit they can from suppliers only to find that new equipment has been ordered, costing thousands of pounds, without competitive quotes being requested or prices and payment terms negotiated.

(The argument that the buyers do not understand the required technical specification is not good enough. If the authorisation procedure is effective, the final selection will require the signature of the person who has responsibility for the investment to confirm it meets the required capabilities and the signature of the buyer to confirm the best deal has been found.)

Name and shame

Frustrated by managers circumnavigating the purchasing department when placing orders, this business runs a monthly list of invoices that have been paid for which there were no purchase orders raised. The list is then circulated to 'name and shame' offenders.

In practice

- Work with the buying department to get the very best value for money you can from your budget!

SALES COPY
ALMOST UNIQUE
Andy Maslen

"Unique" is one of a small but powerful group of words characterized by their magnetic appeal to a certain type of copywriter. Other members of this lexical junta include "fantastic," "exciting," "amazing," and "delighted." As in, "I am delighted to inform you of an exciting new development at XYZ company." Like we care.

Paradoxically, the products I've seen that could truly claim to be unique rarely do so. Perhaps the copywriter didn't notice. Or was unequipped with enough research to discover it. Then there are all those wonderful moments where we find humdrum products described, variously, as "quite," "almost," and "one of the most" unique.

The idea
From a legal publishing firm
A client of mine publishes legal textbooks. The one I have in mind covers the reinsurance market. Reinsurance is that "belt and braces" business where insurance companies take out insurance policies on the risks they're insuring. I'm not sure who insures the reinsurers. Anyway, back to the point. The two major world centers for reinsurance are London and Bermuda.

My client's book is the only one to cover the reinsurance market in depth in both jurisdictions. And as we know, when the word "only" appears, the word "unique" can't be far behind. That single feature provided the platform for the whole brochure, from strapline to headline, body copy to call to action. It worked because it was a) true and b) a compelling benefit to the customer, who would only need to buy one book (they're not cheap).

When you start a new assignment or project your first job is to interrogate the product. In other words, to find out as much about it as there is to find out. Sometimes that's easy. There are spec sheets, press releases, or previous ad campaigns to review. Then there are the limitless possibilities of the web, from Wikipedia to newsgroups, blogs to Google. Ah, dear Google, what did we do before there was you?

From your research you may well find out one unique thing about your product. It's worth talking about, especially if you can find a way to make it sound like a benefit to the buyer. In any case, laying out *why* it's unique is a whole lot more interesting than just slapping the old "unique" sticker on it and hoping some mug will go "Ooh! Look—unique."

In practice

- Do your research. Read anything and everything you can discover that relates to your product. Recently, I found myself on the American Environmental Protection Agency website, downloading PDFs that were exactly what I needed.
- Remember that your reader has seen everything described as "unique" and therefore believes nothing is. Prove it's true.

MANAGING
SET REASONABLE GOALS
Jonathan Gifford

IT IS ONE thing to have an inspiring vision—but can you achieve it? Leaders need to set challenging goals for the organization, but they have to be realistic. An unrealistic goal that the organization cannot achieve can lead to failure.

The idea

John Chen, president and CEO of USA software services company Sybase Inc., says that it is essential to create a good match between an organization's ability and its vision.

"I think what I do best is to match reality with expectations—match the vision of what a company wants to achieve with its execution ability. It's not hard to have a vision, especially when you're in an industry long enough ... From talking to people and through experience, you inherently feel the pulse of the industry. That's why you're in the industry ... The question is, can you get from here to there? ... A lot of businesses fail for that reason. It's not because the individual CEO, president or management team isn't smart enough. It's because they aren't realistic enough."

Gregg Steinhafel is the chairman and CEO of Target Corporation, the USA's second largest discount retailer, behind Wal-Mart. Steinhafel says that the appropriate vision for Target is to be the best in other ways, not the biggest.

"We don't aspire to be as large as Wal-Mart; we know that's not going to happen. We want to be the best retail company we possibly can be. So we're focused on our demographics in servicing our guests the best way we possibly can. We know that if we can do that then we're going to be very successful as well. It's not a zero sum game. It's not as if Wal-Mart wins and everybody else loses. There's a lot of great retail companies and we believe that if we can effectively compete with Wal-Mart and stay true to our strategy, we will be highly successful over the next couple of decades."

In practice

- Leaders should use their experience to set goals that challenge organizations to the limit of their ability, but not beyond.
- Having an ambitious and inspirational goal is not enough; leaders need to understand how the organization will achieve that goal. This involves a realistic assessment of the organization's capabilities.
- It is not essential to be the biggest or even the best. It is essential to deliver products or services extremely well, and to differentiate them sufficiently to command a place in the market.
- Leaders need to make a realistic assessment of what niche their organization can occupy and what it is capable of delivering.

STRATEGY
CONVERGENCE
Jeremy Kourdi

IN CERTAIN INSTANCES, the entry requirements for different markets become very similar, enabling firms to participate easily in multiple industries, spreading risk and gaining benefits of scale.

The idea

As companies grow and establish themselves, they typically acquire a significant number of assets. These factors of production (such as employees, land, or machinery) may have multiple uses, allowing them to be used to produce a variety of products in a cost-effective way. In this way, a valuable competitive edge can be gained when entering new markets.

This tactic was employed by a large number of utility companies in the 1980s and 1990s that, following industry deregulation, realized they had the means of production to operate in the gas, electricity, telephone, and water markets simultaneously. They put their large number of core competencies—including call centers, advanced metering and billing services, and maintenance vehicles—to full use in a variety of markets, increasing their efficiency and turnover.

Are you certain your organization is doing all it can to serve customers, using all the resources at its disposal? By recognizing all the possible uses of assets, an organization can get the most from its resources, spread financial risk, and increase convenience for customers.

In practice

- Customer loyalty and a trusted reputation are valuable resources that can ensure your success when deciding to offer new services.
- Take full advantage of convergence by cross-selling products to customers.

- Hire specialists with expertise in the market you wish to enter; just because your firm is successful in one industry does not guarantee success in another.

SALES
NOT AT YOUR CONVENIENCE
Patrick Forsyth

SOMETIMES SALESPEOPLE FAIL to achieve the results they want, not because they fail to assess what would work best for the client, but more because the best way to sell the product or service is inherently a tad complicated. Whether an idea works needs to be judged first at the customer end of the telescope. If it works for them, then provided whatever it is is cost-effective, then it should usually be made a priority; anything else surely risks diluting effectiveness. Some companies embrace this principle without compromise.

The idea
From Concord Trust Company ...

This organization is a major player in the world of financial services, and specializes in advising wealthy clients on their finances. It certainly does not subscribe to the idea that the way selling is done must be convenient for the sales staff. It may not be: so be it. What matters is that the approach is organized to maximize the likelihood of reaching agreement, and doing so in a way that customers find acceptable. Concord Trust finds that many wealthy people manage their finances on a rather ad hoc basis. So it organizes meetings that get the financial adviser and the client around the table together with the client's accountant, lawyer, or any other professional adviser who can sensibly be involved. Then all the bits of the jigsaw can be considered and discussed together. A question raised by one person may be answered on the spot by someone else, which avoids delays, and a good argument by one participant can be supported by others as the client listens.

This is certainly much more difficult and time-consuming to arrange than just taking the client out to lunch. But it is worth it, in terms of both what can be done and client perception. Managing director Henry Feldman described it to *Professional Marketing* magazine like this: "when professionals do this they immediately transform themselves from railroad managers to transportation professionals in the eyes of their client." The moral here is clear.

In practice

- Selling must take place in whatever way achieves the objectives.
- Resenting the fact that what works best is inconvenient or difficult is not one of the options.
- Ignoring it allows sales to be lost by default.
- If things can be made simpler, fine—if not, so be it. But do not knowingly dilute sales effectiveness.

MANAGING TIME
THE MOST TIME-SAVING OBJECT IN YOUR OFFICE
Patrick Forsyth

ALL SORTS OF things cross your desk: magazines, direct mail, items marked "To read and circulate" and "For information," copies of things that are of no real relevance to you, and minutes of meetings that you wish had never taken place. Much of this pauses for far too long, creating heaps and extra filing trays on your desk and bundles in your briefcase (things to read at home, for instance). It is better to deal with things early rather than later. When they have mounted up, they are always going to be more difficult to get through, and an immediate decision will keep the volume down.

The idea

What is the most time saving object in your office? The WPB. The idea here involves the simple premise of throwing things away. The WPB is, of course, the wastepaper basket. It helps efficiency and time if your desk and office are tidy, if what you need is neatly and accessibly placed—a place for everything and everything in its place—but not if such good order is submerged under sheer quantity of paper, most of it of a "just in case" nature. Clear the clutter and throw unnecessary things away.

In practice

- If you are on a circulation list and do not want to look at something today, then add your name further down the list and pass it on; it will get back to you later when you may be less busy.
- At least check things like a trade magazine at once; maybe you can tear out an article or two and throw the rest away.
- Consider very carefully whether the vast plethora of things that "might be useful" is, in fact, ever likely to be, and either file them or throw them away—regularly.

All such thinking and action help, but most people are conservative and somehow reluctant to throw things away. Unless you are very untypical, there will be things on and around your desk right now that could be thrown out. Have a look, and, as you look, do some throwing. Make a full WPB a target for the end of the day. Imagine it has a scale running down the inside to show how full it is. Such a scale could almost be graduated, not in volume, but in minutes saved.

CULTURE
RESPECT THE CULTURE YOU INHERIT
Jonathan Gifford

EVERY ORGANIZATION HAS its own way of doing things; its own values and beliefs; its own culture. A new leader must respect this.

The idea

Alan Mulally was appointed president and CEO of the Ford Motor Company after having spent all of his working life at The Boeing

Company, where he was vice president of Boeing and CEO of Boeing Commercial Airplanes. He stresses the need to acquire a deep understanding of an organization before attempting to change it.

"I think any time you move into a new organization, it's just so important that you respect the history. You respect the people. You learn as much as you can about it. You seek to understand before you seek to be understood. And then you move very, very decisively but very sure-footedly into a new world. Because you know there is nothing worse than somebody coming in and acting like they know everything when you know they don't. They start handing out all of the assignments and it's just not the way I approach it. And the changes we've made: every one of them has been thoughtful, has been careful, and we've gotten a great response from the team."

Harvard Business School professor, Michael Beers, says that his research shows that effective leaders who move to a new organization should work with the materials that they are given; that they should adapt rather than destroy.

"Effective leaders build on what is already there. I know very few leaders who have succeeded in destroying the past. You have to honor the past ... That does not mean that [organizations] need to continue to do exactly what they did before. Yet leaders must recognize that the identity of people within the firm is critical to the recovery they are trying to fashion. Part of knowing who you are strategically, as well as from a values point of view, is finding a strategy to sustain. Always adapt, but don't destroy."

In practice
- Leaders who move to new organizations should acquire a deep understanding of the organization before they try to change it.
- New colleagues will have spent their working lives immersed in that organization's history and culture; the new leader should learn as much as they can about this history and about their colleagues' perspectives before they embark on major change.
- Leaders should honor the past and adapt existing attitudes and processes to fit the new strategy.

- An organization can be led in a radically new direction and still retain its sense of identity. Some part of the organization's strategy and values should be carried forward in the new vision.

PUBLIC RELATIONS
PRESS YOUR JOURNALIST
Jim Blythe

MOST JOURNALISTS WORK long and often unsocial hours, and are not especially well paid. As a profession, they are often vilified and rarely praised except by their fellow journalists: today's news is wrapping tomorrow's fish, so journalists are constantly under pressure to perform.

Also, journalists do not exist in order to promote corporate products and reputations. Most of them are professional about what they do, and will only publish stories that are accurate, fair, and (above all) newsworthy.

The idea
Tyler Barnett, the owner of the Barnett Ellman PR agency in Los Angeles, sent a compliment to a magazine editor. "Journalists want to know their work is being read by someone, somewhere," he said. "We are all working hard, and can always use a nice compliment to brighten the day."

Make sure you read the journals, magazines, or newspapers you are hoping to place stories in. If your journalist has written a piece that you like, simply email him or her to say so. You don't necessarily need to do this every time, and especially you should not do it only when you want something, but an occasional word of praise will make your path a lot easier when you have something to report.

There is no need to be excessively effusive, either—find something in the article that you genuinely liked, and say so. The chances are other people liked it too, and also the writer himself (or herself) might well have felt proud of it even before your kind comments arrived.

In practice

- Don't be too effusive—it will sound false if you gush all over the place.
- Only give praise when it's deserved, and congratulations when they've been earned.
- Only do this with a journalist with whom you already have a relationship.

SALES

SELL IN COLLABORATION WITH SOMEONE ELSE

Patrick Forsyth

SOMETIMES THERE ARE significant problems in selling. One such is when the status quo is powerful. Customers are using something else that they find satisfactory, and it blinds them to the possibility that you are offering something different and better. However good a salesperson you are, you may conclude that a sufficient degree of credibility can only come from cooperation with someone else.

The idea

A personal initiative from the vice chair of Sony USA ...

A dramatic example of the principle involved here occurred when technology in the music business first moved away from vinyl records with the invention of CDs. Record companies were wedded to the existing technology, and were intent on avoiding change and protecting their present investment in it. Given this block, the answer for those promoting CDs was to take a step back and ask, who is likely to be most interested in a new medium that improves the quality of recorded sound? The answer was the recording artists themselves—the music makers. They gave initial demonstrations to this group, with predictable results: the technology really was better, and they loved it.

Subsequently approaches to the industry, backed by this feedback, persuaded the record company executives first to take a real look at what was being offered, then to adopt it. Not only did sales of recorded music switch quite quickly to CDs; huge sales resulted as people bought second copies of music they already owned in the new format.

In practice

- There are many possibilities here. Ask yourself, who could augment your sales pitch? Customers, outside experts, other staff in your own organization (technical people, perhaps)— all may have something to contribute if you can harness their contribution and support.

COST CUTTING
THAT'S WHAT YOU ORDERED
Anne Hawkins

It's really important to be specific about what you need from your suppliers.

Every £1 you spend on products or services that aren't exactly what you need keeps that shredder busy.

The idea

If suppliers are to get it right, you need to be clear on what you need and you have to communicate this properly.

A company bought in precision-made components from a supplier with an excellent record for quality. Inspected against the drawings, these small components passed first time every time. But the company was having a problem with a high reject-rate on the assemblies into which these components went. Eventually it emerged that while the components agreed to the drawings supplied, these drawings were insufficiently detailed with regard to what subsequently emerged as critical tolerances and finishes on an internal bore. For commercial reasons it would be prohibitively expensive to change the drawings. The solution? The component was brought back in-house and a method developed for creating the bore that would deliver the tolerance and finish required.

The moral of the story?

There is actually more than one. Besides providing a reminder of how important it is to know exactly what it is you want and to communicate this clearly to your suppliers, it's an excellent example of where small may be beautiful—but can certainly be expensive. These components were small so it was assumed they were cheap. Before the problem had been highlighted, whenever the assembly failed test, the component would be removed, thrown in the bin and another one tried until eventually the unit passed.

Had the assembly-worker known that the component cost £44 a time, action to address the problem would hopefully have been taken sooner.

In practice
- If you bring goods into the business that aren't exactly what you need, you're going to end up incurring unnecessary cost so it pays to be precise.
- Buyers are not psychic! Make sure your design team works closely with manufacturing to ascertain precisely what is required and that this is communicated clearly to those in purchasing.

CUSTOMERS
BEING HONEST WITH CUSTOMERS
Jeremy Kourdi

Focusing exclusively on the threat from competing businesses can leave clients feeling alienated and neglected.

The idea
In the early 1980s, soft drinks giant Coca-Cola was concerned by its decreasing market share and rivalry with the soda multinational PepsiCo. The 1980s was a decade that saw a "taste explosion" in the soft drinks market, with the introduction of a wide range of new citrus, diet, and caffeine-free colas. Coke was being outperformed by Pepsi in a series of "blind taste tests."

Rather than focusing on the overall issue of declining popularity, Coca-Cola zeroed in on the issue of losing in the taste tests, ignoring the significance of its image, and consumer attachment to its brand. It launched "New Coke" with a new and improved taste. Although the launch technically went well, Coca-Cola soon found itself facing an angry and emotional reaction to its new formula and image. Thousands of calls were received from people wanting a return to Coke's classic product. Some of the calls were not even from Coke drinkers, but simply Americans wanting a return to a classic cultural symbol. The original Coke was brought back, Coke apologized, and the lessons were learned. Focusing on the threat from an increased number of rivals and on Pepsi's superiority in taste tests meant Coca-Cola had lost sight of the arbiter of competition: the customer.

Making decisions based solely on the actions of competitors, without first researching what matters most to customers, can lead to serious corporate blunders.

In practice
- Work hard constantly to understand as much as possible about your customers; take great care if you are reducing their views to a few simple truths.

- Talk with customers and take every opportunity to engage with them.
- Look at the nature and history of your company: by understanding your brand and product, it is possible to gain an insight into your prospective customer base.
- Use trial launches before significant changes to your product; this reveals potential customer complaints.

MARKETING
LINK TO A CAUSE
Jim Blythe

BUSINESS—AND ESPECIALLY marketing—often gets a bad press. Marketing is often associated with manipulation, persuasion, and separating people from their cash—whereas, of course, marketers see themselves as providing products and services that people want to buy.

Although marketers talk about putting the customers' needs at the center of everything they do, this does not mean that they are Mother Teresa: customer centrality is simply the best way of getting people to part with their money, in a world where they have unprecedented choice. The trick is to get people to spend with us rather than with someone else, while at the same time looking like decent, caring people.

The idea
Cause-related marketing means linking a promotion to a good cause. One of the best-known examples is Tesco's Computers for Schools promotion. This has run every year since 1992: for a period of ten weeks, Tesco stores give a voucher to each customer for every £10 spent in-store. The vouchers can be redeemed by local schools against computer equipment—at the time of writing, over £100 million worth of computers had been supplied.

The promotion serves a number of functions. First, it attracts new customers into Tesco: even if they only stay for the period of the promotion, this represents a substantial chunk of business at a quiet time of year. Second, it is good for community relations—because people give the vouchers to their local school (usually of course their own children's school), Tesco acquires a human, local face. This is no mean feat for a giant multinational chain. Third, customers enjoy the warm glow of giving when they hand over the vouchers, even though the vouchers actually cost them nothing. Finally, Tesco is helping to ensure that the next generation of employees are not only computer literate, but also think well of Tesco.

In practice
- Find a local cause to link with, or set up your promotion in such a way that people can find a local cause for themselves.
- Be specific—offering to pay to some vague or unknown charity does not carry much weight.
- Allow your customers to get the warm glow of giving.
- Time-limit the promotion—otherwise it loses its impact, since it just becomes part of what people expect from you.

COMPETITION
UPSTAGE YOUR COMPETITION
Jim Blythe

SOMETIMES IT BECOMES impossible to compete directly with a rival firm or event. What they are doing is just so far beyond what you can manage that you have no chance at all of attacking them head-on, so the only alternative is to make a guerrilla attack—which in PR terms means upstaging the competition.

Sir Richard Branson is a past master at doing this—turning up at opening days wearing a town crier's outfit, or making a "spoiler" announcement ahead of a competitor's grand press conference. But there is nothing to stop anyone doing it.

The idea

The DJ at one radio station realized that his show would have no chance whatsoever of competing against a major sporting event that was due to clash with it. So he said that, to show his support for the teams, on the day before the match he would sit in every seat in the stadium.

He got permission to do this, and of course the stunt made the local TV news: the shots of him moving from one seat to the next in a 50,000-seat stadium clearly made more interesting TV than yet another interview with the groundsman about the state of the pitch, or with the coaches about the state of readiness of the players.

Timing is essential—doing something on the same day cannot work, because the competitor's event will swamp it. Doing it two days before is too soon, two days after is too late: this DJ got it exactly right by acting on the day before.

Such stunts are hard work and may not always pay off—but it's better than doing nothing in the face of a juggernaut!

In practice

- Recognize when you have no choice but to use guerrilla tactics, i.e., know when direct competition has no chance of working.
- Plan ahead. You will need to think this through and prepare your response.
- Do something that links to your competitor's event, and preferably appears to support it.

COST CUTTING
CHEAPER BY DEFAULT
Anne Hawkins

EVERYTIME ANYONE IN your business uses a resource you incur a cost. So you need to find ways to influence the choices they make.

The idea

Don't just tell people what things cost, also encourage them to make cost-effective choices by default.

Photocopying

Setting printer and photocopier defaults to black and white duplex copies can make savings on paper and cartridge costs.

This college encourages cost-effective photocopying choices not exactly by default, but by charging all printing costs against departmental budgets... except for printing done on the lowest cost-per-copy centralised machine.

Travel

Travel arrangements should default to your preferred hotel partner, or airline or travel agent with whom you've negotiated a corporate rate, or discounts, or retrospective rebates.

Standardisation

Encouraging designers to use standardised parts reduces the cost of holding stock, gives buyers the opportunity to negotiate better discounts, and helps mitigate some of the costly risks associated with new product introduction.

Timing

Scheduling power-intensive activities (e.g. charging up fork-lift trucks) whenever you can to lowest tariff periods will save on your electricity bills.

Requisitions

This manufacturer used to have stores requisition forms that were blank so people would withdraw items from stores, often unaware that there were cheaper alternatives available that were just as fit for purpose. Not only were some choices ill-informed, inaccuracies in completing information (such as the account codes) resulted in difficulties in understanding and managing the spend.

Pre-printed requisition forms listing the preferred choice for the most commonly requested items (together with their account codes) have now replaced the blank forms. Should other items be required, the process requires the authorisation of a more senior manager. This improvement has made the better-value items the default choice and also enhanced the accuracy of management information.

The next improvement? Add the cost of items to the pre-printed list to discourage waste.

In practice
- Look for opportunities to direct the selection of purchases or timing of activities to the most cost-effective choice.
- However, do be careful that in trying to make improvements in for example, purchasing costs, you don't inadvertently end up costing the business more!

COMMUNICATION
ENCOURAGE CANDOR
Jonathan Gifford

IN ORDER TO function as a social group, we often avoid direct communication which might lead to conflict. There is a tendency to reach for social consensus: to gloss over or ignore difficult facts and to emerge with a version of reality that is not too challenging for any member of the group.

Organizations cannot allow this human tendency to disguise the need for radical action on key issues. Colleagues must be encouraged to be frank, honest and "candid".

The idea
The corporate leader who developed the idea of candor in business relations more than any other is Jack Welch, chairman and CEO of General Electric from 1981 to 2001.

Candor, says Welch, is all about asking hard questions. Instead of talking about how difficult the business environment is and congratulating each other on how well we have done under the circumstances, "Now imagine an environment where you take responsibility for candor. You ... would ask questions like: Isn't there a new product or service idea in this business somewhere that we just haven't thought of yet? Can we jump-start this business with an acquisition? This business is taking up so many resources. Why don't we just get the hell out of it?" Welch believes that candor brings more people into a dialogue, which creates an "idea rich" environment. It also speeds things up: "When ideas are in everyone's face, they can be debated rapidly, expanded and enhanced, and acted upon."

Although many corporations have accepted this "in your face" way of conducting business, some national cultures (and many people within any culture) are resistant to the approach, and leaders should bear this in mind.

Jun Tang, president of Microsoft China, highlights the fact that managers may cause offence by speaking too bluntly and causing "loss of face".

"One can hurt someone's feelings forever. American culture is very direct. But [Chinese] people are so sensitive. Sensitivity is part of their 5,000-year-old culture." The problem is not only about managers causing offence to members of the team: employees who bring a problem to the attention of a manager could be seen as implying a criticism of that manager, a suggestion that the manager is in some way responsible.

In practice

- Organizations cannot function successfully with the kind of "social niceties" that are common in everyday life; problems must be addressed frankly and honestly.
- Honest and candid discussions about business issues get to the heart of a problem, reveal stark but realistic choices and speed up business responses. Candor also opens up useful debate by inviting real dialogue about issues.

- In some cultures, and for some people in all cultures, there is real resistance to this kind of candid behavior, which implies criticism and blame.
- The invitation to colleagues to behave with real "candor" must be carefully presented, along with reassurances that frank-speaking will not be misconstrued or penalized. Cultural differences must be taken into account.

SALES
MOTIVATION AS A CATALYST
Patrick Forsyth

IT IS AGAIN the nature of the sales job that it can be repetitive. One call follows another, and many may involve saying essentially the same thing to each customer. I have already recommended tailoring the sales message, but the point remains. Because of this repetition and because there is often a low level of contact with head office, motivation is particularly important for salespersonnel. And quite right too, you may say. It is possible that you would do better if you were better motivated (although you might be highly motivated already, of course). So can you stimulate the motivation process?

The idea
From electronics retail giant Richer Sounds ...

Recently a colleague of mine bought a new television from this retail chain. He was impressed with the service and the selling—it was a purchase that needed to come with some sound advice—and was telling people at a committee meeting we both attend about it in very positive terms. Credit where credit is due: and there is nothing like word-of-mouth recommendation. He had been so impressed, in fact, that he had quizzed one of the sales staff about just why the service was so good. The overall message was that Richer Sounds was a great company to work for.

It was also clear that motivation schemes were well in evidence, and the salesperson described to him one scheme that involved the company Bentley. As an award for sales excellence, one of the team had the use of a quality car for a period. The scheme was clearly well matched to the people it was designed for (and did not result in inappropriate pushy selling that might put customers off). Everyone gained, not least the customer.

This might provide a good example to mention to your manager. If a company like Richer Sounds can go to these lengths, there is surely room for things to be taken further in your organization.

In practice

- This is another area that can only be progressed via sales management.
- A good sales manager can make average salespeople excellent, but it does not just happen. In this case, finding the right incentive (just part of the process) needs careful consideration.

PUBLIC RELATIONS
GIVE A SPEECH
Jim Blythe

THROUGHOUT THE COUNTRY there are organizations such as Rotary Clubs, Chambers of Commerce, Women's Institutes, and even universities where guest speakers are welcome. Trade organizations such as the Chartered Institute of Marketing hold regional events every month at which a guest speaker is invited to present. All of these speech-giving occasions are an opportunity for the speakers to plug their companies by presenting as the expert.

The idea

Contact your local organizations and offer to give a speech. You will probably need to make it accessible for a general audience, and you will certainly need to make it lively and fun.

Most such organizations will be looking for a speech from an expert, on a topic of interest to the membership: you should not try too hard to plug your business, but you will obviously be using anecdotes from your own experience. Structuring the speech is straightforward: begin by telling them what you are going to tell them (i.e., explain what the topic is), then tell them (give them the main content of your speech), then tell them what you just told them (sum up and conclude).

If you aren't used to speaking for an audience, remember that the most effortless-looking speeches are usually the ones that have involved the most preparation beforehand—you need to go over and over what you want to say until you are fully confident. Don't stand stock-still reading from notes, do use marker pens to draw on flip charts or dry-wipe boards, don't use PowerPoint unless you really have no choice—audiences find it extremely boring nowadays. Talk to your audience in the same way you would talk to an individual— crack a few jokes, ask a few questions.

There are plenty of books around to advise you on public speaking, but mostly it comes down to relaxing and just talking about what you know!

In practice
- Prepare well beforehand, and keep it interesting—avoid PowerPoint!
- Provide plenty of opportunity for questions. If the group is small, allow questions as you go along.
- Try not to stick too rigidly to a pre-written script—it's boring.
- Take plenty of business cards and sales information.

SALES
PSYCHOGRAPHIC PROFILING
Jeremy Kourdi

To IMPROVE SALES efficiency, customers can be divided into "groups" according to their personal needs and preferences; new customers can then be assessed and assigned to the appropriate group. This profiling combines psychological and demographic groupings—hence the term "psychographic." This enables the business to cater to customers' specific needs and preferences in a seamless and efficient way. This streamlining of customer knowledge allows companies to triumph in competitive and customer-focused markets.

The idea
"The Key to Happiness" was a self-diagnosis tool developed for Club Med customers. The business found that over 40 percent of customer dissatisfaction was directly linked to customers being recommended (or allowed to choose) the wrong type of location for their holiday. For example, a family would unwittingly choose a resort designed for single people, while a couple wanting to discover the local customs would mistakenly visit an empty island. Further studies revealed Club Med had five customer segments:

- *Tubes*, who like to be comfortable and with their family.
- *Celebrators*, who like to party.
- *Epicureans*, who prefer a high level of comfort.
- *Cultivated guests*, who like to discover the country—its culture, history, and charm.
- *Activists*, who want to get in shape and enjoy sports.

"The Key to Happiness" was a self-service system designed to help customers. It worked by using questions to find out which of the five categories best suited the customer and which location would serve them best. As a result of this system, business grew both in the short term, as customers found what they wanted, and in the long term, as satisfied customers kept returning.

In practice

- Understand your clients. Who are they, and what do they want from your business? Customer feedback and surveys are useful sources of information to help you gather this information.
- Segment your market. Divide your customers into meaningful groups based on their personality, demands, and other relevant factors.
- Brainstorm ways your product can be tailored to best serve the interests of these individual groups.
- Assess each new client, to decide which of the "customer groups" they belong to—and then provide them with a more personalized service.
- Match all the elements of your offer—particularly pricing and extras—to precisely meet the needs of each client segment.
- Ensure that people in your business understand, value, and tailor their work to satisfy each type of customer.
- Be prepared to add new groups as required.

BUSINESS SKILLS
320 GET FEEDBACK
Jonathan Gifford

LEADERS CANNOT MAKE well-informed decisions unless they know what is really happening in an organization. Getting out of the office and meeting people face to face is the best way to achieve this.

The idea

Anne Mulcahy, chairman and former CEO of Xerox Corporation, says that she relies on getting "up close and personal".

"I stay in touch by staying in touch. You've got to be out there. You've got to be visiting your operations. You've got to be doing town meetings. You've got to be doing round-tables. There are plenty of avenues for getting feedback, but there's nothing that substitutes for the dialogue that you can have with people on the ground, with your customers in terms of how they view the company. I think it is really powerful, and it's something that I expect our entire management team to do, as well. This is not an arm's-length exercise. You've got to get up close and personal. You've got to give people permission to give you tough news, not shoot the messenger, thank people for identifying problems early and giving you the opportunity to solve them. So I think part of it is the way you handle candid feedback, but the other part is being present. Nothing replaces sitting around a table and really asking people what's working, what's not working, what's getting in their way, how do we help? I do a lot of that and I think it is the most important thing I do."

Archie Norman, former chief executive and chairman of UK grocery chain Asda, says that when organizations are in difficulty, it is essential to meet people "on the front line":

"In problematic companies, the leader can't rely on the information that is easily and readily available. You've got to go to the front line, the people who are dealing with the customers, and get them to say the things they would never have said to the preceding management or chief executive. Great leaders rarely respect the protocols of hierarchy. Having a drink with a warehouse manager can tell you more about what's going on than all the spreadsheets in the finance department combined."

In practice

- Leaders need accurate feedback about the organization before they can make decisions about change.
- Set-piece "town meetings" or similar structured events are a good way of establishing a feedback process. People need proof that they are being listened to and that their comments are being acted on.
- The most effective way to get real feedback is to get out of the office and talk to colleagues and customers in one-to-one meetings and small round-table sessions.
- Don't pass judgement on what people tell you. Thank them for their views and for giving you the opportunity to address the issues revealed.

SALES COPY
THE RIGHT WAY TO USE NUMBERS
Andy Maslen

FOR SOME PEOPLE, the mere sight of a headline is enough to set off their bulls**t detector. "I can spot marketing speak a mile off," they confidently assert. These are the people who assume that all advertising is lies and that people like me are somewhere below pond life in the intellectual food chain. But ...

Show them the same sales pitch converted into numbers and a fair few of them will, magically, be transformed into believers. "Did you know," they now equally confidently assert, "more than three-quarters of golfers who switched to the Heavy Helga driver now hit the ball 87 percent further?" Nice.

The idea
From *the Times Higher Education*, a newspaper
Media kits are almost the perfect vehicle for numbers-based copywriting. Advertisers, and their agencies, need to know, in detail, how many people read or otherwise consume the media outlet being promoted. They want demographics, shopping habits, income, preferred reading ... you name it, the media kit has to provide it. (Although I did see one that, in essence, said, "You can reach posh people when you advertise in [title]." Judging by the ads they carry, it works.)

For the *Times Higher Education* (*THE*), we wrote and designed a media kit that drew on an extensive reader survey. Our job was to convey the attractiveness of the proposition—advertising in the *Times Higher*, as it's known—without drowning in statistics.

So, we gave percentages, "93 percent of Higher Education and university staff read *THE* because it's easy to read." "*THE* readers authorize the purchase of 87 percent of all student books." "80 percent prefer *THE* for job information."*

We also expressed the numbers graphically, because for a lot of people, pictures are easier to assimilate than percentages. If you say 25 percent, it takes longer for your reader to process than if you show them a cake with a quarter cut out. In fact, this is a good point to remember: wherever you can, unless you're writing a technical document or for statisticians or economists, express percentages as fractions. Prefer two-thirds to 66 percent; three-quarters to 75 percent, and nine in ten to 90 percent.

Numbers have a precision about them that words alone can often lack. This precision, for most people, lowers their resistance to taking in the rest of your message. It's far more effective to talk about "savings of £32.74" for example, than "great savings."

In practice
- Whatever you're writing about, try to discover at least a couple of facts that can be expressed numerically.
- When talking about money, cash values resonate more than percentage savings. (You can hedge your bets by quoting both. I do.)

*Figures reproduced with kind permission of the *Times Higher Education*.

PUBLIC RELATIONS
WATCH TV
Jim Blythe

POPULAR TELEVISION SHOWS offer an almost unlimited chance to pick up PR opportunities. The gradual takeover of television by reality shows and "how-to" shows provides the chance for almost any business to piggyback on a popular program.

For example, cooking shows feature recipes that rarely turn out as they should when one tries them at home: here is an opportunity for a restaurant chef to explain how the TV chefs organize themselves to create a dish. Likewise, an antiques dealer should be able to cash in on the popularity of *Antiques Roadshow*.

Good television is about people and their experiences, and so is good PR. There should be plenty of opportunities for everyone.

The idea

Keep a pen and paper handy when you're watching television. There is a strong likelihood that you will be watching programs that are relevant to the industry you're in, so it should be relatively easy to make a note of anything that strikes you as a possible piggybacking opportunity. You need to be alert so that you grab the opportunity while it is still hot, and before anyone else gets in.

You should be able to make references to most things that happen on the show, but you may need to be careful about using the names of people from it.

News programs also offer opportunities to comment—even if all you do is write to the local paper's letters column, it enables you to raise your profile a bit. Businesses are often lax about putting themselves forward in this way—but that's what PR is all about!

In practice

- Never watch TV (or read a newspaper) without a pen and paper handy.
- Act fast—these leads go cold quickly, and other people sometimes get in quickly, too.
- Be prepared to comment or offer advice on anything relevant to your industry.

COMMUNICATION
WHAT I MEANT TO SAY ...
Patrick Forsyth

THERE IS A problem with communications that has always existed. It is one compounded by people being busy and that has risen in incidence manifold since the advent of email. Probably everyone is aware of wasting time with this: you receive an email. It may be from someone you know and about something you recognize, but your first reaction is to scratch your head for a moment and mutter, *What do they mean, exactly?*

Haste and the informal style of email lead to many messages being dashed off. Something is banged out, a click on Send and the sender goes on to something else. What's the result of this? Many messages are ambiguous or completely unclear. Many of the emails criss-crossing the ether are no more than queries. They are sent only to seek clarification on something already received.

The idea

So resolve to slow down a bit. Think about what you write and make sure it will not cause this problem. Does your message make sense? Not just to you, who are in possession of all the facts, but is it likely to make sense to whomever you are sending it to? The alternative—dashing it off—may seem quicker, but in the long term it isn't. You have to write again to clarify; what is more, such an approach risks wasting other people's time and this may well be resented.

In practice

- Think before you write.
- Go on thinking while you type.
- Take a moment to check everything before you click Send (and spell-checking it too is sensible).
- With email, use the Send Later feature, which allows time for second thoughts.

If we all did this, everyone would save some time.

DELEGATE
Jonathan Gifford

ALL LEADERS HAVE a tendency to assume that they must personally find a solution to every new problem. While leaders will always be responsible for any outcome, they have to delegate the process that achieves that outcome. Successful delegation is a considerable skill.

The reverse side of delegation is the removal of decision-making powers from colleagues in an attempt to legislate against a repetition of past errors. This will not succeed and will begin to erode the organization's ability to think for itself.

The idea

Successful delegation is a great skill: people who take on a task must understand clearly what is required of them, and by when; how their task fits into the organization's overall vision and what parameters they must work within. They must feel both responsible for their task and motivated to carry it out. Lee Iacocca, President and CEO of the USA's Chrysler Corporation in the 1980s, remembers learning about delegation: "You don't know how to delegate," said Iacocca's boss.

"Now don't get me wrong. You're the best guy I've got. Maybe you're even as good as two guys put together. But even so—that's still only two guys. You've got a hundred people working for you right now—what happens when you've got ten thousand?" Iacocca commented: "He taught me to stop trying to do everybody's job. And he taught me how to give other people a goal—and how to motivate them to achieve it. I've always felt that a manager has achieved a great deal when he's able to motivate one other person. When it comes to making a place run, motivation is everything."

John Harvey-Jones, ex-chairman of chemicals company ICI, makes a subtle point about the tendency of organizations to legislate against repeats of previous disasters—with the result that freedom of action is removed from executives.

"A business mistake is made, and it is assumed that the mistake would have been avoided if somebody at a higher position in the organization had known about it or had intervened ... A power that had been delegated previously is therefore removed, usually in quite a small way, by an instruction that in such and such a case the matter is to be referred upwards. Of course that exact case never occurs, or if it does, it occurs in such a way that it is not recognized as being a repeat run of the previous bitter experience. You therefore get an increasing tangle of bureaucratic instructions which seek to legislate for an endless series of unlikely events that have occurred at some time in the organization's past."

In practice

- Leaders must delegate skillfully to their managers and inspire them to motivate their teams in turn.
- Removing managers' discretionary powers in an attempt to prevent repeats of previous errors is unlikely to work. Future situations never exactly repeat past circumstances, and leaders are no better placed to avoid mistakes than their senior team.
- Taking responsibility out of people's hands creates an atmosphere where the team tries to avoid breaking rules as opposed to trying to achieve goals.

SALES
MAKE DESCRIPTION RING A BELL
Patrick Forsyth

THERE CAN BE a problem in describing even the best product in terms that make sense to the customer. This problem is worsened if the product is new and unknown. The advice to salespeople is always to be truly descriptive, but in these circumstances it's easy to become vague and include the words "sort of" early on. Customers tend to be defeated by this. The trick is to find the right way to explain what the product is like, and that starts with the customer.

The idea
From the out-of-this-world world of *Star Trek* ...

The television series *Star Trek* is now a legend across the globe. The original series may have started slowly, but it gained cult status, spawned several spinoffs across many years, and led to a series of successful movies. Financially it became one of the most successful such franchises ever, so perhaps it is difficult now to remember how different it was at its inception from other programs being broadcast at the time. Creator Gene Roddenberry had to find a way of pitching his program idea to the networks. He thought he had a truly novel idea, yet he knew that those he sought to persuade were conservative, and that many of the programs they accepted were close to something already existing—the classic known quantity.

One of the most successful series at the time was *Wagon Train*. That was set in the American West, but the plot and the characters were essentially similar to Roddenberry's idea for a space odyssey. Each episode involved the same tight-knit group moving on to pastures new, and dealt with what happened to them in the new location, and the people they met there. Roddenberry sold *Star Trek* by describing it as *Wagon Train* in space. At the time this was a well-chosen analogy. The programmers understood it, and despite the risk of something so new and different, he got agreement to make the program. The rest, as they say, is history.

In practice
- Just one idea and one key description can create the distinction that is required for sales success.
- Often this is best done not by thinking of how you think your product or service is special, but by finding a good comparison that makes sense to the customer. So boldly go ...

TAKE CONTROL OF YOUR INTERVIEWS
Jim Blythe

JOURNALISTS EXIST TO write news stories. They do not exist to promote your company. This is so obvious it shouldn't need stating, yet many people manage to allow journalists to take control of the interview, and in so doing enable the journalist to create a story out of it by quoting out of context, by directing the interviewee to say something he or she had not intended to reveal, or even by misrepresenting the person's statements.

In fact, the vast majority of journalists are fair-minded and try to give an honest account of the story, but at the end of the day they are under pressure to write the news—and that can sometimes get in the way of fair reporting.

The idea

This idea is from a publisher of a computer magazine—someone who really knows how to deal with journalists!

You need to ensure that the journalist is getting down what you say accurately, so the first question is "Are you recording this, or should I speak slowly so you can take notes of everything?" The best outcome is if the journalist is making a recording, so remember to speak clearly anyway for the tape. Alternatively, have the interview conducted via email. If it is to be done this way, reassure the journalist that you will be giving blunt, honest replies, not PR-speak. Finally, don't be drawn into saying what the reporter wants you to say. They often look for examples of conflict, and will tend to encourage you to reveal plans aimed at damaging your competition, for example.

Think about what you are going to say before the interview begins. This will save disappointment later!

In practice

- Try to ensure that the interview is being recorded in some way other than simple note-taking. This will reduce the chance of accidental or even deliberate misquoting.
- Aim to give interviews by email if possible, but don't use this as an excuse to hand out some standard, sanitized phrases. You certainly don't want to alienate the reporters by using PR-speak.
- Don't be drawn into saying something you didn't intend to say. You can't withdraw a statement once made, and speaking "off the record" is unhelpful and dangerous.
- Don't feel the need to fill a silence.
- Assume that your worst sentence in the interview will be the lead sentence in the finished story. This will focus your mind!

PROFITABILITY
COMPLEXITY BREEDS COST
Anne Hawkins

Do YOU OFFER a wide-range of products or services? ... to many different customers? ... in many different markets? ... do you have lots of different suppliers?

While some diversification may be appropriate to reduce risk, too much can sink the business.

The idea

The complexity of your business will play a key factor in determining how much it costs to run. For example, many businesses claim to make great margins on their spares, but may overlook the additional costs they incur through complexity.

Consider the small local village shop and its inability to negotiate massive discounts from suppliers. To be sustainable there must be a sufficient number of customers prepared to pay a significant convenience premium on enough goods for the owners to make a living. For customers to come through the door, the shop must offer an adequate range of goods to meet their needs. But every time that range is increased so do the costs (e.g. extra money is tied up, extra space is required, there is increased risk of obsolescence either because of sell-by dates or fashion), and hence the convenience premium required to keep the store open increases and ...

A delicate balance.

Don't try to be all things to all people—unless they'll pay you for the privilege.

Premium business

For most businesses it is a great idea to reduce inventory to release cash to either reduce debt (and hence interest costs), or to use profitably elsewhere in the business. But not always. This business supplies a range of components used for repairing oil-drilling equipment in the North Sea. When a rig is down, the customer sends a helicopter to collect the required part.

The cost of the part is virtually irrelevant.

What matters is availability.

If the customer rings and they don't have the part in stock he will call the next person on his list... and may well not call this business first next time. The key success criterion here is product availability with the customer prepared to pay a price that rewards the supplier handsomely for the level of investment and degree of complexity.

In practice
- Reflect on the range of products or services you offer and the diversity of your customer base.
- Review the profitability not just of each product or service you offer but also the categories of customers you serve.

PERFORMANCE
SUPPORT AND CHALLENGE GROUPS
Jeremy Kourdi

ONE OF THE simplest, shortest, and most effective business ideas is to encourage people to establish support and challenge groups. Practiced by many organizations worldwide, these are an indispensable way to build teamwork, productivity, and effectiveness at work.

The idea
A support and challenge group consists of four or five colleagues of a similar level or status, who meet, informally, at regular intervals (perhaps once a month or once a week). Each individual takes a turn for ten minutes or so explaining a challenge or issue that they face. The others listen and then ask questions, helping their colleague understand the key issues and where the solution might lie. This should be done without prescribing a solution; the key is to support the individual and challenge their thinking and assumptions.

The British retail pharmacist chain Boots is among many that have used the technique successfully. Support and challenge groups work for several reasons:

- Speaking about an issue or challenge can help provide perspective and clarify the issues, even without the comments of colleagues.
- The views of others can provide a different approach to a challenge—or simply provide encouragement and strength. Either way, the involvement of others is helpful.
- People gain greater understanding of each issue and the challenges they face. Being aware of common issues encourages people to collaborate more.
- Listening to someone else's challenge enables individuals to sharpen their own thinking and approach.

In practice
- Gather together a group of colleagues, explain the concept

(to provide support and challenge each other's thinking), and arrange to meet regularly.
- One person keeps time—a speaker should take no more than ten minutes to explain their challenge.
- Ensure that the speaker is heard in silence, without interruption.
- Take it in turns to ask questions and comment. A questioning approach is particularly effective.
- Move on to the next individual and repeat the process.

MARKETING
HOW TO GO UPMARKET
Andy Maslen

THERE ARE TIMES when you want to go deliberately upmarket. Perhaps you're selling a very expensive product; or you're selling a cheap product to very expensive people. Either way, you need to strike that elusive tone of voice and style that reassures your reader that they won't be rubbing shoulders with the hoi polloi if they buy from you.

Preserving that sense of exclusivity is about more than using the word "exclusive." In fact, along with "exciting" and "unique," "exclusive" is one of the most overworked old nags in the language, repeatedly pressed into service and weighed down with expectations that it can never deliver.

The idea
From The Economist Group
I have written hundreds of conference promotions for this company, whose delegates are usually charged around £1,000 a place. So not cheap. But, for my client, still an average event in style, content, and delegate profile. When they decided to go truly upmarket, they did without delegate fees altogether. The pitch wasn't, "If you have to ask how much it costs, you can't afford it." It was more like, "If you have to ask whether you can attend, you can't." In other words, it

was all about the exclusivity of the event. Called The Global Agenda, it convened (still does) small groups of extremely influential and powerful individuals. Not just any old CEOs but CEOs of the world's largest corporations. Plus Nobel Prize winners, leading academics, and very senior politicians.

So, an invitation-only event for very important people indeed. The language had to reflect the Economist brand, the unique (there's that word again) character of the meeting, and the participants' own expectations and sense of self-esteem, which we assumed would be high. Here is the opening from the invitation:

> Many speculate about the shape of things to come, but few speak from a position of authority. The corporate and thought leaders invited to take part in this roundtable have, more than most, the experience and insight to make such a claim.

Contrasting the many with the few leaves the reader in no doubt which group he or she belongs to. Referring to the reader in the third person plural—which breaks one of my own cardinal rules—works here, seeming aloof from the grubby business of direct mail selling.

I also deliberately used a slightly arcane vocabulary—"academia," "a crucible for new thinking," "alumni"—to reinforce the sense that this would be no ordinary talking shop.

In practice
- If you are going upmarket, aim for a higher register than you'd normally use—you get to break all the rules about short words, and simple sentences.
- Ask your designer to use a classical serif typeface, Palatino or Perpetua perhaps, with generous margins and leading. Buy the best paper you can afford.

330
TURN A DISADVANTAGE TO AN ADVANTAGE
Jim Blythe

MOST MARKETS ARE in a state of monopolistic competition. This means that one large company controls most of the market, and sets the pace, and the other companies in the market have to follow the leader. Many companies find themselves at a disadvantage when they are competing against the market leader—the leader controls the sources of supply, has the biggest advertising budget, and often controls the distribution network.

This doesn't mean the others can't compete—it just means they need to act more like judo wrestlers, and turn the leader's strengths against it.

The idea
When Avis car hire was founded by Warren Avis in 1946, the company had a total of three cars. By 1953, it was the second-largest car hire company in America behind Hertz. Somehow Avis couldn't catch up with Hertz, so in 1962 the company turned an apparent disadvantage to an advantage by adopting the slogan "We're Number Two—So We Try Harder."

This slogan is extremely powerful on a number of levels. First, it gives the immediate impression that Avis will do more for the customer than will Hertz. Second, it gives the impression that Hertz, as the market leader, is complacent and resting on its laurels. Third, it appeals to people's sympathy for the underdog. Fourth, and perhaps most importantly, it is easily memorable.

The Avis slogan is one of the best known in the world. Nowadays, the company still has not caught up with Hertz, but it is very close behind—if Avis ever did catch Hertz, of course, the slogan would no longer apply.

In practice

- Think about your main disadvantage, compared with the market leader.
- Think about how that disadvantage can be seen as an advantage.
- Express the idea in less than ten words.
- Make it punchy and memorable.

STRATEGY
REINVENT YOURSELF
Jonathan Gifford

IF YOU THINK that a new and more radical strategy is needed, consider "reinventing" yourself and your team.

The idea

After Andrea Jung had already been chairman and CEO of Avon Products Inc. for many years, she realized that the strategies for which she was responsible were not succeeding.

"If you need an example of what is meant by the courage of leadership, this was it. There was a moment when I had to have the humility to undo my own strategies; undo my own team." Her mentor advised her to go home that night and pretend that she had been fired, and then to come in the next morning and imagine that she was an outsider, hired to make fast, tough and objective decisions to save the company. "It was probably some of the most pivotal advice that I have ever received. I came back in the next morning and we did some bold things in terms of radical organizational restructuring. With emotional detachment from existing strategies we made some very tough decisions, and it really breathed a very important new chapter of life into the company."

Wu Xiaobing, president and managing director of pharmaceutical company Wyeth China, uses a similar approach with the whole management team.

During a brainstorm session in which colleagues are encouraged to criticize past decisions, he asks: "If every member of our management team left the company for whatever reasons ... what would a new management team do? Would they be content with the growth rate ... that we've had over the past years? Or would they want to grow even faster, to show they are more capable? If so, then they have to learn two things. First, what did their predecessors do wrong, or not well enough? Secondly, going forward, what will be the important opportunities? So, everyone has to forget his identity and imagine he is a new team member; it doesn't matter what has happened in the past, you can criticize the company fiercely. And indeed, after our brainstorming and discussion, we have been surprised that we had a lot of conclusions and there are many things we haven't done well."

In practice

- If your strategy isn't working, step back and consider a whole new approach.
- Imagine that you are a new leader facing the current situation for the first time; view the current situation objectively and consider more radical solutions.
- Take action as if you were that new leader. Put aside your involvement with previous strategies and approaches.
- The team members already trust you and are loyal to you, so your new direction will be easier for them to embrace than if it was proposed by an outsider.
- Asking colleagues to imagine themselves as a fresh new team assessing the organization's past performance helps the team to examine its own performance critically but positively.

ONLINE MARKETING
PROFILE YOURSELF IN WIKIPEDIA
Jim Blythe

PART OF THE internet revolution has been the proliferation of online information services. People research almost anything online:

students use the internet to research for assignments, buyers use it to source suppliers, and authors use it to create case studies.

One very widely used site is Wikipedia. It is an online encyclopedia (for anybody who doesn't know this already) that is created by its contributors. People who know something about something can write an article for Wikipedia, but must demonstrate that they have researched the topic well and the article is factual.

Obviously this is difficult to police effectively, and no doubt a great deal of stuff appears on Wikipedia without being especially accurate, but it is still a very frequently visited site.

The idea

Wikipedia has a policy of allowing anyone to enter genuine information onto its pages. This does not mean you can insert an advertisement, but it does mean you can put your company history on the site. Note, however, that any other Wikipedia user can edit the article, and although the Wikipedia administrators are fine about people altering articles they will not tolerate malicious editing, vandalism, or outright commercialism.

Wikipedia lends itself to PR, and many firms have written their own entries. This puts the company on the map, and often results in further publicity as the company is cited in articles elsewhere.

In practice

- Be truthful. If you aren't, someone else will be!
- Accept that Wikipedia is, in effect, an open forum. You can't prevent someone else adding to your profile—some company histories on Wikipedia now contain embarrassing revelations about violations of workers' rights or breaches of codes of practice.
- Ensure that visitors to Wikipedia can obtain information from your own website as well.

COMMUNICATION
CONSIDER THE CULTURE
Jim Blythe

WE ARE ALWAYS being told that we live in a multicultural society, yet most of us know relatively little about the other cultures we deal with. This is a particularly acute problem when we are dealing over the telephone, since it requires our telephone staff (sometimes an entire call center full of them) to be culturally sensitive in many different ways to many different cultures.

The problem is exacerbated further by the fact that call centers often have a high staff turnover rate: these are jobs that are stressful, so there is a constant pressure to leave. Making cultural gaffes and annoying the customers simply adds to the stress.

The idea
Aviva is a major financial services player, and consequently the company runs several large call centers. In common with many other companies, Aviva has located some of its call centers in India, where costs are dramatically lower and an educated, English-speaking workforce is readily available. However, the vast majority of this workforce have never been to Britain, and are unlikely ever to do so, so Aviva runs courses on cultural understanding. The courses are not only about what people say, but how they say it: the courses cover issues such as the weather, the state of the roads, current issues in British politics, polite expressions and over-familiar or impolite expressions, and so forth.

The aim is not to allow call center operators to pretend that they are actually British: it is simply to ensure effective communication between call center staff and customers.

In practice
- Identify the cultural groups you might encounter.
- Take advice from a member of the target group—don't rely on your own judgments or published "cultural guides."

- Keep the training going—cultures shift, and anyway there is always more to learn.

BUSINESS SKILLS
SAY SORRY SOMETIMES
Jonathan Gifford

WE WORK INTENSIVELY with our colleagues. Very few leaders will be able to search their hearts and feel that there are not some colleagues to whom they should have said "sorry" on occasions. An apology is a powerful thing that can only improve your relations with your colleagues. Saying "thank you" is pretty good too.

The idea
Marshall Goldsmith is a successful executive coach and business author. He argues compellingly that it is behavioral issues that prevent people from reaching their full potential: anyone who is near the top of their profession has already proven their skills and abilities; it is the way in which they relate to their colleagues that may limit the level of leadership to which they can aspire. His typical coaching technique is to use in-depth 360 degree feedback from executives' colleagues to identify problem areas. Once an executive had acknowledged the need for change (and the great advantages that change will offer), then saying "sorry", says Goldsmith, is the most important next step.

"I regard apologizing as the most magical, healing, restorative gesture human beings can make. It is the centrepiece of my work with executives who want to get better—because without the apology there is no recognition that mistakes have been made, there is no announcement to the world of the intention to change and most importantly there is no emotional contract between you and the people you care about. Saying you're sorry to someone writes that contract in blood."

Goldsmith is talking here about a formal process of behavioral change, which few of us undergo. But it is unlikely that there is not some working relationship you have with a colleague that would not be improved by saying "sorry" for an act or omission of yours.

In practice

- We work closely with our colleagues and have a personal relationship with them.
- We are reluctant to say sorry, but we should not be. Apologizing makes our working relationships better; it acknowledges that leaders are not infallible and creates an emotional bond.
- Because we are all human, it is highly likely that something that a leader has done will have caused unnecessary upset to a colleague.
- Saying thank you is also easy and equally important. A small gesture of thanks can have a disproportionate effect.

CUSTOMERS

PUT VALUE ON INFORMATION ABOUT THE CUSTOMER

Patrick Forsyth

THE IMPORTANCE OF asking questions and listening to the answers has already been stressed. So too has the need to tailor, and be seen to be tailoring, the case you make to an individual customer. One simple mechanism helps you do this, and makes a positive impression on the customer too.

The idea

Catching the details ...

To be fair many salespeople do this, but if they do not, it can send all the wrong signals. Remember first that people's sense of individuality is strong. We all think of ourselves as being unlike other people. And we want others to understand and take these differences into account. Certainly this is true of buyers and sellers.

For example, I wear spectacles, and have just had an eye test. Very thorough it was, too. I would not have been much impressed if I had walked in, perhaps been asked to read a couple of lines of text, and then been told, "Right, I know exactly the prescription you need." I want a thorough check. And believing it is a complex and individual matter, I was pleased to see the optician completing a detailed form as the test progressed. So too with selling. Whenever any degree of complexity is involved, always take notes during your conversation; and remember to base your judgment about complexity on your customer's apparent perception of the situation, not on your own.

It may be polite to ask permission to do this, especially if confidential information is involved, as is often the case in my business. You should always make it clear what is happening. Customers like it, you may need a moment to let your note-taking catch up with the conversation, and where appropriate, it should be a noticeable part of the whole process. Take time too to check what you have written promptly, perhaps highlighting key details in a second color. It is easy to find that after a few days, and after holding several (many?) more customer meetings, you are unsure exactly what some of your notes mean.

In practice

- Now make a note of this: get yourself a notebook or pad and make recording key details part of your routine with customers. One fact remembered rather than overlooked can sometimes lead to the sealing of an agreement that might otherwise be stillborn.

SALES COPY
SATISFY THEIR CRAVINGS
Andy Maslen

WHEN PEOPLE NEED stuff, they will buy it. Just don't expect it to be a particularly motivated customer. Life insurance, new wellington boots, a replacement wastepaper basket: they get bought but not drooled over. Contrast that state of mind to the one when they *want* something. *Much* better. If the want in question is some fundamental human need—sleep for example—it would take an idiot not to be able to connect with their prospects.

Much as people—marketing people especially, I have often noticed—claim to find selling distasteful, without it there is no buying. So being sold to is a good thing. And *if* you're being sold something you really want it's a fantastic thing.

The idea
From a nighttime nanny service
If you have children of your own, this isn't going to be a stretch, and if you haven't children, I still think you'll get it very easily ...

What would it be like to go without a full night's sleep for a year? Or two years? Or three? Not no sleep. Just sleep interrupted every hour or two by a crying, no, make that a screaming, baby. Pick your own noun. Mine would be purgatory. Hell is shorter and probably more accurate. So how wonderful would it be if you received a mailing from a company promising to make this peculiarly horrible pain vanish, literally overnight.

That's exactly what my client was offering. Highly trained and qualified nannies who would sort your baby's sleep problems out for you while you slept. Here's some of the copy that tuned into these sleep-deprived, middle-class parents' nightmare ...

Do you dream of a full night's sleep?

Remember those nights of unbroken sleep? Of waking when *you* were ready, not your little one? We can bring them back for you.

This is the opposite of fact-based copywriting—it's all about emotion. And sometimes it is the easiest to write—no need for AIDCA or any other mechanistic approaches. Your prospects might be frightened rigid by mounting debts; they might be consumed by wanderlust; their heart might race at the mere thought of a gastronomic tour of the world's finest restaurants. Where you can satisfy a craving, a want, rather than just a need, your job is immeasurably easier.

In practice

- As you plan your copy, look hard for the deep-seated cravings that your product satisfies. Just be careful how you phrase it: people don't like their more base desires thrust in their faces.
- Even if your product is a nice to have rather than a must have, if you can find a way to make it *feel* more desirable you engage people's emotions as well as their reason.

SALES
CROSS-SELLING AND UP-SELLING
Jeremy Kourdi

CROSS-SELLING MEANS SELLING additional products to a customer who has already purchased (or signaled their intention to purchase) a product. Cross-selling helps to increase the customer's reliance on the company and to decrease the likelihood of the customer switching to a competitor.

The idea

An idea that first gained momentum in the 1980s, cross-selling involves firms offering a variety of products and services to customers, then using an integrated selling process to market this range to existing clients. For example, if customers trust a firm to provide them with health insurance, they may also trust it to provide car insurance. The company can take advantage of this trust by offering both services, and targeting existing customers with marketing schemes.

Internet-based travel agent Expedia offers an impressively seamless and effective example of cross-selling. When customers complete an online order for a hotel or plane ticket, they are presented with a webpage offering them the opportunity to purchase car hire. Low-cost European airline easyJet uses cross-selling on its website, for example, by offering travel insurance to customers in the process of purchasing a ticket.

However, smaller businesses and offline companies needn't be put off; cross-selling does not need to be a technologically advanced process. Simple integrated sales pitches can be just as effective. For example, having salespeople mention products when taking an order can encourage customers to make multiple purchases.

Cross-selling is similar to up-selling, although there are some key differences. Up-selling is where a salesperson attempts to have the consumer purchase more expensive items, upgrades, or other related add-ons in an attempt to make a better sale. Up-selling usually involves marketing more profitable services or products. Examples of up-selling are adding side dishes to a food order, selling an extended service contract for an appliance, and selling luxury finishing on a vehicle.

In practice
- Ensure the profit from the extra items covers the cost of the time spent selling them.
- Educate sales staff to ensure they have a full understanding of the products they are offering.
- Plan which products to offer to which customers. As with any sale, integrity and honesty (even straightforward openness) usually work best.
- Only attempt to sell products that are clearly linked to a specific purchase the customer has made. This ensures the marketing pitch is more appropriate and less opportunistic.

PUBLIC RELATIONS
THINK SMALL
Jim Blythe

MAJOR MEDIA SUCH as national newspapers and TV news are notoriously difficult to get into. Apart from anything else, they are often bombarded with press releases, most of which are of limited interest. Local media such as local radio news, local TV news, and local newspapers are much easier to approach.

In business-to-business markets the smaller trade journals are also easier to get into, since they are likely to be more specialized and have fewer news-gathering resources.

The idea

Jason Calacanis, founder of *Silicon Alley Reporter* (a small specialist magazine for internet enthusiasts), found that major media outlets were not usually interested in him or his company. He recommends working through small media outlets rather than pitching to the big boys.

Pitching a press release at a smaller medium is usually easier and more likely to succeed. They have more time for you, and in any case the bigger media regularly trawl through the minor magazines looking for stories. This means that your story could well make it into the majors anyway.

Additionally, a small local paper or magazine exists to disseminate local news and human-interest stories, so they are much more likely to accept your piece. They have fewer resources for news gathering, and fewer press releases coming in.

Calacanis also recommends going to blog sites and contributing: either you can send the web link to the media you want to contact, or (fairly probably) they will find it themselves.

In practice

- Choose your media carefully.
- Remember that your press release might be picked up by bigger media, and be prepared to respond as necessary.
- Small specialist magazines rely on contacts with industry, so be prepared to answer questions.

SELF-HELP
GET A LIFE
Jonathan Gifford

LEADERS NEED A life outside work. Working too many hours is counter-productive; quality of work and one's perspective on life both suffer.

Lack of healthy social and family relationships can cause leaders to behave badly and to make poor ethical decisions.

The idea

Tom Stern used to be a stand-up comic; he then launched a highly successful executive search company and found himself so driven by his urge to succeed that his family life suffered. He now considers himself to be "a recovering success addict".

"People who work too much tend to have really bad personal lives. Their families become unhappy, their children have problems that are distracting and emotionally draining, their wives are angry all the time. Obviously, job performance suffers. It's not just how many hours you're putting in or how much you're churning out. There's the quality of your work. And studies show that compulsive workaholism does not produce a better product ... I believe the family is a grounding mechanism. Your family will talk to you in a way people never would in business, especially if you're a high-level executive ... If you're not connecting with your family, you don't have that critical grounding mechanism. And for certain personalities, that can lead to immense arrogance and ethical management issues."

Sharon McDowell-Larsen of the Center for Creative Leadership is a former US Olympic Committee researcher. She reminds us that, in business as in sport, "recovery time" is essential: "Learn from professional athletes. You can actually do more in less time by practicing the art of recovery. Professional athletes understand that pushing themselves at 100% of their capacity 100% of the time results in little or no long-term performance gain. They build time to recharge into their training routines. You can do the same. Do it by finding effective ways to set boundaries. Listen to music on your commute home. Turn off your cellphone and your e-mail during personal or family time. Take up a social activity or a hobby. Relaxing is critical for clear and creative thinking, strong relationships and good health. Know that the time and energy you spend away from work can enhance your productivity and your capacity to deal with things at work."

In practice

- Keep an eye on the hours that you are working—at home as well as in the office.
- Lack of good social relationships is not some kind of unavoidable collateral damage that goes with being successful. Apart from the damage that you are doing to other people, you are damaging your own mental health and your effectiveness as a leader.
- The lack of any balancing input from healthy social relationships can lead to insensitivity and arrogance, which leads to bad decision making and even ethical lapses.
- Leaders need time to relax and reflect. Minor changes in routine can be very effective: use travelling time to "switch off"; make sure that you are not distracted when you are with your family or friends; take up a hobby.

COST CUTTING
DOES ANYONE USE THIS?
Anne Hawkins

IF YOU DO something, it requires time and possibly materials and therefore costs money.

While attention may be paid to the margins made on business done with outside customers, what about your internal ones?

Who do you supply with products or services or information?

What 'value' do they place on these?

Is it worth doing?

The idea
Look critically at how you meet the needs of your internal customers.

A lecturer from a leading university told me how he'd called into the departmental administration office a couple of weeks before the start of the new academic year. Chaos, pandemonium and the onset of multiple breakdowns lay before him. When sensitively enquiring as to the reason behind this, he was told that every year all new students had to be provided with a CD loaded with information from the relevant university websites. This took the staff two weeks of intensive activity.

Why were they doing this?

By the time they had produced the CDs, the information on the websites would have changed... and their customers, the students, were far more adept than they were with IT and would tend to go straight to the website in the first place. Why not just signpost the sites as part of the welcome mail sent to all students?

Now seen as a visionary saviour by staff who were told that this activity was no longer required, the lecturer couldn't wait to tell them his latest idea about rationalising the plethora of consent forms students had to sign on their arrival ...

In practice

- Identify the 'outputs' (products, services and information) you supply to your internal customers.
- 'Walk' your outputs to your customer to ensure you are giving them the service they require, i.e.:
  - what they want
  - in the form they want it
  - in the timescale they need it
  - with the frequency required

If nobody needs it—don't do it!

BRANDING
DEVELOP AN ICON
Jim Blythe

PEOPLE DON'T RELATE to products—they relate to brands. This is a good thing, provided you have a stronger brand than your competitors: but how do you get that stronger brand in the first place?

For strong brand read likable brand. If people feel warm toward the brand, they will in turn feel warm toward the product, which can only be a good thing for immediate sales and future loyalty. One effective way of building likability is to create a memorable icon, a symbol of your brand that will stick in people's minds and be entertaining.

The idea

Dry batteries have been around for over 100 years now: the first ones weighed in at over three pounds, and were used to power telephones, but technology moved on rapidly and zinc-carbon batteries became ubiquitous. At the same time, prices dropped: zinc-carbon batteries were disposable, and were in fact disposed of regularly.

When alkaline batteries appeared, they were a great deal more expensive than zinc-carbon batteries (and still are), so the manufacturers, Duracell, needed a way of demonstrating that the batteries would be cost-effective. Their initial advertising campaign showed a set of electric toy animals that gradually stopped working as their batteries ran down, except of course for the one powered by Duracell copper-top alkaline batteries. This was the Duracell Bunny, a pink toy rabbit banging a drum.

The Duracell Bunny became iconic. People responded well to the "cuddly toy" aspect because of its playfulness, and the memorable advertisements: more importantly, the key benefit of the product came across extremely clearly. More recently, Duracell have been able to do away with the other toys and use only the bunny—it has been seen climbing mountains, canoeing, playing leapfrog, playing soccer, and free running. The advertising was so successful that Ever Ready brought out their own bunny to advertise Energizer, but for legal reasons these ads have not been shown in Europe or Australia.

In practice

* Consider your unique selling proposition—what does your product have that others don't?
* Try to create a playful icon.
* Use your icon in different contexts so that it remains fresh.

SALES
TAKE A LONG-TERM VIEW
Patrick Forsyth

It is an old maxim of the world of selling that the job is not to make a sale, but to make a customer. The implication is that the business you obtain over the longer term is more important than clinching a single deal today, and there is certainly some good sense in this view. Sometimes this philosophy can be taken to extremes, and still make sense.

Let me prefix this idea by summarizing my experience with the cellphone company Vodafone. I have just wasted at least two hours of my time discovering that it cannot supply what I want. I went into a local store to ask, and was told the company could do what I wanted, but only via a bigger store. I emailed the company and (eventually) got a reply saying this was the case. In London a little later, another store told me it could only sort out my problem by telephone. When I was home again, I telephoned. Nobody needs all the details: after endless holding, several transfers, and my demanding to speak to a manager, I was told the company did not do what I wanted at all. You can guess what this experience did for the likelihood of my doing business with Vodafone in the future, especially as at the end of the call I declared my intention to write about my experience, and gave the operative my telephone number so there was a chance for someone else to ring me and try to put things right. I heard nothing.

The idea
From cellphone company Orange ...

After this incident I telephoned Orange. It took one call, one person, and a few minutes. I got a clear explanation, some suggestions, and—and here is the idea—firm advice that I should not buy anything at present. "The cost is disproportionate for what you want," I was told. "You would not feel it was good value." Not only was I not sold anything, I was specifically recommended not to buy anything! Technology should give me new options in the future—and guess where I will be asking about them.

In practice

- The Orange salesperson sacrificed a sale now for a larger sale in future—and some good references in the meantime (including the one in this book!). The moral is clear: customers are more likely to rate, and buy from, people who display this attitude.

PUBLIC RELATIONS
GRAB ONTO SOMETHING UNPOPULAR
Jim Blythe

MOST PR PEOPLE look for the positives, but most news is negative. At the end of 2008, the world headed into a major financial crisis (which had been preceded by a major rise in fuel costs). Most firms tried to mitigate the negatives in the news by putting out counter-stories, basically saying "The world might be going to pot, but we're still solvent."

There could, however, be a much punchier approach waiting if you grab onto the negative news.

The idea

Tell people what you're doing to combat the problem, especially if you have thought of something wild and wacky. For example, if petrol prices have risen, you might have decided to issue bicycles to your employees. If there is a credit crunch, you might run a competition for the most original idea on saving money within the firm. You might decide to make a special offer—for example, in early 2009 restaurateur Peter Ilic abandoned prices on the menus at his top London restaurant and allowed customers to pay what they thought the meal was worth. Obviously, in some cases they would pay very little, but in other cases people paid more than Ilic would have charged, and in any case he got value for money from the exercise simply because of the publicity.

Often these stories have good visual possibilities: employees riding their bikes, the lucky winner of the competition, the restaurateur serving a customer, and so forth. Equally, such ideas are valuable in their own right—putting the staff on bicycles really does save money, and Ilic reported that his restaurant was packed solid with customers. As any restaurateur knows, the key to success is filling the place up seven evenings a week and lunchtimes too.

In practice
- Watch out for disasters and get your response in early.
- Remember you can always back down later, after the story has run.
- Do something out of the ordinary—remember, other people may have the same idea.

COMMUNICATION
USE SYMBOLS
Jonathan Gifford

AN ORGANIZATION'S VISION should be clear, simple and easy to explain. The various strategies that it uses in order to achieve the vision may be more complex, but they must still be understood by everybody. A symbol, image or metaphor is always easier to understand and remember than a detailed argument.

The idea
Franklin Delano Roosevelt served four terms in office as President of the United States of America, from 1933 to 1945; the only American president to serve more than two terms. Roosevelt's long presidency began in the Great Depression and continued throughout World War II.

In these turbulent times, Roosevelt made great use of the media, and in particular of the relatively new medium of radio, to address the American public. He made very effective use of metaphors to get his point across, comparing significant national issues to relatively minor domestic crises in a way that was easy to understand and remember.

In 1941, Britain could no longer afford to pay for the arms and munitions that America had been supplying to support Britain's war with Nazi Germany, but a 1934 Act of Congress prevented America from trading with any other warring nation other than on cash terms. Johnson invented the notion of "Lend-Lease" and sold this to the American public in a disarming way: "Suppose my neighbor's home catches fire, and I have a length of garden hose four or five hundred feet away. If he can take my garden hose and connect it up with his hydrant, I may help him to put out his fire ... I don't say to him before that operation, 'Neighbor, my garden hose cost me $15; you have to pay me $15 for it.' I don't want $15—I want my garden hose back after the fire is over."

Similarly, when the American government needed to sell a record number of War Bonds to finance the continuing war, Roosevelt drew on the image of a community piling sandbags onto the levees of a swollen river to save the town from flooding.

"Today, in the same kind of community effort, only very much larger, the United Nations and their peoples have kept the levees of civilization high enough to prevent the floods of aggression and barbarism and wholesale murder from engulfing us all. The flood has been raging for four years. At last we are beginning to gain on it; but the waters have not yet receded enough for us to relax our sweating work with the sand bags. In this War Bond campaign we are filling bags and placing them against the flood."

In practice
- When addressing large groups of people, keep the message simple.
- Make use of metaphors, symbols and images to get the message across. These are more easily grasped and remembered.

- The central image or metaphor is what will be remembered. The team should have some record of the detail that they can refer to when necessary.

ADVERTISING

MAKE YOUR ADS LOOK LIKE— AND READ LIKE— EDITORIAL
Andy Maslen

THERE ARE TWO schools of thought when it comes to ads. One says make it as vibrant as possible and keep the copy short because nobody reads long copy. (As this is often uttered by copywriters you have to wonder where they get their motivation to come into work from.)

The second school (the old school, if you will) says make your ad resemble editorial, since that is what people buy magazines and newspapers for in the first place, and write as much as possible. Why as much as possible? Because the only people who are going to buy from you are those motivated to do so, and they need and want as much information as possible before making their decision.

The idea
From Lynplan Ltd, who make sofa covers and sell them via mail order

When I came across Lynplan's ad in a Sunday supplement, I couldn't believe my eyes. Here, in late 2008, was a page ad clearly conceived, written, and art-directed by people who don't just want to sell more sofa covers (a laudable enough aim in its own right if that's what you manufacture) but who have bothered to find out what *works*. The ad (miraculously free of the ADVERTISEMENT header some newspapers and magazines insist on for ads with the temerity to comport themselves other than as nightclub flyers) begins with a headline enclosed in speech marks. It reads, "If you've just ordered a new sofa cover, don't read this ... It will break your heart!"

At a stroke they call to the ad their entire target market, that is, people interested in buying sofa covers. Those who have will read because the curiosity factor is so high. Those who haven't will read because they think, rightly, they might learn something to their advantage.

The speech marks are important because they make the headline look like a real person talking. And indeed a real person is talking, as the ad carries a byline, "A special report by John Nesbitt." There follows a detailed account of Lynplan's products, service, even history as a family-run business started by the current managing director's father, a World War II bomb-disposal engineer. My favorite cross-head reads, "The 7 Things You Should Expect From Your Sofa Cover Company." I defy you not to read on.

I counted the words in the body copy and made it 745. Forgive me, Lynplan, if I missed a few. Top marks.

In practice

- Look at the articles in your favorite newspaper or magazine. Remind yourself that this is what you paid to read.
- Try adopting an editorial style for your next ad. Try signing it and writing it as if you were a journalist writing a story, rather than a copywriter writing an ad.

PERFORMANCE
DEVELOPING EMPLOYEE ENGAGEMENT
Jeremy Kourdi

EMPLOYEE ENGAGEMENT IS widely seen as being vital to improving business performance, effectiveness, and productivity. Researchers at Gallup identified several variables that, when satisfied, form the foundation of strong feelings of engagement (see www.gallup.com).

The idea

Business researchers at Gallup identified 12 questions measuring the effect of employee engagement, including such issues as retention, productivity, profitability, customer engagement, and safety. These questions, known as the Q^{12}, measure those factors that leaders, managers, and employees can influence. The questions are based on hundreds of interviews and focus groups, involving thousands of workers in many organizations, at all levels, across a broad range of industries and countries.

In practice

To succeed, it is best to work with a business that possesses experience of administering and delivering Gallup's Q^{12} and can advise on the key issues.

The questions below will help you focus on the challenge of increasing engagement. Consider them either for you or for your team, and rate your response to each question on a scale of 1 (low) to 5 (high).

- Is the team focused on the right things? Is everyone agreed on the priorities and strategy?
- Do the business culture and processes help or hinder collaboration? What changes would improve the situation?
- How well is performance monitored? Does the business merely rely on financial indicators or are there other measures?
- Where do tensions typically arise and where are they likely to arise in the future?
- What is the best way to handle and reconcile tensions when they arise?
- Where is the team succeeding and where do we need to improve (individually, and as a team)?
- Are objectives and processes aligned, consistent, and pulling in the same direction? If not, what needs to change?
- In the last seven days, have you received recognition or praise for doing good work?
- At work, do your opinions seem to count?
- In the last six months, has someone at work talked to you about your progress?
- In the last year, have you had opportunities at work to learn and grow?

ONLINE MARKETING
JOIN LINKEDIN
Jim Blythe

SOCIAL NETWORKING SITES have become very big business indeed, with sites such as Facebook and MySpace linking people all over the world. Apart from linking up old friends, sites such as Facebook enable people to meet new friends through mutual friends.

For businesspeople, the choices are fewer, but one site does exist to provide businesspeople with a way of networking.

The idea

LinkedIn is a networking site for business professionals. It enables people to contact former colleagues, find people who might be of mutual benefit, and provide opportunities to extend one's reputation.

LinkedIn is a way to extend your reputation by using the contacts your colleagues and business associates have. It also enables you to do your friends a favor by putting them in touch with each other—only good things can come of this. You will need to be generous with your time, of course—you should be prepared to offer help to other people on the network, because that is what networking is all about.

There is, of course, nothing to stop you using Facebook or MySpace in a similar way—in each case you can upload pictures of yourself and your business, although you do need to be careful not to be too overtly commercial when using normal social networking sites, since their rules specifically prohibit commercial exploitation of the site. However, no such restrictions apply on LinkedIn: the purpose of the site is to foster business networking.

In practice

- Be prepared to spend some time contributing to the site. In particular, be prepared to help people who contact you through the site—this is about building your reputation, not about selling your products.

- Don't be afraid to ask for help yourself. That's what the site is for.
- Try to involve all your business contacts. The wider the network, the better the results.
- Make sure your business contacts don't mind being added to the site—they will be asked anyway, but it's better coming from you.

MANAGING MEETINGS

AVOIDING MEETING MAYHEM

Patrick Forsyth

MEETINGS CAN BE mayhem. No agenda, no order, confusion and distraction at every turn. Meetings are, or should be, important and, above all, useful. If a "ragged" meeting fails to be constructive, it does no one any good and wastes a considerable amount of time for everyone attending.

The idea

Every meeting must have someone in the chair. More than that, every meeting benefits from a good chair, someone who can lead the meeting, handle the discussion, and generally act to see the objectives of the meeting are met and the agenda is covered in the time allocated. It may be difficult either to take over or to instruct a senior colleague in the art—and it *is* an art—of how to chair a session, but you can at least make sure that any meeting you are to run yourself will be well chaired.

In practice

The benefits of a good chair are considerable:
- The meeting will be better focused on its objectives.
- Discussion can be kept more constructive.
- A thorough review can be assured before decisions are made.
- All sides of an argument can be reflected, and balanced.
- The meeting will be kept more businesslike and less argumentative (even in reviewing contentious issues).

Above all, it will be more likely to run to schedule and achieve the results wanted promptly, efficiently, and without waste of time.

The chairing of a meeting is a skill that must be learned and practiced. It is worth some study. The checklist (Appendix 1 on page 209) will remind you of the essentials, all of which can potentially save time if properly executed.

SALES
LOG OBJECTIONS
Patrick Forsyth

OBJECTIONS ARE UBIQUITOUS in selling. We know we will get some, and we know too, from experience, that they should be regarded as a sign of interest. (No one is going to be bothered to query something they have dismissed out of hand.) We also know that they will vary in topic, nature, and emphasis. Sometimes the same thing crops up repeatedly as a major stumbling block, and on another occasion something might be mentioned in passing, and is not in any sense a major hindrance. What matters is the balance of positive and negative points a customer sees as a case is presented. It is not realistic to try to have nothing on the negative side: when did you last buy something perfect? But the positive side must weigh most heavily in the balance, and what creates that situation may be a number of major points (heavy ones, to stick with the weighing-up analogy), and a number of smaller ones too. Indeed, because it is impossible sometimes to balance one major point with another, several smaller ones may have to do the job.

Whatever else you do, you should be ready for objections.

The idea
Quizzing numbers of salespeople who are good at handling objections shows that this skill does not just happen ...

Occasionally, not often, an objection may surprise you; and if it does, you have to try to be quick on your feet and deal with it. But the majority of objections you receive will be repetitive. The same things recur, and some of them (like price) are common to most selling situations. So make sure that you are ready for them. It is good practice to collect objections—for a week or three, keep a note of every reason people give you for not buying. Then sort them out. Some may need little attention: they will be simple, invalid, or simply so individual that they will rarely or never occur again. The others will fall into various categories. Some will pose the same question, or address the same area, but come at it in a different way. No matter—catalogue the main ones, and check that you are sure how you will deal with them in future. Do you know how to respond? Do you have rebalancing arguments? Can you, where necessary, point out—in an acceptable fashion—that the customer is wrong?

In practice

- Objections should not surprise you. You should be ready for the vast majority of them. This involves undertaking some preparation.

TEAMWORK
INVOLVE THE TEAM
Jonathan Gifford

A TEAM THAT has fully understood the vision and the broad strategy can be trusted to make the right decisions on its own initiative. Such a team is also a hugely effective support system that will "take care of business" in difficult times.

The idea

The British Admiral, Horatio Nelson, victor of the Battle of Trafalgar, is one of Britain's national heroes. By destroying the navies of France and their allies at Trafalgar during the war with revolutionary France, Nelson ensured that Britain would not face invasion from France, across the English Channel. It is Nelson who popularized the idea of a fighting team as a "band of brothers".

Quoting from Shakespeare, Nelson had written earlier in his career about the captains under his command. "Such a gallant set of fellows! Such a band of brothers! My heart swells at the thought of them!"

It was Nelson who forged this team, entertaining the captains in his fleet for informal suppers on board his flag ship; discussing the overall war situation, his strategy and preferred tactics.

As a result, in the smoke and confusion of battle, the band of brothers could be trusted to act on their own initiative, to use the tactics most likely to bring victory, and to have the overall strategic picture constantly in mind.

India's Reliance Industries was founded by Dhirubhai Ambani. His son, Mukesh, recounts the difficulties that the company faced when his father's cousin, a senior company executive, died, soon after which Dhirubhai suffered a stroke.

Mukesh stresses that because he had involved his colleagues in an "open system" of management, there was strength in depth across the organization to cope with the death of a senior executive and the temporary incapacity of the founder.

"That was a huge blow ... two major events in five months. From three of us running the business, for some time, I suddenly became alone ... This is where investing in talent works ... there was no sense of panic. The whole picture was in my head. That was the strength of the open system. If I had kept everything close to my chest, it would have been difficult. We had excellent people across the company ... there was a plan in place. We just kept our heads down and executed it."

In practice

- People can only make a real commitment to an organization's goals when they have been consulted and involved in the process and have committed themselves on a personal level.
- When leaders are open with their teams and involve them in the goal-setting and planning process, the team becomes self-motivating and self-sufficient.
- People who fully understand the organization's goals can be trusted to act on their own initiative; this speeds up decisions and lets the person closest to the action make key tactical decisions.
- An involved team can function successfully for extended periods without input from senior management.

COST CUTTING
DOES SIZE MATTER?
Anne Hawkins

Do you throw away tools because they have lost their size (e.g. drills)?

Have you checked whether these tools could be used in other areas where tolerances are not so critical?

Do you program in the use of expensive specialist cutting-tools (e.g. multi-dimensional reamers) instead of standard tools for straight-forward tasks such as circular interpolation when there is a cheaper one in the tool holder?

The idea

Challenge specifications to make sure you're not wasting your money on unwarranted 'quality'. This principle should be applied throughout your business ... to materials, packaging ... even documentation.

Standardising where possible might get you out of a jam.

Critical differences

This components manufacturer makes a range of products for a particular customer. One part in particular is difficult to make with very tight tolerances on a critical aspect of the design and there had always been a substantial scrap rate on orders for these parts. If it had been possible, the design would have been changed but commercially this was impossible. Therefore (while having strong words with the design department to ensure that the challenging aspects of this design were not replicated in future product lines), it was a question of making the most of a difficult job.

While the business supplies this customer with a wide-range of final components, there is commonality in the initial stages of the process. Some of these components require more critical tolerances than others. Rather than launch orders destined for specific part numbers, the business now initiates manufacture of the generic stage of the design.

At the final point of commonality, the part-built components are tested and sorted with those meeting the highest specification going on to fill orders for the most difficult parts. Others can be used for those products with the less stringent tolerances.

In practice

- Look for instances of 'over-specification' in your business.
  - Do you always need the highest quality tools, equipment and materials for everything you do?
  - Are you doing things 'better' than the customer wants and is prepared to pay for?

And remember that size doesn't necessarily determine cost!

352
USE LANGUAGE YOUR CUSTOMERS CAN UNDERSTAND
Andy Maslen

IF YOU WANTED your four-year-old to wait for you before crossing the road, would you call out, "Darling, do you think, were I to recommend that you refrained from a headlong incursion into the thoroughfare, that you might attend me at the curbside?" I thought not.

Using an appropriate register for your reader is a pretty obvious way of making sure they can understand you. So why do so many organizations make it so hard for the target reader of a piece of copy even to figure it out? It's back to our old friend reader-centricity, I'm afraid (or rather, the lack of it).

The idea
From a service station in West London
When I lived in Chiswick, a leafy part of West London, there was a service station a mile or so away that had clearly become a magnet for drunks on their way home from the pub, looking for a coffee, a packet of fags, or a chocolate fix. Residents tended to complain vociferously to HQ about "noise nuisance" and it had obviously had an effect on the station manager. Right outside the kiosk was a beautifully printed and mounted sign on which were set the immortal lines:

> Out of consideration for our neighbors, would patrons kindly refrain from making undue noise or disturbance when leaving the premises.

Genius! That scores 38.4 percent on the Flesch Reading Ease test. Put it this way, that's harder to understand than the *Harvard Business Review*, a publication with which I feel sure the said patrons were unfamiliar. My question to the author is, do you really imagine that a group of "revelers," staggering noisily from a service station kiosk at midnight, are going to read a sign written like that, let alone figure out what the hell it means?

My translation would be something like,

> Please be quiet when you leave—don't wake our neighbors.
> [FRE score: 100 percent.]

In more obviously commercial arenas I still see plenty of examples of this long-winded style, where every big event is a significant development, and long-term plans are always strategic roadmaps. It makes no sense, literally, to dress up perfectly ordinary sentiments in Sunday best. And remember that everybody can understand Plain English, whatever their level of literacy or intellectual sophistication.

In practice

- Make sure, when you start writing, that you are using the sort of language you'd use if you were talking to your reader face to face.
- Read what you've written out loud. If you sound like a lawyer talking, you need to simplify it.

PUBLIC RELATIONS
GET YOURSELF ON THE EXPERT COMMENTATOR LIST
Jim Blythe

TV AND PRINTED news journalists often need to find an expert who can talk on a given topic. I have a friend who is (he thinks) the only Welsh-speaking astronomer in Wales, so he is always getting called by the Welsh-language TV and radio stations to make a comment about almost anything scientific.

Reporters simply don't have time to start looking for somebody if there is a breaking news story. They need to consult a list, find someone who should be able to say a few words, and contact them within minutes of the story breaking: otherwise they can be scooped by another medium or (worse) might say something stupid because they have not been able to consult an expert.

The idea

Contact your local TV station, radio station, or newspaper and tell them about yourself. It helps if you have an area of expertise that is likely to be newsworthy—for example, if you are an airline pilot, fire safety expert, or finance expert—but obviously your expertise must link to your business, otherwise there will be little or no PR value for you.

You may not be called upon very often, but, when you are, your company name will almost certainly be used (since it explains why you are a credible spokesperson) and your status will be enhanced considerably.

A further plus is that you will usually be paid an appearance fee—nothing big, but almost always worth while. The PR value to you in the eyes of your staff, customers, and financiers is obviously very large indeed—as long as you don't say anything too silly, of course!

In practice

- Be prepared to drop everything to speak at a few moments' notice.
- Get the journalists to brief you beforehand—it may give you a few moments to gather your thoughts.
- Be honest—if you don't know the answer to a question, don't lie about it, just say what you do know.
- Don't try to plug your business. You will get a mention anyway, and if you push it you won't be asked back.

SALES
BIG STRATEGIES
Patrick Forsyth

NOT ONLY ARE some customers different from others (it has already been stressed here that customers need individual treatment); some are also larger than others, in terms of either business received from them or potential. A big customer is sometimes satisfyingly and gratefully simply labeled "big," and no further action is taken. But if the volume of business is already large, that does not mean it cannot be increased. There is an old saying that even the best performance can be improved, and despite the apparent contradiction, this is a sensible attitude to take.

The idea
Analyzing the potential of major customers ...

There is a whole separate literature on major accounts, and on the management of the relationships that go with them (something to investigate if you have such customers). Here, however, is one idea that can quickly create new business possibilities. I like it because in its simplest form it can be worked out on the back of an envelope (even using approximate figures).

The necessary analysis simply takes the value of a large customer's business and splits the figure across two axes of a matrix. One axis lists products (or product areas) one by one, and the other lists buying points one by one. For example, for my own business I could list consulting, training (or perhaps several separate areas of training: sales, making presentations, business writing), and writing. Then I could list the various buying points in a client company. There are various ways to do this, but in my case I'd probably opt for function—the marketing department, HR, and more—or location: for instance offices in London and Manchester, or London, New York, and Singapore.

In practice
How is this useful?

- If you do this, you'll find some boxes of the matrix show a higher value than others. A great deal of product A might be sold in London, but (surprisingly?) little of product B, for instance.
- Or there might be total gaps—nothing being sold in particular areas of a large customer's organization.

- Asking why can identify opportunities and provide targets for future selling. Maybe there are new contacts to be investigated; maybe you can get an introduction from one part of the company to another.
- Exploring the details in this way almost always provides some food for thought. Just saying, "These figures are good," doesn't help you identify how they could be still better.

CUSTOMERS
CUSTOMER BONDING
Jeremy Kourdi

As BUSINESS COMPETITION becomes increasingly fierce, firms should not only focus on attracting new customers, they should also use rewards to retain existing clients and get more out of them, which will also attract more clients.

The idea
Many industries are characterized by the fight not only to attract customers but also to retain their continuing support once captured. An example of using information to enhance customer bonding and improve competitiveness is customer loyalty schemes. These schemes have long been a feature of marketing programs, with a recent example being Air Miles. There has been a large growth in the number and type of firms offering loyalty programs. These range from bookstores, such as WH Smith in Britain, which has a sophisticated database of millions of customers, through to credit card companies and telephone operators such as MCI in the USA, which pioneered the friends and family discount. For MCI, this single measure, undertaken with relatively modest advertising expenditure (5 percent of the market leader, AT&T), resulted in its market share growing by 4 percent despite fierce competition.

The inventiveness of loyalty programs is constantly surprising, revealing the brand values of the companies and the threat they pose to competitors. For example, Virgin Atlantic introduced an ingenious loyalty scheme for customer bonding, to reduce the time that it takes to get new customers. Virgin offers privileges to those involved in competitors' loyalty schemes, offering a free companion ticket to any British Airways frequent flyer who has accumulated 10,000 miles. This has the added advantage of reinforcing perceptions of the Virgin brand as being dynamic and flexible.

In practice

- Create customer loyalty schemes to encourage repeat business and build up a positive brand image among your client base.
- Focus on your competitors when creating a loyalty program. What are they offering, and what can you offer that is better and more enticing for the customer?
- Be creative with loyalty programs and other methods of customer bonding. It is an area with many possibilities for innovation—take advantage of them.
- Ask customer-facing employees how best to enhance customer loyalty.

REWARDS
BE FAIR
Jonathan Gifford

PEOPLE ARE VERY sensitive to what is "fair". This applies to what they feel is reasonable to expect from them and to what rewards they are offered. Rewards within the organization need to be consistent.

The idea

Jonah Lehrer, neuroscientist and author on the psychology of decision making, describes "the ultimatum game": a key experiment into human selfishness and altruism.

One of two people ("the proposer") is given $10. He or she is then asked to make an offer of any proportion of the money to the other person ("the responder"); if the offer is accepted, both parties keep the money. It was assumed that the proposer would act selfishly and offer a minimal amount and that the responder would react rationally and take any offer as better than nothing. But, as Lehrer reports, "The researchers soon realized that their predictions were all wrong. Instead of swallowing their pride and pocketing a small profit, responders typically rejected any offer they perceived as unfair. Furthermore, proposers anticipated this angry rejection and typically tendered an offer of around five dollars. This was such a stunning result that nobody really believed it." "The fact is," says Lehrer, "that we can imagine how the other person will feel about an unfair offer. Our brains have become hard-wired to see things from the other person's perspective."

David Packard made a speech to Hewlett Packard managers in the 1960s in which he talked about the responsibilities of leaders: "Tolerance is tremendously significant. Unless you are tolerant of the people under you, you really can't do a good job of being a supervisor. You must have understanding—understanding of the little things that affect people. You must have a sense of fairness, and you must know what it is reasonable to expect of your people."

The American psychologist Frederick Herzberg's "Two factor theory" of job satisfaction suggests that people are made unhappy by what they see as bad or unfair things in their working environment, to a greater extent than they are made happy by things that are satisfactory. Preventing people from being dissatisfied is just as important as concentrating on their motivation.

John Harvey-Jones, previously chairman of ICI, confirms the importance of fairness: "Certainly my own personal experience tends to confirm Herzberg's theory that monetary reward is not in itself an incentive, but poor or unfair reward is a major disincentive ... Relative rewards within the organization, unless demonstrably fairly apportioned, have the same effect."

In practice

- People have an innate sense of what is fair. This applies to whether what they are being asked to do is "reasonable" and whether they are being treated "fairly".
- Leaders must ask people to make exceptional efforts; a key function of leadership is to assess what can reasonably be demanded.
- Rewards must be fair and be seen to be fair. An unfair reward can be disproportionately de-motivating.
- Not all rewards need to be financial, but people are equally sensitive about whether praise or other intangible rewards have been fairly allocated.

MARKETING
EDUCATE YOUR CUSTOMERS
Jim Blythe

WHEN A PRODUCT is new, and often when it isn't, people need a certain amount of help in working out how to use it. This goes beyond including an instruction manual—sometimes there are circumstances in which the product might be used differently from the way it has been used in the past. For example, Heinz Salad Cream is now promoted as a recipe ingredient, as well as for its original use as a salad dressing.

Showing the product in use is one thing—showing it in the use context is another, and sometimes people need to be given a whole new idea for an activity involving your product.

The idea
During Britains's post-war boom of the 1950s and 1960s, Rowntree's chocolate manufacturing company were looking for a new way to shift chocolate. They came up with the idea for a chocolate-covered after-dinner mint. The only problem was that people were not (at

that time) in the habit of giving dinner parties at home. Socializing usually took place outside the home, in pubs or coffee bars, rather than over a home-cooked meal.

Rowntree's therefore had to show people how to have a dinner party. The early advertisements for After Eight mints showed people enjoying a dinner together, with the hostess bringing food out from the kitchen and the guests complimenting her on the meal. The concept of an after-dinner chocolate did not exist prior to After Eights, and in fact for most people the idea of having a dinner party did not exist, either.

For Rowntree's, the combination of creating a whole new way of eating chocolate and also of encouraging a new group of people to have dinner parties meant having an entire market to themselves. No 1960s dinner party was considered to be complete unless After Eights were offered, and indeed many guests would bring them along as a gift in order to ensure that they would be on offer.

In practice
- Consider both the occasion and the product use.
- Don't be afraid to innovate—just because nobody else has done it does not mean that it's a bad idea.
- Get the concept across clearly in your advertising—show people how it's done.
- Show people—don't just tell them.

VALUES
STICK TO THE VALUES
Jonathan Gifford

AN ORGANIZATION'S VALUES dictate how the organization deals with its members and customers and with the outside world in general. Ensuring that everyone in the organization adheres to those values guarantees that colleagues behave appropriately towards each other and towards customers, and that business is conducted in an ethical and honest manner wherever it operates.

The idea

Gerard Kleisterlee, president and CEO of Philips, the multinational Dutch electronics company, talks about how the company's values transcend national borders: that they must apply to any market in which the company does business.

"In 2001/2002, we updated our values. We describe them today as the four Ds—we delight our customers, deliver great results, develop our people, and depend on each other. Although we have not formulated any typical values, things like business ethics, integrity, honesty, and so on are all part of our business principles. We believe that they are self-evident. But the four 'Ds' are our transcendent culture, be it in Asia, the United States or Europe."

Kenneth Yu, Managing Director of 3M China, points out that in the early days of the company's operations in China, the country's environmental laws were less strict than they were in the United States, so that it would have been quite legal for the company to relax its usual environmental policies. The company decided to stick to its values and its standard procedures, even though this cost them business at first.

"In the early days, people said when you do business in a developing economy, you do it differently ... but when it comes to business ethics, there is no compromise ... We did lose business in the early days. We'd rather lose a customer than taint our squeaky-clean image ... Environmental law here, although it is getting tougher, isn't like in the US. At the beginning, we raised eyebrows. Over time it has given 3M a lot of good publicity, and we eventually got benefits from the host government in the area."

In practice

- An organization's values dictate how it deals with its own members, with customers and with the outside world. It is the leader's job to make sure that those values are clearly understood throughout the organization and that they are not forgotten.

- It should not be necessary to remind colleagues to do business in an ethical way, but leaders must ensure that basic standards of honesty and integrity never slip.
- International organizations will do business in places with different cultures and legislation. The company's values should not change in different contexts.

SALES
TAKE YOUR TIME
Patrick Forsyth

MANY PRODUCTS AND services are non-standard. A kitchen can be designed and tailored to fit your needs and your house, a landscape gardener works in a similar way, many computer systems and consultancy of all sorts are bespoke. To a degree this is one of the strengths of such products, and one of the things that persuades the customer and prompts purchase.

But there is a danger. If the customer does not believe the product or service is really bespoke (when that is what they want), but suspects what they are being offered is actually just a standard option, then a unique aspect of it is negated and selling becomes that much more difficult. Even if there is a "good fit," they may believe they are being short-changed; certainly perception of price may well change.

The idea
This is a common problem in consultancy, which is part of my own work portfolio ...

There are two stages to making bespoke suggestions. The first is identifying the individual circumstances, the second making a specific suggestion based on observation and some sort of survey. Often the second involves a written proposal. For example: the kitchen supplier must draw up and submit drawings and costs, and the consultant must propose how work will be carried out and write a detailed proposal. In both cases the instinct in terms of customer service is to jump to it and do this promptly.

The idea here is simple: take your time.

In practice

- Of course, you must check how urgently the proposal is needed, and make sure what you do will be satisfactory to the customer, but the time taken will be seen as in direct relationship to the degree of tailoring involved. If the proposal is based on a thorough survey, well described and presented, and delivered some time after the survey (even if it only takes a moment to customize it), the customer will assume it to be truly bespoke. It will be seen as having higher value than a standard offering.
- Allow sufficient time to show that some thought has gone into them, and your proposals may be valued more highly.

CRISIS MANAGEMENT
BRING YOUR ENEMIES INSIDE THE TENT
Jim Blythe

THERE IS AN old saying that it is better to have your enemies inside the tent p***ing out than outside the tent p***ing in. Any large company, and most smaller companies, develop enemies one way or another—dissatisfied customers, disgruntled pressure groups, unpaid creditors, revenge-seeking ex-employees, and honest people who have an honest grievance.

In some cases, one or several of these people will set up a website dedicated to vilifying the company. Such websites are called McNitemares after the McDonald's shadow website, and although they operate on a relatively low level they can still be extremely damaging to companies.

The idea

Royal Dutch Shell is an Anglo-Dutch oil company—in fact it is one of the Big 7 companies in the oil business. As such, it has major involvement in the exploitation of North Sea oil and has many offshore facilities in the North Sea for this purpose.

One such was the Brent Spar storage facility. In 1991, Brent Spar had reached the end of its useful life, and was in fact slightly damaged (during installation), so it was doubtful whether it could realistically be salvaged. Shell conducted a scientific study that showed that the least risky way of disposing of Brent Spar, both from an environmental viewpoint and for the safety of workers, was to tow it to deep water in the Atlantic and sink it, using explosives.

Greenpeace disagreed. They occupied the rig for several weeks, and when they were evacuated they held a press conference in Aberdeen: as is often the case, the protest groups have slicker PR than do the companies they protest against. Over the ensuing weeks, Shell petrol stations and offices were boycotted or even attacked, and Shell staff were sometimes abused.

Shell eventually backed down and had the rig dismantled. Their PR people then looked for ways to prevent any such action taking place in future—and the result was the TellShell website.

TellShell is a site that offers an open forum for discussion of anything related to Shell, its activities, its employees, and so forth. The site is moderated by Shell to remove anything libellous or simply malicious, but the intention is to promote genuine debate. The running costs are relatively low, and the effect is powerful in terms of flagging up problems before they get out of hand. It also provides Shell with a source of free advice for avoiding further PR disasters.

In practice

- Ensure that the site is well publicized on your main website and elsewhere.
- Be genuinely open and honest on the site—otherwise someone will soon set up a credible rival site.

- Moderate the site to ensure that it doesn't simply become a ranting-shop.
- Get your senior people to visit the site occasionally, both to comment and to be aware of the issues.

EXECUTION
IMPLEMENTATION
Jonathan Gifford

YOUR COMPETITORS' STRATEGIES will be very much like your own. The organization that best executes its strategy will be successful.

The idea
Frank Zhou, general manager of pharmaceutical company Abbott International China, argues that execution is especially important in markets such as China.

"My view is that in China, execution is a big issue. All the pharmaceutical multinationals have more or less similar strategies: They all know that China is a huge market, they all need to invest here and they all know we need to bring different product lines into China. However, what makes a company successful in the end is determined by whether or not it can be really good at doing what it wants to do ... In terms of accessing the market, retaining talent, establishing ethical standards and communicating with your head office, if you can do better than your competitors on these things, you will achieve better results ... We need to focus more on details, and to follow through and get things done."

As Jack Welch, previous CEO of General Electric, said, "I don't want to oversimplify strategy. But you just shouldn't agonize over it. Find the right aha and set the direction, put the right people in place, and work like crazy to execute better than anyone else, finding best practices and improving them every day."

In practice

- You and your competitors are likely (for good reasons) to have similar strategies. The organization that executes its strategy best will succeed.
- The organization's strategy does not have to be radical or even original.
- How well the strategy is implemented is probably more significant than the originality or detail of the strategy itself.

CASH FLOW
GET IT INVOICED!

Anne Hawkins

DOES YOUR BUSINESS have a get-it-out-the-door mentality?

Does everyone breathe a sigh of relief and head for the coffee-machine as the lorry disappears down the road on its way to the customer?

Haven't you forgotten something?

The idea

Not only do you want the customer to pay you for what you do—you also want him to pay for it as soon as possible. The longer you have to wait, the more capital you need to invest in the business just to keep it turning and hence the more you're going to have to spend on interest payments.

To get the money in as fast as possible not only do you have to try to negotiate the shortest credit periods you can ... you also have to raise an invoice!

You'd be surprised how often this gets overlooked or put aside to deal with later when there's a quiet moment to 'catch up with the paperwork'. If invoices are not raised promptly and accurately you're going to pay the price for it later when you come to try to collect that all-important cash. Even delaying a day can end up costing you money. But there can be other reasons than procrastination for delays in invoicing.

Changes in the market—Development costs
Many businesses have lived through an era when they could invoice the customer for development work before entering the production phase. However, most markets now require suppliers to spread the recovery of these costs over an agreed initial quantity of production items. This means that the business has to finance the costs incurred for development over a longer time period, increasing their business investment and hence their interest costs. And of course if the customer then moves their schedules out to the right...

Management focus—Milestone payments
Some longer-term contracts allow progress payments to be invoiced and paid upon reaching given milestones. While those involved in delivering the contract may well be avidly pouring over Gantt charts to map their progress, do they understand the commercial terms of the contract? Do they have their priorities right? A critical part of project-management is to understand where the trigger-points for invoicing are and put systems in place to make sure the trigger is pulled.

... and look out for those TBAs!

In practice
- Focus on your destination—the customer paying you for all your hard work.
- Most customers will not pay without an invoice.
- Look at the various ways invoices should be being triggered by your business and ensure there are no obstacles in the way.
- Once you've invoiced make sure you collect the cash!

CUSTOMERS
USING CUSTOMER INFORMATION
Jeremy Kourdi

SEAMLESSLY GATHERED INFORMATION can be used to save costs, to provide a tailor-made service to individual clients, and to sell more—often using the internet.

The idea

The American online retailer Amazon.com has redefined bookselling. Its culture appreciates the potential of technology, with the company using information in four key ways:

1. *To minimize risks* by analyzing information from millions of customers to see how and when they purchase, enabling Amazon.com to reduce the level of risk.
2. *To reduce costs* by using technology to control the way it manages its inventory and suppliers.
3. *To add value and help customers* by offering reviews of books and free downloadable information, and by treating its home page as an individual storefront for each customer—for example by tailoring lists of suggested titles that the customer may enjoy based on previous purchases.
4. *To innovate.* Amazon believes that, to rival its competitors, an innovative approach is essential in order to improve the value and service offered to consumers.

What matters is not simply what information exists, but how that information is used to build competitive advantage. Interestingly, many other retailing companies have now followed Amazon's lead. For example, Apple's iTunes and iStore have done for music retailing what Amazon did for bookselling, using many of the same principles.

In practice

- Treat each customer as an individual. For example, music retailer iTunes tracks the purchases of individual clients and provides a customized webpage designed to introduce a client to new buying opportunities that appeal to his/her personal taste.

- Use the internet to provide information for the individual—even if your business does not carry out its primary operations online. By collecting customers' email addresses, a business can develop a highly valuable and intimate marketing strategy.
- Smaller businesses and freelance workers may be able to research more in-depth information on each client. This can then be organized into an accessible database, with subheadings for each client covering all areas of relevant information.
- If your organization is unable to seamlessly track consumer trends, use incentives such as free products for customers who volunteer their information. Similarly, you should also provide rewards for customers who agree to receive information on your organization—the marketing should be entertaining, lively, appropriate, and relevant.

SALES
THE SMALL PRINT
Patrick Forsyth

MANY A DEAL has foundered on the small print. The customer likes the product, they want to buy the product, maybe even at some stage they actually intend to do so, then—suddenly—they decline. Something about the terms of the deal destroyed their intent.

The idea
From the conference industry ...

The terms and conditions you state for contracts must protect your financial position as supplier, and in particular, protect your profitability. At the same time it is important that they:

- Are communicated clearly and prevent misunderstandings.

- Project efficiency.
- Enhance the client relationship (for which they must be seen as acceptable and necessary).
- Encourage conversion of business effectively and promptly.
- Link to any other necessary arrangements and documentation.

I first worked on the detail of what is best here during some research with the Meetings Industry Association. The key here and elsewhere is that when discussing terms and conditions you should never apologize. Stress the mutual advantages of clearly specified contract conditions. Talk about working together, and if necessary use a checklist to ensure you deal with everything systematically. Specifically you may want to evolve a step-by-step way of introducing and describing terms and conditions, and making them stick. This is the kind of progression involved:

- Introduce the concept of contractual agreement. You need to consider the timing of this in the context of your type of business, but it is usually best early on rather than later.
- Make clear the detail. You must be careful to spell it out accurately, and not assume the customer is familiar with everything, least of all figures, costings, and timing. Always check understanding (this may need only a simple question).
- Document your side of the arrangements. Tell the customer what you will do, and follow it up efficiently and promptly in a way that sets the pattern for clear written communications. Make it easy for the customer (you set out the details), but ask for confirmation, chase if necessary to get it, and keep clear records throughout the process if it takes any amount of time.

In practice
- Adopt the appropriate manner throughout the process, and make it clear that none of this is a negative procedure.
- Stress the advantages to the customer of having things clear. Link to any follow-up, and ultimately this includes invoicing. (Here it is most important that the invoice reflects—accurately—the agreed detail, and is straightforward and clear.)

BE DECISIVE
Jonathan Gifford

THERE WILL NEVER be enough information to guarantee that you have made the right decision. At some point, leaders must trust their experience and their instinct and seize the moment.

The idea

Making decisions is the defining aspect of leadership. There has never been a leader who made only right decisions. An effective decision made at the right moment is far better than no decision at all. A forceful exponent of this school of thinking was George S. Patton, the US Army General who led the armored dash across France towards Germany after Allied forces had established a beachhead in Normandy, in north-western France, in order to launch a land attack on Germany and bring an end to the Second World War.

His experiences in the First World War, during which he witnessed the futility of trench warfare, convinced him of the need to keep an attacking force constantly on the move. Patton was convinced that establishing a defensive line was what lost battles and got soldiers killed.

"Attack rapidly, ruthlessly, viciously, without rest—however tired and hungry you may be, the enemy will be more tired; more hungry." This aggressive, take-the-fight-to-the-enemy approach led to one of Patton's most famous quotations: "A good plan, violently executed now, is better than a perfect plan next week."

Lee Iacocca, president and CEO of the USA's Chrysler Corporation in the 1980s, offers a modern, corporate version of this philosophy:

"If I had to sum up in one word the qualities that make a good manager, I'd say that it all comes down to decisiveness. You can use the fanciest computer in the world and you can gather all the charts and numbers, but in the end you have to bring all your information together, set up a timetable, and act ... Too many managers let themselves get weighed down in their decision making ... at some point you've got to take that leap of faith. First, because even the right decision is wrong if it's made too late. Second, because in most cases there's no such thing as certainty."

In practice

- Events move increasingly quickly; leaders do not have the luxury of waiting in order to make a better-informed decision.
- Delay can lead to the loss of a key opportunity or the establishment of a potentially overwhelming threat.
- With all of the information that is available to you at the time, with the advice of your peers and your organization, and based on your lifetime's experience, make a decision.
- Not to make a decision is a choice in itself. You are as accountable for non-decisions as you are for decisions.
- It is better to make a timely decision based on the best information available, and to repair any damage done later, if necessary, than not to make a decision and to be at the mercy of events.

ABOUT THE AUTHORS

Jim Blythe is a former company director, sales manager, and marketing consultant. He is now a business author and lecturer, and a senior examiner for the Chartered Institute of Marketing.

Patrick Forsyth runs Touchstone Training and Consultancy, an independent firm specializing in marketing, management and communications skills. He is also a successful author whose books appear in more than 25 languages.

Jonathan Gifford is a businessman, historian and author, whose writing focuses primarily on the human aspects of leadership and management. He is the author of *History Lessons: What business and management can learn from the great leaders of history.*

Anne Hawkins works as a freelance trainer renowned for her expertise in explaining financial matters in relevant, practical and commonsense terms. As an author, her books have been translated and appreciated internationally.

Jeremy Kourdi is successful businesss writer and advisor. During his career he has worked with the Economist Group, HSBC, London Business School, IMD and the Chartered Management Institute.

Andy Maslen runs Sunfish, an independent copywriting agency specializing in direct and digital marketing as well as B2B corporate communications. He is also the author of *Write to Sell* and *The Copywriting Sourcebook.*